CHILE:
An Attempt at
"Historic Compromise"
The Real Story of the
Allende Years

Jorge Palacios

BANNER PRESS
CHICAGO, 1979

U.S. Edition published by:
BANNER PRESS
PO Box 6469
Chicago, IL 60680
November, 1979

ISBN 0-916650-11-1
Library of Congress Card Catalogue Number 79-55190

This book is dedicated to our beloved and unforgettable Comrade Guillermo Arévalo, trade union leader and member of the Central Committee of the Revolutionary Communist Party of Chile, who was tortured to death without uttering a single word that could serve the fascists.

CONTENTS

PART III
ECONOMIC POLICY OF THE
POPULAR UNITY GOVERNMENT

PART IV
THE BOURGEOIS INSTITUTIONS CONFRONTED BY THE ALLENDE GOVERNMENT

PART V
CONTRADICTIONS WITHIN THE FORCES OF THE OPPOSITION AND OF THE GOVERNMENT

PART VI
PROSPECTS FOR THE STRUGGLE
AGAINST THE FASCIST MILITARY JUNTA.

Introduction

Chile is painfully notorious throughout the world for the devastating earthquakes that break out every six years or so. On September 11, 1973, however, the Chilean people became victim of a calamity much worse than all these disasters taken together: the military coup d'état. In a country of only ten million inhabitants, over 30,000 persons were murdered during the first six months of the dictatorship alone; more than 150,000 people went through the jails or the concentration camps. More than half a million Chileans had to leave the country because of political persecution or economic repression. The most brutal and sophisticated tortures, copied from the most sanguinary regimes, are used systematically as a "normal" method of interrogation or as a means of revenge or intimidation.

But the repression does not only express itself through direct violence against individuals. It resulted in the total destruction of the bourgeois democratic institutions and guarantees that had existed for decades in Chile. The Parliament, the elections, the legal activities of all parties, the United Workers' Central, almost every single press and radio organ as well as the television programmes not under the control of the dictatorship have been suppressed. Even humanitarian organizations set up by the Church to assist the families of the persecuted have been dissolved.

Out of the 110 articles of the constitution in force before the coup d'état, hardly more than a dozen remain in application. Through the decree Law No. 28 of November 16, 1973, "The government junta has taken over the constituent, legislative and executive powers." Whenever one of these decrees violates the constitution, the latter is considered to be amended by such a decree, by virtue of the "constituent" power that the junta has attributed to itself. The most rigorous legislation and legal procedures have been used as a "legal" cover-up for the repressive trials: those of military courts operating in wartime. But even these laws and procedures of extreme harshness have not been respected, and in practice, absolute arbitrariness reigns supreme in matters of repression. More than three years after the coup d'état, the country is still under the state of siege: martial law as well as a permanent curfew through the night.

The most basic trade union rights have been abolished: rights to petition, to strike, to elect leaders and to hold meetings. As far as this last right is concerned, it is not only forbidden to meet in public places, but an authorization is demanded even to hold private meetings of more than six persons. Tens of thousands of workers have been dismissed from their jobs without any recognition of the legal recourse to which they were entitled in such cases.

The military authorities interfere in education at all levels. The autonomy of the universities has been completely suppressed. Military administrators have been nominated in replacement of the rectors and between 25 and 60 percent (depending on which university centre) of the students and faculty have been expelled. A large number of chairs as well as entire fields have been arbitrarily suppressed because they were considered subversive. Just as during the mediaeval period, a policy of burning allegedly subversive books and literature has been initiated.

The arbitrary actions of the Chilean fascist military against the most elementary human rights have earned the condemnation of many governments and international bodies, including the United Nations, the Organization of American States, the International Labour Organization, etc. Leopoldo Torres, General Secretary of the Catholic Jurists' Movement and member of the International Jurists' Commission, declared after the inquiry held in October 1973, when the repression had just begun, that: " . . . The situation and the criminal actions of the Chilean junta can be characterized as an attempted genocide, according to the definition of the United Nations Convention."

The destruction of the institutions and of the most elementary rights provided by the bourgeois democracy in Chile, together with the crimes, tortures and repression carried out by the fascist junta, represent just one side of the coin. All this repression is used in order to drastically and brutally expropriate the workers and large middle sectors of craftsmen, manufacturers and tradesmen for the benefit of internal as well as imperialist monopoly capital and of the landed oligarchy. The economic genocide carried out against the people by the junta is even worse than the repressive genocide.

The fascist junta has not only striven to provide the big internal exploiters and the foreign investors with cheap labour by means of repression. It has also effected the most monstrous transfer of purchasing power from the workers to big capital ever seen in our times. The part of the "wage earners" in the income distribution has fallen from $15,328 million during the 1970-1973 period to only $6,275 million for the period of 1974-1976. In other words, the workers have lost $9,053 million, a fall of about 60 percent. As for the "small businessmen and independent workers", they have lost $179 million in income.

One of the devices used to expropriate the workers and the middle strata for the benefit of big capital is the application of discriminatory taxes. The two social sectors just mentioned bore the cost of a more than $400 million tax raise, while the latifundists, the national monopolies and foreign capital benefited from a tax reduction of a similar amount. Another expropriation system is to proclaim "freedom of pricing" which, because of the monopolistic structure of the main branches of production, has resulted in ever faster soaring prices. Just in the twelve months that followed the coup d'état inflation rose by more than 1,000 percent. In the meantime, the fascist military has continuously raised the rate of the dollar (twice a month, if not more often), thus favouring the imperialist monopolies and the big bourgeois exporters as well as escalating the inflation process. Finally, expropriation was carried out through drastic cutbacks in public expenditure and in every budget relating to welfare services. One only needs to say that in 1977, the public health budget was reduced by half while the army budget was multiplied by four.

As was to be expected, the steep drop in the purchasing power of the broad masses of the people, the tax increase that they suffered together with the middle strata, the tightening of credit for the small and medium manufacturers and tradesmen and the elimination of the protective tariff walls on imported goods, all this has generated a severe recession in productive and trade activities as well as a massive process of failures for the small and medium enterprises. This was also deliberately sought by the fascist junta in order to promote the concentration of capital in the hands of the monopolistic sectors. This concentration was complemented with the restitution to their former owners (or the sale to new investors) of the firms nationalized by the Allende government and of the nationalized agricultural estates, as well as with huge compensation payments to the imperialist monopolies affected by the reforms of the said government. In 1976, 25 percent of the lands expropriated under the Frei and Allende governments had already been given back to their former owners: more than 2.97 million acres. Of a total of 494 enterprises (mainly factories) put under state control, 457 have already been restored. Even businesses created as state corporations before the Allende government have been handed over to the private sector. At the same time, more than $500 million has been paid out to the U.S. monopolies affected by the reforms of the Allende government, either in the form of compensation payments or of tax reductions.

Even if the bankruptcy of the small and medium enterprises was part of the junta's policy of serving big capital, as with the brutal lowering of the standard of living of the masses, the fascist military has been bending over backwards in its slavishness to the promoters of the coup d'état, causing a severe and almost uncontrollable economic crisis. An unbridled inflation and a most serious recession have combined to destroy the Chilean economy, giving rise to the worst crisis in the history of this country. In 1975, the gross national product had already declined by 15 percent, reaching the lowest point since 1969, and the real national income had sunk by at least 26 percent, making the per capita income lower than that of ten years ago. Industrial production alone registered a fall of 23 percent in 1975. Failures now begin to hit even large corporations, including the financial concerns where the pets of the regime used to speculate.

What the Pinochet government has done in Chile is widely known and condemned throughout the world. The liberal British weekly *The Observer* sums up the general opinion in an article entitled "No to General Pinochet", when it says that the latter "appears to be not only a cruel tyrant, but also an incompetent administrator". Also generally known are the economic and political, national as well as international, interests which formed a coalition in order to overthrow the Allende government. As far as the U.S. Senate Commission led by Church is concerned, it made us familiar with even the details of the role played by the CIA in preparing the overthrow of the Allende government. A large number of books, pamphlets, articles and films have come out to describe and analyze the political, economic and military offensive launched by the most reactionary circles of Chile and assisted by the US government in order to put an end to the reformist experiment attempted by the Popular Unity after it had gained the Presidency of the Republic in 1970.

But the more the facts come to light about the legal and illegal, open and underground, institutional and frankly subversive reactionary offensive waged by means of propaganda and sabotage, criminal attempts and armed actions that put an end to that peculiar experiment of "socialism", the more inconceivable to everyone is the attitude of the Allende government and of the leading members of the political parties supporting it. In particular, one cannot explain the attitude of the so-called "Communist" Party of Chile which claims to be Marxist and which played a leading role in the activities of both the Popular Unity and the government. One cannot figure out why this government, with half the population on its side, particularly with the most vital and decisive sections of it, the workers and the peasants, did not mobilize them to smash the reactionary offensive. One cannot explain the government's attachment and submission to the laws and institutions that were not only controlled and used by the subversive opposition, but that were also continuously violated by them according to their putschist plans. The government's attitude towards the Armed Forces is also inconceivable. These Armed Forces were dependent on imperialism and were known to be repressive. Their putschist efforts and even their aborted coup d'état attempts were ever more evident. However, the government professed (and propagated amongst the people) an unlimited confidence in the army and granted it excessive powers. One cannot explain the constant efforts by the Popular Unity government and leadership to extinguish the vigorous fighting spirit exhibited by the masses of the people, which included the use of repression on certain occasions. One cannot figure out why the government did not take advantage of the economic blockade and other forms of aggression by the U.S. government in order to develop an anti-imperialist popular mobilization which could have had repercussions on the continent. Finally, one cannot explain the desperate efforts made (in particular by the leaders of the "C"P) to enter into a pact (which was in fact a surrender offering, a compromise on key points of the government programme) with the Christian Democratic Party, which was in fact manipulated by a team of known agents of U.S. imperialism led by Frei and some of the active organizers of the coup d'état. Were the leaders of the "C"P, the real inspirers of the Popular Unity and of the government's policy, so naive that they believed that they could march to socialism by promoting the political and economic "suicide" of the ruling circles, and this by remaining within the framework of the law? Did they believe in the "constitutional" and "purely professional" spirit of an army which had massacred more than 10,000 workers since the beginning of the century and which, faced in 1964 with the possibility of Allende being elected, made many offers to the U.S Embassy to stage a coup d'état? Moreover, when faced with the furious and multiform offensive of the opposition forces and with putschist schemes, did they put their confidence in the "legalist spirit" of the Chileans to defend the government when they scorned any attempt to appeal to the masses? All these questions and many others remain without any answer from those who continue to pretend that under the Allende government there was a real attempt to establish socialism in Chile. The policy of the Popular Unity leaders (particularly those of the "C"P) who claim to be Marxists is even more paradoxical if we consider that the reactionary opposition forces, together with the CIA, developed their offensive against the Allende government with tactics much closer to "Marxist" tactics than those of the so-called Marxists: they combined legal and illegal struggle, open and underground work, they mobilized the masses around their demands but with the clear intention of overthrowing the government, they used the laws and institutions against it and they bypassed them when it suited their aims, etc.

In this book, we intend to clarify the reasons behind all these "mysteries" stemming from the basic policies of the Popular Unity and its government. In order to do so, it is essential to denounce the real motivations behind the two basic formulations, the two pillars of the Chilean "C"P's strategy that were decisive in this experience: the so-called "peaceful road" to power, and the efforts made to achieve a sort of "historic compromise" with the leaders of the pro-Yankee populist forces. The "mistakes" involved in such a strategy and its ever more evident bankruptcy — evident of course for those who sincerely believed that they were marching to socialism because of Allende's electoral victory — gave rise to intense struggles within the Popular Unity. This increased the confusion, the paralyzation, and in the final analysis, the vulnerability of the Allende government. But the most fundamental mistake was to believe that through the "peaceful road" and the "historic compromise", the "C"P leaders wanted to achieve genuine socialism, and that these were just "erroneous" strategies and "opportunist deviations" followed by them. In this manner, the real reactionary and fully conscious origin of the politics carried by the Chilean "C" P leaders was not seen through, nor was their servile subordination to the strategy put forward by the Soviet Union in Latin America in order to contend for hegemony with the United States. Their plan to establish in Chile alone a counterfeit socialism as in the USSR and in the countries of the Warsaw Treaty also remained unexposed. It is precisely because this strategy, based on reactionary motivations was considered as a "mistake", as a pure "opportunist deviation", and because it was combated as such that it was able to maintain itself as a dominant trend within the Popular Unity and the government. This led to the present tragedy.

As soon as we consider the model of "socialism" advocated by the pro-Soviet leaders of the Chilean "C"P (a state capitalism similar to that created as a result of the degeneration of socialism in the USSR and in the Eastern European countries dependent on her), the "peaceful road" strategy that they preach to the people becomes fully coherent and clear. It is precisely because they only want to replace one system of exploitation by another and because they wish to substitute a bureaucratic bourgeoisie issued from their ranks for the traditional big bourgeoisie and some monopolies, that they are forced, first and foremost, to oppose the revolutionary mobilization of the people and anything that could lead them to the seizure of political power. Therefore, they were forced to maintain the laws and institutions of the bourgeois state and to make sure that they were not destroyed by the people in their revolutionary offensive. This would have meant the failure of their plan to replace one system of exploitation and oppression by another. That is why they limited themselves to bringing pressure on the traditional sectors of the bourgeoisie by demagogically mobilizing the masses, but only in order to bargain on the basis of their capacity to maintain the people within the limits of the existing laws and institutions and to blackmail the bourgeoisie with the threat that the people might come under genuine revolutionary leadership. But they are as much afraid as the traditional bourgeoisie that the people will really embark on the revolutionary road. The necessity to oppose revolution in order to pave the way for a farce of socialism is the essence of the "peaceful road" to "socialism" advocated by the sham communists as a strategy for the people. If the pro-Soviet so-called communists, in preaching this strategy, have completely abandoned Marxism, it has to be very clear that it is not because of simple ideological deviations or mistakes, but because their aims themselves are anti-Marxist and reactionary. It would therefore be quite naive and vain to try and convince them of their opportunism.

On the other hand, it must be clearly seen that the strategy put forward by these sham communists of following the "peaceful road" to power is one thing, and that the methods they use when the time comes to establish their state capitalism under socialist disguise are quite another. The "peaceful road" formulation is designed to prevent the people from rebelling and seizing power through violence, but it does not in the least prevent these sham communists from calling in their armed forces to maintain their own political power, as they did in Czechoslovakia or in Angola; it does not prevent them from using armed mercenaries as in

Zaire nor from resorting to a coup d'état by the infiltration of the bourgeois armed forces, as they tried to do in the Congo; it does not hinder them from infiltrating anti-imperialist governments as they did in Cuba. Even though the goal is always the same (regimes of state exploitation of the people with Soviet social-imperialism pulling the strings), the methods differ according to time and place. Where there is direct domination by the USSR, social-imperialism resorts to armed intervention (as in Czechoslovakia) to crush any attempt at independence or at subversion of state capitalism. In the regions where the domination of the other superpower, U.S. imperialism, is relatively weak, as in Africa and certain regions of Asia, state power is also seized through violence, even though the USSR acts in an underhanded manner. On the other hand, in Western Europe and in America, where U.S. influence predominates, it seems that the strategy is to avoid open challenge (for the time being) with U.S. imperialism and with the forces that are close to it and not to establish a "socialist" model of the Eastern European type. Instead, an alliance is forced with the populist sectors under United States' influence in order to infiltrate the government and state apparatus and engage in joint exploitation of the people together with the ruling circles or a section of them at the expense of the others. This is the precise mission the pro-Soviet so-called communists had (and still have) to accomplish in Chile. From there stems their active promotion of the line of "peaceful road", preventing any mobilization of the people aimed at blocking the road to the reactionary offensive. That is why, at the same time, they made an active use of the devastating effects of this offensive in order to impose, at all costs, a pact with Frei and his team. This very orientation explains why today they are still actively opposing any resistance meant to *overthrow* the Chilean military junta and they are putting forward as the "only alternative" the replacement of the dictatorship by a Christian Democratic government in which they hope to participate, even if it is only in the far future. Thus, they remain loyal to the basis of their strategy: "peaceful road" forbidding the people to rebel against the dictatorship, and "historic compromise" with the pro-Yankee populist forces. While under the Allende government, they preferred to sacrifice the people to fascism instead of letting them fight and open the way to power, today, they prefer their submission to the dictatorship and the prolongation of their sufferings to the possibility of an insurrection which could make their plan fail. They only accept the replacement of this open dictatorship with a "veiled dictatorship" that would keep the bourgeois state apparatus intact, including the Armed Forces which exercise the dictatorship.

Besides the basic theses that we have just formulated, we show in this book that the Soviet Union openly disregarded the possibility of openly defending the Allende regime (economically and still less militarily) because it did not correspond to the strategic model they proposed for Latin America. We show how the Popular Unity government, under "C"P hegemony, would not have led to genuine socialism even if it had been successful in implementing its programme, unless the people, under revolutionary leadership, would have rebelled and fought against its opportunist leadership. We also refute the cynical line of the "C"P leadership according to which it is the "ultra-leftists" who are responsible for the failure of the Allende government. This line is designed to cover up their open sabotage of any real advance towards socialism as well as their own responsibility for the rise of fascism. We show that the middle strata turned against the Allende government not because of simple tactical mistakes in dealing with them, but because of the control of political power by the most reactionary strata and because the opportunist leadership of the Popular Unity refused to lead the people in fighting the reactionaries. In the various chapters, we give detailed analysis of the character of the Chilean Armed Forces, showing their repressive and anti-people history and providing detailed denunciation of the praising campaigns organized for them by the "C"P in particular. We show their dependence on U.S. imperialism and refute the thesis according to which they were "constitutionalist" beyond and above any class role. We also refute the thesis that "it is just a handful of traitors who misled them away from their purely professional role" and that "until the last few months, they were reluctant to unleash a coup d'état".

Besides the interest and opinions that the theses defended in this work may arouse, we made a particular effort to prove everything we assert with extensive and detailed quotations based on a thorough re-reading of all the main newspapers of the government and opposition during the three years of the Allende government as well as of a large number of publications that came out during this period and since the coup d'état. Thus, for those who do not agree with the conclusions that we draw, this study will have at least some documentary value. This documentary analysis comprises a study of the origin of the "peaceful road" thesis in Chile as well as an extensive account of documents dealing with the manner in which Allende's victory was used, in Chile and abroad, in order to promote this thesis. Based on these documents, we also analyze the economic policy of the Allende government, the nationalization process, the crisis of the state economy, the effects of the economic sabotage perpetrated by the opposition and the U.S. government, the magnitude of the reforms applied by the government, and the powerful interests that the government was hitting at. We also carry out a documented analysis of the conflict between the two superpowers (the United States and the Soviet Union) about Chile as well as the expression of this conflict within the country. We examine chronologically the use made by the opposition of the Parliament, the courts, the Contraloria (General Audit) of Republic and other institutions to obstruct all action of the Executive and prepare its overthrow. We include a documentary analysis on the CIA's activity in preparing the coup d'état, particularly within the army. We provide a well-documented study on the political contradictions and differences operating within the various political forces comprising the opposition, the Popular Unity and other anti-putschist forces besides it. In this respect, we include a critical analysis of the weaknesses of the leftist opposition to the dominant line in the Popular Unity and the government. Finally, we further analyze the positions of the various political forces and their activities during the three years that followed the coup d'état, on the basis of their documents and their practical activity.

Even though such an investigation requires a considerable effort (particularly in exile conditions) so that it is based on objective evidence, it is not an uncommitted work, a pure sociological analysis. It is an effort to develop a Marxist-Leninist analysis of the concrete reality of our country and of what took place there. First and foremost, we want to assert that it is not Marxism nor socialism that failed in Chile, and, that this theory, by ridding itself of its falsifiers and combined with the heroic fighting capacity of our people, will lead us to national liberation and genuine socialism.

Jorge Palacios
January, 1977

Part I
Ideological Background to the Political Failure of the Popular Unity

Chapter I
Prehistory of the "Chilean Road" to Socialism

In order to understand the origins of the "Chilean road" to socialism, it is essential to analyze the legal and constitutional context in which the Chilean politics developed and the role played by the pro-Soviet "Communist" Party of Chile.

Chile appeared as an exceptional country in Latin America. It was considered as "the England of Latin America" because for a long time, a certain bourgeois democratic legality and institutionality remained in force. Indeed, despite the fact that almost all the constitutions which governed Chile have been imposed through military pressures, it can be said that there was an old tradition of legalism and bourgeois democracy in this country. Even though the anti-communist repression launched by the Gonzales Videla government, and continued during almost the entire following one, was violating the spirit of the constitution, it was nevertheless legislated through the Parliament: the so-called Law to Defend Democracy.

On the other hand, the bourgeois democratic traditions played a decisive role in the arguments put forward by the leaders of the "Communist" Party of Chile when they were propagating their theory on the so-called "peaceful road" to socialism. But to a large extent, these traditions owe their existence precisely to the influence of this party and the reformist character of the opposition policy it followed for decades in Chile.

1. The Whys and Wherefores of Bourgeois Democracy in Chile

The "Communist" Party of Chile was born a few years after the victory of the socialist revolution in Russia. It deeply integrated with the proletariat of the saltpetre mines operated by imperialist companies. Its founder, Luis Emilio Recabarren, was a great organizer of the working class press in the country. Later on, with the relatively fast industrial development of Chile in the context of dependent countries, its militant activity spread throughout the country. Its growing influence is explained by the prestige of the Bolshevik Revolution of Lenin and Stalin's time and by its role as the builder of the first workers' organizations that took up the demands of the workers and peasants.

Later on, on the eve of the Second World War, the party began to play a leading role in the bourgeois electoral and parliamentary politics, using its mass influence for the creation of broad anti-fascist fronts that were to bring to the Presidency of the Republic the first men who did not belong to the traditional right-wing parties.

Finally, after the war, the party reinforced its bureaucratic and propaganda apparatus. In 1947, it obtained the first significant portion of the vote in the country, winning almost 100,000 votes in the municipal elections before it was outlawed. In 1965, it got almost 300,000 votes, representing then 12.4 per cent of the total. In 1967, it reached 14,7 percent with 341,700 votes, and in 1969, on the eve of the elections that were to bring about the triumph of Allende, it won 15.9 percent of the total votes, with 380,700. As for the Socialist Party, under the hegemony of the "C"P since the 1950's, it got between 250,000 and 300,000 votes in the last three elections just mentioned.

Until the birth of groups of Cuban inspiration and the Revolutionary Communist Party of Chile in the 1960's, the old "Communist" Party of Chile had the prestige of being the only spokesman for the masses of workers and peasants and undoubtedly it was the only party with genuine roots in these classes. The only ones who had ever questioned this role were some weak and isolated Trotskyite groups and a Socialist Party internally undermined by numerous factions and without any clear and consistent alternative line. Furthermore, during the 1950's, after a short-lived populist deviation which caused a large number of its rank and file to split and support General Carlos Ibanez for President (1952-1958), the Socialist Party submitted entirely to the electoral blocs and the strategy put forward by the "C"P.

Because of its mass influence and the hegemony of its class collaborationist politics over the traditional left-wing forces, the "Communist" Party of Chile has been largely responsible for the preservation of the legal and institutional system of exploitation that remained in force until the coup d'état. The maintenance of the bourgeois legality and institutionality until September 11, 1973, allowed the ruling classes to enrich themselves and to exploit the people without the risks involved in resorting to an open and brutal dictatorship that could have aroused a revolutionary opposition as a counterpart. Moreover, as a supplement to this legality and this institutionality and as the real foundation of the regime of exploitation, the ruling classes relied on the Armed Forces and the police, ready to violently suppress any protest that would bypass the limits acceptable and constitute a potential threat to the regime. In fact, any vigorous popular protest against the worst forms of exploitation was always considered as a threat to the system of exploitation and brutally suppressed. Thus the people, lacking a revolutionary orientation, were held for many years "between the sword and the wall": between the sword of the military and the wall of an institutionality and legality basically opposed to their interests.

In this context, the docile opposition into which the leadership of the Chilean "C"P had misled the left explains, to a large extent, the whys and wherefores of the survival of certain relatively stable forms of bourgeois democracy in our country. Far from jeopardizing the regime of exploitation, the Chilean "C"P, one of the most influential in the capitalist world (if not the most influential) considering the population of the country, played an important role in its preservation. This was done by promoting respect for and submission to the existing laws and institutions, by launching, within such a framework, purely economist and conciliating actions to support their demands, by reducing any aspiration for power to mere electoralist attempts during the presidential elections every six years, and finally, once defeated in these elections, by acquiescing to collaborate with the government to form a legalist opposition within the limits tolerated by the ruling classes.

Many honest rank and file militants of the Chilean "C"P who were told that the democratic traditions of Chile were making possible the seizure of power through the "peaceful road" would be quite surprised to learn that in the main these traditions were maintained because they were inefficient as revolutionaries, and nay more, because they were successful in leading broad strata of the population into a purely reformist road. It is precisely because of this that the Chilean "C"P was allowed to send its leaders to Parliament, even though it was claiming to be "Marxist". It is because of this that it was permitted to set up enterprises of a capitalist type belonging to the party, to openly control a series of trade union organizations, to create with other forces a whole movement based on electoral politics and to set up a legal bureaucratic party machine with printing press, journals and radios, with political quarters, and hiring thousands of officials. But later, the "reward" for all these successes materialized in the electoral conquest of the Presidency of the Republic was to be the destruction in fire and blood of all that had been gained during half a century of patient and peaceful work.

Had the militants of the Chilean "C"P been consistent with Marxism, as they claimed to be, they would have understood that the elections in which they believed so much as a means of taking power were nothing but security valves for the exploitation system. They represented the possible variations of a rigid system and their sole use was to maintain the illusion that it was possible to rely on such mechanisms to change the system against the will of the ruling classes. However, as the facts have eloquently shown, those who controlled power had no intention of tolerating a real modification to *their* system that would harm their interests and privileges without opposing it by force. Not only that, it was glaring that they were ready to even destroy *their* institutionality and legality as soon as they would be used against their interests.

Even the election results to which the sham Marxists were attributing some magical power were no more than the thermometer that comes with any security valve. Those holding power and the main instruments of production were using them to periodically assess the level reached by the opposition — channelled and institutionalized through the electoral system — and to determine what concessions or restrictions were necessary. And more importantly, the election results were used by them in order to establish a limit beyond which it was dangerous that the opposition, even institutionalized, use the system to promote its own interests. As it is shown by the manoeuvres deployed to prevent Allende from becoming President of the Republic, this limit came to the fore when the latter took over the executive power and showed willingness to use it in order to undertake reforms that were going to hit hard at the interests of the ruling classes. Under such conditions, the previous benefits of the electoral system as a moderating element designed only to keep the people off the revolutionary path had, to a certain extent, transformed into their opposite: into a threat to the ruling classes.

The exploitation of legality within the framework of the bourgeois institutions and the dissemination of opportunist ideology amongst the masses by the Chilean "C"P leaders were two complementary aspects of the same reality, two sides of the same coin. However, the existence of such a bourgeois democracy and the possibility to enter the Parliament were the central arguments of the revisionist trend dominating the Chilean "C"P: the possibility for the people to seize political power through the "peaceful road". Thus, they were presenting as a specific and essential feature of the Chilean political process something which was basically the consequence of their class collaborationist politics, allowing U.S. imperialism and local reactionaries to exploit the people without having to resort to open dictatorship. They were subjectively transforming a temporary particularity of this process, a result of the lack of revolutionary leadership, into an alleged "law" governing this process.

In order to understand how the experience of the Popular Unity government and the "Chilean road" to socialism so much talked about were arrived at, it is now necessary to briefly look into the policy of the "Communist" Party of Chile which paved the way to such an experience.

2. The Policy of Popular Fronts

After the formation of anti-fascist fronts just before the Second World War, the Chilean "C"P followed a policy of broad alliance with other bourgeois political forces and succeeded in creating the electoral conditions that brought their candidates into the government. These united front alliances were a correct response to the rise of world fascism as well as an important method to unite (in dependent countries such as Chile) broad sectors under the hegemony of the proletariat; however, in our country, they actually remained under the leadership of the bourgeoisie. Moreover, the Chilean "C"P leadership, which was supposed to guarantee proletarian hegemony over the united front, was entirely dominated by bourgeois ideas and the party was put in the service of the rising bourgeois sectors.

The first of these anti-fascist coalitions to win victory was the Popular Front, which presented Pedro Aguirre Cerda as candidate for the Presidency of the Republic in 1938. This candidate, the first president to be elected with the support of the "C"P, was a member of the Radical Party, led by a hodgepodge of right-wing elements with various others of social-democratic tendency. During the election campaign, a modest reformist programme was put forward in which were proposed reforms to the Labour Code, the unionization of the peasants, the dissolution of the National Agricultural Society (organization of the big landlords) and the reorganization of the administration. At no time did the "C"P leaders propose, even in their own documents as an independent line, a programme for people's democratic transformations. They never advocated a genuine revolutionary strategy of seizing power otherwise than through elections. They simply submitted to the modest programme of the bourgeois candidate and they accepted elections as the only road to power. When Aguirre Cerda was elected, none of the points in the programme was implemented, and as far as the most important one was concerned, the unionization of the peasants, the "C"P leaders agreed with the government to postpone it indefinitely.

Later, after the Second World War had broken out, the Chilean "C"P (according to confessions made afterwards by its own leaders) "fell" into the anti-Marxist deviation initiated by Browder, the then General Secretary of the "Communist" Party of the United States. His thesis was that after the defeat of fascism, there would be an agreement between the victorious capitalist countries and the socialist camp. According to him, this agreement would bring about a tremendous improvement of the living conditions of the masses, rapid industrialization and independence of the countries oppressed by imperialism, and a long period of peace making possible a peaceful transition to socialism. Browder was actually a predecessor for the opportunist theses later put forward by Nikita Khrushchov. He himself recognizes this in 1960 when he says: "Nikita Khrushchov has now adopted the 'heresy' for which I was expelled from the CP in 1945. It is the same line, almost word for word, that I defended fifteen years ago. Thus," he concludes, "my crime has been converted, at least for the time being, into the new orthodoxy."

It is in this way that the Anti-Fascist National Union was understood by the "C"P leaders strongly influenced by Browderism, as an almost total renunciation, not only of the struggle for power, but of class struggle itself.

In an article published in *Principios,* theoretical organ of the Central Committee of the "C"P of Chile, Humberto Abarca, national leader, praises the reactionary politician Cruz Coke for the "largeness of mind" and "clarity" that he exhibited when he said in a meeting that "the division between right and left is artificial. To pose the problem of class struggle in this manner is wrong. We have to give a new sense to capitalism, because Chile needs capital".

As for Carlos Contreras Labarca, General Secretary of the "C"P, he shamelessly quotes the *Wall Street Journal,* daily newspaper of the American bankers, to "demonstrate" that "our countries hope that the United States and the great powers will follow a policy aimed at developing our economies and improving the standard of living and consumption capacity of our populations; and this is not based on declarations or vague hopes, but on serious facts."

Later, under the presidency of Juan Antonio Rios, also elected by the votes of the old Chilean "C"P. Elias Lafertte, leader and founder of the party, presented the following programme in 1945, in a report submitted to the Sixteenth Plenum of the Central Committee: "an agrarian reform within the existing juridical framework, trying," he adds, "to be as beneficial as possible to the peasant masses and not to the big landlords." To achieve this, he proposes to expropriate the big landlords "with reasonable compensation and to hand over the land to the peasants who will pay for it on a long term basis." As anti-imperialist measures, this draft programme only proposes: "The revision of the concessions made to the large foreign companies in order to ensure a greater respect of national sovereignty and life of the natives", claiming, however, that in the meantime, "we must attract foreign capital so that it fulfils the role it is assigned to by the good neighbour policy".

The aspirations of the "C"P leaders to gain power were thus reduced to becoming members of some ministerial cabinet together with "all democratic parties and sectors, without exception". In order to achieve this, they devote "maximum energy" according to their own words, to convince the opposition parties (including the party of the President of the Republic) to enter the government. "Our party," says Senator Lafertte, "made every possible effort to convince the leaders of the Radical Party and the Socialist Party of the necessity to give up their policy of opposing the President of the Republic and to achieve an agreement with him so as to promote a progressive policy."

3. The Line of the Post-War Period

Six months after these declarations, at the end of 1945, the Thirteenth Congress of the "Communist" Party of Chile was held. According to the official history, the Browderite and opportunist line was then "swept away". In fact, once the war was over and the conciliation dreams of Browder were smashed by real life, once Browder himself had been severely criticized by the International Communist Movement because of his arch-opportunism and once the contradictions between the Soviet Union and the United States had sharpened, it was then recognized that the "C"P of Chile "had suffered from alien influence which had led it to opportunist deviations" and that "these erroneous views had temporarily weakened the fighting spirit of the party, endangered the independence of its politics and prevented it from playing its role as the leader and the vanguard." However, the report submitted to this Congress contains no revolutionary strategy or programme to replace the previous line recognized as opportunist. On the contrary, in this very report, Contrera

Labarca, General Secretary of the "C"P, continues to beg that his party should be admitted into the bourgeois government, following the old tradition of the party leadership. "The CP," he says, "considers its participation in this cabinet as essential and will fight along with the people to enter this government." Regarding imperialism the "revision of the foreign concessions" put forward by Elias Lafertte is not even raised during the Thirteenth Congress. On the contrary, Contrera Labarca upholds that "the doors of Chile must be opened to foreign capital."

On international politics, it is said that "the guarantee for peace and international security, for the reconstruction of a world of independence, democracy and well-being" would be "the unity between the three great powers: the United States, England and the Soviet Union."

In the middle of 1946, the Chilean "C"P launches a new election campaign in support of Gonzales Videla of the Radical Party, nominated during a convention involving a number of parties. If the problem of "division of large estates" (which, of course, never took place) is raised, absolutely no anti-imperialist measures are put forward, and quite the contrary, the policy of "Good Neighbourhood" is persistently advocated as "a means to win over the collaboration of the United States".

In the beginning of the Gonzales Videla government, the "C"P leaders finally obtain participation in a ministerial cabinet, as they had hoped and begged for a long time: they are put in charge of three departments. This immediately results in frenzied calls for class conciliation, under the hoax that it is necessary to "increase production" and to support a government in which the "communists" are participating. The demands of the masses are restrained in the most scandalous and open manner. In the beginning of 1947, the General Secretary of the "C"P writes: "The provocateur elements are being expelled from the trade union organizations. The working class understands its responsibility as a leading force in front of the government. The workers have enthusiastically supported the call of the Communist Party to increase production and to solve their problems and fulfil their needs by making full use of all the necessary procedures and by resorting to strike only as an exceptional measure." In the report to the Sixth Congress of the Santiago region, the "C"P says : "Faced with the immediate task of collaborating with the government in the battle to increase production, the Confederation of Chilean Workers and our Party have solemnly declared that — without giving up the sacred right to strike — it would be used only as the ultimate resort, after all other means of agreement with the employers and enterprises will have been exhausted." The report castigates the "irresponsible provocateurs" who "want the working class to launch improvised and artificial strikes against the government". Galo Gonzales, later to become General Secretary of the "C"P, upholds that "the Party will make all possible efforts to ensure that the labour conflicts will be solved in harmony between the employers and the workers".

Despite these great services rendered by the leadership of the "C"P to the bourgeois government, the communist ministers were expelled from the government after the municipal elections of 1947 in which the "C"P got a large number of votes. The government legislated the "unionization" of the peasants in order to prevent any real organization in the countryside. Quite upset, a leader of the old "C"P commented: "We are faced with a paradoxical thing. The communists are forced out of the government because the people support them more warmly with every passing day." It is obvious that such a paradox is incomprehensible only to those who never reasoned from a genuinely Marxist standpoint.

Despite their expulsion from the government, the "C"P leaders carried on with their politics of conciliation with the latter: "We will support all the measures taken by the government for the implementation of the Programme. We will not engage in opposition for opposition's sake. (?) We will develop a constructive and realistic policy." As usual, the question of taking power and developing a revolutionary strategy in order to do so was completely left out of the declarations of these "communist" leaders.

In October 1947, Gonzales Videla used the army and the police to encircle the coal miners of Lota who were on a legal strike and he issued a compulsory back-to-work decree. He forbade the members of Parliament to enter the zone and imposed censorship on the left-wing press. He requisitioned food from the homes of the strikers and he established summary courts on warships. Thousands of the strikers' families were forcibly removed to every corner of the country and they were left there, deprived of the most basic necessities. A series of arrests was launched throughout the country against the activists of the "Communist" Party who were jailed or put under home surveillance, or thrown in concentration camps. All those suspected of being members of the party were expelled from their jobs. The following year, the Parliament approved legislation called "The Law to Defend Democracy" depriving all "C"P members of their civil and political rights and providing for jail terms as well as other hard measures to deal with any party activity, propaganda or organizing.

Later, the sharpening of the contradictions between the United States and the Soviet Union and the obvious role of U.S. imperialism in the repression that was rampant in Chile resulted in some progress in the programme of the "Communist" Party of Chile. Thus, in 1949, a "Programme for National Salvation" was developed. It considered the expropriation without compensation of the large land estates, the free nationalization of the public utility companies and the sources of raw materials in the hands of the United States, and the expropriation of private banks and insurance companies. There were also other measures to improve the standard of living of the people and for the democratization of the country. However, even if this political manifesto advocates the "overthrow of the present government and its replacement with a democratic, representative government", there is no definition for this new type of government, no explanation as to the role of the proletariat in it and no revolutionary strategy is developed for the seizure of political power.

The systematic persecutions launched by Gonzales Videla reduced the number of the members of the old "C"P to less than 3,000, half of whom were newcomers, recruited during the repression period. The others, trained for electoralist and economist struggle, could not resist such a repression and left the party.

Under such circumstances, with the hard lessons of the

repression, the struggle between opposing trends within the "C"P leadership came up all the more strongly. One tendency, the minority, upheld the necessity to overthrow the Gonzales Videla dictatorship. The other one, for its part, only wished to restore legality by making pledges to the ruling classes that its true aim was to respect the bourgeois democratic laws and institutions. The rightists within the "C"P leadership, taking advantage of the fact that their opponents were dispersed all over the country, began to co-opt into the leading bodies all sorts of elements having ideas similar to theirs and who had been members of the Central Committee annex commissions. These individuals, many of whom were former Trotskyites, were linked with the Freemasonry or had taken open anti-communist stands, were to take over the key positions in the leadership. Because of these manoeuvres, the opponents of conciliation became a minority in the leading bodies and began to develop factional activities from the National Organizing Commission of the "C"P and from a work group created by the commission. However, isolated from the masses and even from the party rank and file, they undertook a series of putschist actions against the dictatorship. These actions were used by their opponents in order to discredit them and finally, in 1950, they were expelled from the party.

The consequences of the takeover of the "C"P leadership by the most right-wing faction did not take long to come. In the middle of that year, they developed a document-programme known as the "Emergency Plan", which is a definite regression compared to the previous "Plan for National Salvation". The slogan for the nationalization of the imperialist enterprises was replaced by that of "protection, in terms convenient to the country, of the national production against imperialist competition. Suspension of the payment of the external debt as long as the crisis persists. Obligation for the companies to have their administration in Chile itself." The agrarian reform was reduced to the "obligation to cultivate the non-exploited lands. Assistance to all cultivators, big or small, interested in increasing production. Requisition, during the periods of crisis, of the uncultivated lands that their owners refuse to put in production. . . ."

Galo Gonzales, General Secretary of the Chilean "C"P, justified these concessions compared to the previous programme with the unity that must be built, because "all the activities of the party and all the people's struggles must be merged, linked and developed on the basis of the struggle for peace."

Just before the 1952 presidential elections, in which Salvador Allende was presented for the first time, the "C"P united with a section of the Socialist Party, and under the pressure of this ally, it came back to the slogans calling for the agrarian reform and the nationalization of foreign enterprises.

During the elections, a large number of the "C"P activists were deleted from the electoral lists because of the "Law to Defend Democracy". Allende suffered his first defeat and only got 5.45 percent of the vote. General Carlos Ibanez triumphed. This man had already been head of a dictatorial government during the world crisis and was responsible for large-scale penetration of North American capital in Chile. Even though it had denounced these facts during the election campaign, the Political Commission of the "C"P said, after the victory of Ibanez: "The Communist Party is willing to make a resolute contribution so that the government of Mr. Carlos Ibanez can act for the benefit of the country. It will support all practical measures that this government will adopt for the benefit of the people and the nation." And, forgetting as usual the problem of taking power: "Our attitude, inspired by the sole desire of serving the people, will be one of patriotic collaboration to solve problems and of patriotic and constructive opposition to government actions inconvenient to the masses of the people and to Chile." Even after one year of the reactionary Carlos Ibanez government which was continuing to implement the repressive legislation of the previous government, the leadership of the "C"P stated, in *Principios,* theoretical organ of its Central Committee: "Our goal is to try to harmoniously solve the conflicts between labour and capital by using all possible means. And we advocate resorting to strike, a right recognized by the Labour Code, only after all other means have failed."

4. The Twentieth Congress of the CPSU and the "Peaceful Road"

The opportunist line of the "C"P leaders was to receive, later, an international support from the Soviet leaders when the orientation revising Marxism adopted during the Twentieth Congress of the CPSU became public. When the Twentieth Congress of the CPSU was held, the leaders of the "C"P of Chile had not held a congress for eleven years. However, a few months after the political turn in the USSR, the Tenth Congress of the "C"P *(1)* was hastily held without any prior discussion only to impose, in Chile, the theses formulated by Khrushchov, in particular those concerning the "peaceful road" to socialism. It must be remembered that during the Twentieth Congress of the CPSU, Khrushchov and other ideologues of modern revisionism raised the slogan of "using the parliamentary road for the transition to socialism" and declared that: "Today, the international and national conditions favourable for the working class of a series of capitalist countries to accomplish the socialist revolution through the peaceful road are being created."

In January 1961, in *Principios,* Luis Corvalan declared, echoing the Soviets, that: "The great merit of the Twentieth Congress of the CPSU is that it re-established the validity of the peaceful road rejected by the Communist Movement after Lenin's death, even as an exceptional possibility. . ." And in the issue No. 35 of the same magazine, giving a good illustration of his tailism regarding the Soviets, he said: "This question *(the peaceful road)* has been raised from the prominent tribune of the Twentieth Congress of the CPSU. In Chile itself, we had demonstrated the possibility of using the parliamentary road to lead the people's forces to power *(?)*. But this question was not sufficiently clear to us. Now, we clearly see that such a possibility also exists for us in Chile; if we destroy the anti-democratic handiwork of Gonzales Videla and democratize the country, there is no doubt that new promising perspectives will open before us for the unity of broad strata for the democratic transformation of our society, without waiting for nor creating a situation favourable to insurrection. . ."

From the Twentieth Congress of the CPSU onward, the activities of the "C"P leaders were centred around the restitution of the "C"P's legal and electoral rights so that it could arrive at government through the "peaceful road". Allende's election was nothing but the culminating point, as well as the tragic conclusion, of this path. In 1957, the year following the Twentieth Congress of the CPSU, Luis Corvalan, already General Secretary of the "C"P, issued a statement calling upon the reactionaries to restore the civil rights of the "C"P. This statement is a monstrous abjuration of the basic principles of Marxism. During the Twenty-Fourth Plenum of the Central Committee, he declared: "We want and demand our civil liberties. And we solemnly declare that once we will be free to operate in the political life, we will not be of any threat to any respectable interest. We are in favour of solving everything democratically, in accordance with the majority of the country and within the free play of all parties and trends. We do not advocate today the substitution of collective property for the private property of the Chilean capitalists. And when tomorrow we will move over to this task, we think that it will also have to be done with the agreement of the majority of Chileans, through the peaceful road and securing the rights and welfare of the capitalists, that is providing them with due compensation." Naturally, after such a commitment, the civil rights of the "C"P were restored. A party with such an orientation represented no danger for the exploiters and their system. On the contrary, it was rendering them an invaluable service by bringing the masses of the people under its influence to "set the pace" for the legalist and electoralist political manoeuvrings that would never seriously jeopardize their power. It is tempting to quote here an ironical comment made by Marx and Engels concerning a similar attitude of the German Social-Democratic Party: *"Let the Party therefore prove,"* they write, *"by its humble and lowly manner that it has once and for all laid aside the 'improprieties and excesses' which occasioned the Anti-Socialist Law. If it voluntarily promises that it intends to act only within the limits of this law, Bismarck and the bourgeoisie will surely have the kindness to repeal it, as it will then be superfluous!" (2)* But in the case of Chile, there had not even been the *"improprieties and excesses"* on the part of the "C"P, and Gonzales Videla, as he confided to an English reporter of the *New Chronicle,* had launched the repression against this party because he believed that a new world war, this time between the United States and the Soviet Union, would break out in the coming months and he wanted to be one of the first Latin American leaders to side with the United States.

Under the governments that followed that of Carlos Ibanez, those of Jorge Alessandri and Eduardo Frei, the leaders of the Chilean "C"P persisted in implementing a policy of putting a brake on class struggle and developing a conciliatory opposition to the government of the moment. *"For everyone knows,"* Lenin writes, *"that the history of all revolutions the world over reveals an inevitable rather than accidental transformation of the class struggle into civil war." (3)* Therefore, the basic role of these sham Marxists was indeed to pit themselves against class struggle in order to prevent any evolution towards civil war and so that they could continue their dreams of peacefully taking power.

These conciliatory politics led President Alessandri, a government representative of the most reactionary circles of the country, to issue a certificate of good behaviour to the leaders of the "C"P, declaring at the end of his mandate that during his administration, there had been no serious problem with this party, because it was an organization respectful of the laws and democratic life.

During the Frei administration, they continued to practise a basically verbal opposition and to obstruct, in fact, the struggles of the people. At the end of 1967, following the guide-lines and demands of the American-controlled financial organization, the International Monetary Fund, the Frei government put forward a wage readjustment plan aimed at shifting onto the back of the workers the effects of the crisis seriously aggravated during the last years of its administration. On December 13, 1967, Luis Corvalan said, referring to this readjustment plan: "In general, to vote in favour of this project means to turn on the green light for this retrogressive policy. To vote against it does not amount to refusing any wage legislation. It means voting against the retrogressive policy of the government and creating conditions so that it will table a different plan." After this readjustment plan was unanimously rejected, the government tabled before the Parliament a plan described by the "C"P leaders as "more reactionary than the previous one". However, after secret negotiations with the Christian-Democratic leaders, the "C"P members of Parliament turned on the "green light" for this second plan by voting for its inclusion on the agenda. In order to justify this betrayal of the workers' interests before public opinion, they said that the negative aspects of the plan would be eliminated during the article by article discussion in Parliament. This was but a sham and hypocritical justification aimed at concealing their compromise with the Frei government, since they knew perfectly well that the traditional left did not have enough votes to change these articles once the plan was on the agenda. Thus, in May 1968, the plan was approved just as the government had wished.

Later, these conciliatory activities became even more evident as the 1970 presidential elections were drawing near. In December 1969, Luis Figueroa, a member of the Political Commission of the "C"P and president of the United Workers' Central (Central Unica de Trabajadores — CUT), signed an agreement on behalf of this central that included almost all the organized workers accepting a minimum wage of 12 escudos per day. On December 5, *El Siglo* (daily journal of the "C"P) had published a paragraph concerning the protracted strike at the FENSA steel plant, saying: "The workers are demanding a raise of 75 per cent, with a minimum of 28 escudos per day, which is hardly enough to live." Yet, without any mobilization or struggle, they committed all the CUT members to accept, through the compromise signed by Figueroa, a minimum wage of less than half of what they had described as "hardly enough to live".

Naturally, the agreement signed by Figueroa and the government was warmly praised by the reactionary circles. The journal *El Mercurio,* mouthpiece of the monopoly bourgeoisie and the American firms, declared on December 5, 1969: "It must be recognized that it *(the agreement)* reflects an atmosphere different from that we have been accustomed to during the debates on readjustment. . . On this occasion, the United Workers' Central has contributed to avoid the atmosphere that it usually takes upon itself to cultivate on such occasions. . . . The said agreement also includes some hope for social peace and a pledge from the CUT leaders." On the same day, *Diario Ilustrado,* representing the most reactionary oligarchy, wrote: "It is very good to see how easily the government could come to full agreement with the CUT . . . It is good because this could mean a sort of 'entente' between the government and the CUT." For his part, the Minister of the Interior in the Frei government said about the agreement that "it sets an example, in our difficult times, for many other sectors which have not yet reached a true understanding. It is for this reason that I wish to express my gratitude to the CUT for its responsibility and seriousness. . . . "

Finally, in the middle of 1970, when the workers responded to the decline of their standard of living imposed by the compromise between Figueroa and the government with a national strike, the "C"P leaders again contrived with the government so that during the strike, any manifestation of fighting spirit would be suppressed in order to make sure that the coming presidential elections would not be prejudiced. On July 9, the president of the governing party said: "The provocateurs of the ultra-left make it necessary to have an agreement between the various political forces for the appropriate completion of the electoral process. Tomorrow, I hope to meet with the radicals, the communists and the socialists". On July 16, the same leader stated in *La Segunda:* "I had discussion with the communists and the socialists concerning the CUT strike as well as with the student leaders in order to maintain social peace and not to disturb the order." The result of these conversations was the intimate collaboration between some "C"P activists and the police "Mobile Group" in directly suppressing the workers who marched in the streets on the day the strike took place in order to stage a more militant protest. The day after the strike, *El Siglo,* telling the reactionaries how it was capable of stifling the mass struggles, referred to "the Sunday aspect of the people and districts, people in discussion in the streets and on the sidewalks, children playing and women taking sunbaths" during the strike.

The pretext continuously used by the "C"P leaders to suppress any fighting spirit of the masses of the people was that of a "threatening coup d'état" by the ultra-right which was already unhappy because of the reforms affecting their interests carried out by the Christian-Democrats. This threat, just like the fable of the wolf, is used by the "C"P leaders every time there is an upsurge of the people's struggles. But curiously enough, these "Marxists" do not use these threats of coup d'état in order to mobilize the masses and prepare them ideologically and materially so that they can face the alleged putschist attempts, but rather to make them abandon all "exaggerated" demands and any fighting mobilization and patiently wait for the presidential elections that will enable them to implement a policy favourable to the people. The "C"P leaders stuck to such a policy in order to avert the threat (real, this time) of a coup d'état during the Allende administration. We all know the consequences. The difference is that this time, they entrusted the wolf itself (the reactionary Armed Forces) with the mission of preventing the so dreadful coup d'état.

Chapter II
The Ideology of Defeat:
The "Peaceful Road to Power"

As we have pointed out in the beginning of this book, the dominant line in the "C"P of Chile was an opportunist line, both in its programme and in its concrete political activities, and this had been the case long before the Twentieth Congress of the CPSU. During this period, however, these purely reformist activities and lines were not systematized as a thesis revising Marxism.

On the other hand, these reformist lines and political practices coexisted within the old "C"P (and they did so "peacefully" until the Twentieth Congress) with a certain theoretical education of the party activists on the basis of the works of Marx, Engels, Lenin Stalin and Mao or of Marxist revolutionary history. While in the Cadres Schools all this was studied, the political line was condemning the activists to engage in economist struggles, in election battles, in ceaseless money-raising campaigns, in propaganda work for this very line, and in purely reformist activities aimed, in the final analysis, at winning some votes in the elections. At no time was there a relation between the teachings of the Marxist classics or the revolutionary history and what was required from the Chilean "communists". There was also no relation between their programme, for example, and the minimal conditions required from a party to be admitted in the Communist International of Lenin. These conditions were never met.

The truth is that this contradiction was concealed and veiled by various circumstances. During the decade prior to the Second World War, a misunderstanding and a wrong application of the policy of anti-fascist united fronts (negating the principle of both unity and struggle within these fronts and the necessity of proletarian leadership over them) allowed opportunism to make its way in various places through these correct alliances. This is precisely what happened in Chile. On the other hand, during and immediately after the war, the opportunist and anti-Marxist trend initiated by Browder had tremendous influence in Latin America. Finally, concerning Chile, the dominant reformist and opportunist trends were not seen through because of the ban against the "C"P and the legal persecution of its activists and their work. It was this illegal status and these persecutions (1947-1957) as well as the necessity to organize underground, and the reactionary propaganda that called the "C"P activists "subversive" that conferred a revolutionary aureole upon this party. Also, there was the idea of "doing something" to overthrow the Gonzales Videla government which was circulated amongst a large number of militants and even some leaders. But this was only a state of mind on the part of those who had been betrayed by Gonzales Videla and wanted to take revenge, or rumours spread once in a while to "raise the morale" of the activists until legality would be restored. These leaders never presented a consistent policy aimed at developing class struggle so as to achieve this goal. The official policy was to wage struggles for demands, to participate in elections under the cover of other forces and to protest against repressive measures, begging for the restoration of the previous legal rights of the "C"P.

Finally, the struggle opposing the tendency of a tiny group of "C"P activists (and some leaders) who organized putschist actions against the government and that of the remaining leadership who only wanted the restoration of legality and of the right to run in the elections at whatever cost resulted in a split. After the expulsion of this small rebellious group, the domination of the most rightist and opportunist trend within the "C"P was complete.

However, the contradiction between such leaders and a large number of activists who honestly considered themselves Marxist, who had suffered from the reactionary repression and who had access to Marxist literature had in no way been suppressed nor resolved. This contradiction was brought in the open when the ruling classes legalized the "C"P again and when the anti-Marxist theses deprived of any originality, put forward in the past by Bernstein and Kautsky, became the international line set by "the prominent tribune of the Twentieth Congress of the CPSU". This congress was held in 1956 and the Chilean "C"P was given back its legal status the following year. From the Twentieth Congress of the CPSU onward. the leaders of the "C"P, and especially Luis Corvalan, its present Secretary General, began, following the Soviet revisionist ideologues, to systematize and to publicly promote an opportunist *political theory* aimed at justifying and pursuing the opportunist *political practice* which had in fact been theirs for many years. In this manner, while they were beginning to "theorize" and hoping to justify their parliamentary cretinism, their respect of bourgeois legality and their opportunist line through writings, they only highlighted their extreme opportunism before their activists who, although profoundly dissatisfied with their political activity within the "C"P, were unable to understand the anti-Marxist ideological roots of such an opportunism.

1. Corvalan's Arguments

In February 1961, the "C"P leadership published a pamphlet entitled *Our Revolutionary Road,* which was a collection of various articles by Corvalan defending the theses of the Twentieth Congress of the CPSU. In this pamphlet, he was defending the idea that in Chile, a "peaceful road" to socialism was possible. Pretending that he was applying Marxism to the conditions of Chile in a "creative" and "original" way, Corvalan was in fact only plagiarizing the opportunist nonsense of Khrushchov, who, on the other hand, was just repeating the rotten arguments put forward by the old renegades already repudiated by Marx, Engels, Lenin and Stalin.

Quoting, for example, the Soviet neo-revisionist Kusinen, Corvalan tries to justify the "peaceful road" to power for Chile by arguing that Marx had admitted this possibility for England and the United States in 1872. And he does so with all the dishonesty characteristic of the conscious opportunists, because he certainly knows what Lenin himself wrote on this question: *"The argument that Marx in the seventies allowed for the possibility of a peaceful transition to socialism in England and America is completely fallacious, or, to put it bluntly, dishonest in that it is juggling with quotations and references. Firstly, Marx regarded it as an exception even then. Secondly, in those days monopoly capitalism, i.e. imperialism, did not exist. Thirdly, in England and America there was no military clique then — as there is now — serving as the chief apparatus of the bourgeois state machine."* (4) Let us just add that the factors pointed out by Lenin in order to refute the fraudulent utilization of Marx's quotation by Kautsky, i.e. militarism, imperialism, etc., not only have not decreased in importance, but have taken monstrous proportions. Thus, the swindle of Corvalan, who is also *"juggling with quotations and references",* is even worse than that of Kautsky.

In another article, conscious of the fact that the entire historical experience goes against his wrong thesis of "peaceful road" to socialism, Corvalan completely reverses the Marxist theory of knowledge and writes: "Even though there has been no example of socialist revolution through the peaceful road, it was not necessary to rely on historical precedents to establish the thesis that this road is possible. If, to develop any Marxist-Leninist thesis." he adds, "it was necessary to have practical proof of it, a complete realization, the classics of Marxism would have never been able to develop many of their theses." Of course, the occurrence of a fact is not necessary for us to foresee it. Marx and his followers foresaw the socialist society at a time when it had not materialized in any country. However, if the prediction of a new fact is to be scientific, it has to be based on events, conditions and historical laws that make it possible and necessary. Otherwise, such a prediction is only the expression of either wishful thinking or the conscious intention to mislead with false declarations. As for the possibility of a peaceful transition to socialism, as we have seen, the factors opposing it not only did not shrivel, but intensified in our era. Therefore, the declarations of Corvalan and those who are docile followers of the falsifiers governing the USSR have no basis either in theory or in practice. They are nothing but lies and speculations in the service of an opportunist line.

In another part of his writings, Corvalan puts forward another view to defend his bourgeois pacifism that will lead the disarmed

Chilean people to massacre. This view implies another complete falsification of the Marxist theory of the state. He says: "The proletariat and its party have never been supporters of violence for the sake of violence", in order to justify the necessity to use peaceful means to take power. Thus, as nobody, except a few mental patients, is for "violence for the sake of violence", in fact the meaning of this clever short sentence of Corvalan is that he refuses to recognize the violence inherent to the bourgeois state. This is why he adds: "if the ruling classes resort to violence, it is possible that the people's movement will be forced to follow another path, the armed struggle."

Thus for Corvalan, violence only exists when the ruling classes resort to prison and massacre as their usual policy. When they do not do these things on a daily basis, when there is a façade of bourgeois democracy, according to Corvalan, we are in a "normal" situation, having nothing to do with violence, and therefore, the people have no right to use it in order to liberate themselves. But anyone fairly versed in Marxism or opening his eyes to reality knew that in Chile (as in any bourgeois regime) the people were subjected to constant violence under a bourgeois dictatorship wearing a democratic mask. It was not a question of future violence, to which they did not respond with the other road Corvalan talks about anyway, but a question of actual daily and permanent violence. That violence was not only expressed in the periodic massacres which occur even in the most "democratic" capitalist societies, but also in the subjection of the people to wretchedness, unemployment, malnutrition, insanitary housing conditions, premature death, and in short, to the conditions inherent to the system of exploitation. Or is it that Mr. Corvalan believes that the Chilean people have voluntarily accepted, because they like them, the misery and ferocious exploitation to which they are subjected? The truth is that they were forced to accept this through violence. This was imposed upon them precisely by a state which, although bourgeois democratic in form, is nevertheless, as Lenin puts it: *"a special organization of force; . . . an organization of violence for the suppression of some class".(5)* Thus, whenever the people fight more intensely to liberate themselves from the daily "violence" inherent to the system of exploitation, this veiled and hypocritical violence transforms itself into deliberate massacres, jailings and tortures. It is therefore not a situation, as Corvalan suggests, where the reactionaries *may* resort to violence and where, in such a case only, it would be justified to give up the peaceful means. Class dictatorship and violence, open and brutal as today, or veiled by some apparent "democratic guarantees", have always existed in Chile under the different regimes of exploitation.

Corvalan reveals his class nature in another text and he is led to adapt himself to the bourgeois society and to "forget" the permanent violence that crushes the Chilean people. After having asserted with the utmost frivolity that the armed struggle to overthrow the Chilean ruling classes "would last a maximum of a few days or a few weeks" because "no government would be able to sustain a stoppage of the main activities during one month", he states that "peaceful revolution corresponds to the interests of the working class and the masses of the people". We ask: if, as Corvalan says, a few weeks of struggle is enough for the people to liberate themselves from their exploiters, why is it that he prolongs their sufferings for decades and decades? Corvalan answers with no less original and absurd arguments: "In practice", he says, "the Chilean people's movement, given the concrete historical conditions of this country" *(he probably refers to the protracted opportunist influence of his party)*, "has for a long time developed along the peaceful road, since the period of the Popular Fronts, for twenty-five years." And he adds: "If the Chilean people's movement has marched for years on the peaceful road, why is it only now and not before that objections are spreading in certain left-wing circles?" The very fact that Corvalan asks such a question shows to what extent these sham communists are integrated in the bourgeois society. They are incapable of understanding that the masses of the people are questioning a "road to power" that has maintained them in misery and exploitation for over half a century. And, a further aberration, they use the fact that an error has been maintained for a long time in order to justify the necessity of perpetuating it. Following this logic, when we will celebrate the centennial of the failure of the "peaceful road" to power, Corvalan's argument advocating the persistence along this road will be even more valid.

The fact of the matter is that with his arguments, Corvalan exhibits both his adventurist mind and his ultra-right opportunism, claiming on the one hand that it is possible to overthrow the ruling classes in a few weeks, and presenting on the other hand the prolonged failure of the peaceful road as an argument to justify the very policy that has prevented the people from liberating themselves. The tragic experience the Chilean people have gone through since the fascist coup d'état has the virtue of showing the falseness of both these assertions: it was not possible to overthrow the power of the ruling classes through the peaceful road in order to establish a kind of state capitalism (let alone using such a road to establish genuine socialism), and neither was it possible for the people's violence to obliterate in a few weeks the violence unleashed by the ruling classes.

The concrete form of the "peaceful road" to socialism in Chile, as advocated by Corvalan, was to use the elections to take power. Showing once again that he has completely betrayed the Marxist theory on the nature of the bourgeois state and on the necessity to destroy it, as Marx, Engels and Lenin said, in order to establish the dictatorship of the proletariat, Corvalan gives as an example to illustrate the possiblility of taking power through the "peaceful road" the "resounding electoral victories" won by the "C"P in supporting bourgeois candidates! The fact that Gonzales Videla viciously suppressed the "C"P after he had been elected by its votes was not even used by him for pondering over the little significance of such "resounding victories" in the service of the bourgeoisie. On the contrary, on the basis of these examples, he concludes that it is possible to gain power "through the electoral process" in order to use "the presidential regime to bring about important changes of all sorts, with the free play of all parties and trends". Thus, in 1961, the theory was already clearly formulated that was to bring about the disaster spearheaded ten years later by the Popular Unity, the main victim of which was to be the Chilean people.

2. The Marxist-Leninist Opposition

After the Twentieth Congress of the CPSU, when the Chilean "C"P leaders began to openly formulate their revisionist theories, some activists of the party, honest and loyal to Marxism-Leninism, began to oppose them. On the occasion of a congress held during the 1960's, a large number of activists and even whole units took positions opposing the official line and criticizing the merely reformist, legalist and economist activity into which the leaders were dragging the party. The ideological discussion was mainly centred around the opportunist theory of the "peaceful road" to socialism, transformed into the official line by the "C"P leadership.

However, the struggle developed during this congress was in no way capable of changing the opportunist positions. The bureaucracy of the pro-Soviet revisionist leaders was exercising a powerful control over the key organs of the "C"P. They were thus able to slavishly mobilize themselves to silence all those disagreeing with them by resorting to threats and pressures, corruption and other manoeuvres and to prevent them from being delegates to the regional and local congresses.

Later, in 1963, the publication of the material of the Communist Party of China and the Party of Labour of Albania against modern revisionism was of invaluable assistance to the Marxist-Leninists who had begun to regroup within the parties manipulated by the pro-Soviet revisionists. This polemic assisted them in reaffirming their opinions against the widespread distortions of Marxism, in providing new arguments for the ideological struggle with the important support of parties already in power, and finally, in showing that these deviations were not only a national and local problem, but a world-wide counter-current launched by the Soviet leaders. Thus, with this polemic, a group named "Espartaco" (Spartacus) constituted itself within the Chilean "C"P in 1963 and began to publish and disseminate the Chinese and Albanian publications in Chile, in open opposition to and rebellion against the opportunist leaders of the party.

The struggle against these leaders and their anti-Marxist line within the "C"P showed the people waging it that such leaders were not honestly mistaken leaders, but fully conscious traitors to Marxism-Leninism and unconditional agents of the USSR chieftains. They never accepted a frank discussion within the ranks of the old "C"P with those in disagreement with them, and not even with those who agreed with them but had doubts. In their fight against the Marxist-Leninists, they were content with slandering them, attempting to corrupt them, threatening and assaulting them, and with forbidding them to give their views. All this served to show that within the old "C"P, the minimal conditions of internal democracy necessary to have the Marxist-Leninist line adopted did not exist because the bureaucrats sold out to the Soviet chieftains had received the order to impose their anti-Marxist fabrications at whatever cost. Therefore, the only alternative was to pull the honest activists away from the "C"P and to create a genuine Marxist-Leninist party.

At the end of 1963, the internal struggle led to a split from the "C"P and to the birth of a Marxist-Leninist group that kept the name "Spartacus", forerunner of the Revolutionary Communist Party of Chile. When it started engaging in activities as an independent group, "Spartacus" also had to wage a fight against the Trotskyites who were trying to take advantage of the struggle against revisionism to infiltrate the newly born organization so as to take control of it. It also had to fight the Cuban leaders and their followers who were attempting, in a hypocritical and veiled manner, to serve revisionism by putting up the mask of ultra-"left" positions apparently different from those of the Soviet leaders. They rendered to the latter and their Latin American lackeys an invaluable service in that a number of petty-bourgeois elements, dissatisfied with the reformism of the pro-Soviet parties, were led to adopt various forms of armed struggle without any links with the masses and doomed to be defeated and wiped out. At the same time, they actively preached that for the seizure of power, it was not necessary to build genuine proletarian parties and united fronts led by the proletariat. In this manner, they caused a large number of people who could have played a positive role within the Marxist-Leninist parties to be drawn away from the masses of the people, thus clearing the way for the poisonous influence of revisionism and leading these people to unavoidable death at the hands of the reactionary armed forces under Yankee-imperialist advice. Thus, the "guerrilla foci" (and their later variations: urban guerrillas, expropriations, terrorism, etc.) smashed throughout Latin America were used by the revisionists in order to discredit "armed struggle" in general and to strengthen their arguments for a peaceful and reformist line. Finally, as Fidel Castro and the other Cuban leaders increasingly revealed themselves to be lackeys of Soviet social-imperialism, they forced the groups close to them to openly put themselves in the service of the Latin American revisionist parties. In fact, these groups, by maintaining secondary differences with the revisionists and putting forward positions in appearance more radical, served to rally those who were dissatisfied with revisionism, to prevent them from opposing it on a correct basis within the masses, and to maintain them in fact linked with opportunist politics on the main questions. The politics of the MIR leadership in Chile, particularly during the Popular Unity government, are a good example of this.

The "Spartacus" group not only worked directly among the masses and led numerous struggles, but it also carried out propaganda work and ideological education. From its birth it published a daily journal called *Combate* and a theoretical review called *Principios Marxista-Leninistas,* as well as a large number of factory newspapers, pamphlets, etc. In the second issue of the mentioned review (May-June 1964), I was asked by the leadership of "Spartacus" to write a detailed article entitled *The Peaceful Road of Corvalan: Counter-Revolutionary Road.* Already in this article, six years before the experience of the Popular Unity government, the farce of the "peaceful road" to socialism was refuted and the tragedy to which it would lead the Chilean people if implemented was foreseen.

The "Spartacus" group, in the context of the international struggle against modern revisionism, also started to establish links with the Marxist-Leninist organizations which had just been born in Latin America and other parts of the world and especially with the Communist Party of China and the Party of Labour of Albania which had always upheld the banner of Marxism-Leninism. These contacts had a prodigious importance for the transformation of "Spartacus" from a political group into a Marxist-Leninist communist party.

The long interview that the greatest revolutionary leader and Marxist theoretician of our times, Comrade Mao Tsetung, had with the leaders of "Spartacus" at the end of 1964 was particularly decisive for the building of this Marxist-Leninist communist party. During the interview, Comrade Mao gave us great encouragement for the arduous struggle that we had undertaken. He showed us that although in the beginning we were few in numbers, we would undoubtedly be successful if we remained loyal to principles and linked ourselves with the masses. He warned us that we would have to suffer setbacks and he taught us to draw lessons from them, taking examples from the history of his own Party and the revolution in his own country. He urged us to closely unite with the masses, particularly the workers and the peasants, and to lead them as well as learn from them. Finally, he particularly exhorted us to study the concrete conditions of our country in the light of Marxism-Leninism so as to better fight revisionism without falling into dogmatism and without mechanically copying from foreign experiences.

3. The Birth of a Genuine Communist Party

The "Spartacus" group, with the clear goal of establishing a genuine Marxist-Leninist communist party of Chile, set itself three basic tasks in order to achieve this goal: firstly, the development of a long-term programme for the Chilean revolution that would lead the masses of the people on the revolutionary road and at the same time politically and ideologically unite those joining the Party. Secondly, spreading the "Spartacus" organization over the entire national territory, in the Leninist organizational form (basic units, local and regional committees). Thirdly, having in its ranks a large majority of activists from working class and peasant origin. These basic conditions were met in 1964-65. They were achieved in the active and fighting participation of "Spartacus" in the struggles of the workers, peasants, students and other people against the fraudulent pro-Yankee reformist politics of the Frei government.

In February 1966, the Founding Congress of the Revolutionary Communist Party of Chile *(Partido Comunista Revolucionario — PCR)* was held in Santiago, in absolute secrecy. Ninety-three delegates from the various regional committees created in the country and amongst whom the workers and peasants pre-dominated attended the congress. The Communist Rebel Union, a Marxist-Leninist organization from the northern part of the country created for the same ideological and political reasons as "Spartacus", also sent delegates to the Congress. There were also fraternal delegations from the Marxist-Leninist parties and organizations of Argentina, Bolivia, Brazil, Ecuador and Peru who, on the basis of their experience, made important contributions to the Congress and the birth of the Party.

The PCR, since its inception, had as a basic prerequisite for joining its ranks the acceptance of its ideology and main political line. It systematically refused to engage in uncontrolled recruitment, neither in the form of mergers with groups based on fundamentally different principles or line, nor through unprincipled proselytism. Just like "Spartacus", it decided to maintain a basically underground structure. It firmly opposed organizing the Party and carrying out its activities in the manner of the bourgeois parties, that is on the basis of public meetings, public quarters, rallies of activists, commercial type of propaganda, large number of officials, open militancy, etc. One can use the bourgeois laws and institutions in the service of an essentially revolutionary policy, but without submitting and adapting to them, because that would compromise the political independence of the Party and the security of its illegal work. The fact that the struggles of the PCR and its integration with the masses have not been known in their full breadth and depth is due, among other things, to these characteristics, let alone the deliberate will of the right-wing and traditional left-wing forces to block any information about the Party. The PCR does not want to engage in glamourous actions of a publicity type, and that is why, as well as for security reasons aimed at making the struggle more efficient, it does not claim as its own all the struggles that it leads and it even less tries to appropriate the struggles of others. However, larger and larger strata within the masses — and that is the most important — know its activities and its positions, developed by living with the masses, sharing their struggles, their weals and woes, and building the Party in their midst. Thus, the development of the PCR and its influence are solid, profound and stable, and the Party is not subject to the fluctuations suffered by the bourgeois parties that base their influence on demagogical propaganda aimed at manipulating the people "from the outside", without really uniting with them and serving their real interests.

While intensifying its activities among the masses, the PCR has developed to serve this task a broad work of propaganda and political education of the masses. In addition to numerous theoretical and political pamphlets, it has published various periodicals disseminated throughout the nation such as *Espartaco, Denuncia Popular (Popular Accusation),* and *El Pueblo (The People),* which is still published underground today. From May 1968 to the 1973 coup d'état, twenty-five issues of a theoretical review *(Causa Marxista-Leninista)* have been published. This review even spread its influence outside of Chile, since a number of its articles have been reprinted in other countries.

The Leninist underground structure of the PCR and its loyalty to principles, on both the organizational and the political levels, made it possible for it to be today in Chile, under the ferocious fascist dictatorship, far ahead of all the others, in better conditions to organize the resistance against the dictatorship. Almost all its activities and leaders are inside the country; all its basic organizations and its auxiliary commissions have maintained their operations by making the changes necessary to adapt to the new conditions of repression; the number of its activists that the organs of repression have been able to identify is extremely small. On the other hand, these activists were prepared to fight in such conditions and they displayed the highest sense of revolutionary morality before the repression. It is for these reasons that the PCR, far from being destroyed, has considerably developed since the coup d'état, from the point of view of both its militancy and its links with the masses. While the parties exclusively adapted to the legal style of activity (public quarters, officials, commercial type propaganda, etc.) have completely disintegrated, the PCR, with its method of direct work amongst the masses, of underground activity and simple propaganda within the reach of the workers, and with its experience of illegal work, is developing like a fish in the water. Another factor that has contributed to the upsurge of the PCR in the present conditions (the most difficult one can imagine for a work of opposition to and struggle against the ruling classes) is the fact that the broad masses are beginning to recognize that it has always followed a basically correct line, denouncing the farce of the "peaceful electoral road" to socialism and warning the people against the reactionary Armed Forces and against the fascist coup d'etat. On the other hand, the masses of the people who want to organize themselves and fight against the fascist dictatorship have increasing faith in the PCR because they know the efficiency of its organization and of its underground methods of work. All this has made it possible for the Party to play an important role in the organization of the resistance, in the underground propaganda against the fascist military junta, in the assistance to the victims of the persecution and their families in the organization of the first struggles against the dictatorship and in the ideological struggle against the opportunist leaders who led the people into the dramatic situation in which they are now.

Chapter III
Sowers of Illusions

As it is obvious, the electoral victory of Salvador Allende in 1970 only strengthened the opportunist line advocated by the leaders of the "C"P. Many of those who had doubts about the "peaceful" and "electoral" possibilities of seizing power from the Chilean ruling classes were dragged into the euphoria of the 1970 electoral victory. This illusion was further strengthened by the failure of the CIA and the ultra-right circles to prevent Allende from taking office after his election.

However, the "C"P leaders not only propagated their anti-Marxist theses ever since Allende's election and during the first year of his administration, when a number of economic and political successes were apparently registered, but they continued to deceive the people during the three years of the UP government, until the very day of the coup d'état. Moreover, as opportunist diehards, they disregard the terrible sufferings into which they plunged the Chilean people and they persist, even today, in asserting the validity of their theses on the "peaceful road" to power and "socialism". They have not only declared through *Radio Moscow* that the three years of the Allende regime have proven the validity of their theses, but in a recent document, they even attributed the failure of their anti-Marxist offspring in Chile to the MIR and the "ultra-leftists".

It is therefore important, in the present work attempting to analyze the reasons for the failure of the so-called "Chilean road to socialism", to give examples of the deceptive pacifist, legalist and reformist illusions actively propagated by the "C"P leaders and to show their influence on the ruling circles of the other parties comprising the Popular Unity. To show to what extent this deceptive campaign has persisted, we have decided to illustrate it separately, although with indications allowing to relate it to the events analyzed later. Of course, the number of examples is far greater than we have been able to collect in exile, without easy access to the news media that existed in Chile during the Allende government. Nevertheless, they are more than enough to assess the responsibility of the sham communists in the events of Chile.

It is appropriate to emphasize here a point on which we will insist throughout this book, since it is a key point to understand the reactionary, as opposed to simply erroneous, nature of the strategy advocated by the "C"P leaders: the maintenance of the bourgeois state and their attempts to take it from the inside were inherent to the sham "socialism" that they wanted to impose upon Chile. It was indeed impossible for those who only intended to establish their state capitalism to rely on the revolutionary mobilization of the people. Their only aim was to create a new bureaucratic bourgeoisie through broadening the public sector, either at the expense of some of the old exploiters, or in association with others, and to have a joint exploitation of the Chilean people by the two superpowers. Their very nature, as a new developing bureaucratic bourgeoisie (exploiting and oppressing the people), did not allow them, in their fight against Yankee imperialism and those holding power internally, to mobilize the people for a genuine revolutionary struggle for the seizure of power. Such a genuine revolutionary mobilization would not have allowed them to take the place of the old exploiters and to consolidate their domination, even under socialist disguise. That is why the sham Marxists cannot destroy the bourgeois state and can only aspire to using it in their attempt to replace certain ruling forces within that state and to share domination with others. That is why, although they were contending with these forces for power and control over the economy, they united with them to protect and preserve the regime whenever it was threatened.

This necessity to preserve the regime of exploitation and the bourgeois state is, on every occasion, the main axis of all their politics. Therefore, even when their allegedly socialist attempt was crumbling from all sides as a result of the implacable reactionary offensive, and especially during it, they could not stop sowing illusions on the existing system and fulfilling their role of sabotaging any people's struggle for fear that the masses would respond to the offensive on their own account. Although it was difficult for them to replace the old ruling strata, they were not ignorant that a genuine seizure of power by a people breaking away from reformism and legalism and determined to smash the bourgeois state apparatus would make it even more difficult for them to establish the state capitalism that they wanted. It is important to keep in mind that in essence, according to Lenin's definition, the revisionists are the servants of the big bourgeoisie and their role is to safeguard the bourgeois order, even when they become disloyal and ungrateful servants (especially since the rise of social-imperialism) who would like to take the place of their masters and become exploiters themselves. For such people, an eventual mass struggle independent of their conciliating line in response to the arch-reactionary imperialist offensive launched in Chile against the UP government was even more dangerous than the temporary victory of the old exploiters and the establishment of fascism. Because of this opportunist logic, their strategy was always to oppose the mobilization of the masses of the people, to uncompromisingly defend the system with its reactionary laws and institutions, and to desperately seek an alliance with the CD that would allow them to have a share in the exploitation of the people. As soon as everything was lost, they actively engaged in demobilizing the people and in preventing any resistance to the coup d'état so that once in exile, they could continue, for propaganda purposes, to take advantage of the sufferings into which they led the Chilean people and to seek an alliance with the CD.

The facts that we are relating show, in part, how the false theories inspired by the Soviet leaders since the Twentieth Congress became propaganda themes in the service of an opportunist line.

1. Eulogy of the "Peaceful Road"

In October 1970, one month after the electoral victory of Salvador Allende, Corvalan stated during a meeting held in Montevideo (Uruguay): "We won in an election battle, a ground on which it is very difficult to win. This shows that the roads and forms of the revolutionary process have their originality in every country. Many did not believe in this possibility. In the very camp of the left we saw, in the beginning, incredulous people. Some opposed it. The 'ultra-leftists' squarely fought against the policy followed. The results have proven that we were right." (6) It is not useless to relate the faith of certain people in the pacifist sermons of Corvalan to the fact that today, Uruguay is also under the jackboot of a fascist dictatorship.

Two months later, the same Corvalan declared to the Plenum of the Central Committee: "Comrades, life has shown the correctness of our politics. We were right in promoting the unity of all left-wing forces. We were right in upholding the real possibility of taking over the government through the unarmed road. Our ideological fight against the rightist and ultra-leftist positions was an essential element in the struggle for the unity of the people." (7)

In January 1971, Volodia Teitelboim, a member of the "C"P Secretariat, declared to the First National Assembly of the United Workers' Central (CUT): "For the first time a people has arrived to power through the narrow and apparently impossible and impracticable pass of the polls. The Chilean people's movement has enriched social practice with this new creative contribution to the history of the struggle for emancipation of the workers." (8) It should be noted here that Teitelboim no longer speaks of a takeover of just a government, but of power itself. Depending on the occasions and the public, the "C"P leaders will put forward one or the other of these two notions so as to pass them off as synonyms and create maximum confusion on this matter.

On March 8, 1971, an article by Jorge Insunza, a member of the Central Committee of the "C"P, appeared in the daily *El Siglo.* Later, this article was to be reprinted in the issue No. 138 of *Principios,* theoretical review of this party. In an attempt to explain the success of the "peaceful road", the article says: "What has happened until now is that the people were able to accumulate such a strength (and to neutralize other forces) that it was impossible for the reactionaries to resort to armed violence, despite all their desire and efforts to do so."

And it adds: "The theoretical possibility to bind the hands of the enemy, on the basis of accumulating a potential strength of such magnitude that its presence and the public evidence of its readiness to fight are enough to quell the resistance of the reactionaries, has been concretized in Chile."

Further, this "great" theoretician declares: "These facts confirm beyond doubt that the reactionary classes do not give up power unless they are pushed off, but at the same time, they negate the dogmatic views on the question of revolutionary violence, the views according to which revolutionary violence is reduced mainly or exclusively to armed violence ('political power grows out of the barrel of a gun'), relegating to a secondary position the strength of the masses, and with it mass work and mass struggle, in order to give the primary role (and sometimes the only role) to conspiratorial work. The experience the Chilean people's movement has lived through until now shows that it is wrong to develop a policy while living in the expectance of confrontations and while solely and exclusively considering as such the armed confrontations." Thus, this shameless falsifier of Marxism describes revolutionary violence not as armed struggle by the masses for the seizure of power, but as the passive expectance of a confrontation by a group of conspirators, isolated from the people. However, what the man says after this exposes even more the role played by the "C"P leaders in stifling any mass mobilization against the putschist attempts. In fact, they turned this stifling of mass mobilization into *their* "anti-putschist" policy. Referring to such a mobilization that some political circles were trying to develop, he says: "With this, the definite fact that a confrontation is in process is hidden, the strength of the enemy is overestimated *(we can see that now!),* and it is made easier for them to mobilize enough forces to take the struggle against the popular government onto the military ground, which is undoubtedly the ground that they would prefer today." For this remarkable "Marxist", thus, the way to avoid the armed coup prepared by U.S. imperialism and internal reaction was to prevent the people from preparing themselves for confrontation. In line with this was the demobilizing slogan raised by the "C"P leadership to "confront", later, the imminent coup d'état: "No to civil war". This nonsense, obvious not only to those who claimed to be Marxist but also to the blindest politician of any tendency, can only be explained by what we have pointed out earlier, by the panic that struck these candidates for succession to the old bourgeoisie at the idea of any fighting mass mobilization that could threaten them also in the future.

Finally, this follower of Mahatma Gandhi concludes: "There are elements in the revolutionary camp, mainly those who took ultra-left positions during the pre-electoral period, who are unable or unwilling to overcome the dogmatic conceptions that life has destroyed. They insist on the question of revolutionary violence in a narrow manner and thus facilitate the manoeuvres to blame the people for the origin of violence which the class enemy has interest in provoking." Now, having in mind the events of Chile and the facts confessed by the American CIA which started preparing the coup d'état right from the time Allende was elected, it is possible to assess the results of these politics which pretended to emotionally impress the reactionaries with mere pacifist declarations. It seems that they believed they could apply the Soviet techniques of painless birth-giving to Chilean politics by persuading imperialism and the big bourgeoisie to let themselves be cooked up in the sauce of the laws and institutions of the bourgeois state.

Near the end of 1971, in October, a comment by Eduardo Labarca, a leader of the "C"P and expert of panegyrics glorifying Corvalan, appeared in *El Siglo*. This comment was on the book entitled *Roads of Victory,* by Corvalan. It stated: "In January 1961, ten years and nine months ago, the General Secretary of the Communist Party, Luis Corvalan, wrote: 'As for Chile, we, communists, based precisely on the concrete conditions of our country, had come to the conclusion that the most probable road for revolutionary development was the peaceful road.' " And Labarca further continues: "In 1963, the General Secretary of the CP added: 'Regarding the elections, it is not only those of the parliamentary type that may come up as a favourable conjuncture for a decisive victory of the working class and people in their struggle for the conquest of political power. Although the Communist Party of Chile and its allies of FRAP can improve their position in the Parliament, it is not precisely in that direction that their perspectives are best. They link the possibilities of their victory to the presidential elections because the executive power, through the huge quantity of its prerogatives, is the centre of political power.' "

"The strength of Corvalan's book," Labarca comments, "is that its content has been confirmed by the events. It is a tested commodity: here is (for those who have doubts) the Chilean people's government."

And he concludes: "In commenting on *Roads of Victory*, it seems useless to line up epithets to praise a party and a leader who have brought a line of such clarity to the workers and the people. It is enough to simply point out one thing: the entire fundamental thesis contained in these reports and works has been confirmed by the historical reality of Chile." *(9)*

In 1972, Corvalan gave a long interview to this so lucid journalist. It was published under the title "Corvalan 27 hours". It is interesting to quote certain views contained in this interview because Corvalan persists in his anti-Marxist line although the offensive of the arch-reactionaries to overthrow the government has already been vigorously unleashed. Here are some of these views:

"Undoubtedly, the Cabinet in which the three branches of the Armed Forces are and where the working class has a remarkable presence is an unsurmountable barrier against subversion."

"I think that the Armed Forces, beyond attacks, flatteries and pressures, will maintain a correct attitude."

"As a party, we have made our contribution, acknowledged the world over, concerning the possibility of taking political power through the unarmed road. . . . I think that no party has made a greater contribution on this front."

"I also believe that what we have done in terms of the agrarian reform, the nationalization of the banks and of a series of enterprises in the public utility sector is irreversible." *(All these, and even some corporations nationalized before the UP, have been given back to Chilean or foreign private interests by the Military Junta.)*

"We have always upheld the possibility of succeeding and creating in Chile a people's government and of opening the way for revolution otherwise than with guns. And the facts have proven our thesis was and is realistic."

"We are 'pro-Soviet' . . . The Central Committee of the Communist Party of China sent us a letter in 1964, violently attacking, in abusing terms, the orientation of our Party. They considered it an illusion that the Chilean people could take power without arms. Moreover, they recruited here and there a few turncoats in order to try and split us."

And he concludes with this sentence which deserves a monument: "The possibility of failure does not torment the mind of any communist, including mine."

Again in March 1973, during a mass meeting to sum up the parliamentary elections recently held, Corvalan stated: "Social revolution is possible without armed confrontation and it is our duty to the people to make every effort so that this possibility keeps broadening." *(10)*

In May 1973, right during the full final offensive of the putschists and less than four months from the coup d'Etat, the convocation to the Fifteenth National Congress of the "C"P stated: "The theses on the possibility of marching towards socialism along the unarmed road remain valid. Their materialization is feasible because only an extremely small minority, a portion of the opposition (the openly fascist trend) want to deviate the course of events away from the institutional framework." *(11)*

To conclude this series of "lucid prophecies", we will only add the opinion of Volodia Teitelboim, published on the very same day as the coup d'état, on September 11, 1973, in the daily newspaper of the Italian "C"P, *L'Unita:* "The right wing is trying to mobilize the relatives of some general or admiral, but the vast majority of the army remain loyal to the deep sentiment of their constitutional mission."

2. "C"P's Influence on Allende and the Popular Unity

This absurd and unjustifiable confidence in the "peaceful road" to power and the Armed Forces propagated for years (before and during the Allende government, and even now, after the coup d'état) naturally also influenced the other political trends comprising the Popular Unity and the President of the Republic himself. If those who were claiming to be "communists" and "Marxists" publicly and repeatedly abjured the basic principles of Marxism on the character of the state and the reactionary armed forces, it is not surprising that similar positions were often taken up by other political circles, such as the Movement for United Popular Action *(Movimiento de Accion Popular Unitaria — MAPU)*, the Christian Left *(La Izquierda Cristiana — IC)*, the Independent Popular Action *(Accion Popular Independiente —API)* and the Radical Party *(Partido Radical — PR)*, none of which had any pretension to have a Marxist analysis of society (except for the MAPU at a certain period). This was also the case for some leading sections of the Socialist Party of social-democratic inspiration, and for the President of the Republic himself. However, to the honour of the majority of these organizations, it must be pointed out that in all of them, trends came up that somehow understood that an armed confrontation was coming up and tried to get prepared; some of them even tried to get some sections of the masses to get prepared. Even President Allende, as we will show later, supported the idea of not relying solely on the Armed Forces, and although he rejected any formation of civilian armed groups, he advocated the setting up of a vast network of people's committees which, in collaboration with the Armed Forces, would block the way to the putschists. The "C"P leadership squarely opposed this idea. In fact, the "C"P was the only party that remained monolithic in its opportunist positions.

Thus, in the resolutions of a meeting of the First Santiago District of the Popular Unity, published in *El Siglo* on January 9, 1971, one can read under the title "The Army is a Model for America and the World": "It is firmly rooted in its constitutional, professional and democratic traditions. The attempt against Chief Commander of the Army, General René Schneider, is a proof of what we say. The right-wing circles believed that the Chilean legislation, created by the bourgeoisie, would be used by them only if they would be the winners. When they lost, they no longer wanted to play by the democratic rules, which only proves their lack of strength. They knew that the army would not participate in this double play."

Later, on March 31, 1971, the same "C"P paper carried a statement by the Political Commission of the SP saying: "The ultra-right hopes to win over a section of the army, but they forget that it is not the Brazilian army, which rebelled against Janios Quadros and Goulart. They want to knock on the doors of the barracks, but they forget that this is not Indonesia, but Chile. This army is the people in uniforms. If some fanatics want to strike a blow on the people's order and achievements, they will face an army which will defend the new democracy and the government in unity with the people."

On June 1, 1971, the same paper printed a statement by the Political Commission of the MAPU. It said: "We first believe that the army will play a positive role in the process of developing our national independence, perfecting our democracy and building socialism in this country . . . The development of the tasks of national liberation will inevitably bring the army closer to the people, and united together in the same fatherland, they will become an impassable wall for the enemies of Chile. . . We believe that in this matter, any simplistic analogy with the role that other armies have played in other revolutionary processes can lead to erroneous conclusions. Similarly, a schematic theoretical analysis on the historical role of the state and its armed apparatus in class societies can lead to dogmatic theses that mechanically link the ruling classes to their institutional instruments of domination. . . The fundamental fact is that our army has shown in practice an absolute loyalty to the letter and spirit of its traditions now that the bourgeoisie, which ruled for so long, has been forever thrown out of the government." And a few months earlier, MAPU had declared itself Marxist-Leninist!

At the end of June, the National Political Command of the Popular Unity declared: "The Popular Unity is aware that the best defence the government can have is the vigilant and fighting attitude of the masses as well as the firmness of the democratic and professional traditions of the Armed Forces and the Carabineros. While maintaining the previous provisions, the Popular Unity will investigate the means to improve and promote the plans of the Executive aimed at providing more men and material for the Carabineros and the judiciary police." *(12)*

The President of the Republic himself, Salvador Allende, was one of the main victims of these absurd and deceptive theses on the "peaceful road" to socialism and on the "professional", "democratic" and "constitutionalist" role of the Army, new version of the old opportunist theses pushed by the Soviet leaders and parroted by their Chilean agents. Until the day of his heroic death, when he still believed that he had the support of a loyal section of the Armed Forces, he upheld and propagated the belief that he could rely on them. He was a victim of this tragic error (tragic for him and for the Chilean people) because of his low level of Marxist education, which he humbly recognized himself, because of his own tradition as a legalist parliamentary leader, and because of the influence that both the "C"P leaders and an eminently bourgeois organization, the Freemasonry (of which he was a high-ranking member), had on his ideas.

Although his subsequent attitude showed that what he lacked was certainly not the courage to defend his beliefs, numerous facts illustrate how he was influenced by the poisonous ideas of the anti-Marxist theses propagated for decades by the sham "communists". In fact, they were able, with the farce of "creative Marxism" invented by Khrushchov in order to peddle the most rotten opportunist theses, to convince him that Chile, for the first time in history, had ushered in a new road to socialism. At the National Stadium (tragically transformed a few years later into a concentration camp by the Military Junta), during the ceremony held at the beginning of November 1970 on the occasion of his accession to the Presidency of the Republic, he declared: "Chile undertakes its march towards socialism without having suffered the tragic experience of a fratricidal war. And this fact, in all its greatness, conditions the road that this government will follow in its work of transformation. The people's will makes our tasks legitimate. My government will respond to this confidence by making the democratic tradition of our people real and concrete." *(13)*

And at the end of November 1970, speaking before the Plenum of the Central Committee of the so-called "Communist" Party of Chile, he said: "What we have done and achieved in Chile has not been achieved, until now, in another country which is capable of taking power with legal means, in order to initiate the revolution. The Chilean people is the only people, on this continent and in the world, that has done this." *(14)*

Later, on May 21, 1971, in his first message to the Congress of the Republic, he would tell the representatives of those who, already, were actively working to overthrow him: "Just like Russia, Chile is faced with the necessity of experimenting with a new way of building the socialist society: our revolutionary road, the pluralist road, foreseen by the classics of Marxism, has never been experimented before. . . Once again history allows us to break from the past and to build a new model society, not only where it was most likely to be expected theoretically, but where the conditions most favourable for its success have been created. Chile is today the first country in the world called upon to experiment with a second model of transition to socialist society." *(15)*

Until the end of his government, he never stopped praising the Armed Forces and he categorically opposed the arming of the people against the putschists. In March 1971, for example, he declared to the peasants of the Cautin province: "I said, I uphold, and I reaffirm: the people's government has promised (and such is my word to the country) that in Chile, there will be no Armed Forces other than the forces of the armed institutions of the Army, the Navy, the Air Force and the Carabineros. The people do not need means of defence other than their unity and their respect for the Armed Forces and the Fatherland." *(16)*

On October 6, 1971, he reiterated: "In this country, there are no other Armed Forces than those established by the political constitution, that is the Navy, the Army and the Air Force. Therefore, any armed group trying to take action is creating problems for the government." He then pointed out: "Formal instructions have been given so that these armed groups, upon their arrest, be detained, handed over to the courts, and judged according to the state internal security legislation. I add that the government will be implacable and will have no consideration as to the number or the political affiliation of the people involved in manoeuvres of this type." *(17)*

On March 20, 1971, Allende declared to foreign correspondents: "The Chilean Armed Forces are professional forces. . . These professional Armed Forces with a technical capacity and a moral credibility throughout our history must fulfil an important role in the entire economic process of Chile. They must be linked to the process of national progress. . . I am not flattering them. Why? Because they have the dignity of their own responsibility. The Chilean Armed Forces are professional forces, respectful of the constitution and the law, and I am, as provided by the constitution, the Supreme Commander of the Chilean Armed Forces and I am assuming this responsibility through dialogue with them, a dialogue in the service of Chile and the people." *(18)* Two days later, he declared: "The Armed Forces are the people in uniforms and as the Supreme Commander of these, I feel proud of their past, present and future in the service of the Fatherland." *(19)*

At the end of May, *El Siglo* published the lecture given by Allende at Concepcion University. In it, he shows that he is in fact aware of the contradiction between the ideas of the sham communists that he had adopted and Marxism: "I emphasize," he says, "and I do so with vigour and patriotism, the attitude of the Armed Forces and the Carabineros of Chile. You traditionally know it and I do not need to repeat it. You have read, as I have, the book of Lenin, *The State and Revolution*. I have studied it many times during my life and we find in it the theoretical conception about the armed forces that the revolutionaries like Lenin have. But Chile is going through a stage which is glaringly proving how different our Armed Forces are. They are professional armed forces, and in the balance of forces, the fact that I am President of Chile is precisely in favour of the loyalty of the Armed Forces and the Carabineros, and that is because of the people's will and the people themselves." Further, he points out: "There are also millions of human beings watching the Chilean experience with a passionate interest. They basically regard it from the facts that have happened on this continent, where many thought that the only possibility was the *foquismo (20),* the armed struggle, the insurrection and the people's army. Would you deny that they are doctrinaires, that there are socialist countries where sixty percent of the land belong to private owners, as it is the case in Yugoslavia, Poland and Rumania? And they are socialist countries, Comrades!. . ." *(21)*

Later, on August 20, 1971, speaking at the ceremony of Oath to the Flag of the Tacna regiment, Allende declares: "Next Monday, in fulfilment of a pleasant obligation, I will travel across various countries of Latin America. I will take to these countries the affectionate and fraternal greetings of the Chilean people. I will also carry your voice, your voice of peace and dignity, of work and sacrifice. I will be able to say, with all the pride of being Chilean and Supreme Commander of the Armed Forces of the Fatherland, that Chile can be in security because it has confidence in its Armed Forces that are professional and respectful of the civilian power that came out of the people's will, that have achieved their desire of being ever more Chilean and in the service of Chile." *(22)*

Although he already knew about the subversive activities developing within the army and even though two military plots had already aborted, President Allende still continued to cling, during the last two months of his government, to the illusions about the loyalty of the Armed Forces. On August 11, 1973, when he received the oath of the new cabinet that he had to form with the Chief Commanders of the Armed Forces in a vain attempt to prevent the final offensive of the opposition, President Allende declared: "And I must repeat before the nation what I always said: in this country, there will be no armed forces other than those established by the constitution and the law. In this country, the hierarchy of the command will be maintained *(the Commander-in-Chief of the Armed Forces was no other than Pinochet, who was feverishly preparing the coup d'état)*. In this country, the Armed Forces, the Carabineros and the judiciary police have written in the history of the democratic development their loyalty and their attachment to the civilian power. That is why the government will reject any attempt at subversive infiltration of the Armed Forces, the Carabineros and the judiciary police." And he once again stated, expressing his desires rather than the truth: "The Armed Forces have been and will be with the government. . . We need a government based on moral strength and resolution to have the constitution and the law respected, a government that strengthens the functions of the state. And what is better than a Cabinet in which the Armed Forces, the administration and the workers are repre-sented?" *(23)*

Finally, on September 6, 1973, only four days before the coup d'état, Allende still upheld that: "The government has insisted on the fact that the Chilean reality cannot be distorted with a false antagonism between the people and the Armed Forces. These institutions must maintain their integrity and their professional character to fulfill the lofty responsibilities required for the defence and the security of the nation." *(24)*

3. International Speculation on the "Chilean Road"

The opportunist offspring generated by the Soviets in Chile through the "pro-Soviet" leadership of the "C"P was peddled throughout the world as a proof of the correctness of the theses on the "peaceful road" to socialism as formulated in the USSR at the Twentieth Congress of the CPSU. As it seems, Chile was to be the guinea pig for the attempts at domination by the two superpowers. It first served as a pilot country for the experimenting of the U.S. policy under the signboard of the Alliance for Progress, and then, for the Soviet attempts at creating a state capitalism under socialist disguise within the framework of the bourgeois state. Hence, as soon as Allende was elected, all the pro-Soviet "C"P's and the individuals linked with them began to use this experience (which ended so sadly) for the benefit of the politics they advocated in their own countries. After the coup d'état in Chile, the necessity to hide the total collapse of the Soviet theses largely explains the gigantic campaign undertaken by the USSR and her cronies to denounce the brutalities of the Chilean Military Junta, a "compassion" which they did not display in face of the military coups and repression in Indonesia, in Iran, in Cambodia under Lon Nol, and recently, in face of the coup d'état in Argentina. We will give some partial examples of how Allende's electoral victory was used to propagate the anti-Marxist theses in other countries.

Shortly after Allende's victory, the Dominican revisionist "C"P newspaper, *El Popular,* points out: "The victory confirms the success of the line drawn by the Communist Party of Chile, in the sense that this country had gathered the conditions so that the anti-imperialist and anti-feudal revolutionary forces could win power without resorting to revolutionary violence as a prerequisite, but only in case it would be necessary to defend the victory of the people against the violence of reaction. This victory," they conclude, "is a serious setback for the ultra-leftist groups that negated such a possibility." *(25)*

In Caracas (Venezuela), Federico Alvarez writes in this country's "C"P magazine, *Deslinde:* "What was too much for many people was the essential tactical formulation of this programme: in Chile, the CP said, victory will come through electoral victory. We have a bulk of traditions, an institutional armature and a network of mass organizations that allow us to attempt to seize power without the necessity of taking up the gun as long as the enemy respects the rules of the game. They demanded the right to develop a line based on their situation while many obstinately tried to impose foreign schemes upon them. Time has shown that they were right." (26)

For his part, the Argentine revisionist leader, Benito Marianetti, writes: "Today, more than ever, it is necessary to defend the new victorious forces of the sister country. And the best way to do it is to tell our own people and workers what is the project of these forces, their programme, how they intend to reach their goals and how they came to power." (27)

In Ecuador, Edmundo Rivadeneira says, on behalf of the sham communists: "For this victory, I rejoice because of my ideology and because I lived four years in Chile, which is a sort of second fatherland to me. I think that the Chilean victory confirms that it is necessary for revolutionary action to comply with the objective and real conditions of each people. It shows that it is perfectly possible to take over the government without locking oneself in hard and unilateral politics which, to my mind, mainly scare the people away and weaken the revolutionary movements." (28)

At the Twentieth Congress of the "C"P of Uruguay, it is Volodia Teitelboim who takes the floor to use (as all revisionists) some alleged particularities of the Chilean process to negate the basic principles of Marxism, already embodied in the Communist Manifesto. He states: "Certain critics of the communist movement had upheld that it was absolutely impossible to take power otherwise than with guns. Perhaps, in certain countries, this thesis continues to be valid. The error is to make an absolute out of it, to turn it into a compulsory, general dogma. On this question, which has been the focus of an acute polemic within many revolutionary movements, certain people pretended, among other things, that the impossibility of the peaceful road was proven by the fact that it had never succeeded before. With this logic, America would have never been discovered. We think that to think in this way negates the dialectical essence of Marxism and the law without which both life and social transformations would be inconceivable, that is the law of change. This method is suffering from the metaphysical spirit. They cling to schemes of the past, to the petrifying and mummifying postulate according to which nothing can be that has not already existed." *(29)* It must be remembered that this original theoretician, on the very day of the coup d'état, made declarations in Italy calling to have confidence in the Armed Forces and that even today, after all that has happened as a result of the anti-Marxist line pushed by him and his friends, he is cynical or stupid enough to claim on *Radio Moscow* that "the three years of the Allende government prove that the peaceful road was possible in this country". In such cases, it is difficult to decide whether to have a polemic against him or just treat him as mentally deranged.

However, the "Chilean road to socialism" was not only waved in Latin America for the benefit of the opportunist lines that facilitated the setting up of military dictatorships almost everywhere on the continent. It has also been largely used in Europe and other countries of the world.

Corvalan himself "theorizes" in issue No. 10 (1970) of *Prague International Review,* in which he says: "The constitution of November 3 of the government presided by the socialist Salvador Allende and made up by all the organizations forming the UP bloc   ushers in a new stage in the history of Chile. It represents a fundamental change in the direction of the country. The fatherland of O'Higgins and Recabarren embarks on the road of profound revolutionary transformations, the road of national and social liberation, of advanced democracy and socialism."

And he carries on: "This climate of Latin American recognition and solidarity, plus the fact that this victory has been achieved through roads that no one can openly question, and, of course, the gravitation towards socialism and democracy on the world level, all this .explains why imperialism and the reactionaries of all Latin America cannot but accept the new situation that has been created in Chile."

After the "acceptance" of the events of Chile by U.S. imperialism and the reactionaries (in his own imagination, of course), Corvalan carries on to highlight the source of his project that was to lead to fascism: "The 'Chilean case' comes to demonstrate that the roads and methods of the revolutionary process have their own particularities in every country. It proves that the thesis proclaimed by the Twentieth Congress of the CPSU and adopted by the Conference of the Communist Movement in 1960 is not precisely nonsense: the working class and other forces struggling for socialism can take power and achieve revolutionary changes without necessarily taking up arms. . . In this struggle," he adds, "the party and the communist youth had to face open and hidden enemies, the straightforward reactionaries and those hiding under ultra-left disguise. The latter propagated the slogan 'gun instead of ballot' and lavished all sorts of insults on the communists: 'cowards', 'reformists', 'conservatives', 'traditionalist', 'only interested in parliamentary seats', 'bourgeoisified', 'defenders of order', to give just a few of the epithets stuck onto certain leaders and activists of the party. . . But all this has been useless. The party and the communist youth, fully convinced of the correctness of their line, stood firm and active, united as one man." *(30)* Let us see now who was right: those who were giving them these well-deserved epithets (although too soft), or Corvalan and his cronies who stuck to their opportunist line until failure and who continue to do so even now, after this failure?

In France, the socialist leader Claude Estier draws lessons from Chile for all Europe when he states: "The Chilean experience is, in a certain way, a lesson for all the Europeans whom it has taught that the left can get to power through the democratic road. For us, it is a matter of great satisfaction to see that the union of the left dedicated to the fight within legality leads to victory. The events of Chile have greatly enhanced our conviction that we must fight along the legal road, particularly in countries like France and Italy, where violence would have no support. When I was his guest, Allende insisted on the fact that he had to struggle during eighteen years before he became president. He told me that patience was necessary in the struggle to bring about the victory of the left." *(31)*

In December 1970, *El Siglo* reprinted the view of Gunther Jahn, First Secretary of the German Free Youth in the GDR.

This young revisionist bureaucrat declares: "The victory of the Chilean people confirms beyond any doubt that the political power of imperialism and internal reaction can be overthrown through hard class struggle, but along the peaceful road, on the basis of the unity of all the anti-imperialist popular forces." And he continues with a lecture on "creative Marxism": "This example shows that it is in the unity of action between the communists, the socialists, the social-democrats, the independents, etc. that the strength and the invincible power of the people take roots. Just like the history of our people and the GDR, the victory of the Chilean people confirms that the main task in the struggle against imperialism and internal reaction, against colonialism and neo-colonialism, for social progress in the capitalist states and in the developing anti-imperialist forces." He then draws the conclusions for the entire world: "Thus, the UP has set an example as to the road for revolutionary transformations not only for the Latin American countries, but also for other countries of Asia and Africa as well as for imperialist Europe."

Finally, he concludes, as Corvalan, by pointing out the origin of the line that led to "victory" in Chile: "Thus, the validity of the strategy and tactics for class struggle as developed by the communist and workers' parties in Moscow, in 1960, is proven in a most impressive and irrefutable way." *(32)*

The Soviets, on the other hand, are more moderate, since the UP did not fully comply with the road they set for the Chilean "C"P, that is to arrive to government in alliance with the Christian Democracy. Rasnitdov Sharaf Rasnidovitch, alternate member of the Political Bureau of the CPSU, said before the Plenum of the Central Committee of the Socialist Party of Chile: "The coming to power of a people's government in Chile is a serious blow to the positions of imperialism and reaction, not only in Chile, but also throughout the American continent." *(33)* During the Plenum, Walter Roman, a member of the Central Committee of the Rumanian "C"P said: "Your experience shows once again that the achievement of unity of action between the SP and the CP, the union of all the popular, democratic and creative forces of the nation represent the motive force and the guarantee for victory in the struggle for democracy, social progress and national independence. The successes achieved through a road of your own, that you have yourselves opened and that have had such profound repercussions on every continent demonstrate that things are changing in this world and that they are changing for the better, comrades. For this historic demonstration", he concluded, "we express with deep emotion our gratitude to the Chilean people, to their most progressive forces." *(34)*

In France, François Mitterand, after Allende's victory, claims: "In Chile, there is an original political experience which is unquestionably leading the country to socialism." *(35)* And on another occasion: "The Chilean regime represents the experience closest to what could happen in France." *(36)*

Similar opinions are given in all the press organs of the traditional left. In France, for example, the central organ of the SP, dated April 7, 1971, writes in a comment about Chile: "It is an example which makes all the reactionaries extremely sad, which shows that from now on, a time can come when the people may decide to choose socialism through the democratic road; it shows at the same time that the fatalism of the violent revolution does not exist and it repeats to the socialists what the people are expecting from them. There is no question of an improved copy of what others have done, but of the most audacious option within the framework of democratic rules."

"Chile is not France", the paper concludes, "and it is far from France. However, its experience deserves to be studied and thought about. For a number of years, the reconciliation of socialism and freedom has been a great problem, inasmuch as we can think of socialism without freedom. In any case, Chile proclaims a profound identity between the two." *(37)*

On May 6, 1971 *El Siglo* reprinted an article from *Le Nouvel Observateur,* saying: "Chile is the only country in Latin America where it can be said that the socialist power (once again confirmed by the last elections) has not been gained with the gun, but with the ballot."

On October 19, *El Siglo* reproduced the views of the Italian deputy Lelio Basso, first published in *L'Unita,* stating: "My impression is that the Chilean experience is of world significance. It is the first time that the working class parties are capable of seizing the government by using the instruments of bourgeois democracy while declaring, at the same time, that they want to use these instruments to build socialism."

The following month, on November 25, René Andrieu, editor of *L'Humanité*, declares: "Undoubtedly, Chile is not France. However, what is happening there concerns all progressive people the world over. And more particularly so, perhaps, those of our country. The experience of the Popular Unity contains a number of lessons that could be used by the French left . . . The fact that armed struggle has been necessary in Cuba for winning independence and that perhaps it will be necessary in the future in another country of this continent, does not mean that it will be compulsory at all times and places. It is preferable to try, when the conditions allow it, to take power through the electoral road."

Of course, after the coup d'état, none of these panegyrists of the "Chilean road to socialism" has drawn correct lessons as to what has happened to Chile, let alone using the opportunity to adopt correct Marxist positions and wage a world-wide campaign in defence of them, as they did to defend the wrong line initiated by the Chilean "C"P. On the contrary, they have fabricated (particularly the leaders of the pro-Soviet "communist" parties) an even more rightist line promoted by the leaders of social-imperialism as a means to gain power in the U.S. sphere of influence: this line is to push for an alliance of the pro-Yankee political forces with the traditional left and to reject the head-on clash between these two in the electoral competition for government. The champions of this line in Europe are the leaders of the Italian, French and Spanish "communist" parties. Carrillo in Spain is seeking an alliance with no less than the monarchists. Berlinguer in Italy although he had almost half the vote in 1976, is refusing to form a government with the socialists and other forces and he claims that he will wait until the CD decides to join them in the government. Finally, Marchais, in France, is talking about a people's front and he is waging a polemic against Mitterrand who is establishing a front "of the left". This rightist trend, even more so than that which led to the failure of the Chilean experience, expresses itself in the open and public rejection of the fundamental Marxist concept of the dictatorship of the proletariat, in the acceptance of the links with the military block set up by the U.S. through NATO, and even in certain criticisms against the Soviet leaders for the ferocious fascist dictatorship that they exercise in their country. Despite these disagreements with the Soviets (more fake than real), they are nevertheless the most loyal representatives of their strategy for the infiltration of the Western world governments, strategy that the Chilean "C"P has been unable to apply, which explains the meagre support the Popular Unity got from the Soviets.

Part II
Superpower Contention
in Chile

Chapter IV
The Strategy of Social-Imperialism
in Chile

Both the experience of the UP and its outcome are impossible to understand completely and accurately if one ignores international politics and, more concretely, the fight between the two world superpowers (the United States and the USSR) to divide the world into spheres of influence and domination. This contention goes on everywhere, in the ideological, political, economic and military fields; its particular intensity, in one of these fields or in all of them, depends on the country in question (on its strategic, economic or political importance) and on the actual historical moment.

1. The Establishment of State Capitalism

The ultimate goal of Soviet strategy in countries such as those of Latin America does not differ from the model which the USSR has imposed *manu militari* on the member countries of the Warsaw Pact. That is, state capitalism, run by a bureaucratic bourgeoisie which carries on in this form the exploitation formerly practised by the old bourgeoisie (sometimes allying itself with certain sections of the latter) demagogically presented as "socialism". These new bureaucratic bourgeoisies are composed mainly of the cadres of the pro-Soviet "communist" parties, which play (before and after power is won) the role of "fifth column" of the social-imperialist bureaucratic bourgeoisie which governs in the USSR, and facilitate its military, ideological, economic and political expansion. This does not mean that, in the process of development of these local bureaucratic bourgeoisies (as the example of Czechoslovakia shows), contradictions cannot arise with Soviet social-imperialism. The concentration of economic and political power which state capitalism allows, as well as a certain capacity for centralization and for economic planning and the demagogic pretext that "we are building socialism", allow a ferocious dictatorship of the fascist type to be exercised over the masses of the people. This dictatorship has gone to such extremes in the USSR and the countries dominated by it that even some pro-Soviet "communist" parties, such as the Italian party, the French party and others, albeit for electoral reasons, have been forced not only to recognize its existence but also to "condemn" it publicly.

In such "socialist" countries, all the features of the capitalist system exist, disguised under the legal fiction of ownership by the state, by the "whole people". The direct producer is deprived of the means of production, he is paid wages, his labour power is a commodity sold at a price set by the employer, the representative of the state bourgeoisie. The upper bureaucracy amasses fabulous profits, sharing amongst itself all the surplus-value created by the workers. In order to lay hold of the surplus-value, the upper bureaucracy not only maintains enormous differences in the rates of pay, but also, because of the need to preserve the fiction of the non-existence of profits and of individual gain, it must use the most devious and corrupt practices to enrich itself: kickbacks, the black market, embezzlement of goods, underground enterprises and many other practices which are everyday things in these countries. Finally, there are privileges which the very exercise of power there confers: it makes it possible to demand — through flattery or through terror — services, gifts, favours and even forced labour. These mechanisms operate with special force in the USSR because of the enormous amount of wealth which the state monopoly bourgeoisie has laid hold of there, because of its social-imperialist character. For example, there is one member of the Central Committee of the CPSU who, on his own, managed to embezzle funds in the value of half a million rubles, that is, the equivalent of what the average worker would earn in four centuries. *(38)*

The relations which the USSR maintains with the member countries of the Council for Mutual Economic Aid (COMECON) and of the Warsaw Pact are an indication of the relations which it aspires to establish, little by little, with other countries which fall under the control of pro-Soviet bureaucratic bourgeoisies. In these countries, the theory of "limited sovereignty", propagated by the Soviet rulers to justify their invasion of Czechoslovakia, is enforced. This means that both their internal and their external policy is subject to the dictates of the rulers of the USSR, who, under the pretext of defending a "socialist" system (which ceased to exist there a long time ago, and which the people consequently have no interest in defending), arrogate to themselves the right to intervene militarily. They go so far as to plan to suppress the formal aspects of political sovereignty, and certain theoreticians of social-imperialism talk about the necessity of an "international political superstructure" for these countries, that is, direct government of them by the Soviets, behind the screen of a few local puppets.

The political vassalage of the countries dominated by the USSR is nothing other than the instrument for ferocious imperialist-type exploitation of these countries. Because of the Soviet military domination of these countries, this exploitation is carried out by using, in the most shameless way, all the usual methods of the imperialist countries: buying raw materials at low prices, selling manufactured products at very high prices (higher than world market prices), investing in their enterprises to make profits, forcing these countries to invest in Soviet enterprises, etc. In order to better carry out the various forms of exploitation of these countries, the USSR, in the name of the "international division of labour", forbids them to develop certain branches of production and forces them to produce what Soviet industry needs. What is more, their distorted industrial development depends completely on Soviet supply, which accounts for 96 percent of their oil, 97 percent of their coal, 80 percent of their iron and two-thirds of their cereal grain. Not content with that, the monopoly bureaucrats of the USSR plan in future to completely annex the economies of these countries, maintaining in this respect that: "The borders of the national states are (too) narrow for the development of the productive forces. It is necessary to establish a system of common property within the larger community." *(39)* In this manner the Soviet monopolist and social-imperialist bourgeoisie is preparing to absorb totally the economies of these countries, while on its own territory it shares the exploitation of the people with the big international trusts which it has permitted to invest in the USSR, such as the German firm Krupp, FIAT of Italy, Renault of France, and Japanese and U.S. companies.

Statistics show that between 1955 and 1973, the USSR caused five East European countries to lose $19 billion through unequal trade. Between 1954 and 1974 the export of capital to COMECON, just in the form of "economic aid", exceeded $10 billion, and the Soviets boasted that they had interfered in more than 1,300 enterprises in these countries. Following the U.S. imperialist model, they have already created a super-bank within COMECON, the International Investment Bank, 40 percent of whose capital is Soviet, through which they carry on the plunder and control of the East European countries under their domination; in the same way, since 1972 they have been creating multinational economic trusts, such as "Intertextilmach" and "Interatomenergo".

Soviet social-imperialism has also extended the tentacles of its imperialist exploitation to the Third World countries, and is hoping to create in these countries the political conditions which allow it to apply the methods it uses on its COMECON neighbours. From 1954 to 1972, the USSR exported more than $13 billion in capital to Asia, Africa and Latin America, becoming involved in about 1,000 enterprises and taking out more than $19 billion in raw materials at low prices: sugar, cotton, rubber, oil, mineral ores, etc. At the same time, it sold them, between 1955 and 1973, more than $16 billion worth of industrial products at high prices, making, in the same period, more than $11 billion in profits, just through unequal trade. Not content with these traditional forms of exploitation proper to all imperialism, they are beginning to suggest, as they did in issue number 8 of the journal *Komunist* of 1973, that the "new form of cooperation", to which priority must be given "in a more and more resolute manner", is the creation of "joint-stock enterprises" with the USSR, with the goal of "gradually deepening specialization and cooperation in production", and of "sharing gradually and step by step in the socialist division of labour". They added, unblushingly, that the plan for the "economic integration" of COMECON was open to the developing countries. Thus they bare-facedly show their future colonialist-type plans for the Third World. *(40)*

Although the ruling circles of the USSR are trying everywhere to set up political systems similar to those of the Warsaw Pact countries, which are so favourable to their interests, the tactical paths which they advocate vary according to the position which the country in question occupies in the world context, as well as according to its internal characteristics. In countries such as those of Western Europe, where there are powerful capitalist interests allied to U.S. imperialism, as well as powerful social-democratic forces serving these interests, Soviet penetration through the so-called "communist" parties which serve its policy is conceived in a gradual way. In these countries, there is no question at this time of contending for government with the pro-Yankee forces, through a closed bloc of the "left". Rather, the effort is made to constrain these forces to ally themselves with the "C"P in order to get into government with them. The way to force them to share government with the "C"P is to patiently accumulate mass influence and electoral strength. If the pact is accepted, the USSR will *de facto* force U.S. imperialism to share with it its involvement in these countries, in the parts of the world corresponding to the U.S. sphere of influence. Meanwhile, the camp of the countries under Soviet control will remain closed to U.S. influence and under the firm control of social-imperialism. On the other hand, if a fascist regime opposes the attempts to impose a sharing of government, its repressive and anti-democratic nature will be used to discredit the traditional capitalist system and imperialism and thus to build up strength to demand the restoration of bourgeois democracy and to be able to begin again the process we have described.

This policy, however, is not the sole policy, nor is it the same for all countries and in all circumstances. In some countries, the Soviets have used attempts at coup d'état, as in the Sudan or in China with Lin Piao, for example, or military intervention as in Angola.

The nature of the alliance with the pro-Yankee populist or social-democratic forces, which the "communist" parties want to establish as a protective shield to get into government, is determined precisely by the reactionary nature of the regime they want to set up. Winning government power through a "left" bloc (as the case of Chile has just proved) tends to divide and polarize the forces and can only be defended by opposing the armed apparatus of the traditional bourgeoisie and eventual imperialist intervention, by mobilizing and arming the people to destroy the bourgeois state apparatus and to preserve national independence. But regimes of the type which hold power in the Warsaw Pact countries, and the reproduction of a system of imperialist exploitation such as social-imperialism practices against them, *are incompatible with any revolutionary mobilization of the people.* Moreover, at the present time the USSR does not have the strength to impose such regimes through armed intervention in countries which are key points for U.S. imperialism and which the latter could defend even at the price of a war with the USSR. As a result, at the present time, the advance toward the Eastern European-style "socialist" model requires, as a first step, the preservation of the bourgeois state apparatus against the people, the strengthening of this apparatus through the advance toward state capitalism, the infiltration of this apparatus thanks to the relative tolerance of the traditional bourgeois forces. The basic elements of this strategy are: the winning of widespread mass influence by the pro-Soviet "C"P, by taking advantage of the capitalist crisis and by practising demagogy; the effort to infiltrate the bourgeois armed forces; and the attempts to establish an alliance with the populist or social-democratic forces, which contend with the "C"P for large popular and middle sections.

In the face of this revisionist strategy, more important than ever is the idea formulated by Mao Tsetung, in accordance with the basic theses of the Marxist classics, when he stated: *"Without a people's army the people have nothing."* To impose state capitalism, to subordinate the country to social-imperialist exploitation, it is necessary to have armed forces of the type which exist in the capitalist regimes: foreign to the masses of the people and opposed to them. Exactly the opposite of the Marxist concept of the people in arms. That is why, for the phony communists, it is indispensable to preserve the bourgeois armed forces, to win them over to their cause and/or to restructure them little by little in order to put them at their service. Never must they be destroyed by the people in arms. The discussion which

Khrushchov had with an Albanian leader during his last visit to Albania (before the break between the two countries and the two parties) is symptomatic in this regard. In his travels throughout the country, Khrushchov saw peasants working with rifles on their shoulders; he asked how it was possible that people who did not belong to the Armed Forces were allowed to bear arms. The reply was that in Albania, socialism is defended not only by the People's Army, but also by arming the entire people. Khrushchov still insisted, pointing out that this would create a serious problem if all these armed people turned against the government. The Albanian leader answered that, for such a thing to happen, the government would have to be implementing a policy opposed to the interests of the people and that, in such a situation, it would be very positive for them to turn their guns against the government. Khrushchov did not open his mouth again on this subject during the whole trip.

The strategy conceived by the Soviet rulers to penetrate Latin America is similar to the one we described above. Although these countries do not have as much importance for U.S. imperialism on the military, economic and political levels as does Europe, they are neighbours of the U.S. and have sometimes been defined as its "backyard". Consequently, the U.S. government does not seem prepared to tolerate there any regimes of the type the USSR has created in Eastern Europe without doing its utmost to block such regimes. This is why it is reasonable for the USSR to act very cautiously and gradually in this region, seeking to infiltrate their governments, their states and their armies, which prop them up, through an alliance with mass-based political forces that oppose social-imperialism under the orders of the U.S.

2. The Line of Alliance with Pro-Yankee Populism

In Chile, for example, the strategy drawn up by the Soviet rulers, of an alliance between the "C"P which they control and bourgeois forces which have great influence over the middle sections and some sections of the workers, is old. It had already begun with the people's fronts and the alliances with the Radical Party (and other minor forces) when the latter was a really influential party. With a truly masochistic tenacity, the "C"P leaders sought these alliances despite the fact that the candidates of the RP, once elected to the Presidency of the Republic, turned their backs on them, forgot all their electoral promises, and went so far as to persecute them ferociously. Later, when the CDP had been chosen by the State Department as its favourite, and had received the investments necessary to make it the most important political force in the country, the "C"P leaders never stopped trying to make an alliance with it. For these leaders, despite their oath of faithfulness to the SP, their alliance with the latter is only a means of obtaining another alliance with the CDP, the alliance that the Soviet leaders demand of them.

The above can be demonstrated by numerous and varied examples from both before and after the Allende government. In this chapter, we will merely mention a few examples of this policy from before the UP government. Before the 1964 presidential election, when the CDP stood out as the favourite of the U.S. government, the efforts of Corvalan and Co. to run together in this election were already beginning. The leadership of the "C"P (and I, like all those who still worked in the "C"P, was a direct witness of this) carried on consultations in the basic organizations (something like a poll to measure the resistance which would come up) on the possibility of running in the presidential election united with the CDP. What is more, although Frei was clearly the favourite of the U.S. for its so-called Alliance for Progress policy, Corvalan, despite his FRAP allies, personally took steps for Frei, who had already announced his candidacy for the Presidency of the Republic, to travel to the USSR. In the same period, and despite the total resistance which the base of the "C"P had shown toward an alliance of this type, the "C"P Political Commission declared at the beginning of 1963 that "there are several factors favouring a joining of forces by means of an agreement between the Christian Democratic Party and FRAP". The agreement, however, failed, because on the orders of their U.S. backers, the CDP leaders made public statements against the "communists" and against the USSR. Moreover, the leadership of the "C"P, amongst whose rank and file was born a Marxist-Leninist opposition precisely at the end of 1963, did not risk carrying on any further the pressure designed to obtain an alliance with the CDP.

Later, under the Frei government, although they were

formally in the opposition, they continued to cooperate with the government in all decisive matters, with a view to obtaining the alliance that was coveted and demanded (by the USSR) for 1970. We will not stress what we have already pointed out in the first chapter (p. 43 ff.) about the shameful betrayal of the interests of the workers by the "C"P and CUT leaders and their parliamentarians, through their support for the Frei government at the time of the readjustment plans of 1967-1968 and 1969-1970. It is enough to say that at that time they took a position to the right even of the Radical Party. In the same way, they adopted an attitude of servile and loathsome collaboration with the CDP government during the national strike which, under pressure from the base, the leadership of the CUT had to approve at the end of the Frei government (p. 43ff).

But even before these events we find Orlando Millas, member of the Secretariat of the "C"P, on a visit to Cuba in 1966 for the anniversary of July 26, flying into a rage to the point of publicly criticizing no lesser person than his host, Fidel Castro, because Castro made bold, in his traditional speech on this occasion, to criticize the economic aid granted by the USSR to the pro-Yankee Frei regime. In July 1967, Corvalan made an open appeal to the CDP during a luncheon he gave for the political editors of the press and radio. He stated: "The people were very wise in not electing Allende in 1964, because, we now think, it would have been difficult to keep him in power due to the aggressiveness of Argentina, to the situation in Brazil and to the aggressive interventionist line of the United States." And he added: "It seems to us that Gumucio (then President of the CDP) could succeed Allende as the candidate of the left. We have already told Comrade Allende that we will not continue to support him, because it is necessary that the next presidential campaign be fought with a new face."

In 1967 a trend appeared in the CDP, following the defeat in the elections in April of that year, which demanded a recti-fication of government policy. That same month, at a meeting of the National Council of the CDP, a Politico-Technical Commission was appointed, whose task was to plan a new political strategy for the last stage of the Frei government, that is, for the years 1967 to 1970. This commission was chaired by

Jacques Chonchol, Vice-President of the National Institute for the Development of Agriculture and Animal Husbandry (INDAP), who harboured strong sympathies for the methods of Cuba, where he had participated in agrarian reforms as an FAO technician. The commission wrote a report entitled: "Proposals for political action in the period 1967-1970 in a non-capitalist path of development." The plan, in reality, was a "golden bridge" of the left trends in the CDP, which at that time controlled the leadership of the party, to obtain the support of FRAP for their party's candidate in 1970. It was, essentially, a plan of reforms, more advanced than those of the Frei government, designed to attenuate the most abusive forms of capitalism within the framework of the bourgeois state. It contained important similarities with the programme set out by the "C"P and its FRAP allies. However, the ideas of the "rebel wing of the CDP, which inspired the writing of the plan, were (as its subsequent evolution showed) more advanced than those it could express in this document. The document had to be subject to a series of restrictions imposed by the Frei wing. The latter agreed, provisionally and with bad grace, in order to avoid a deep split in the party which would have weakened its electoral base even more and caused it to lose the interest entertained in it by the imperialist circles.

Without setting forth a socialist ideal, the report maintains: "We Christian Democrats desire economic growth that will take us away from, rather than compromising us further in, the capitalist criteria . . . " and it attributed the poverty and backwardness of the country "to the inefficiency and injustice of the capitalist system", stating in conclusion that "all the supporters of the CDP have declared themselves against the rebuilding of capitalism or the establishment of neo-capitalism." To "set us apart" from capitalism, the report proposes a sort of Yugoslav-style "socialism", through setting up "community enterprises" in which the means of production would belong to the workers, although the workers would not have the right to monopolize them and would have to work in conformity with a National Economic Plan. The various enterprises would participate in a sort of capital market organized by the state. With respect to imperialism, the Frei wing did not allow them at that time to plan the nationalization of the imperialist firms, but did allow formulas for state participation (in joint enterprises with foreign capital) that would be less harmful to the interests of Chile than those implemented by the Frei government. On the question of agrarian reform, the report merely planned to carry it out without discussing methods.

Even though it did not name them, the report contained open appeals for unity with the forces that were joined together in FRAP. It said it was necessary "to try to carry on a democratic and constructive dialogue with the various national and political forces and in particular with those which may support us in the implementation of this programme". And at another point it states: "We must consolidate stable social and electoral support through the creation of an alliance between the people and the progressive middle class." Knowing how the wing which wrote the report opposed any alliance with the right, it is easy to guess to whom these appeals for unity were addressed.

The leadership of the "C"P immediately echoed these appeals, which coincided with its strategy of alliance with the CDP. In issue number 124 of the "C"P theoretical journal *Principios* (March-April 1968), there appeared an article by the "C"P member of Parliament and economist Jose Cademartori, entitled: "The Non-Capitalist Path in Chile." This article and the concepts expressed in it were sanctioned shortly after in an interview given by Luis Corvalan to the newspaper *La Segunda* on April 26, 1968. The article attempted to answer three questions: 1) "Does the non-capitalist path correspond to a real historical phenomenon, or is it, on the contrary, an abstract, utopian formulation, bearing no relation to the practice and experience of the peoples?" 2) "Is the non-capitalist path a formulation opposed to socialism, a solution distinct from socialism, or is it a road which in fact ends in or can lead to socialism?" 3) "Is the non-capitalist path possible in Chile, as one of the forms of transition to socialism?" To the first of these questions, Cademartori answers: " . . . the non-capitalist path is put forward as a real historical problem, and is entirely linked with the stage that numerous underdeveloped countries in the world are going through at present . . . the non-capitalist path is not a utopian, unreal concept, a whim, but corresponds to new historical phenomena proper to the stage we are presently going through . . . New forms of transition to socialism are now emerging. The non-capitalist path," he concludes, "is precisely one of these forms, one of these access routes to socialism which are appearing, in present historical conditions, in a number of countries which are liquidating capitalism or its chances of existence." Further on, defining the "non-capitalist path", he states: "it expresses itself in a series of structural and political reforms, the goal of which is to liquidate or limit the basis of private ownership of the means of production." To the second question, as to whether or not the non-capitalist path is a form of transition to socialism he answers: "(F)rom all that we have said, we can conclude that the non-capitalist path is not a solution distinct from socialism, not a third road, but a policy which, borne along by the struggle of the masses and developed to its final consequences, leads to the establishment of socialist society." Finally, he answers the questions: "Is the non-capitalist path possible in Chile? Is it or is it not the most probable form of transition to socialism in our country? And, if the reply is affirmative, is the idea which certain circles in the CDP have formulated to this effect correct?" On this question, laying claim to this opportunist idea, which falsifies Marxism, as part of the "C"P programme, he states: " . . . we are for socialism . . . However, starting now, as an immediate problem, what we want is 'a new, more democratic, non-capitalist path which, instead of accentuating the power of the capitalist strata, extends and increases only those efforts undertaken until now for independent development, efforts which promote major growth of the economic and cultural life of the country, the basis of which requires the deepest democratization and a government of a new type, led by the working class.' (*Party Programme,* p. 46) . . . As can be seen," he adds, "since 1962 we have established the possibility of the non-capitalist path in Chile, as a mode of transition to socialism, which bars the path to capitalist development of the country." Then, trying to demonstrate that there is no difference between FRAP and the CDP, he adds that FRAP "in two presidential campaigns (1958 and 1964) has presented consistent anti-imperialist, anti-monopoly and democratic programmes, oriented towards a socialist perspective. These were programmes of non-capitalist development. Similar programmes," he adds, "are upheld by the Popular Socialist Party, the Social-Democratic Party and broad independent left-wing nuclei."

Finally, Cademartori mentions the opportunist strategy advocated by the "C"P leadership to attain this equally opportunist goal, through which they wanted to unite with pro-Yankee reformism. "The motor of this path," he states, "is a new state regime, characterized by new social classes being in power." How will this be obtained? According to Cademartori: "by ensuring the majority participation of elements of these (popular) classes and social strata in Parliament, in the municipalities and in other political and administrative organs", that is, by electoral means.

After these ideological embraces and kisses of the CDP by the leadership of the "C"P, in the framework of a complete betrayal of Marxist principles, came the reaction of Frei and his team, demanded by their U.S. advisers. The latter insisted that Frei block any alliance of the CDP with FRAP for the 1970 presidential elections. However, the Frei faction, because of its subjection to imperialist interests and its populist demagogy, faced a complex situation. It was not in a position to present a rightist candidate coming from within its own ranks (and still less to support a candidate of the right), because this would have brought about chaos within its ranks and a sharp decrease in the popular vote for the CDP. Furthermore, the right, much embittered by certain reforms which were affecting its interests, by the mass movement unleashed by these reforms, and by the anti-oligarchic demagogy of the CDP government, was not disposed to support any Christian-Democratic candidate. There was, therefore, only one solution open to Frei and his team: to firmly take control of the party in order to avoid its entering as such into an alliance with FRAP; and to present a candidacy with a programme resembling that of the traditional left, a programme liable to take votes away from the left or, at best, liable to win the left's unconditional support for the CDP standard-bearer and programme, like the support the right gave Frei in 1964.

The CDP was floundering in this period in the midst of the

sharp struggle which was stirred up in its ranks by the veiled pressure by each of the two superpowers to put the CDP in its service. Frei and his team, out of respect for those who had financed their half-failed populism, had to keep the CDP away from the pro-Soviet "Marxist" currents; Corvalan, from his side, obeying the Soviet orders, had the opposite mission: to unite with these populist currents and draw them toward his false Marxism in order to get into the government with their protection and impose a deal on U.S. imperialism. The "rebel" currents within the CDP were applying pressure to discuss a common candidacy with FRAP, and some leaders, not as idealist as their rank and file, saw the possibility of restoring the CDP's fortunes and once again taking the Presidency of the Republic, this time with the support of the left.

However, as we have pointed out, Frei's categorical commitment (then as now) toward his "generous" U.S. patrons was at all costs to prevent being used as a "Trojan horse" for Soviet penetration in the Chilean government through a CDP-FRAP pact. The CIA undertook to remind Frei publicly of his commitment by having a poster put up with Frei's picture and the statements he made when he was a candidate opposing any alliance with the "C"P. Thus, on January 6, 1968, in a meeting of the National Council organized by Frei and his team, Rafael Gumucio, leader of the "rebel" wing, was removed from the presidency of the CDP and replaced by Jaime Castillo, a rabid opponent of the "C"P who had collaborated in publications of the CIA. In April 1968, the "rebels", united with a third trend, intermediate between themselves and the Frei group, brought back Radomiro Tomic from the United States, where he had been serving as ambassador. Tomic launched his candidacy for the Presidency of the Republic, making it conditional on obtaining the support of FRAP. "Personally," stated Tomic, "I am in favour of thoroughly trying out an understanding of all the political and social forces which believe in the need to give Chile basic institutions that are more appropriate than those that have survived from the past, and which are, furthermore, willing to replace the capitalist structures with a communal economy, communal enterprise and a communal society."

However, just as Frei was incapable of bringing the CDP back to an alliance with the right, the "C"P leadership (despite its wishes) met within FRAP insurmountable obstacles to pushing it into supporting a CDP candidate. In particular, the SP, its main ally within FRAP, flatly refused to support a CDP candidate. What is more, until the Plenum held in June 1969, it even opposed organizations like the Radical Party and the small Social-Democratic Party entering FRAP, finally having to back down on this point. The SP, knowing the leanings of the "C"P leadership, justifiably feared losing its role of privileged ally, as well as the candidacy of one of its own members for the Presidency of the Republic. Thus Corvalan was incapable of making an alliance with the CDP in accordance with the Soviet instructions, for he was afraid of causing disintegration within FRAP if he imposed an alliance around a CDP candidate. Faced with these difficulties, the only solution for Corvalan and Co. was to try to draw the CDP into preliminary discussions with FRAP for the purpose of designating a candidate and overcoming the resistance of the SP. This was why he rejected, even more vigorously than the SP, the candidacy of Tomic, who had tried to present the left with a *fait accompli* by demanding support for his candidacy. It was in this context that Corvalan's slogan was popularized: "With Tomic, not even to Mass." The U.S. State Department showed a growing uneasiness about all this, because the Christian-Democratic youth organized a march from Valparaiso to Santiago, with the FRAP youth, to protest against U.S. intervention in Vietnam. In December 1968, the "C"P leadership issued a "People's Manifesto" in which it persisted in its appeals to the CDP. This document states: "Chile needs an anti-imperialist and anti-oligarchic people's government having the support of the majority of the nation, composed of all the parties and trends which come together in a programme of revolutionary changes . . . We declare ourselves, therefore, for a people's government of several classes, a broad, strong, revolutionary, active government, to ensure the country democratic stability and accelerated social, economic and political progress and to give our people full freedom . . . In the conditions of our country, the broader this government, the more revolutionary, firm and effective it will be . . ." The "C"P leadership then states who can participate in this government:

". . . those who work in the Communist, Socialist, Popular Socialist Union and Social-Democratic Parties, or who support their principles. But they are also found within other political trends. They make up the majority in the Radical Party and are an important part of the Christian Democratic Party. To unite all these forces around common goals is the task for today."

At the beginning of 1969, Nixon announced the end of the Alliance for Progress policy, considered paternalistic and unrealistic, the end of the use of reforms as bait to promote U.S. interests, and once again brandished the stick. In March 1969, the government committed a brutal massacre of homeless people who were attempting to occupy land at Puerto Montt. In the May 1969 parliamentary elections, the CDP again declined, this time to about 31 percent of the vote. The "C"P obtained 380,000 votes, moving up to 15.9 percent from the 12.4 percent it had received in the previous election. The National Party and the Socialist Party also increased their vote. The situation was tending to polarize to the detriment of the CDP. Tomic then renounced his presidential candidacy, stating: "The refusal of the Communists, and to a lesser extent of the Socialists, was public and repeated ('trenchant', to use the expression that pleases *El Siglo)* both towards me personally and towards the CDP as a united party. It is clear," he added, "that the Socialists and Communists are only a part of the people and of the left; but is equally clear that there is no popular unity without them." The withdrawal of Tomic's candidacy gave a second wind to the "C"P leadership in its efforts to lead them into pre-electoral discussions with FRAP, and at the Plenum of the CC held in April 1969, Corvalan reiterated: "In practice, we offered the country a Socialist-Communist government in 1964. All that was said to attribute our defeat in the elections of that year to the enemy's campaign of mystification is a partial explanation which does not go to the root of the problem. From the enemy, we must expect the worst. The truth is that the country was not then in a position to give us majority support so that Communists and Socialists alone would lead its destiny. We consider that this situation has not sufficiently changed, and as a result we must go for a people's movement and for a government with a broader social and political base." And he added: "We say it very clearly: we are proponents of an understanding between FRAP and other popular forces, including the Radical Party . . . " Finally, he tried to put pressure on the CDP by threatening it with a split, and he said, referring to the circles in the CDP that were unhappy with Frei: "This Christian Democratic faction is a progressive popular trend. It has not been able to act under Mr. Frei's government. We consider that it has many things to do in the people's movement."

In the CDP, on the other hand, the voices of the supporters of unity with FRAP were being heard, voices such as that of Senator Renan Fuentealba, who dared denounce the intervention of the U.S. embassy in the pre-electoral process. To avert these threats, Frei, together with the corps of CDP bureaucrats, organized another meeting of the National Council of the Party on May 3, 1969; by a vote of 233 to 215, the National Council decided to reject the appeals of FRAP for unity and to face the presidential election alone. After this resolution, a group of student supporters and some trade union and peasant branches of the CDP, headed by a few of the "rebel" leaders who had contributed to the writing of the report on the "non-capitalist path", split and formed the Movement for United Popular Action (MAPU), which entered into contact with FRAP. However, this did not constitute a very important numerical loss for a party like the CDP, which, despite its setback, still received more than 700,000 votes in 1969.

In August 1969, another meeting of the CDP National Council decided to again present the candidacy of Radomiro Tomic for the Presidency of the Republic, with a programme similar to FRAP's. This meant that Frei, unable to persuade his party to support the right, resigned himself to a candidacy that would prevent deeper division of the party and take votes away from FRAP. However, he and his team stayed out of the electoral campaign in favour of Tomic. The CIA and its bosses did not show much enthusiasm for Tomic, who, according to CIA reports, was "to the left of President Frei" and "was unhappy about campaigning on the Frei government's record and at one point made overtures to the Marxist left." According to the report of the United States Senate: "The CIA felt it was not in a position to support Tomic actively because ambassadorial 'ground rules' of the previous years had prevented the CIA from dealing with the Christian Democrats." Further on, we read: "The Agency believed that Alessandri, the apparent front runner, needed more than money; he needed help in managing his campaign." *(41)* Apparently Frei had at the time temporarily lost the confidence of the U.S. governmental circles for not having been able to put a brake on the mass struggle, nor on the opposition in the CDP, nor on the economic crisis of the last years of his government.

In June 1969, at a Plenum of its CC, the SP ratified its clear and sharp refusal to support Tomic. The leaders of the "C"P desperately tried to salvage an electoral alliance with the CDP in accordance with the Soviet orders, or at least to present a candidate who would attract CDP votes. Throughout 1969, when each party in FRAP presented its pre-candidate, they waged an intensive campaign in favour of Gumucio and of Chonchol, two former CDP cadres who for this reason had been admitted into MAPU. At the same time, they encouraged the manoeuvres within the SP of those who were trying to overthrow Salvador Allende, the candidate who (as will be seen later) had the greatest chance of uniting the various forces in FRAP around himself. They did not succeed and on January 22, 1970, they reluctantly had to accept Salvador Allende as the sole FRAP candidate in the presidential election.

However, they continued (despite intensified repression) to support the Frei government in all decisive matters. When the threat arose of a coup d'état by General Roberto Viaux, in October 1969, the "C"P and the CUT, which it led, were the first organizations to meet in the Palace of Government to offer their unconditional support to Frei against an alleged coup d'état. Moreover, in the course of these events they voted against the laying of constitutional charges against the Minister of the Interior, a measure demanded by journalists because of the arbitrary censorship of the press, radio and television imposed by the government to hide the shameful agreement it reached with the putschists.

3. The Policy of Social-Imperialism Toward the Victory of the Popular Unity.

Salvador Allende's victory in the 1970 election caused deep disarray and concern amongst the Soviet rulers. In the same way, the U.S., which believed that Alessandri would win with 40 percent of the vote, was not expecting a UP victory. We have already pointed out that the Soviet line, which the "C"P leaders failed to implement, was for the traditional left (including the "C"P) to get into government in coalition with the CDP, that is, in an agreement with U.S. imperialism. They did not want, nor were they prepared to assume, in other Latin American countries, the risks and the economic bloodletting which the ill-timed turn of the Cuban government toward pro-Soviet "Marxism" had brought about. Open support on their part for a regime like the UP, which called itself "Marxist" and on the road to "socialism", which was seen around the world as implementing the theses of the 20th Congress, and in which the pro-Soviet "Communists" were participating, all this right in the U.S. imperialist geopolitical zone, represented an open challenge to U.S. imperialism. Such a challenge could mean that the U.S. would arrogate to itself the right to intervene in any conflict which might arise in Eastern Europe (like the Czechoslovakia conflict, for example), a region of Europe where the USSR had serious potential problems, such as the succession to Tito in Yugoslavia, and the leanings toward independence of Romania and other countries. We must remember that the United States government remained neutral toward the invasion of Czechoslovakia, recognizing the right of social-imperialism to domination. Similarly, it must be remembered that one of the causes of the fall of Khrushchov was his adventurism in installing missiles in Cuba, an act which pushed the USSR to within an inch of war with the U.S. — it was able to avoid war only by accepting not only the withdrawal of these missiles under threat of an ultimatum, but also the humiliation of allowing the U.S. to inspect the ships effecting the transfer.

Because of these considerations and others, the policy of the Soviet rulers toward the Allende government was aloof and extremely cautious, both in their designs for economic penetration and in their financial aid or political support for the government. This aloofness increased as the government went into crisis and began to suffer heavy blows from the offensive destined to overthrow it.

This policy of the USSR toward Chile under Allende is confirmed by numerous accounts and concrete facts, which further exposes the hypocrisy of the protest campaign organized after the coup d'état. Already, in regard to the election campaign, Kerry, the U.S. ambassador to Chile, had stated (according to ITT documents brought to light by the U.S. Senate Subcommittee which investigated the involvement of multinational enterprises in Chile): "With respect to Russia, I discount the part the Russians have played in Allende's election."

With respect to the credits granted by the Eastern European countries and the USSR at the beginning of the Allende government, when there was still some hope for it, they were granted under conditions equal to or worse than the credits of U.S. imperialism. That is, they were linked with projects favouring the creditor countries, and often at a rate of interest higher than that normally in effect on the international market. This caused a real scandal within the UP commissions which had to go to these countries to negotiate. In particular, these countries charged higher-than-normal rates of interest on the short-term loans that were most urgent for the acquisition of things indispensable to the functioning of the economy: they profited from the fact that these loans were extremely urgent for the Chilean government and from the blockade enforced by international financial organizations dependent on the United States. Both the "socialist" countries of COMECON and countries with reactionary governments like Spain and West Germany, which were tempted by the attractive offers that the Chilean government had to make to break the blockade, participated in this speculation at the expense of very serious difficulties in Chile.

However, in the very critical moments at the end of 1972 when President Allende himself had to go to the USSR to ask for a credit of $500 million that was absolutely essential to cover the balance of payments deficit, this credit was refused by Brezhnev himself. This fact is attested by Joan E. Garcés, one of the closest collaborators of Allende, in his book on Chile after the coup d'ètat. *(42)* He refused, even though Allende was forced to sign a Joint Communique in which he appeared to subscribe to the formulations of Soviet international policy dealing with regions very distant from the Latin American continent, as, for example: on the European Conference on Security and Economic Cooperation, on the reunification of Germany, on the Middle East, and even on Bangladesh. What is more, Allende was forced to make serious concessions on the firm and traditional Chilean policy of defending the 200-nautical-mile territorial sea, which both the USSR and the U.S. were fighting, and to make a commitment to "harmonize their positions and mutually collaborate . . . taking into account the interests of all states". The $500 million credit was requested not for ambitious development projects but for the urgent acquisition of food and raw materials, intended to soften the economic catastrophe which was preparing the ground for the military coup.

Furthermore, the United States had previously received a formal guarantee that the Soviet government would not grant substantial aid to the Allende government. At the meeting held on October 21, 1971 between the committee of multinational firms having interests in Chile and the U.S. Secretary of State to organize an offensive against the UP government, William Rogers indicated that he had talked to the Russian Minister of Foreign Affairs to see whether or not Moscow would finance Chile as it had financed Cuba. He added: "Russia denies having such a plan." One can also read the ITT document examined by the U.S. Senate; Allende's collaborator Joan E. Garcés also cites this document in the book mentioned above. Furthermore, at the precise moment when the U.S. copper companies were committing aggression against Chile, Kosygin announced his plan to exploit Siberian copper in collaboration with these same companies.

At the same time, a large portion of the credits obtained from the Eastern European countries was not used, either because they were not asked for in time to figure in the production plans of these countries; or because the anarchy which reigned in the UP economy prevented the sending of studies demanded by the creditor countries prior to the allocation of funds; or because it was thought these credits were not suitable. On November 28, 1972, the CDP member of Parliament Claudio Huepe, basing his case on a publication of the Production and Development Corporation (CORFO), denounced the non-utilization of 95.2 percent of the credits from the "socialist camp".

As far as commercial or technical relations with the USSR during the Allende government are concerned, these were so minimal that the right-wing press, extremely careful to denounce any interference in this field, had almost nothing to speculate upon. During the three years of the Allende government, the newspaper *El Mercurio* denounced only the activity of a few Russian fishing boats rented by the government, publicizing the protest of the leaders of the fishermen's corporation; the visit of a 16-man Soviet delegation to conclude economic agreements; the signing, at the end of March 1972, of an agreement for the purchase of 5,000 tractors in the USSR; and Chile's sending back to the USSR 125 graders which were unsuited to the Chilean soil and defective. The most serious denunciation seemed to concern the acceptance by the government of Soviet technicians in the national copper enterprises. At the end of June 1973, the Christian Democratic senator Juan de Dios Carmona protested the hiring of 36 advisors and 10 interpreters, by virtue of an agreement with the "Tsvetmetpromexport" firm of Moscow, for salaries of $844 and $470 a month respectively, which far exceeded the legal maximum equal to 20 times the minimum subsistence level. In December 1972 the CDP had already sent a letter to President Allende questioning "access by Soviet technicians to industrial secrets and to the experiments of large national mining enterprises, thus favouring so strong a potential competitor as the USSR". In the same letter, the CDP also asked: "Is it true that the Soviet Union, in its position of 'big brother', a position assigned for the first time to a foreign country by a President of the Republic of Chile, grants us credits with strings attached, something you and the parties of the Popular Unity used to criticize so harshly?" *(43)*

On the subject of arms purchases from the USSR, here was an attempt which, it seems, was rejected by the USSR, or in any case did not materialize, when in May 1973 the Commander-in-Chief of the Armed Forces, General Carlos Prats, visited the

Soviet Union accompanied by Generals Bonilla and Benavides. Symptomatically, as Joan E. Garcès points out in his book, "the right-wing military men decided on May 25, just when Prats was in Europe and Pinochet was replacing him as Commander-in-Chief of the Army, to organize a coup d'état." It is difficult to see the real meaning of this trip, which came at a time that could not have been less opportune, for the putschist circles, incited by the CIA and the Pentagon, had been very active for a long time; and one of the most unpardonable things for the U.S. is arms purchases from the USSR. Was it an unsuccessful attempt to threaten the U.S., so that it would stop arousing the putschists in the Army? If that was the intended goal, the effect was exactly the opposite, as facts soon showed. In any event, it was an unusual initiative, taken in a moment of extreme difficulty; it did not correspond to the usual policy of the Chilean government, which had never attempted to buy arms in the Warsaw Pact countries, and still less did it correspond to the intentions of the USSR and of these countries. In this field, as in any other field which would signal an intention by the USSR to resolutely support the Chilean government, neither the Pentagon nor the White House had any worries, at least in the short term. The intelligence reports they had available indicated with total clarity that neither the USSR nor the Eastern European countries were thinking of supporting the Chilean government, either militarily or economically. The U.S. government, as the report of the U.S. Senate on the activities of the CIA in Chile found, made use of regular studies by the intelligence services, called National Intelligence Estimates (NIE's), which were drawn up not only by the CIA but also by the State Department's Bureau of Intelligence and Research (INR). These studies were analyzed by a special board of the U.S. government. The NIE sent in 1969 predicted that any new administration established in Chile would explore the establishment of better relations with the "communist" and "socialist" countries. In addition, it pointed out that Allende in particular would take this step, but it also stated that he would be prevented from going too far in this direction due to Chilean nationalism, which would energetically oppose any subordination whether to Moscow or Havana or to Washington. Allende, the report continues, would strengthen

Chile's relations with the "socialist" and "communist" countries over the years. However, he would be careful not to subordinate Chile's interests to any "communist" or "socialist" power and not to break links with non-"communist" countries, to whose aid he would continue to resort. The 1971 and 1972 NIE's stated that Allende was charting an independent and nationalistic course. In short, Allende, the report points out, was committed to a policy of non-alignment. *(44)*

A 1970 NIE predicted that Allende would establish relations with Cuba as soon as he was elected. However a 1971 NIE described the state of Chilean-Cuban relations as one of ideological distance and closer economic ties. It also pointed out that, despite Allende's longstanding personal relationship with Castro, he had refrained from excessive overtures to him. A 1972 NIE, moreover, recognized that Havana had been circumspect about trying to use Chile as a base for promoting revolution throughout Latin America. *(45)*

In 1970, the reports still show a certain concern about the expansion of Soviet influence in Chile under Allende, and about the establishment of a major Soviet military presence. However a 1971 NIE predicted that the Soviet Union would not be certain of its ability to make a decisive impact, given Allende's desire for independence, although it continued to exploit its influence in the Chilean government through the "Communist" Party of Chile. The same NIE states that neither Allende nor the Chilean military would tolerate a permanent Soviet military presence in Chile. *(46)*

Finally, a 1972 NIE centring on the Soviet attitude toward the Allende regime maintained that it was "characterized by caution and restraint". This attitude, added the report, was "due to Soviet reluctance to antagonize the U.S." and, more importantly, to a Soviet desire to avoid with Allende "the type of open-ended commitment for aid that they had entered into with Castro". An intelligence note prepared by the State Department stated that a Soviet-Chilean communique, issued following Allende's visit to the USSR in December 1972, "reflected Moscow's decision to continue a cautious policy toward Chile and to avoid a major open-ended commitment of aid to Allende. According to the intelligence note, the Soviets apparently advised Allende to negotiate his differences with the U.S." *(47)*

This attitude of the Soviet social-imperialist rulers toward the Allende government is fully consistent with their decision to support only a government of collaboration with U.S. imperialism, through a UP-CDP alliance, in Chile. This also explains why the "C"P leaders sought in an obsessive manner to ally themselves with the CDP during the Allende government, as a strategic goal and not as a mere tactic. They pursued this goal before Allende's election, during the Allende government, and they are continuing today, after the military coup, to push this same policy.

4. The Pursuit of a UP-CDP Pact During the Allende Government

This policy (conducive to joint exploitation of Chile by social-imperialism and U.S. imperialism, offering the latter, in exchange for this co-government, the paralysis of the mass struggle, which the CDP never obtained during its administration) began with the pressure that the "C"P leaders put on Allende to convince him to sign the constitutional guarantees demanded by the CDP to approve his nomination as President in the Congress.

One of the pillars of this policy was to convince Allende that he could count on the Army's spirit of "constitutionalism", "democracy" and "professionalism". For this purpose, they used as a smokescreen the only or almost the only high military leader on whom they had any influence, General Carlos Prats. At the same time, in an effort as desperate as it was fruitless, they tried to broaden their influence in the Army High Command, where the U.S., due to all the links it had established with the military over the decades, had an overwhelming advantage over them. In fact, this second "C"P failure, added to the first — the impossibility of leading the UP into a pact with the CDP (more because of the influence of Frei and his team within the CDP than because of the resistance of some circles in the UP) — also conditioned the distant and cautious attitude of the USSR toward the Chilean experience. In any case, the fact that Prats held the post of

Commander-in-Chief of the Armed Forces was a permanent threat to the numerous putschist trends which were fighting for hegemony within the Army. It was feared he might draw part of the Army into supporting the government: united with the people's resistance, this faction would have represented a serious obstacle to the putschists' plans. It was not by chance that *Radio Moscow* announced after the coup d'état that Prats was marching south at the head of troops faithful to the government. Nor was it by chance that the Military Junta decided to assassinate Prats in Buenos Aires, where he took refuge following the coup (he worked there in the firm of a powerful industrialist closely linked to the Soviets, José Gelbard, who, being Peron's Minister of the Economy, had a three-hour-long conversation with Brezhnev during a trip to the USSR). Nor was it by chance that the setting up of a hierarchy for the coup d'état, thenceforth led by Prats' replacement as Commander-in-Chief of the Armed Forces, Augusto Pinochet, was accomplished during Prats' trip to the USSR, and that the coup d'état materialized after his retirement from the Army. Pinochet himself, in statements to *Radio Agriculture* of Santiago on September 3, 1974, said: "It would have been enough that one department, that a single unit, not carry out the orders coming from Santiago for the country to be plunged immediately into a civil war." This possibility of a people's resistance uniting with a part of the Army that would be faithful to the government frightened the "C"P leading group as much as it frightened Pinochet, if not more. This is why the "C"P leaders opposed the initiative of the masses in crushing the employers' strike in October 1972 and hastened to impose their "solution", a "solution" full of concessions to the opposition, through a military cabinet. For the same reason, they constantly opposed the plan of Allende, who, despite his confidence in the Armed Forces, was setting up a whole system of defence based on the people's mass organizations, a system that might have worked in conjunction with the loyal sections of the Army against any attempted putsch. Expressing Allende's opinion on this subject, Joan E. Garces, his closest adviser, maintains: "The Armed Forces-people's organizations link-up could be conceived of and implemented starting in 1970 on condition that it correspond to the goals of the anti-putschist movement in the Army: to avoid civil war by defending and strengthening the political and social institutions based on democratic principles that permitted the free expression of the popular will. The need for it could be established, because it was legitimized by the legal responsibilities incumbent on the government and by the UP programme, as well as by existing legal provisions. It will suffice to refer to the Civil Defence Act of 1945, which provided for coordination between the workers' trade unions and other civil organizations on the one hand; and Carabineros and Armed Forces on the other, to prevent or prepare for exceptional situations and situations of national emergency. Civil Defence under the command of the Ministry of the Interior and its regional representatives, that is, under strictly *political* government leadership, not military." And Garces adds: "The UP counted on its legitimacy as holder of government, and on the will of the temporarily predominant section within the Armed Forces and the Carabineros, to defend democratic institutions against subversion and sabotage. It counted on the organized trade unions throughout the country and on legal instruments to put together in time a whole network, as elaborate and vast as they might desire, to prevent actions of sabotage and subversion which, for three years, were the principal means used by the counter-revolution to disrupt the socio-economic mechanisms of social integration and equilibrium." And then he adds: "The mass counterpart of the policy in regard to the Armed Forces was the goal of various initiatives by President Allende beginning in January 1971; not only in private, such as his speech to the Plenum of the CC of the CP in June of that year, but also in public. On February 29, 1971, at Punta Arenas, where he had gone with three commanders-in-chief to visit the military bases of the region, in a speech in the covered stadium that was broadcast on the radio and partially reproduced in the press, Allende declared that it was necessary to organize the masses of the people in order to give the military dissuasion policy of the UP its own social base." And Garces then points out: "If the rank and file and the supporters of the workers' parties had counted on new forms of action (which was most difficult), if the circumstances made it necessary to distribute arms, this would have been done, for it was implicitly provided for in the government's plans, as President Allende publicly showed on June 29, 1973. But this required prior preparation of the citizens for new forms of fighting, distinct from the merely electoral forms." Garces concludes: "Such were, in summary, the central theses which shaped the speech of President Allende on February 29, 1971 . . ." and he adds: "Even on June 5, 1973, amongst Allende's recommendations to the political committee of the UP, one can read: **1)** Mass front: people's organization to resist the confrontation three-four months forward." And we add a final commentary by this political adviser of Allende's, who was not exactly known for his sympathy towards the supporters of people's armed struggle for power, but who, on the contrary, tried throughout his work to show that this road was not applicable to Chile: "And in these circumstances," he adds, "what a cruel contrast! During the whole of 1971 and 1972 the entire left-wing press denounced the fact that the right was organizing in paramilitary fashion, that its urban residential zones were prepared for centrally led and coordinated civil actions, that there were alert exercises and psychological adaptation exercises, etc. And for more than two years the left knew about and publicly described, in full detail and with ample information, the civil organizations which were preparing the bourgeois insurrection. But the workers' districts, the factories, the headquarters of the workers' parties organized nothing similar . . . *in defence* of democratic freedoms, of the legally constituted government, and lastly, of its own *raison d'être,* the interests of the working class," *(48)*

It must be said, furthermore, that although President Allende went in person to the Plenum of the CC of the "C"P to put this problem to them, the "C"P leaders categorically rejected this defence organization of the masses. For this reason they were criticized even by the Soviet rulers, Judas-like hypocrites who want to wash their hands so that no one pins their responsibility on them. The "C"P leaders rejected Allende's plan because they were less honest than Allende, because it did not conform with their plans for state capitalism and because they were more lucid then Allende's close advisor Garces. They knew, however, that the Armed Forces were essentially in the service of Yankee imperialism, despite their constant praise for their "professionalism" and their "constitutionalism", and that there were only two solutions: either destroy the Armed Forces, which they in no way wanted to do, or neutralize them, by reaching an agreement with imperialism through the CDP, which moreover was the demand of their Soviet mentors. Consequently, the "C"P leaders were also not unaware that as much as they might be "defensive" in the beginning, the mass organizations proposed by President Allende would inevitably escape their control, becoming an antagonistic fighting force against the opposition bloc, to the extent that the latter pushed forward its subversive actions, and in the end, against the Armed Forces, to the extent that the latter showed evidence of putschist intentions. Thus, such mass organizations, under the possible influence of revolutionary ideas and of the existing high level of fighting spirit, threatened to become instruments of a policy opposed to the "C"P leaders' intentions to conciliate with and to preserve the system so as to build their farce of "socialism" on this basis. This is why the "C"P leaders categorically opposed not only organizations of this type which, as Garces himself points out, would eventually have been provided with arms, but also the innocent, electoralist-type Popular Unity Committees, which they managed to dissolve after having used them for the last time in the elections of April 1971. Garces, as well as analysts further to the left in Allende's government, seemingly did not understand that the "C"P leaders and the international reactionary centre which directed them were much further to the right than he and President Allende. There is a big difference between sincerely aspiring to socialism, while applying erroneous methods to obtain it, and pretending to want socialism in order to establish an oppressive state capitalism, as the "C"P leaders intend to do.

This blind obedience to the Soviet watchword of alliance with the CDP made them oppose not only the formation of mass defence organizations but also President Allende's much more innocent idea of calling a special referendum, which would bring out popular support for the basic points of the UP programme. A referendum of this type would mean that the UP, by relying directly on the support of the masses of the people, would free itself from the CDP's work to obstruct any government initiative, obstruction which grew out of the CDP's growing tendency to adopt the firm style of opposition practised by the right. But the tactic of the "C"P leaders was precisely to profit from the growing number of obstacles which the government was meeting in its path in order to put pressure on it and to convince their reticent UP allies of the necessity of reaching an agreement with the CDP at all costs. A successful referendum held the danger of reproducing, in an even riskier form, the strategy which the Soviets judged unacceptable for Chile (and for Italy and France today): the implementation of reforms on the basis of a left bloc that would confront an opposition including the populist sections manipulated by U.S. imperialism. Or, in other words, they were opposed to an attitude of openly challenging the U.S. in its sphere of influence, instead of collaborating with it partly through willingness and partly through force, which was the goal of the Soviets.

Unfortunately, the "C"P leadership succeeded in drawing the leaders of the other UP parties into opposing the referendum initiative, even though the other leaders gave different arguments for rejecting it (and so did the "C"P leaders, as a tactic). Garces makes the following comment on this question: "Each initiative by Allende to reach legislative agreement with the CDP was only the solution he was driven to after the rejection by the UP political committee of what he considered the most correct course to solve the problem: to ask the country to take a definite stand, through a referendum, on the means necessary for the government to continue to implement the UP common programme." And he goes on to give examples which show just how clever this tactic of the "communist" leaders was. "The Allende-Tomic talks of December 1971 followed the rejection by the UP of the referendum proposals made by the President of the Republic in June, July and August of the same year. The negotiations with the President of the CDP, R. Fuentealba, in May 1972, followed the rejection of the referendum proposal made to the UP by Allende after the defeat in the Colchagua and O'Higgins by-elections in January of the same year. The talks with the CDP in July-August 1973 were requested by President Allende after all the parties in the government coalition had refused, in June, to settle the main conflict with Parliament, the nationalization of enterprises, through a general consultation." And he adds: "In proportion as the revolutionary process advanced without the UP having a clear majority in Parliament, the CDP's role as arbitrator grew under conditions more and more unfavourable to the working class parties." But this was exactly what Corvalan and his cronies wanted! "The Communist Party in particular," Garces states, "thought that it *(the referendum)* was bound to fail. Its General Secretary, Luis Corvalan, argued this way, and summed it up in a very popular phrase: 'We'll lose from here to Penco.' " *(49)* Here we see nothing less than the party which has placed its confidence in elections in order to win power, opposing an electoral consultation on the subject of the UP programme and totally subordinating this programme to a high-level deal with the CDP. This was in January 1972. But even before (when the UP had just obtained more than 50 percent of the vote in the April 1971 elections), in July 1971, another possibility for electoral consultation came up on a measure as important and as much in demand by public opinion as the nationalization of copper. All the members of Parliament, from the extreme right to the UP, including the CDP, were forced to vote for the constitutional reform that made possible the nationalization of the big copper mining industry. However, some articles of the initial government bill were deleted by the parliamentary majority and the President vetoed this deletion and proposed that the UP instead of promulgating the pruned-down bill Parliament had passed, call a referendum in support of the original bill. But the parties in the UP opposed this. "The Communist Party," says Garcés, "declared itself absolutely opposed to referring the promulgation of the mines nationalization bill, flatly rejecting the calling of a referendum." *(50)* Especially at that time, after the UP had obtained more than 50 percent of the vote a few months before, there was no doubt that the referendum would have been won, particularly since it concerned a reform so much desired by the people as the nationalization of copper. But the "C"P leadership opposed it (and opposed it "flatly") at a time when, from all evidence, the future argument of Corvalan — "We'll lose from here to Penco" — was not valid. What the "C"P leaders rejected, therefore, was not a possible defeat, but on the contrary a victory, for the implementation of this procedure would have made the alliance they were seeking with the CDP more difficult. It was therefore completely accurate to say that the "C"P leadership (although for aims relatively different from those of the opposition) was an accomplice in the policy of obstruction and blockade against the Allende government, a policy that would create the conditions for its overthrow. This fact, as well as the hidden motives of such an action, are even more obvious when one considers the point at which (finally!) the "C"P leadership decided to accept the idea of calling a referendum. They did so in September 1973, when everyone could see that the coup d'état was imminent and that the *demand* to call a referendum *was being put forward precisely by the Christian Democrats.* They did so on this occasion, when there were in fact the greatest chances that the government would lose and when this referendum was one of the ultimatums addressed to the Executive by Frei and his group. That they did so at this precise moment is natural and consistent with their strategy, for the referendum had changed from a chance to escape the blackmail of the pro-imperialist faction of the CDP to a condition for an eventual agreement with this faction, a goal sought by the leaders of the "C"P and of the USSR.

But the sabotage against the government by those who orchestrated the policy of social-imperialism in Chile was not only in their opposition to everything that would mean relying on the masses of the people. This sabotage also came up (again in view of a pact with the CDP) each time that President Allende tried to take more severe measures against military men caught plotting. In August 1973, for example, barely two months after the *tancazo (51),* the "democratic" and "constitutionalist" Chilean Army gave birth to another attempted putsch, led by Generals Bonilla, Nuno, Baeza, Arellano, Javier Palacios and Torres de la Cruz. What was the attitude of the "C"P leadership? According to Joan E. Garces, "The General Secretary of the CP, Luis Corvalan, stated his disagreement when, on August 21 and 23, Allende informed him of his intention to retire, that same week, six Army generals who were known to head a plot." "The Socialist Party, MAPU and the Christian Left," reports Garces, "wished the government to adopt offensive measures and fully assume the risk of armed confrontation. But the Communist Party's analysis of the situation and its preference were very different: still trying to avoid civil war, the CP looked towards the Christian Democrats and sought to unite their votes in Parliament with the UP votes in order to declare a 'State of Seige'." *(52)* During this period, the CDP leadership tried to use blackmail against the government by demanding, as a condition of voting in favour of the State of Seige, that the government approve the CDP's constitutional reform to cancel the government's nationalizations, which Allende flatly refused to do. The Minister of Justice, Sergio Insunza, a member of the "C"P leadership, then reduced the planned State of Seige to only three months in order to reach an agreement with the CDP, and asked Garces "not to use his influence to convince the President to continue to demand from the CDP all the legal powers, without exception, that the constitution grants, in order to deal with the alert that the military coup had just created." "A useless preoccupation," adds Garces, for "sixty hours later, the CDP said that it would refuse even three months, that it would grant the government no extraordinary powers against subversion."

Strangely, the Commander-in-Chief of the Armed Forces, General Prats, was of the same opinion as the "C"P leadership and maintained to President Allende that: "We can only prepare the counter-coup." To which President Allende (according to Garces) replied: "General, everything depends on the force with which they deliver the first coup!" * Finally, faced with an imminent coup d'état and the rejection by the Frei faction of the CDP, which now officially controlled the party, of any agreement with the UP, Prats deserted his post by resigning his commission as Commander-in-Chief of the Armed Forces and putting himself into retirement, following a few provocations by people in the opposition and by military wives. He did so, according to his letter of resignation, so as "not to become a factor for the disruption of institutional discipline and for disturbance of the law, nor to serve as a pretext to those who

---

* Translator's note: The literal meaning of 'coup' (as in "coup d'état") is 'a blow'

want to overthrow the constitutional government . . ." A strange way to achieve all that! A few weeks after Prats' resignation, the coup d'état was carried out.

In the middle of 1972, after the initial calm of the first year of UP government, the efforts of the "C"P leadership to obtain an agreement with the CDP were intensified in the face of the growing crisis and of the opposition offensive. Within the UP there was a dangerous (for the goals of the "C"P) nervous irritation with the official tactic. On May 12, in Concepcion, a militant demonstration took place which was forbidden by the "communist" Intendant; all the local UP forces took part, except, naturally, those of the "C"P. The demonstration was violently repressed, and the police forces assassinated a supporter of "Spartacus", youth organization of the RCP, in the street. The "C"P leadership tolerated verbal disagreements with its line, but not the insubordination of its allies, especially when the latter were with the masses. The next month, in June 1972, the UP held the Lo Curro meeting in order to debate the differences which had come up between a number of organizations in the UP and the official line imposed by the "C"P. At this meeting, the "C"P leadership, through a member of its Secretariat, Orlando Millas, proposed that what had been achieved be "consolidated" and that the reforms not be deepened. The SP, MAPU and the Christian Left, on the other hand, wanted to continue the progress of reforms "towards socialism". They believed this goal could be achieved not by organizing the struggle for power but by carrying on with expropriations. At Lo Curro, however, the line of the "C"P leadership won out. Even President Allende, who was planning his trip to the USSR to desperately ask for help (which, as we have seen, would be refused him), took the side of the "C"P leadership.

However, what the "C"P leaders had in the back of their minds was not only to "consolidate" the achievements and not continue the march forward, but to go backward in order to reach a point of agreement with the CDP. They proposed a retreat on the number of firms that would be transferred to the public sector, on the refusal to apply the policy demanded by the Yankee organization for economic control of the Latin American countries (called the International Monetary Fund), on the policy of indexing wages and salaries to the exorbitant rise in the cost of living, etc. With regard to agrarian reform, they proposed to stabilize what had already been expropriated and to go no further forward. Resorting to verbal trickery to hide this proposed retreat, and at the same time showing whom he was obeying, Victor Diaz, member of the CC of the "C"P, stated in an interview on June 22, 1972: "To consolidate is to advance, and to the same extent, an agreement with the Christian Democrats, an eventuality that is becoming possible, would be a positive thing." (53) On his part, Volodia Teitelboim, in order to impose the compromise with the CDP that the "C"P leaders wanted, took up the "terror campaign" as his own and wrote: "We want for this country neither the fate of invaded Vietnam, nor of Santo Domingo, nor of Guatemala. We want the problems of our nation to be resolved by the majority, knowing that this struggle cannot cross the limits beyond which it will jump the institutional rails and careen down a road of no return . . . We believe that people are playing with fire . . . The secret marriage which, in the name of the law, we maintain with violence, seems horrible to me. We are against any form of violence that could embroil the country in a fratricidal struggle. But just as it takes two to fight, it also takes two to avoid the quarrel. And on this question we think that the responsibility does not belong only to the UP but also to the CDP and to all those . . . who consider that just men can save the country from . . . catastrophe." (54) Statements like that, of a "profound Marxist content", which became more and more pronounced during Teitelboim's senatorial campaign, earned him the following question from a National Party leader during a televised debate: "Are you a communist candidate for the Senate or for Archbishop of Santiago?"

Shortly after the Lo Curro meeting, as an expression of the victory of the "C"P position, Orlando Millas was named Minister of Finance. At the same time, Luis Figueroa, President of the CUT and leader of the "C"P, was named Minister of Labour in order to more efficiently put the brakes on the workers' struggle. From his ministry, without consulting his allies, Millas sent to Parliament a bill in which he reduced to just over 40 the number of firms to be transferred to the public sector (at the beginning, the UP had spoken of 250 firms, then of 140, later of 90, a number that was finally reduced by Millas to about 42). In addition, he accepted for some state enterprises the CDP thesis of transforming them into "workers' enterprises", owned by the workers. At the same time, he entered into relations with the International Monetary Fund, which were expressly condemned by the UP programme, submitted to its demands (monetary devaluation, wage and salary freeze, restriction of credit, etc.), and thus obtained a $42.5 million credit. What is more, in order to please their hypothetical interlocutors of the CDP, the "C"P leaders ordered violent repression against the shantytown of Lo Hermida. Following orders emanating from the offices of the Undersecretariat of the Interior, Daniel Vergara, a member of the "C"P, descended on this shantytown at five o'clock in the morning on August 4, 1972 with more than 350 policemen armed with submachine guns, as the subsequent inquiry ordered by President Allende showed. One inhabitant was killed and dozens of others wounded by bullets. One of those who led the operation was the deputy head of the civil police, Carlos Toro, a member of the "C"P. The "C"P newspapers had run the front page headline: "Let's Calm Down the Leftists!"

Following the repression and the economic measures taken by Millas without consultation, various parties in the UP protested. After having observed, following Allende's trip to the USSR, that their bosses were turning their backs on them, the "C"P leaders' haste to obtain an agreement with the CDP turned into real despair. They no longer deigned to consult their allies and staged a real coup d'état inside the UP. Later they would split MAPU (which had moved away from their positions following an internal congress) using elements they had infiltrated into it. At the end of January 1973, the SP stated: "With respect to the statement made by the Minister of the Economy, Orlando Millas, and the announcement of a bill sent to the National Congress on the delimitation of the public sector, the mixed sector and the enterprises designated 'special cases' (these were the workers' enterprises promised by Millas to the CDP), the Political Commission of the Socialist Party has resolved to state publicly that these decisions were not the subject of any consultation with our party and that, furthermore, we are not in agreement with their content." The Christian Left, for its part, criticized the government for having taken up, despite the differences of opinion existing on this question within the UP, "the futile discussions with the CDP" and for having announced "the bases of a new economic policy, the UP leaders only being informed of such a policy several days later".

However, the content of the criticism by some parties in the UP of the policy of the "C"P leaders was not aimed at the real motives of this policy, nor did it offer a correct solution. Often, influenced by Trotskyist ideas, they maintained that the "errors" of the "C"P policy grew out of its refusal to advance immediately towards socialism (which was obvious, but not only immediately) and that, for this reason, the "C"P leaders wanted an alliance with sections of the non-monopoly bourgeoisie and with the middle sections, to set them against the monopoly bourgeoisie, imperialism and the landlords, thus conceiving the revolution in stages. These ideas, entirely correct in the case of Chile, but correct as a strategy for a united front led by the proletariat, had however nothing to do with the strategy of the "C"P leading group. The latter did not seek an alliance with certain non-monopoly sections of the bourgeoisie and with the middle sections (which would have been correct) to fight and annihilate the main enemies mentioned above. On the contrary, it tried to put pressure on the monopolist sections of the bourgeoisie, on the imperialist firms and on the landlords, (by threatening them with isolation) to thus obtain an alliance with these same dominant sections at the expense of the interests of the workers and of the middle sections. To realize this, one has only to consider the policy proposed by Millas. The reduction in the number of monopoly enterprises slated for transfer to the public sector was a measure to benefit not the middle sections but the big bourgeoisie. The limits on the expropriation of big land estates, and the opposition to their reserves being reduced from a base of 80 irrigated hectares to 40 hectares, were not to favour the middle peasants but the big landlords. The guarantees given to imperialism for the creation of joint ventures with the state were in favour of the U.S. monopolies. The implementation of the policy of the International Monetary Fund, directly opposed to the middle bourgeoisie and the workers, was favourable to the big imperialist interests. Lastly, the holding back and the repression of any mass mobilization and the strict adherence to the institutions and laws of the bourgeois state favoured only the imperialist circles of the big bourgeoisie and the landlords, who controlled state power. Although the "C"P leaders wanted to take the place of these dominant sections as a bureaucratic bourgeoisie, they were incapable of doing so under the conditions in Chile; and hence, in accordance with the strategy of social-imperialism, what they wanted was an alliance with these dominant sections or part of them in order to develop state capitalism. This policy has nothing to do with the formation of an anti-imperialist, anti-monopolist and anti-landlord national united front led by the proletariat to isolate and annihilate these enemies and for the people to win power. The teachings of Lenin on phony "communism" must not be forgotten: *"The opportunists are bourgeois enemies of the proletarian revolution, who in peaceful times carry on their bourgeois work in secret, concealing themselves within the workers' parties, while in time of crisis, they immediately prove to be open allies of the* entire *united bourgeoisie, from the conservative to the most radical and democratic part of the latter, from the free-thinkers to the religious and clerical sections. Anyone who has failed to understand this truth* after *the events we have gone through is hopelessly deceiving both himself and the workers." (55)* It was precisely the "secret" work done by "concealing themselves within the workers' parties" that made the honest sections of the traditional Chilean left forget the true character of those who falsify Marxism, first to become allies of all the exploiters, and later, exploiters themselves. The latter tendency has notably grown in our era, when phony "communists" have taken power and established state capitalism in a number of countries.

The policy of Orlando Millas which we have described, begun in the middle of 1972, carried on in 1973, although, instead of reaching an agreement with them, the CDP launched an open offensive in the employers' strike of October 1972 with the aim of overthrowing the government. This strike offered the "C"P leadership favourable conditions for obtaining the surrender of the government and the agreement with the CDP that it coveted.

However, its plans ran into an obstacle: the strike gave rise to intense militancy and mobilization of the people and was defeated by the firm attitude of the working class in particular. However, at a time when it was fully possible and necessary to launch a counter-offensive to smash the retreating putschist circles, the "C"P leaders managed to transform the people's victory into a defeat for the government. A cabinet was appointed including the Armed Forces, who were credited with the "solution" of the already disintegrating strike; the people were demobilized by resorting to the March 1973 elections as a means of smoothing over the conflicts with the opposition, and shameful concessions were made with the defeated, with the organizers of the strike. Economic guarantees were given so as to keep the paper monopoly in the private sector (one of the main watchwords of the opposition); *Radio Agriculture* of Los Angeles and the newspaper *El Sur* of Concepcion, which were being run by the government because they had incited subversion, were given back; the powers of the JAP's *(56)* and those which the industrial cordons *(57)* had won in the struggle against the strike were cancelled; the trial of the strike leaders was cancelled and a guarantee was given that there would be no reprisals against the participants; guarantees were given that transport would remain in the private sector; a commitment was made to give back the commercial establishments and industrial enterprises that had been occupied by the workers after being paralyzed or to avoid their being paralyzed; the wholesale trading company CODINA, really a centre used by the opposition to create shortages and black market, was taken off the list of firms to be expropriated; and so on. In addition to the measures which were made public, there were secret agreements by Millas with the CDP, which, as we have seen, were not even known to the parties of the UP.

What finally happened after this policy of betrayal of the people's interests, with a view to a pact with the CDP, was carried out? The "C"P leadership itself clearly showed what happened in a document that appeared in March 1976, in which it stated: "In June 1972, when Senator Renan Fuentealba was president of the CDP, that party and the UP were on the verge of signing a set of agreements that were to be implemented into law. The possibility presented itself of putting into practice both the UP programme and the programme supported by Radomiro Tomic during the presidential campaign. Such convergences enraged the fascists who are today temporarily in power. At the very moment when this patriotic agreement was going to be signed, Frei himself used every means to demand the annulment of this act." That the pact existed is absolutely certain, but the conditions under which the "C"P leaders maintain it would have been signed are absolutely false, for, as we have seen, the agreement was not based on the UP programme, nor on the most advanced of the reforms in the Tomic programme, but on shameful concessions to the imperialist and reactionary interests that Frei supported. It was with him that the "C"P leaders sought agreement, using the sections of the CDP closest to the UP as instruments to this end. The proof of this is that Frei was able to impose his annulment without the left wing of the CDP struggling to demand the implementation of these reforms. The intuition of broad middle strata and of workers in the CDP, who are aware of the oppressive, exploiting systems which exist in the USSR and its Warsaw Pact "allies", and who confuse these systems with "socialism" and "communism", allowed and today still allow Frei and his team to oppose an alliance with a coalition in which the pro-Soviet "C"P leadership would play a dominant role. Naturally, Frei used this confusion among the CDP rank and file and did not let his real motives show through: to serve the policy of U.S. imperialism and the internal reactionary forces.

The reason why we have included the efforts of the "C"P leaders to obtain an alliance with the CDP at all costs in this chapter where we are analyzing the contention of the superpowers in Chile, is that their policy is directly imposed as a strategy by the Soviet rulers. Corvalan defines himself and his party as "pro-Soviet", but the truth is that they are much more than that. A "pro" is one who spontaneously admires an institution or a person (a football team or a performer) but the relations of Corvalan and the other "C"P leaders with the Soviet bureaucrats are not relations of mere admiration but of dependence and subordination. Furthermore, this leading group is one of the most servile and unquestioning toward the Soviet leaders in the entire world. We have already pointed out in the first part of this book how the Chilean "C"P, which had gone about 11 years without holding a congress, held one a few months after the Twentieth Congress of the CPSU for the sole purpose of transposing the line approved in the USSR to Chile. There were cases in which the list of members of the Central Committee of the "C"P was learned by listening to *Radio Moscow* before they were "elected" in a congress taking place in Chile. In the framework of the polemic by the Marxist-Leninists against modern revisionism, not only did they align themselves without any debate with the positions of the Soviet leadership, but they forced all their leaders and important trade union cadres to write articles against the communist parties of Albania and China. During the Soviet invasion of Czechoslovakia, they were the first party in the world to give their public approval to this invasion. Furthermore, they publicly attacked the Cuban leaders when in the beginning, the latter sometimes demonstrated their independence from the Soviets.

The line of alliance with the CDP, which they followed in an blindly obsessed manner, was only an application of the orders of the Soviet leaders. It was the Soviet line for Chile (and on some points, for Latin America) faithfully carried out by their agents in our country. In this sense, the leaders of the Chilean "C"P were the precursors (unfortunate precursors, to be sure) of the "historic compromise" of Berlinguer in Italy, and of the line which Marchais in France and Carrillo in Spain stubbornly implement, despite the traits of independence which they try to show toward the USSR. The events in Chile explain in some way a fact that surprises many people in Europe and which was noted, for example, by Jean-Pierre Vigier, an ex-member of the CC of the French "C"P, writing in *Le Monde* of July 22, 1976: "Things have reached a point where we are witnessing the amazing spectacle of a big workers' party *(the Italian "C"P)* making desperate efforts not to come to power." If one thinks about this, it is the same logic that inspired the Chilean "C"P, and it is normal that this should be the case, because the two obey the same leading centre.

Faithfulness to this foreign line also explains the form in which the situation in Chile unfolded following the launching of the coup d'état. After the failure of the pact with Fuentealba, after the resignation of Prats, their lever in the Army, after the official takeover of the CDP by the Frei faction, and faced with evidence that a coup d'état was inevitable, the efforts of the "C"P leaders were aimed at preventing any kind of resistance to the coup d'état. Politically, they did this by giving even more forcefully the suicidal and demobilizing slogan: "No to civil war". This slogan obviously did absolutely nothing to hold back the military putschists, who obeyed the slogans of circles very different from the "C"P, but did hold back the popular strata that wanted to resist the coup, as well as sections of the Armed Forces that were potentially faithful to the government. And this was no mere slogan. For months after the coup d'état, one could meet "C"P militants in exile who, in their naivete, praised the "foresight" of their leaders who, weeks before the coup d'état, had made them turn in the few guns they had stocked in some factories. For example, the leaders of the coal miners' union, members of the "C"P, who headed a powerful proletarian organization and who because of their work had access to lots of dynamite, waited in vain in their trade union offices for instructions from their leaders (who undoubtedly were already holed up in some embassy), while the military hesitated to go into these mines, expecting stiff resistance. Finally the military found them in these offices and shot them on the spot. Lastly, the main leader of the CUT, Jorge Godoy, a leading member of the "C"P, was presented by the Military Junta on the television networks, during the days when the coup d'état was being executed, to make an appeal to cease all resistance and collaborate. Such treason cannot be justified under the pretext of any pressure, no matter what, for those who believe they are revolutionaries. What was the cause of this shameful attitude of the leaders of the "C"P of facilitating the coup d'état by destroying and discouraging any possibility of resistance? *It was that they believed that a few months after the overthrow of the Allende government, the Army would give the presidential mandate back to Frei,* who had even got himself elected president of the Senate in order to claim a "legal" right of succession recognized by the constitution, for he thought he could receive the presidential mandate that way. In this manner, after the failure of their strategy to prevent a coup d'état through an alliance with the CDP under the Allende government, the "C"P leaders prepared to carry on their pressure for such an alliance from exile by offering themselves as collaborators of Frei and his team. To achieve this, they had to demonstrate their ability to hold back all resistance to the coup d'état and even more so all threat of civil war based on a potential split in the Armed Forces. What neither they nor Frei counted on was that the military putschists wanted to stay in power. In spite of everything, they have not abandoned their strategy and persist in it, although in much more difficult conditions, despite rejection by the Frei wing, which is not unaware that such an alliance is unacceptable to the U.S. and that the possibility of such an alliance in the past was one of the reasons for the coup d'état.

Chapter V
The U.S. Policy towards the
Popular Unity Government

1. The Failure of the Alliance for Progress

In order to understand the policy of the U.S. in regard to the Allende government, it is essential to analyze both the changes which took place beginning in 1969 in the government and the policy of the United States, and the fate that the policy applied by the Democratic administrations during the Frei government suffered in Chile. During the Kennedy administration, Chile was chosen as a pilot country to test the so-called Alliance for Progress policy. Two fundamental objectives were pursued through this policy: on the one hand, to contribute to the development of dependent capitalism, putting the most profitable sector of manufacturing industry under the control of U.S. investors; on the other hand, on the basis of this capitalist development subordinated to monopoly capital, to enlarge the market for machinery, technology, raw materials, spare parts, etc., for certain sectors of U.S. industry. On the political level, it was a question of using the reforms necessary for this capitalist development (some of which went against the interests of the landed oligarchy and of certain national monopolies) to develop a populist movement through intensive demagogic publicity. This movement would act as a brake on any revolutionary opposition and on the exacerbation of nationalist anti-imperialist tendencies.

This policy of the Democratic group in the U.S. basically represented the interests of advanced industries like electronics, petrochemicals, precision machinery, etc., as well as the service industries and the big trading firms. These monopolies had an interest both in investing in a Latin American market expanded by regional treaties, and, on the basis of capitalist development, in selling what they were producing in the U.S. For example, these groups were unhappy when the Import-Export Bank refused the Allende government a credit of $21 million it had asked for in order to buy three Boeing aircraft for the Chilean National Airline. The *New York Times,* a representative of these interests, published an article on September 2, 1971, which stated: "Unemployed aircraft workers in Seattle will scarcely be pleased to learn that the United States' move against Chile will increase employment in the Ilyushin plants of the Soviet Union if Chile is forced to turn to the only alternative source of long-range commercial jet aircraft . . . " The *Washington Post,* another paper characterized by its opposition to the coup d'état in Chile and to the Military Junta, declared in this regard: "It's not only toward Chile that the United States is brandishing the stick, but toward the whole of Latin America and the entire world."

Expressing these opinions, the president of the National Association of Manufacturers stated: "There can be no greater error than to believe that our export business depends on the economic retardation of other countries. Our main obstacle in the export business with Latin America is the people's lack of purchasing power. This market is growing not through an increase in raw material wealth, but through industrialization. History shows that when the people of any country develop their industry profitably, their consumption grows, creating a greater demand for foreign and domestic goods. The best consumers are not the countries producing mainly raw materials, but the industrially developed ones." In 1943, a report published by the same association had already pointed out: "It must always be remembered that the economic value of trade between the United States and other countries increases in proportion to the development of the countries traded with. There is a widespread opinion that if the nations which formerly had little or no industrial activity were to develop extensive industry, they would as a result reduce the export market for American industries. However, this is not a necessary result. An abundance of statistics shows that, as industry develops, purchasing power also increases and with it the demand for imports. It therefore follows that efforts to raise the standard of living of the backward countries through intensive use of their resources are profitable for the United States." Albert Hirschman, a member of the

Governing Board of the Federal Reserve System, stated: "Probably, the most important reason for our lack of anxiety over industrialization abroad rests in the composition of our exports. Unlike a country such as the United Kingdom, our exports typically consist of items suited both to increasing production (machines, equipment, or other investments) and to high or growing income levels (automobiles and other durable goods). That is why our exports not only are not threatened by industrialization abroad, but on the contrary benefit considerably from the expansion of production and the raising of incomes in other regions of the world. This is in marked contrast with what is happening in industrial countries whose exports are based mainly on items such as textiles, which are one of the first things to be produced by countries that industrialize. Furthermore," he added, "the United States exports substantial quantities of industrial raw materials such as cotton, oil, etc., and these exports directly benefit from industrial expansion abroad." (58)

In any case, the Alliance for Progress policy also called for U.S. investments in the most profitable developing industries. Thus, profits were made in two ways from the process of industrialization in Latin America: by increasing the sale of capitalist goods and luxury products, as well as raw materials, and by directly appropriating the most lucrative part of this development.

It is for the traditional monopolies, engaged in the extraction of raw materials in the dependent countries, that the industrial development of these countries is undesirable, for it brings with it both the demand for higher wages in the firms through which they exploit these resources, and a tendency to recover the resources in order to use them in developing the industry of the country. This is why these monopolies are generally opposed to a more liberal policy which would allow the workers to fight for higher incomes and to any capitalist development inside the dependent countries. This is why their favourite political allies are the big landlords and the national monopolies, forces which hold back capitalist development in opposing it and are prepared to make fewer concessions to the workers and to practice harsher repression.

Having discovered that it was impossible to rely on the traditional parties of the oligarchic and monopolist right, due to their extremely retrogressive nature and opposition to all reform, the Kennedy administration began to seek the support of new, more dynamic class strata and a different political force as the instrument of its plans. Thus, beginning in 1961 (the year in which the U.S. government elaborated its formulation of the Alliance for Progress at the conference of chancellors in Punta del Este, Uruguay), the Kennedy administration explored the possibility of using the Radical Party or the Christian Democratic Party for its new policy. The following year it had already decided in favour of the latter.

In light of the facts known to all concerning the aid and the loans granted to the Frei government by international credit organizations in which the U.S. has decisive influence, and of the secret facts, partly revealed in the U.S. Senate report on CIA involvement in Chile, it is clear that the CDP is virtually a creature of the CIA and of the U.S. government. This despite the fact that many of its supporters come from the ranks of the people. Deceived by multi-million dollar propaganda, they must have been the most surprised to learn the origin of the economic resources which their leaders spent to make the CDP the largest party in Chile both in influence and in electoral strength.

The support of the United States for the CDP, as we have pointed out, has two basic aspects: the open economic "aid" given by U.S.-controlled credit organizations, and the secret support given by the CIA and, through it, by the multinational corporations. As to the first aspect, suffice it to say that during the Frei government the external debt rose to about $3.13 billion as of December 31, 1970. The director of the U.S. Economic Mission to Chile, Sidney Weintraub, was correct when he pointed out on October 2, 1969 that: "Chile represents approximately 3.5 percent of the population of Latin America, and in recent years it has received about 12 percent of United States economic aid to Latin America. Obviously Chile has received preferential treatment . . . Chile has received more aid per capita than practically any other country in the world."

As to the secret aid of the CIA, which it admitted to before the U.S. Senate Committee that investigated its involvement in

Chile, the CDP benefited from projects promoted and financed by the CIA beginning in the 1950s, projects aimed at the peasants, the slum-dwellers, the organized workers and the students. All this activity was later directed in favour of the CDP. However, direct aid began in 1962 with a CIA grant of an initial sum of $230,000 to establish the CDP, to use the CIA's own expression. It was in this way that in the municipal elections of April 1963, this party became the most influential in Chile, with 22.7 percent of the vote. Prior to this, the National Phalange, the party which had given birth to the CDP and from which its first leaders had come, had obtained barely 3.9 percent of the vote in 1949 and had dropped to 2.8 percent in 1953. Later, $3 million were given to the CDP for the Frei presidential campaign in 1964. In addition, according to the Yankee Senate report, the CIA financed groups of pro-CDP students, women, professionals, slum-dwellers and peasants. This involvement (of which Mr. Frei, with supreme cynicism, claims to have been unaware) reached its peak, as the U.S. Senate report recognizes, with the formation in the U.S. capital of an "election committee" to give the campaign an "American-style" orientation. This committee included no less than the Assistant Secretary of State for Inter-American Affairs, Thomas Mann; the head of the CIA Western Hemisphere Mission, Desmond Fitzgerald; and Ralph Dungan and McGeorge Bundy, representatives of the White House. A parallel committee, fully coordinated with the one formed in Washington, was organized in Chile with embassy representatives and the heads of the local CIA station. *(59)*

However, to judge the magnitude of financial aid to the CDP, two aspects must be considered: first, that these were the contributions admitted to by the CIA; and second, that since they were secret contributions, these dollars were exchanged on the black market where they are worth several times the official rate. Under the Allende government, the CIA admits having exchanged them at five times their official rate, but at certain periods the difference was much greater. Suffice it to say that in some months under this government the minimum wage of a worker could be paid with one dollar sold on the black market. In regard to the amount of the aid, some journalists, like Bernard

Collier of the *New York Times,* maintain that about one million dollars a month left the U.S. throughout most of the 1964 election campaign. As to the aid from the Christian Democratic Parties of Europe to Frei, Collier puts it at $20 million minimum. To all this, one must add the aid of $1.5 million offered the Frei campaign by the representatives of multinational corporations having interests in Chile. This aid (as the CIA modestly admitted) was granted to the CDP on its advice, through a "businessman".

As a result of this massive support, Frei obtained 56.09 percent of the vote in the 1964 presidential election, and the certainty of this victory allowed the U.S. embassy and the CIA to reject, on the eve of the election, no less than three offers of coup d'état that were made to them by various "democratic" and "constitutionalist" Chilean army circles in the event that Allende won.

The secret CIA aid continued during the Frei administration in order to politically support his work in the service of U.S. policy. In 1965, the 303 Committee, precursor of the 40 Committee (which is in charge of the CIA) authorized the granting of $175,000 to support a group of candidates selected by the U.S. embassy to run in the parliamentary elections at the end of March in the same year. In these elections, the CDP became the majority party in the Senate and gained an absolute majority of votes in the Chamber of Deputies. Thus, the conditions for the implementation of the so-called Alliance for Progress policy were nearly perfect. However, not satisfied with direct support of the CDP, the CIA launched its own "anti-communist propaganda campaign" (before and after the presidential elections and admits having spent an additional $2 million on 20 secret projects carried out between 1964 and 1970. These projects included organizing a popular movement amongst the slum-dwellers and the peasants (for this purpose three pro-CDP trade union federations were created during this period in the countryside); supporting an anti-communist womens' group; encouraging opposition trends in the CUT; financing numerous posters and propaganda of all types; and, lastly, giving heavy financial support to the newspaper *El Mercurio,* whose editorials the CIA admits having inspired on a daily basis. *(60)*

Of course, all this spending was not done out of pure love of "democracy", nor was it wasted. Frei had to "pay back" by promoting the profits of the U.S. monopolies and their penetration of the Chilean economy, and, in general, by implementing the reforms that the so-called Alliance for Progress policy, advocated for Chile. Following the directives of this policy, Frei strengthened the state corporations with which U.S. investors wanted to associate in joint ventures. He implemented several partnerships of this type, making shameful concessions to the imperialist interests. He spurred agrarian reform (as well as the unionization of the peasantry and a minimum wage for peasants) in order to develop capitalism in the countryside, a reform demanded by the U.S., not to help the peasantry, but to expand the consumer market for the U.S.-backed industries. He improved the training of manpower for these industries through apprenticeship courses. He spurred fiscal reform to facilitate the financing of an entire infrastructure necessary to the development of dependent capitalism. Lastly, he promoted the entry of Chile into the Andes Pact and other regional continental agreements, a measure also demanded by the U.S. capitalists investing in industry in order to expand their sales market.

Similarly, at the demand of his promoters, Frei tried to develop a populist movement designed to support the pro-Yankee reformism that he called "Revolution in Freedom"; this movement he developed particularly among the non-proletarian strata of the shantytown-dwellers, housewives, peasants, students, etc. It was developed through activities that were inexpensive for the government, such as handicraft courses, production cooperatives, summer work for students, housewives' associations, etc., and by means of an intensive demagogic propaganda campaign that presented the government's policy as "revolutionary" and "anti-oligarchic" while praising the "generous" U.S. aid given through the Alliance for Progress.

In addition, Frei acted in full accord with the wishes of the investors represented by the U.S. Democratic administration (who were different from traditional investors interested only in grabbing raw materials) by throwing the doors wide open to the penetration of their capital in the most profitable industries. This plan to take over the manufacturing industry corresponded to an investment policy applied almost everywhere in Latin America, a policy served by the very reforms promoted by the so-called Alliance for Progress. According to the U.S. Department of Commerce publication *Survey of Current Business,* "U.S. private direct investment in the Latin American manufacturing sector increased from $1.52 billion in 1960 to $6.46 billion in 1973."

For Chile, from the beginning of the Frei administration to the end of 1969, the investments totalled more than $320 million. Investments in manufacturing industry (in relation to investment in other sectors of the economy) grew from about 3 percent in 1953 to 7.8 percent at the beginning of the Christian Democratic administration, and later to about 14 percent in 1968. However, in the case of Chile, these figures do not give a clear picture of the Yankee efforts to take over the manufacturing industry, due to the already existing big investments in the copper mines. The investments in manufacturing industry grew faster than in all the other countries of the Andes Pact, rising from $22 million in 1960 to $68 million in 1969, that is, more than 300 percent. At the same time, the U.S. rapidly outstripped other countries in the relative importance of their investments in industry. U.S. capital rose from 59 percent of total foreign investment in 1964 to 75 percent in 1968.

Frei paid back the "generous" U.S. aid for his candidacy and his government not only by facilitating the penetration of the Chilean economy and by faithfully applying the Alliance for Progress policy, but also by allowing the Yankee monopolies an unprecedented increase in their profits in Chile. During the Frei administration, their profits exceeded a billion dollars, and the average monthly profits were twice those recorded in the 32-year period previous to his administration. This means that during the Frei administration the U.S. monopolies made declared profits almost equal to the total of their investments in Chile. Among the measures Frei took to facilitate the intensification of U.S. plunder of Chile's resources was the setting up of a few joint ventures under conditions shamefully favourable to foreign capital. Amongst these, let us give the example of the joint venture formed between the state and a few U.S. monopolies that exploited Chilean copper, a venture that Frei (with a certain black humour) called the "Chileanization of copper". The Frei government "Chileanized" the El Teniente mine by buying 51 percent of the shares for $80 million. Kennecott, the owner of the mine, agreed to lend this sum to the newly-formed joint company for 15 years at a 4.5 percent interest rate payable in dollars and exempt from all taxation: thus Kennecott gained $35.5 million more. However, what was most monstrous about the deal was that the book value of the business in which the government was acquiring a 51 percent interest was only $65 million in 1963, and no further investments had been made in it. The mine installations were Kennecott's only contribution to the operation of "Chileanization". Therefore, by paying $80 million for half the shares (51 percent), the government was graciously crediting the U.S. monopoly with $160 million when it had only invested $65 million. It was with reason that the U.S. publication *Hanson's American Letter*, written for investors in Latin America, stated: "It must be admitted that Frei has done so much for foreign investors in Chile (far surpassing their greatest hopes) that U.S. companies are starting to be as optimistic as former investors in Cuba used to be before Castro arrived on the scene." And the publication adds: "Chile is the Latin American republic most preferred by Washington and, it goes without saying, Frei is Washington's favourite customer." Further on, the same publication gives one of the reasons for its love for Frei when it states: "No government of the extreme right could have treated U.S. businesses with the generosity that Frei has shown in signing the agreements (referring to the agreements on the "Chileanization" of copper). The conditions, favourable to a fault, revealed such a lack of balance and judgement and were so contrary to Chile's interests that they provoked near hilarity in Washington."

Because of its extreme servility toward U.S. imperialist interests, amongst other reasons, the Frei administration led the country into acute economic crisis in the final years of its term. This despite the enormous credits it had available, and despite an extremely favourable international price for copper on the world market, which had brought it an extra $200 million a year. There were other factors in this crisis: the fact that through incomplete agrarian reform, the Frei government was not successful in solving the crisis of the agrarian economy, but on the contrary touched off a powerful and militant peasant movement; the fact that it tied the country to an enormous external debt, which reached almost $3 billion in 1969, consuming just in interest and amortization payments about half the total currency reserves; the fact that because of its pro-Yankee reforms and demagogic attitude it lost the confidence of the national monopolist circles and of the capitalist circles influenced by the national monopolies. Thus, even though the Frei administration had very little effect on their interests, it could not count on them in applying its policy for investments and growth of production.

As a result of these factors, amongst others, the average annual growth rate of industry, which had been about 7 percent for the first two years of the Frei government, dropped to a 2.3 percent average for the last four years. At the same time, industrial sales declined and the national product growth rate fell. The consumer price index recorded an annual increase of 36 percent at the end of the Frei administration and the unemployment rate exceeded 8 percent of the labour force.

At the same time, the populist movement created at the prompting of the United States failed in its political objectives, that is, failed to hold back the development of class struggle. As the class struggle grew, the electoral influence of the CDP declined, despite the millions of dollars invested to promote it, to resist its opponents and to promote the mass movements in support of it. From 42.3 percent of the vote it received in the 1965 parliamentary elections, the CDP dropped to 35.6 percent in the 1967 municipal councillors' elections. Later, in the 1969 parliamentary elections, it received only 29.7 percent of the vote.

In regard to the mass struggles, despite the constant assistance that the "C"P trade union bureaucracy gave the Frei government to hold the struggles back, more than 2,000 conflicts took place in 1967, involving more than two million strike days. During the first eight months of 1968, this figure rose to 4.5 million strike days. In the countryside also, where strikes had been the exception in the past (five strikes in 1963 and only 39 in 1964), a powerful and militant movement was unleashed and the process of occupying land began. In the years 1966, 1967 and 1968 there were 1,688 peasant strikes, in which about 100,000 farm workers participated. In the three months from August to October 1969, there were more than 7,000 workers on legal strike in the countryside and more than 26,000 on illegal strike, according to Labour Ministry data. The Christian Democratic government was forced to throw off its demagogic mask and use violent repression. Amongst the widely-varied forms of repression were two massacres: one against the miners of the El Salvador copper mine, where, on March 11, 1966 eight people were assassinated by troops and more than 60 wounded; and the other, involving eight deaths and 26 wounded, against homeless people who had occupied vacant lands in the southern town of Puerto Montt. The temporary houses they had built were burnt with all their furniture.

Finally, the economic crisis and the repression the CDP had unleashed, as well as its accelerating electoral decline, caused severe crisis within the party itself, as progressive trends appeared which challenged the government's policy.

Thus we see that the pilot test carried out in Chile for the Alliance for Progress policy, an experiment that had its leaders dreaming of an era of at least 30 years of Christian Democratic government, had failed two years after it had begun, even inside the CDP. This fact is of prime importance to understand the change in U.S. government policy toward the Popular Unity, which would succeed the Frei government.

The Popular Unity was no longer up against the reformist policy of the Democratic administration, which, as we have said, was inspired by certain monopolies whose interests differed from those of the monopolies which had traditionally exploited Chile. It should not be forgotten that Kennedy, the man who inspired the Alliance for Progress, was assassinated precisely because of contradictions between monopolies. Once elected President of the United States, Nixon sent Nelson Rockefeller to Latin America to investigate the results of the Alliance for Progress policy. During his trip Rockefeller was confronted by militant protests by the people of the countries he visited. After Rockefeller had written his report, President Nixon gave a speech indicating the general line of what would be his policy. The report of the U.S. Senate on CIA involvement in Chile points out in this regard: As early as 1969, President Nixon announced a new policy toward Latin America, labelled by him 'Action for Progress'. It was to replace the Alliance for Progress which the President characterized as paternalistic and unrealistic. Instead, the United States was to seek 'mature partnership' with Latin American countries, emphasizing trade not aid. The reformist trappings of the Alliance were to be dropped; the United States announced itself prepared to deal with pragmatic foreign governments. (61) In essence, this was a get-tough policy. The policy of penetrating manufacturing industry was maintained, but at the same time the interests of the traditional monopolies operating in extractive industries were defended. The development of the people's struggles was met not with a pretense of reforms and populist programmes but with direct repression. To this end, Rockefeller recommended in his report that the Armed Forces be directly promoted into power when the bourgeois parties fail. Consequently, it was not by chance that Nixon's coming to power was followed by a series of coups d'état in Latin America. The Popular Unity government took over when this process was already in full swing.

The Allende government tried to win over or at least to neutralize the monopolist groups interested in investing in the manufacturing industry by concentrating its anti-imperialism on the mining monopolies operating in Chile as well as on the monopolies that controlled the public utilities (ITT). With a number of industrial firms, the government nationalized that part of the firm which represented Chilean investment and entered into a joint venture with U.S. investors, offering them very advantageous conditions. This was the case with companies engaged in automobile assembly in Chile and with electronics, metallurgical, petrochemical and other firms. For example, in March 1971 an agreement was reached with the Radio Corporation of America (RCA) through the Production Development Corporation (CORFO). The government bought shares held by Chilean capitalists and formed a joint enterprise with the U.S. monopoly, which continued to control 49 percent of the shares. A similar agreement was concluded in the INSA tire manufacturing firm. Also in March 1971, an agreement was reached with U.S. capitalists to form a joint enterprise in mining and steel called the Pacific Steel Company. The state would control 35.7 percent of the shares of this company, Armco Steel Corporation 34.3 percent, and the Electrometallurgical Company (Rockefeller group capital) 30 percent. In addition, in the chemical industry, the investments of the U.S. Dow Chemical monopoly were maintained.

These measures were not isolated, but corresponded to a clearly defined policy of the UP government. The Finance Minister, Americo Zorrilla, a member of the Secretariat of the Central Committee of the "C"P, stated in a speech to a meeting of governors of the Interamerican Development Bank on May 11, 1971: "In the framework of the Chilean revolutionary process, both external financing and foreign capital investment must play a role. Oriented toward priority goals, responding to economic necessities, and complementing our own internal effort, foreign investment will be the source of a dynamism greater than that which it has traditionally given rise to." And he added: "For these foreign investments the vast field of the mixed and private sectors is open, on condition that the state give its approval by guaranteeing both its legitimate interest and a prospective orientation favourable to the development of the country." The offer of such investments to the Americans was one of the inducements that the USSR offered the U.S. with a view to joint domination of the Chilean people. For his part, Chancellor Clodomiro Almeyda had pointed out to U.S. Secretary of State William Rogers in April 1971: "that it was not correct that the Chilean government opposed foreign investment. Only the basic resources," he maintained, "must remain in the hands of the state, but there are other economic categories and sectors in which foreign investments are perfectly possible." As an example, he mentioned the agreement with the Radio Corporation of America.

2. Nixon and Kissinger Intervene in Favour of a Coup d'État

The policy of the U.S. government toward the Allende government did not fit into the framework of the reformist and semi-liberal trend that the Kennedy administration followed in

Chile. In accordance with the recommendations made by Rockefeller in his report on Latin America, it was characterized by a hard-line attitude and suppression of the reforms. The need to establish the difference between these two policies neatly explains the "mystery" that a group in the U.S. Senate decided to investigate the CIA and expose its involvement in Chile. This group carried out the desire of a group of Democratic senators led by Church, a former candidate for the presidency of the United States, to establish the difference between the two policies for electoral purposes. Although it certainly hid many aspects of the activities of the CIA and was completely silent about the participation of the Pentagon through the DIA (Defence Intelligence Agency), the Senate Committee was concerned to show that U.S. involvement under Kennedy and Johnson was different from the involvement that Nixon carried on. The Kennedy-Johnson involvement was described as *preventive,* ensuring Frei's victory and subsequent support for his administration, and at the same time *reformist,* that is, designed to alienate the people from "communism" rather than to repress it. In the words of the Church Commission: "Arguably, the 1964 election project was part of a 'progressive' approach to Chile. The project was justified, if perhaps not actually sustained, by the desire to elect democratic reformers." In the case of Nixon and Kissinger, as the Senate report clearly establishes, involvement was aimed exclusively at overthrowing the Allende government. Although the former appraisal certainly does not characterize the general attitude of the Kennedy and Johnson administrations, which intensified the war against Vietnam and Laos, tried to invade Cuba and intervened in the Dominican Republic, it basically corresponds to the policy applied during the Frei government in Chile. It is also true that the Nixon government, after the election of Allende, did its utmost to overthrow him, although for the sake of form it maintained a hypocritically tolerant attitude toward him.

Various factors entered into play in this get-tough approach of the U.S. government. In the first place the fact that the Republicans represent, to a greater extent than the Democrats, monopolies that are linked to raw material extraction and to the exploitation of public utilities (ITT, for example), monopolies whose aggressiveness, opposition to capitalist development in other countries, and alliance with the most repressive elements in the dependent countries are well known. In addition, one must consider the fact that the reformist policy and populism with which the U.S. imperialists and their agents tried to hold back the class struggle during the Frei administration had failed. Finally, one must take account of the fact that the UP government came to power at a difficult time for the U.S. economy. On top of their mounting setbacks in Vietnam and Cambodia, which would later force the U.S. imperialists to withdraw in defeat from these countries, came the start of a serious economic crisis which would eventually engulf the entire capitalist world. As a study appearing in the January 1973 issue of the *Latin America Empire Report*, published by NACLA (North American Congress of Latin America), pointed out: "1970 marked the culmination of the difficult situation that the American economy had already been going through for some time. Inflation was becoming uncontrollable, the unemployment index reached high figures, gold reserves were steadily dwindling, the U.S. share in world trade was down, and for the first time in nearly a hundred years, the trade balance was running a deficit. While this was happening to the U.S. economy, the countries of Western Europe and Japan appeared as examples of prosperity in full bloom: high rates of industrial growth, a growing share of international trade, increasing investment abroad, etc. The 'aggressiveness' of the European and Japanese competition must have heightened U.S. sensitivity toward the programme of the UP in Chile, which included the nationalization of substantial American interests."

The same study adds: "The 'New Economic Policy' established by the Nixon government to confront the poor economic situation implied the need to exercise greater pressure on foreign governments (particularly in the underdeveloped world) so as to ensure the interests of U.S. investments, which more than ever were confronted with the need to strengthen their position in the face of the expansion of European and Japanese capital."

Although it is certain that the efforts of the U.S. government to overthrow Allende came in the context of the serious economic crisis in the U.S., and that the crisis influenced the U.S. aggressiveness (particularly in regard to the blockade) against Chile, the basic motivation of the U.S. government in overthrowing him was eminently political.

The pace of the economic aggression was set by the Treasury Department, led by the ultra-conservative Democrat John Connally, who had links with a number of multinational firms with interests in Chile. Connally told *Business Week* in July 1971 that the United States could take a hard-line approach toward Latin America in economic and trading matters because "we haven't any friends there anyway". The reaction, which we shall call "economic", of reprisals against the Allende programme, inspired violent editorials in newspapers linked to the affected interests. The *News Washington Daily* of August 13, 1971, said: "If we allow the Marxist Allende to nationalize without compensation, this will create a precedent endangering the billions of American dollars invested in the mines, oilfields and industries of Latin America. Furthermore, since these assets are insured by government agencies, it will be the American taxpayer who will pay for the damage." This was certainly true, at least insofar as the big copper mining firms and ITT were concerned, and it helped the affected firms to commit the U.S. government (if not the taxpayers) to opposition to Allende. The investments of these firms in Chile were protected by insurance policies with a United States government agency called OPIC (Overseas Private Investment Corporation), a branch of the AID. This agency had to indemnify Kennecott, Anaconda Copper and ITT in the amount of more than $400 million because they had been expropriated without what they considered fair compensation. This sum exceeded the financial capacity of the agency, and the government had to take charge of the debt.

However, despite the opinions of many journalists who let themselves be taken in or want to be taken in by what was most ostensible (the blocking of certain credits for Chile), the most destructive blows against the Allende government came from the internal, secret work of the CIA and the Pentagon aimed at dislocating the Chilean economy, at coordinating and strengthening the opposition to the Allende government and at preparing the coup d'état together with the Armed Forces. In this sense, it must be said that the most merciless attack against the

Allende government came directly from the U.S. government which pretended to be tolerant and neutral. This attack hit the "Achilles' heel" of the UP: its lack of control of power, which prevented it from firmly stopping subversive opposition and from strengthening the economy in the transition to state capitalism, which prevented it from holding back the "destabilizing" factors that would facilitate the military coup d'état. It is easy to understand that those who (like the "C"P leaders) contributed decisively to its overthrow with their wrong strategy for the winning of power and by their sabotage against the consolidation of the UP government, carried out with a view to their planned alliance with the CDP, have an interest in attributing its failure to supposedly invincible external factors (such as the blockade). However, internal economic and political stability based on firm control of power by the people, would have well allowed these external factors to be overcome: obviously this was incompatible with the plans of the phony "communists". The blockade was effective and caused serious damage to the Chilean economy because the UP was unable to consolidate the economy, basically because it did not control power and was at the mercy of those who did hold it. On the other hand, the work of the CIA and the Pentagon, although it was the embodiment of external aggression, was effective because it hit directly at (the most decisive) internal contradictions that the Allende government faced.

The decision of the U.S. government not to stop at forcing the Chilean government to pay compensation or causing problems for it in trade or international credit, but to directly overthrow it, *was a decision based mainly on political reasons.* It was a political decision, fundamentally aimed at preventing "socialism", of the style of the Eastern European countries dependent on the USSR, from being consolidated in Chile; and, more concretely, at blocking the first step toward such a model, a step, set forth by the Soviet rulers, consisting of an alliance of the CDP with a conglomerate such as the UP in which the pro-Soviet "C"P would play a dominant role. Awareness of this danger and of the necessity to avoid it at all costs prevented the U.S. government from applying a strategy of wearing down and discrediting the UP without resorting to a coup d'état (a stategy which was also perfectly feasible and even more logical, given the excellent results achieved thanks to it). This process would certainly have led to the possibility of overthrowing the UP in the presidential elections of 1976 in the same way that it had attained power. And let it not be said that the Chilean extreme right circles were capable of bringing a coup d'état by themselves and that the U.S. had to accept a *fait accompli;* because of its influence in the decisive leading circles of the CDP, as well as in the Army, and because of the resistance to the putschist solution by the group opposed to Frei within the CDP, the U.S. government could largely prevent the carrying out of a coup d'état.

The fact that the decision to intervene in Chile to overthrow the Allende government in the shortest possible time was eminently political and moreover was *based on strategic considerations of international politics* emerges from the intelligence reports on Chile sent by the CIA and other departments to the U.S. government during the UP administration. There is an apparent paradox in these reports: the more reassuring they were for the U.S. government (because they recorded the economic and political failure of the attempts to consolidate Soviet-style "socialism"), the more the efforts to push forward the coup d'état were intensified at the insistence of the U.S. government. Obviously, as we shall see later, the fear was no longer that the UP experiment would succeed as a political example, nor was it of the alleged intentions of the USSR and the COMECON countries to support the UP at all costs; *rather, the fear was of the possible solutions to which the Allende government and the UP leadership might resort (precisely because of their failure) to hold on to government. That is, the U.S. government feared the alliance with the CDP.*

In July 1970 one of the most alarmist of the NIE's was sent. It pointed out that an Allende victory would mean the gradual establishment of a classical Marxist-Leninist regime in Chile. It would be a Chilean version of a Soviet-style Eastern European state. However, it predicted that democracy would probably survive in Chile for two or three years to come and that Allende would have a long way to go to lead Chile to Marxist socialism during the six years of his administration. To do this, he would have to surmount some very important obstacles, such as Chile's security forces, the Christian Democratic Party, some elements of organized labour, the congress and the Catholic Church. Lastly, it states that Allende expected progress on basic bread and butter issues which would afford him an opportunity to secure control of the congress in the 1973 election and thereby enable him to impose a socialist state of the Marxist variety by the peaceful road. *(62)*

An NIE sent later, one month before Allende's electoral victory, stated that if Allende were to win the election, he would almost certainly take measures against U.S. business interests in Chile and challenge U.S. policies in the hemisphere. The NIE predicted, however, that Allende would probably not seek a break with the U.S. over the next two years. *(63)*

Finally, still in 1970, there was issued what the Senate Report on CIA intervention in Chile calls: "the most direct report concerning the threat an Allende regime would pose to the United States". This report was issued September 7 and was sent not only to the CIA, but also to a group called the Interdepartmental Group for Inter-American Affairs, made up of representatives of the CIA, the State Department, the Defense Department and the White House. The Report concluded that the United States had no vital interests in Chile; the world military balance of power would not be significantly altered by an Allende regime, and an Allende victory in Chile would not pose any likely threat to the peace of the region. The Report noted, however, that an Allende victory "would be extremely costly on the political and psychological levels". The political cohesion of the hemisphere would be threatened by the challenge that the Allende government would represent for the OAS. "Chain reactions are bound to occur in other countries. An Allende victory," the Report concluded, "would represent a psychological setback to the U.S. as well as a definite advance for the Marxist idea." *(64)* As can be seen, the major preoccupying factors were eminently political and it was these factors which motivated the pre-emptory and urgent order issued after Allende's election to overthrow him by a coup d'état.

Once Allende was installed in office, the reports became visibly more optimistic for the U.S. However, the offensive against the

Chilean government was waged still more strongly. An NIE written in August 1971, after nine months of Allende government, stated that the domination of Marxist politics in Chile was not inevitable and that Allende had a long way to go to achieve this. It also said that Allende would probably be impelled to use political techniques of increasingly dubious legality to maintain his coalition in power, even though he would certainly prefer to adher to constitutional means. Up to that point, the NIE pointed out, Allende had scrupulously observed constitutional forms and was enjoying great popularity in Chile (65).

An NIE written after 10 months of Allende government stated that relations between the U.S. and Chile were dominated by the problems of nationalization, although Allende himself seemed to wish to avoid a confrontation (66).

A report prepared shortly before Allende's victory had indicated that Chile had long been a relatively open country for leftists and would become even more so under Allende. Despite this, the report notes that Allende would be cautious in providing assistance to extremists for fear of provoking a military reaction in his own country. However, the same report observed that the degree to which revolutionary groups would be allowed to use Chile as a base of operations would be limited by the orthodox communist party which opposed violent groups. A Report on the same subject, prepared in June 1971, stated that, contrary to some earlier indications that Allende might provide clandestine assistance to neighbouring insurgency movements, evidence to date suggested that he had been sensitive to the concerns of neighbouring governments and had sought to avoid action which would strain bilateral relations. Chile had warned Argentine and Mexican exiles that they could reside in Chile only if they did not engage in political activities; and some of the more politically active Brazilian political exiles had been invited to leave the country. The Report predicted in conclusion that it was unlikely Allende would financially support or train exiles to facilitate the export of insurgency (67).

An NIE issued in June 1972 stated that the future prospects for democracy in Chile seemed to be better than at any time since the start of the Allende government. It observed that the traditional political system in Chile continued to demonstrate remarkable resiliency. Legislative, student, and trade union elections continued to take place in normal fashion, with pro-government forces accepting the results when they were adverse. The NIE pointed out that the CDP and the National Party had used their combined control of both houses of congress to stall government initiatives and to pass legislation designed to curtail Allende's powers. In addition, the opposition press had been able to resist government intimidation and persisted in denouncing the government. The report concluded that : "the most likely course of events in Chile for the next year or so would be moves by Allende toward slowing the pace of his revolution in order to accommodate the opposition and to preserve the gains he had already made." *(68)* It should be pointed out that it was from this very moment that the CIA increased its contributions to organizations which a few months later would promote the first big offensive to overthrow the government: the strike of October 1972. On the 29th of that month came the failure of the first attempt at talks between the CDP and the government to reach an agreement; and within the UP, faced with this initial failure to reach agreement with the CDP, Orlando Millas' line of retreat, designed to open the way to this agreement, was imposed.

Another 1972 report noted that Allende, to date, had sought to avoid irreparable damage in his relations with Washington. And the report points out that although the major problem concerning U.S.-Chilean relations continued to be that of compensation for the nationalization of U.S. companies, Allende had taken pains to stress publicly his desire for amicable relations. In addition, a report the following year stated that Allende had kept lines open to Washington on possible Chilean compensation for the expropriation of U.S. copper companies *(69)*.

Finally, one last NIE sent in September 1973, just before the overthrow of Allende, demonstrated in its conclusion the central preoccupation of the U.S. government. The NIE focused on the probability of the Allende regime maintaining power. It concluded that at that juncture the most likely course of events in Chile seemed to be a political standoff. It noted that Allende had not consolidated the power of his Marxist regime; that the bulk of low-income Chileans believed that he had improved their conditions and represented their interests; and the growth in support for his coalition reflected his political ability as well as the popularity of his measures. The NIE noted, however, "that the growing polarization of the Chilean society was wearing away the Chilean predilection for political compromise." Nevertheless, the analysts predicted that there was only an outside chance that the military would move to force Allende from office *(70)*.

As can be seen, the trend of the intelligence reports is evidently more and more "reassuring" for the U.S. government: the USSR is maintaining a "cautious" position and is not trying to support the Allende government at all; the government, for its part, is avoiding interference in neighbouring countries and is not helping subversive movements there; the bourgeois institutions are continuing to function; the government is running into obstacles in the application of its model of "socialism"; moreover, the U.S. has no vital interests in Chile and the world military balance of forces has not been significantly changed by the UP victory. What is more, the last reports observe that the UP sees the possibility of setting up its state capitalist model receding; and since CIA activity was a decisive factor in its aggravation, the U.S. government must certainly have been well aware of the very serious economic crisis which was afflicting the country since 1972. Why not hope, then, that the intensification of the crisis would lead to the thorough discrediting of the government, so as to overthrow it in the 1976 elections? Why did the CIA seek untiringly and urgently to organize a coup d'état, until it finally succeeded in unleashing one?

The authors of the Senate Report on CIA activity in Chile asked themselves these questions. In fact, they note that: "At the same time as the Chile NIE's were becoming less shrill, the 40 Committee authorized greater amounts of money for covert operations in Chile. The amounts authorized by the 40 Committee rose from $1.5 million in 1970 to $3.6 million in 1971, $2.5 million in 1972, and, during the first eight months of 1973, $1.2 million. Covert action decisions," they comment, "were not . . . entirely consistent with intelligence estimates." *(71)* At another point, they state: "A review of the intelligence judgements on Chile offered by U.S. analysts during the critical period from 1970-1973 has not established whether these judgements were taken into account when U.S. policy-makers formulated and approved U.S. covert operations. This examination of the relevant intelligence estimates and memoranda has established that the judgements of the analysts suggested caution and restraint while the political imperatives demanded action." *(72)*

In fact, the Senate Report points out: "The reaction in Washington to Allende's victory was immediate. The 40 Committee met on September 8 and 14 to discuss what action should be taken prior to the October 24 congressional vote (which would ratify Allende's election). On September 15, President Nixon informed CIA Director Richard Helms that an Allende regime in Chile would not be acceptable to the United States and instructed the CIA to play a direct role in organizing a military *coup d'état* in Chile to prevent Allende's accession to the Presidency." *(73)* According to the Senate Report, the 40 Committee met "on 23 separate occasions between March 1970 and October 1973 to authorize funds for covert activities in Chile. During this period, the Committee authorized a total of $8.8 million for CIA covert activities in Chile." *(74)* On September 15, 1970, Nixon, Kissinger and Richard Helms, Director of the CIA, participated in a meeting at the White House to deal with the "case of Chile". According to Helms' handwritten notes, President Nixon stated: "One chance in ten, maybe, but Chile must be saved . . . There is no getting concerned over the cost of the operation . . . There is no taking into account the risks stemming from it . . . $100 million available, and more if necessary . . . work full time, with the best men available . . . work out a plan with solutions . . . make the *(Chilean)* economy scream . . . 48 hours to come up with a strategy . . ." *(75)*

In his statements to the U.S. Senate Committee, Richard Helms declared that he left this meeting with "the impression that the President had made it very clear that he wanted us to do something. He didn't much care how and he was ready to provide all necessary funds . . .It was an order that left us *carte blanche* . . . So much so that if ever I had full power to act on leaving the President's office, it was on that day." *(76)* For his part, Kissinger "does not remember that the instructions were as precise as

Helms says they were," (his poor memory is natural), but he stated: "What mainly came out of the September 15 meeting was that Helms was encouraged to do everything in his power to prevent Allende from taking over . . . It is clear that President Nixon wanted Helms to encourage the Chilean Army to act in collaboration with us or to take the initiative itself in preventing Allende from coming to power." (77)

The other CIA agents and officials who participated in organizing the coup d'état in Chile emphasized the extreme pressure to which they were subjected by the U.S. government to carry out their mission. Thomas Karamessines, head of the "secret services" of the CIA, maintained: "Kissinger left me in no doubt about the fact that he was under maximum pressure for this mission to succeed and that he in turn was putting maximum pressure on us to achieve this." (78) The assistant head of the "Western Hemisphere" section of the CIA stated: ". . . (This pressure) was the most crushing of any that I have witnessed during the time that I have been working; it went to the limits of the bearable." The supreme head of this section, William Broe, maintained: "I have never gone through so hard a period as when we were dealing with the Chilean business. I must say that it was absolutely constant . . . the pressure didn't stop for a single moment . . . It came from the White House." (79)

Why did the White House, from the beginning until the fall of Allende, have this firm determination to overthrow him? Why this pressure and urgency that were surprising and unexpected even to CIA agents?

Some of the most obvious reasons (and of course, ones that he wanted to express) were contained in an informal interview of Kissinger by several journalists on September 16, 1970. Because it was forbidden to transcribe this interview, the various versions differ a little, but they do not differ in the ideas which all the journalists picked out, except that some journalists omitted some statements that others recorded. Reconstructing the interview from the different versions, Kissinger's views were the following: It is now easy to see that if Allende takes power in Chile, there is a strong possibility that within a few years he will establish a sort of communist government. In this case we will have a communist government and not on a coastal island, lacking traditional relations with and impact on Latin America, but in one of the big countries on the continent. This communist government could unite for example with Argentina, with which it shares a long border; or with Peru, which has gone in a direction that makes our relations with it difficult; or with Bolivia, which even before these events had gone in a more leftist and anti-American direction.

Thus (continued Kissinger), I think we would be fooling ourselves to believe that if Allende takes power, he won't present enormous problems for us, for the democratic and pro-American forces in Latin America and undoubtedly in the whole Western Hemisphere. What would happen to the Western Hemisphere Defence Committee, to the Organization of American States, is very problematical . . . Political developments in Chile are very serious for U.S. interests because of their effects in France and Italy. We are following the events very closely. This is one of those situations that aren't exactly happy for American interests . . . Right at this moment, (Latin) America has a great deal of influence.

There is a complementary point of view in the Senate report on CIA activity in Chile. This view links the problem posed by Allende's victory in Chile to the world struggle between the U.S. and the USSR (something Kissinger did not do, but which is implicit in his reasoning). The report states: "Another rationale for U.S. involvement in the internal affairs of Chile was offered by a high-ranking official who testified before the Committee. He spoke of Chile's position in a world-wide strategic chess game in 1970. In this analogy, Portugal might be a bishop, Chile a couple of pawns, perhaps more. In the world-wide strategic chess game, once a position was lost, a series of consequences followed. U.S. enemies would proceed to exploit that new opportunity, and our ability to cope with the challenge would be limited by any American loss." *(80)*

It seems, therefore, that the U.S. government proposed to overthrow the Allende government first of all in order to ensure the balance of power in its conflict with Soviet social-imperialism, rather than to defend the interests of one expropriated monopoly or another. But this was obviously not due to the importance of Chile in its own right, since the intelligence reports judged that the U.S. "had no vital interests in Chile; the world military balance of power would not be significantly altered by an Allende regime, and an Allende victory in Chile would not pose any likely threat to the peace of the region." The problem was that: "Chain reactions are bound to occur in other countries," for "an Allende victory would represent a psychological setback to the U.S. as well as a definite advance for the Marxist idea." Where did this "Marxist" idea that opened the way for the Allende victory come from? Everyone knows: from the Twentieth Congress of the CPSU. Furthermore, this conclusion is explicit in the Kissinger interview in which he speaks of the dangers for the whole Western Hemisphere.

However, these conclusions are only a part of the truth. They can explain the quick decision of the U.S. government to attack the Chilean economy from inside and from outside and to encourage a military coup after the election of Allende. However, if the U.S. government feared the maintenance of a Soviet model of "socialism", even though it would be developed by the peaceful road, this did not justify its persisting through to the end by means of the most extreme pressure with a strategy aimed at overthrowing Allende by a coup d'état. On the one hand, it was obvious that, having achieved its goal, the U.S. would be discredited by this new example of brutal interference in another country, which is what in fact happened. In addition, and more importantly, Chile from 1972 on was no longer a model for anyone, even for the Chileans. How could a country that had reached more than 1 percent inflation per day, with an enormous trading deficit, with uncontrolled issue of currency, with state enterprises working at a loss, with a financial deficit estimated in 1973 at more than 40 percent of its total spending, etc., be a model! Even within the Popular Unity it was admitted that the next presidential election was lost. This was the main argument that the "C"P and other parties used to refuse to call a referendum. It must be asked, then, why the U.S did not change strategy when Chile was breaking all its own records in many indices that showed the seriousness of the crisis. Why did they not profit by the *negative* model that Chile offered, in order to cause a chain reaction opposite to the one it feared, showing the failure of the "socialist" model and the peaceful road? Why did they not wait for the certain defeat of this model in the elections of 1976?

It may be argued that they feared the UP leadership and the government would officially turn to violent methods to remain in power, or that the UP would gain influence in the Armed Forces, thus helping it to stay in power. However all the concrete facts militate against this idea, at least insofar as official means are concerned. The CIA and the Pentagon knew better than anyone that the government did not have support in the Army, because they had worked there actively; moreover, facts showed it. The intelligence reports emphasized the constitutionalist inclinations of Allende and the most important leaders of the UP. As far as the "C"P leaders were concerned, even Frei assured that they would prevent the government from straying from the path of legality. The Vice-President of ITT relates the conversation he had over lunch with Frei on December 10, 1971, as follows: "Concerning the future of the Allende government, whether it would remain on its present course, or be pulled by the left-wing extremists to a policy of violence and dictatorship, Eduardo Frei did not want to predict. He did comment that the only strongly disciplined political force in the country was the Communist Party, and while the opposition parties were now tending to unify, they could not be compared as a disciplined group with the Communists. Furthermore, that Allende would be unlikely to abandon such a hard-core group." *(81)* For the rest, the reports of the CIA itself spoke of "the orthodox Communist Party in Chile which opposed violence-prone groups". Even the little children in Chile knew this. Therefore, it is clear that the U.S. was not afraid that the Allende government would try to solve its problems and stay in power by force.

How could they have feared such a thing, in reality, given the hegemony within the UP of "communists" who, in the midst of the most unbridled reactionary violence, formulated only pious calls for peace and gave as their main slogan: *"No to civil war!"*.

All these considerations force us to ask the question again: why did the U.S. government implacably keep up the pressure for a coup d'état right until the end?

By studying the events in Chile, one can reach the conclusion that the U.S. government maintained its plan to organize a coup d'état at all costs on the one hand *to head off the powerful development of the class struggle and the trend, at the end of the Allende government, toward the organization of a political formation opposed to the dominant reformism; and, on the other hand, to avoid the risk of a sort of preview of the Italian "historic compromise":* an alliance between the UP and the CDP. However, in the longer term, the first factor was particularly important since the formation of a UP-CDP governing coalition would quickly have radicalized against it those political sectors of the UP which already had a critical attitude toward its opportunist conduct; these sectors, linked to an increasingly militant mass movement, could have opened the way to an increasingly influential revolutionary trend.

Although the fear of a UP-CDP alliance was jealously hidden, it is possible to draw this conclusion from the ideas contained in the U.S. Senate report and in the statements of members of the U.S. government. It follows, for example, from Kissinger's allusions to the dangers of the UP experiment in Chile for the Western Hemisphere, and in particular for Italy and France. Kissinger's threats against the Italian Christian Democrats agreeing to form a coalition government with the Italian "Communists" are well known; so is the decision taken by the governments of France, West Germany and the United States, made public in a *Time* magazine interview with Helmut Schmidt on July 16, 1976, to cut off all economic aid to Italy if such a thing ever occurred. The same conclusion can be drawn from the intelligence report quoted above, which the U.S. government had before their eyes in June 1972, at the time of one of the most important attempts to reach an agreement between the Allende government and the CDP. The report stated: "the most likely course of events in Chile for the next year or so would be moves by Allende toward slowing the pace of his revolution in order to accomodate the opposition and to preserve the gains he had already made." We have already pointed out that this report was followed by substantial CIA assistance in organizing and assisting the October 1972 strike and that they succeeded in causing the CDP-government talks to be broken off. After that, the "C"P leadership tried desperately, even brushing up against its allies, to truncate the UP programme in order to facilitate the CDP-UP pact.

In the opinions expressed in the last NIE sent before the coup d'état, the central preoccupation with the pact with the CDP, the only chance of survival the UP had left, once again appears. The NIE notes with relief "that the growing polarization of the Chilean society was wearing away the Chilean predilection for political compromise". (One of the essential tasks of the CIA was to encourage this polarization.) Despite this remark, and perhaps fearing that the "Chilean predilection for political compromise" would win out anyway, they continued to believe that the solution lay in the Armed Forces driving out Allende by force.

It should be pointed out that the U.S. government feared a compromise because it did not have complete confidence in Frei. They feared that his unbridled ambition, of which they were more aware than anyone and which they had generously "fed", could push him into accepting a compromise despite all their warnings. Before Allende even took on his mandate, Frei had hesitated to openly foment a coup d'état to stop him from doing so, because he hypocritically wanted to maintain his "constitutionalist" and "democratic" image. The ITT report (exposed in the U.S. Senate inquiry into the participation of that multinational firm in the attempts to overthrow Allende) states: "President Eduardo Frei wants to stop Allende and has said so to intimates. But he wants to do it constitutionally — i.e., either through a congressional vote upset or an internal crisis requiring military intervention . . .

"All previous evaluations of Frei's weaknesses in a crisis are being confirmed. Worse, it has been established beyond any doubt that he is double-dealing to preserve his own stature and image as the leader of Latin American democracy. For instance: he told some of his ministers he'd be more than willing to be removed by the military. This would absolve him from any involvement in a coup that, in turn, would upset Allende. Then, he turned right around and told the military chiefs he is totally against a coup." On September 21, the U.S. ambassador to Chile, Edward Kerry, thought it proper to send a message to Frei through the Defence Minister himself; in this message he tells

Frei that if Allende takes over the Presidency, Frei "should know that we won't let a screw or a nut into Chile under Allende. As long as Allende is in power, we will do everything in our power to condemn Chile and Chileans to the greatest deprivation and poverty, as a long-term policy to reinforce the harsh features of a communist society in Chile. Consequently, if Frei expects something other than total poverty, than seeing Chile totally cast down, he is operating under an illusion." Without any doubt, this warning was not intended to explain to Frei the obstacles that Allende would meet from the U.S. (which could only have made Frei rejoice for his future) but to take away any hope that the U.S. would be more tolerant toward the Chilean government if the CDP supported it.

To the "honour" of Frei's faithfulness to the U.S. government, it must be said that he made every possible effort (even if he did so "behind the scenes" so as not to compromise his political image) to assist the coup d'état attempts aimed at preventing Allende's nomination from being ratified by the Congress, including the one that culminated in the assassination of the Commander-in-Chief of the Armed Forces. Following his instructions, his Minister of the Economy publicly painted the picture of a deep economic crisis caused by the defiance aroused by Allende's victory amongst employers; this to stir up the military. That is, he divulged the initial effects of the campaign to sabotage the economy, a campaign inspired by the multinational corporations and by the most reactionary interests in the country to bring about a coup d'état. But Frei did not want to sacrifice the image that would give him the best chance of replacing the overthrown government. At a time when the U.S. government was demanding *everything* of him in order to calm its worries, he did not want to accept the tarnishing of his pristine image of "legalism" and preferred to act only in back rooms. He would never be completely forgiven this, either by the fascist military or by the U.S. government, which knows how to expose itself when its vital interests are at stake.

If to this entire portrait of the hesitations of its right-hand man, is added the fact — serious for the U.S. government — that Frei was not even able to convince his party to refuse to ratify Allende's nomination as President in the Congress, it is perfectly natural to suppose that they were seriously afraid the "C"P leaders, and through them the Soviets, would succeed in leading the CDP into a compromise with the government coalition. Hence their only certain reserve was the Army, and they decided without hesitation to continue to work for the coup d'état right through to the end.

Today, Frei and his team in the CDP are desperately trying to regain the confidence of the U.S. government and the Armed Forces to return to power, publicly guaranteeing that they will not be led into a compromise that would allow the "C"P to return to power or at least to legal activity in Chile through an alliance with them. Patricio Aylwin, president of the CDP and Frei's right-hand man, told the Spanish magazine *Cambio 16* on June 21, 1976 that to rebuild a democratic government in Chile "one must count on the support of the Christian Democrats, the old radicals, the social democrats and the liberal right". And then he utters a threat by maintaining that: "If Chile has no democratic way out in the short term, we are heading toward communism, for the junta is a regime that creates polarization." He clearly says that: "Democracy cannot co-exist with non-democrats. When the communists come in, democracy goes out." And he adds: "In my country it is unthinkable not to be aware of the Armed Forces phenomenon. If they are admitted as a political factor, one must count on their participation, and we know that they exclude the communists. This is why to be an ally of the communists is equivalent to renouncing democracy."

3. The Social and Economic Conditions that Facilitated the Coup d'Etat

In coordination with the work within the Army and in close collaboration with the political opposition to the government, with the multinationals and with the U.S. government, the CIA made every effort to create the social and economic conditions necessary for the unleashing of the coup d'état. This is what they euphemistically called the "destabilization" of the Allende government. In this chapter, we will not examine the activities of the opposition forces under the direct guidance of the CIA, because this question is dealt with in the chapter concerning the economic policy of the Popular Unity government. Here, we will only deal with the direct economic sabotage of the U.S. and its propaganda campaign.

On September 29, 1970, the 40 Committee got together and created a larger committee to organize the "destabilization" of the Allende regime. This committee included William V. Broe, head of the CIA section responsible for operations in the Western Hemisphere, as well as representatives of the State Department, the Treasury Board and the National Security Council. On the same day, William Broe sent the following plan to Edward Gerrity, First Vice-President of ITT:

1. *Banks should not renew credits or should delay in doing so.*

2. *Companies should drag their feet in sending money, in making deliveries, in shipping spare parts, etc.*

3. *Savings and loan companies there are in trouble. If pressure were applied they would have to shut their doors, thereby creating stronger pressure.*

4. *We should withdraw all technical help and should not promise any technical assistance in the future. Companies in a position to do so should close their doors.*

5. *A list of companies was provided and it was suggested that we approach them as indicated. I was told that, of all the companies involved, ours alone had been responsive and understood the problem. The visitor added that money was not a problem.*

He indicated that certain steps were being taken but that he was looking for additional help aimed at inducing economic collapse. I discussed the suggestions with Guilfoyle. He contacted a couple of companies who said they had been given advice which is directly contrary to the suggestions I received.

Realistically I do not see how we can induce others involved to follow the plan suggested. We can contact key companies for their reactions and make suggestions in the hope that they might cooperate. Information we received today from other sources indicates that there is a growing economic crisis in any case (82).

After Allende had set up his government, the last point recommended above had already been concretized. A committee of powerful multinationals had been set up in order to sabotage the Chilean economy. This committee included, among others, Ford Motors, Anaconda Corp., ITT (International Telephone and Telegraph Corporation), the Bank of America, the First National City Bank, Firestone Tire and Rubber Corp., Grace and Co., Ralston Purina, Charles Pfizer and Co., Dow Chemical Co., Kennecott Copper Co., and Bethlehem Steel Corp.

According to the report on ITT's intervention in Chile, the multinationals were secretly aware that it was necessary to provoke an economic crisis in order to pave the way for the military coup. On September 29, 1970, the notes of ITT's First Vice-President indicate: "A more realistic hope among those who want to block Allende is that a swiftly deteriorating economy (bank runs, plant bankruptcies, etc.) will touch off a wave of violence resulting in a military coup . . . *(The)* military will not act . . . unless internal conditions require their intervention . . . More important, massive unemployment and unrest might produce enough violence to force the military to move."

On September 28, 1971, ITT submitted an 18-point programme to the U.S. government aimed at organizing the downfall of the Allende government before April 1972. Here is the plan:

1. *Continue loan restrictions in the international banks such as those the Export/Import Bank has already exhibited.*

2. *Quietly have large U.S. private banks do the same.*

3. *Confer with foreign banking sources with the same thing in mind.*

4. *Delay buying from Chile over the next six months. Use U.S. copper stockpile instead of buying from Chile.*

5. *Bring about a scarcity of U.S. dollars in Chile.*

6. *Discuss with CIA how it can assist the six-month squeeze.*

7. *Get to reliable sources within the Chilean Military. Delay fuel delivery to Navy and gasoline to Air Force. (This would have to be carefully handled, otherwise would be dangerous. However, a false delay could build up their planned discontent against Allende, thus, bring about necessity of his removal.)*

8. *Probably will be necessary to give dollar assistance to the crippled news media because this factor is quickly going down the drain and* El Mercurio, *an outspoken opponent, could be wiped out on a moments notice.*

9. *Help disrupt Allende's UNCTAD plans.*

10. *Expropriations and nationalization of U.S. private investment without full and immediate indemnification is directly detrimental to the U.S. balance of payments. It serves to disrupt the equilibrium and faith in the dollar.*

The U.S. government is doing everything possible to balance the budget, strengthen the dollar, and keep U.S. manufacturers competitive in the world market. At the same time, some foreign governments are discriminating against U.S. private investment while simultaneously demanding preferential treatment in our markets, and also requesting soft loans from U.S.-supported banks.

11. *The IADB Charter (Sec.2-a-iii) stipulates loans should be made to "supplement private investment." The opposite is taking place: IADB loans are* displacing *private investments.*

12. *U.S. manufacturers should stop or delay shipments of small arms and ammunition to Chile. Last week the following shipment from* Remington *was flown out of Miami on ALFE: 75,000 — 38; 44,000 — 22; 50,000 — 32.*

This went to the Ministry of Interior, Departmento Abastamiento del Estado for the Secret Police.

13. *Chile's recent travel restrictions are detrimental to U.S. trade. Chileans are well known as one of the greatest travelers in Latin America. There should be some retaliation which could be imposed.*

14. *Chilean action against UPI should be blasted by the Inter-American Press Association and U.S. press in general.* (The Washington Post *even criticized U.S. tough policy on Chile. They should be made to eat their editorial now that UPI has been closed.)*

El Mercurio *of Santiago remains alive and continues criticism of Allende. Some aid should be considered for this paper.*

15. *In a meeting with Assistant Secretary of State Charles A. Meyer and his staff only a few days ago — September 28 — we were informed that up to $1 million (U.S. dollars) are going into Chile* each month *from funds in the "Aid pipeline!" We believe this U.S. taxpayer money to the Marxist government should be terminated.*

16. *Also, we were told that funds in several "Inter-American Development Bank pipelines," not previously utilized, were re-*

allocated into a so-called earthquake emergency fund and made available to Chile. Considering the U.S. heavy contribution to the IADB, and the lack of a real emergency, such action should not have been permitted; and, if possible, should now be rescinded.

17. It is noted that Chile's annual exports to the U.S. are valued at $154 million (U.S. dollars). As many U.S. markets as possible should be closed to Chile. Likewise, any U.S. exports of special importance to Allende should be delayed or stopped.

18. The U.S. should consult with other governments whose nationals are suffering from the Chilean Marxists. This would include countries to which Chile owes money. Allende's treasury reserve is depleting rapidly and he has already suggested a moratorium on servicing his foreign debt.

Elsewhere, the same document indicates that the U.S. plans were aimed at sharpening the internal contradictions and taking advantage of Allende's loss of control in order to overthrow his government:

Also, there is the beginning of concern on the part of the Military. They see the Chile scene slowly crumbling and realize that, before economic chaos takes place, the Armed Forces will have to step in and restore order. There are also signs of anxiety within the Chilean Navy, which traditionally is quite an elite group.

The possible deterrent forces which can thwart Allende and which remain intact are:

1. Military

2. Judiciary

3. Civil Service

4. A crippled news media

5. Fragment of the legislative branch

During the crucial period, these forces must be utilized to every advantage against Allende's continued success (83).

ITT is precisely listing the key sectors of the bourgeois state apparatus over which the Popular Unity did not have any control and that it had to confont in order to implement its plan for reforms.

Because of the reactionary governments, Chile has developed a heavily foreign-dependent economy, particularly in regard to

U.S. imperialism. For many years, the balance of payments has accumulated deficits. For the 1961-1965 five-year period, the average annual deficit has been $168.4 million; for 1966-1970, it reached $77.6 million, and in 1971, $312 million. Traditionally, these deficits were offset by foreign loans, particularly from the U.S. Thus, the foreign debt increased from $569 million in 1958 to $3.13 million in 1970, the year during which Allende took over. On the other hand, exports only increased by 48 percent (in real terms) during the sixties.

Chile needed these credits to buy from abroad (mainly from the U.S.) machines and spare parts for its industries, food to make up for the chronic deficit caused by the stagnation of her agriculture, as well as raw materials, fertilizer and chemicals in general. The U.S. ruling circles knew that by withholding their loans, given the excessive demand generated as a result of the actions taken by the UP government in this direction and given the sabotage of industrial expansion by the employers, they would cause a complete drain of the country's foreign currency reserves. This is what happened. On top of all this, as an additional factor increasing the deficit, there was the steep drop of copper prices on the international market, which in 1971 alone resulted in a decrease of $140 million in the inflow of foreign currency. Finally, the rising prices of imported goods brought about another loss of some $120 million.

Chile's dependence towards the U.S. was primarily quantitative, since it was there that Chile used to get the bulk of its credit (78.4 percent of the short-term commercial credit in 1970). But there was also a qualitative dependence, in the sense that machinery bought from the U.S. needed spare parts and often raw materials and fuel from the same market. For example, at the end of 1971, the Chilean Minister of the Economy estimated that one-third of the diesel trucks at the Chuquicamata mine, 33 percent of the state buses, 30 percent of the private buses and 21 percent of the taxi cars could not operate for lack of spare parts or tires.

Aware of this dependent nature of the Chilean economy, the U.S. government, in collusion with the CIA and the multinationals, organized a blockade of credits and subsidies to Chile to assist the internal offensive of the opposition aimed at intensifying the crisis.

The U.S. Import-Export Bank was one of Chile's main suppliers of short-term credit used for purchasing U.S. goods and services. According to the U.S. Senate Report: "U.S. Import-Export Bank credits, which had totalled $234 million in 1967 and $29 million in 1969, dropped to zero in 1971." *(84)* Furthermore, at the beginning of 1971, this Bank turned down a credit application of $21 million made by the Chilean government to buy three Boeing passenger airplanes for the National Airline. At that time, one could not even use the pretext of the refusal to pay compensation to the copper corporations, since they had not been nationalized yet. Furthermore, the Import-Export Bank was the organization which used to provide insurance for the loans granted by the private banks as well as for exports. These insurance policies were serviced by the Foreign Credit Insurance Association, affiliated to the Bank. Not only did the Import-Export Bank decide to cut the credits, but at the end of 1970, it arbitrarily reduced Chile's credit quotation from "B" to "D" (the lowest economic solvency quotation) in order to discourage the banks from lending to Chile. Consequently, in 1972, the imports from the U.S. went from the usual 40 percent of the total to only 15 percent.

For its part, the Inter-American Development Bank (IDB), which since 1959 had granted 59 credits totalling $310 million to Chile ($46 million in 1970 alone), decided to reduce its credit to $2 million in 1972, despite the fact that the Chilean government, between 1971 and 1972, had paid back some $16 million on its old debt to this very bank. However, credits of $11 million were maintained for two Chilean universities dominated by the opposition forces.

For its part, the World Bank (International Bank for Reconstruction and Development), which had lent $234.65 million since its foundation in 1944, refused to authorize any credit at all during the Popular Unity government.

As far as the Inter-American Development Agency (IDA) is concerned, after having lent some $400 million since 1964, the year Frei took over, it reduced its credits to $2.5 million in 1971 and 1972, and these were applied to some U.S. penetration programmes called "technical assistance programmes". The

Chilean government, however, had inherited from the previous governments a series of debts to this Agency, which in June 1971 amounted to $500 million payable in dollars and $30 million payable in escudos.

The U.S. hard line in the credit institutions over which they had influence had an impact on the behaviour of the private banks. In the past, Chile relied on short-term credits from these banks for more than $200 million. During the Allende government, $35 million only was available.

The balance of payments deficit caused by the suspension of international credit combined with the internal sabotage: in 1971 alone, the outflow of capital resulted in an additional drain of some $270 million. Thus the balance of payments deficit, which amounted to $312 million in 1971, reached $644 million in 1972.

These measures of the multinationals and the U.S. government aimed at sharpening the crisis in Chile were supplemented by the special offensive waged by two U.S. firms after their expropriation: Kennecott and Anaconda, until then involved in the exploitation of Chilean copper. In February 1972, Kennecott froze the accounts of several Chilean agencies in New York. Later on, Anaconda did the same. Court actions were even taken in the countries purchasing copper from Chile, such as France, Switzerland, Germany and Italy, so that a freeze would be declared on the payments pending the judgement of international courts on the issue of compensation. This created obstacles for Chile's copper sales.

As for the renegotiation of the external debt that President Allende had asked for since November 9, 1971, only the United States adopted a harder line during the second renegotiation at the end of 1972. In February of that year, Chile's 13 creditor countries met in Paris. The Allende government asked for a moratorium on payments and the renegotiation of the enormous debt still outstanding as of 1971. Despite the pressure exerted by the U.S., the other creditors agreed to renegotiate Chile's external debt. Seventy percent of the Chilean debt as of 1971 — some $165 million, of which $62 million was owed to the U.S. — was postponed. The U.S. finally agreed to sign the agreement along with the others on April 19. The position of the U.S. gradually became harder as the Chilean government became weaker. In December 1972, during the bilateral discussions for renegotiation, the U.S. government representatives declared that any agreement would be conditional on the payment of "fair compensation" to the nationalized copper companies. Finally, in March 1973, during another bilateral session, U.S. representative John Crimmings interrupted the talks declaring that "the United States has no time to waste".

Despite the efforts of the U.S. government and the multinationals to sabotage the Chilean economy, it must be realized that this form of aggression could only be effective because the Popular Unity had no control over state power. With a firm control over the state, and through this, over the economy, and with a genuine anti-imperialist, resolute and fighting policy, these difficulties could have been overcome. To overemphasize the importance of the "external blockade" as a factor responsible for the failure of the Allende government is to conceal the position of the "C"P leaders and to hide *their* responsibility in this failure. The fact is that Chile not only achieved a relative success in the first renegotiation of its external debt, but it also obtained substantial credits from other countries and thus began to liberate itself from the one-sided dependence on U.S. credit. The Minister of Finance himself, Orlando Millas, recognized this on November 15, 1972, in his report to the Joint Commission on the Budget appointed by the congress: "Decisive changes have taken place in the structure of our external financing. While at the beginning of this government the United States accounted for 78.4 percent of our total short-term financing, this high concentration no longer exists. A much more diversified structure has been created in which the United States, for example, accounts for only 6.6 percent of the total. The volume of credits obtained presently amounts to $490 million and is highly diversified. In particular, one should note the case of the Soviet Union, which provided $103 million, Australia, which provided $29 million, West Germany and France, which provided $28 million and $36 million respectively, Spain, which provided $15 million and Mexico, which provided $26 million, etc." As for long-term external financing, he said: "We also achieved significant results in increasing its amount and in diversifying it considerably. Let us mention the agreements with

Brazil ($10 million), Mexico ($20 million), Peru and Argentina, the terms of which exceed eight and a half years and which allowed us, through aggregate financing, to purchase more than $40 million worth of equipment and machinery. Special financing agreements of great importance have been made with some West European countries such as France, Spain and others. In particular, Chile appreciates the features of the credits offered by Sweden, the Netherlands and Finland. As for the financing of investments from the socialist countries, we have made a big step forward. Credits totalling $446 million have been obtained with amortization periods extending from 5 to 20 years: $259 million from the Soviet Union, $55.5 million from the People's Republic of China, $35 million from Poland, $25 million from Bulgaria, $22 million from Hungary, $20 million from the German Democratic Republic, $20 million from Rumania, $5 million from Czechoslovakia, $5 million from the People's Democratic Republic of Korea, etc." (85) In addition, during the first semester of 1973, some $662 million of short-term credits were obtained from these same sources.

Analysis of these various sources which were to compensate for the blockade imposed by the U.S. shows that first of all, the amount of credit obtained could have been still higher if Chile had been able to stabilize its economy through firm control over state power. Secondly, taking into account the renegotiation of the external debt and the origin of the credits, we can see that the idea of the U.S. government to choke the Chilean economy would eventually have backfired against its proponent, since it did not have the smallest influence even on countries very close to the United States. Among the countries which granted credits to the Allende government, there are some which are not exactly progressive, such as Spain, West Germany, Japan, France, Argentina and Brazil.

The failure to use these credits, in particular the long-term ones, resulted, among other things, from the acute crisis and anarchy that plagued the Chilean economy while the government, faced with economic and political aggression, could find neither the instruments nor the authority to confront it. Of the long-term loans obtained in 1972 which aroused the pride of the Minister of Finance, only $192 million were used.

As for the short-term credits, they had to be obtained at very high rates of interest because of the emergency situation created by the need to satisfy the demand for basic necessities that could not be produced in the country. Therefore, their amortization contributed to accelerating even more the outflow of currency. Of the short-term loans mentioned above, the $662 million obtained in 1973 remained unused.

Finally, concerning the situation created as a result of the closing down of the usual markets for machinery, spare parts and other equipment relatively hard to obtain from other countries (even though this is not impossible, because one can almost always get them from third parties), it must be noted that such a situation had to be expected if the nationalization of U.S. companies was planned and that one had to be prepared to face it. Or is it that one was naive enough to believe that the U.S. would applaud or remain indifferent when its interests were hit?

As opposed to this, not only did the UP government not use enough firmness and authority to deal with the consequences of the blockade, but it adopted a weak "anti-imperialist" policy and took a compromising and defensive stand. Once again the conciliating influence of the "C"P leadership can be seen: as we know, these leaders were obediently following the line of the Soviets of not seeking a confrontation with imperialism but a compromise that would even include the formation of a coalition government with the main imperialist agents, that is, Frei and his team. It was along the same lines that President Allende was advised by his assistant, the "sociologist" Joan E. Garces. This man thought that the U.S. imperialists wanted the Allende government to adopt a resolutely anti-imperialist policy so that they could organize to quickly overthrow it. The concrete result of the conciliatory attitude, however, was that the U.S. used every means except direct armed intervention to overthrow the Chilean government, and succeeded despite all conciliation attempts; conversely, the Chilean government gave up the myriad possibilities that a firm anti-imperialist attitude, based on the mobilization of the people, would have offered it.

Contrary to what Garces believed, the whole U.S. policy was based on avoiding the mistake that they made in Cuba, where they had aroused an anti-imperialist movement of the broad masses which until now has prevented them, despite an attempt at invasion, from regaining control over the government of that country. Because of this, they were forced to accept a government which, a few miles away from their territory, has not only nationalized the U.S. interests but also represents an important base for Soviet social-imperialism. This defeat of U.S. imperialism in Cuba is certainly not due to the fact that the Soviet Union is ready to defend this country at all costs (this has been clearly shown by the missiles incident in 1962), but, as we have pointed out, to the fact that the Cuban people were prepared to fight and had a high anti-imperialist consciousness. Fearing the anti-imperialist mobilization of the people in Chile, Ambassador Kerry gave the following advice in 1970: "This 'cut-off' *(of aid to Chile)* will be denied by State, who will say, as it has in the past, 'there has been no shut down of aid to Chile; the programme is under review.' " He also said: "there are several alternatives of action, the main ones being to provoke Allende and cause a rupture in our relations with Chile, thus, lose all without a try. The second would be to try to live with Allende — not appease him — take a firm line, but attempt to negotiate at every turn." He concludes: "The second alternative seems to be the one the U.S. will take." *(86)*

Garces himself, in his book written after the coup d'état *(Allende and the Chilean Experience)* draws conclusions absolutely opposed to those which follow from the facts he himself presents when he quotes Nachmanoff, the main adviser of Kissinger. Nachmanoff describes the U.S. policy towards the Allende government in this way: "It is important to avoid open challenges to Allende which would have the effect, in the Administration's view, of strengthening him. (It is preferable to exert pressure on Chile in such a manner that its government looks like the one provoking the United States. This would then allow direct actions. — *note by Garces)* Basically, Nachmanoff describes the U.S. policy now as being quiet but strong, doing nothing to provoke Allende. If Allende should attack the United States, however, then our government would reply in kind." *(87)* From this, Garces concludes that the position of the Chilean government was correct, "avoiding battle on the open ground where they wanted to take it." However, his conclusions about the U.S. strategy only consider the appearance of what he quotes in order to support his reasoning. As described by the Senate Report on the CIA activities in Chile, the U.S. policy was basically three-fold: a "cool but correct" public posture, "extensive clandestine activities", and "economic pressure". These last two aspects, hidden by the hypocritical "cool but correct" official attitude, were aimed at preparing the overthrow of the government. The same report describes their effects in this manner: "The United States cut off economic aid, denied credits, and made efforts — partially successful — to enlist the cooperation of international financial institutions and private firms in tightening the economic 'squeeze' on Chile. That international 'squeeze' intensified the effect of the economic measures taken by oppositional groups within Chile, particularly the crippling strikes in the mining and transportation sectors. For instance, the combined effect of the foreign credit squeeze and domestic copper strikes on Chile's foreign exchange position was devastating." *(88)*

Thus, the U.S. strategy was to squeeze the economy from within and from without as well as, through "extensive clandestine activities", to prepare the forceful solution, the military coup. This military coup, in any case, is central to the strategy. The economic offensive against Chile was not launched simply to discredit the UP experience, but to prepare such a coup d'état. The CIA Headquarters clearly indicated this in 1970: "In order to overthrow Allende with a coup, we must take a firm and consistant attitude . . . We must continue to exert the utmost pressure and use every means possible." It is therefore obvious that Nachmanoff's plan only refers to a diplomatic strategy. The U.S. government, which was waging a destructive, putschist offensive on the economic and propaganda fronts against the Allende government, was not interested in arousing internal and international public opinion and in providing the Allende government with a good stimulant for a campaign against the United States by publicly attacking it. The U.S. Senate Report indicates: "The 'cool but correct' overt posture denied the Allende government a handy foreign enemy to use as a domestic and international rallying point." *(89)* Since it was *assumed* that the Allende government would respond to the ferocious economic aggression and to the ever more intense putschist activities, it was preferable that the first public attack come from Chile and that the *official* U.S. attitude appear to be only a reply to such an attack. And if the Chilean government, because of the "cool but correct" U.S. official attitude, quietly let itself be stabbed in the back and bled to death, this was even better. *That* was the real objective of the U.S. government, and not, as Garces pretends, that the Chilean government would throw the first rock so that the U.S. could counter-attack. The quieter this duel involving the United States once again in dirty manoeuvres and aggression against a small country, the better it would be for the U.S. government. We can see, then, what great service to the Allende government was rendered by those who, like Garces, discouraged it from undertaking a wide-scale open mobilization against U.S. imperialism. Chile suffered all the consequences of an imperialist aggression which used every means, except direct invasion, but she benefited from none of the advantages that would have derived from an anti-imperialist mobilization of the people. Of course, the "C"P leadership championed this crippled and emasculated position, since they feared the mobilization of the people more than they feared imperialism and its agents, with whom, in fact, they wanted to have an alliance. This is one of the reasons why, after the articles of the constitutional reform dealing with the nationalization of copper had been vetoed, the "C"P leaders opposed President Allende's proposal to have a referendum on the issue. They were afraid that such a referendum would stimulate the anti-imperialist movement and interfere with their plan to have a pact with the Christian Democrats.

The Chilean ruling circles, like the U.S. government, were extremely conscious how dangerous it would be for them if the government and the Popular Unity were to raise the flag of a broad mass mobilization against U.S. imperialism. Such a mobilization would have involved large sections of the population and possibly some nationalist sections of the Army, and it would have completely isolated those who attempted to oppose it. This explains why the constitutional reform to nationalize copper was *unanimously* approved in Parliament. It was also because of their fear of such an anti-imperialist mobilization that the Chilean ruling circles protested when the Export-Import Bank prematurely refused the credit solicited by the Allende government to buy airplanes for the National Airline. *El Mercurio,* the most faithful press servant of the U.S. interests, wrote about this question as follows on August 17, 1971: "This U.S. policy jeopardizes inter-American relations and is a repetition of an old historical error *(A reference to Cuba)* which we thought had been understood." The National Party, for its part, declared: "Such attitudes and declarations as those we are reporting can only contribute to the deterioration of international relations and to making the solution of problems difficult . . . They reflect a deplorable lack of judgement and an ignorance of the Chilean reality." The clearest warning, however, came in a declaration of the Christian Democrats published on August 16, 1971, in *La Prensa,* organ of Frei's group: "The decision for which the chairman of the Export-Import Bank seems to be responsible has all the ugly features of a provocation . . . Thus once again, prematurely, the U.S. government appears identified with private interests, forgetting the superior political interests . . . It is a mystery for no one (and the various U.S. missions in Chile must have informed their government about this) that within the government of our country, there are two tendencies which, for the moment at least, are in co-existence. One wants to lead the Chilean revolution by respecting the constitution, without internal violence nor international crisis. The other wants to provoke a violent rupture which, necessarily, has to be considered also on the international level. They are the ones demanding or simply announcing that the expropriated firms should not be indemnified. The Export-Import Bank has started to play into the hands of this trend which wants nothing more than to provoke such reactions."

The Industrial Development Society, the main corporate organization of the Chilean big bourgeoisie, wrote to the chairman of the Export-Import Bank: "Chile is going through a process of profound economic and social changes which radically affect its economic position and consequently the situation of its manufacturers. Therefore, our professional organization — the oldest in the Americas — is engaged in minimizing the cost of these changes and in insuring that they take place within the framework of freedom and democracy, with full respect for the fundamental guarantees. This is why, faced with the refusal of the Export-Import Bank to grant this loan, we cannot, as private investors, and because of our respect for our noble democratic tradition, accept that such resolutions be subordinated to decisions that our government might take within the framework of the juridical regime that the country has democratically worked out for itself."

Thus we have *El Mercurio,* the National Party, the wing of the Christian Democratic Party led by Frei and the Industrial Development Society, that is, the entire civilian command of the putschist conspiracy against the Allende government, all advising the U.S. government not to make the mistake of "premature" aggression that might assist the section of the Popular Unity that wants to develop a firm fighting anti-imperialist policy. It is therefore such a policy that frightens the sections that are most servile to imperialism and most opposed to the Allende government. At the same time, it is clear that both the "C"P leaders and Garces, through his advice, have contributed to placing the Allende government in a position most favourable to U.S. imperialism. Later on, when economic aggression much worse than the refusal to lend $21 million to purchase airplanes took place, all these people remained silent, since they were then convinced that the government was not considering to organize a powerful anti-imperialist people's movement.

The arguments expressed by Garces and the "C"P leaders in order to reject a firm anti-imperialist policy result from a defeatist attitude toward the might of U.S. imperialism. Garces says: "Since the United States has adopted an indirect strategy against Chile, few things could be more favourable to their success than the adoption of a direct strategy by the weakest party in this confrontation . . . This would make the victory of the counter-revolution easiest, quickest and most complete." *(90)* Nevertheless, historical experience shows exactly the opposite. Only peoples who have developed a staunch and consistent anti-imperialist struggle have won important victories and even their total liberation. It is absolutely ridiculous and inconsistent to feel defeated in advance by imperialism and, despite this, to undertake reforms that hit at its interests. The only possible logic for the defeatists is to resign themselves to oppression and exploitation. *"Those who have a slavish soul,"* Marx said, *"deserve to be slaves."* Or can we pretend to fool the U.S. monopolies and government or rely on a moment of "goodwill" on their part so that they let themselves be expropriated without putting up a fight? On this front, the straightforward defeatist logic (caused by fear of the people) pushed by the phony "communist" leaders who are pressing for an alliance with the pro-imperialist forces and remain satisfied, in countries like Chile, with a joint exploitation with imperialism, is much more consistent. But on the other hand, to present defeatism as a strategy makes no sense and leads precisely and inevitably to the present sufferings of the Chilean people. It is the same logic that was behind the "solidarity" with Vietnam and Cambodia exhibited by those who were highlighting the sufferings caused to these people by imperialist aggression instead of praising their heroic struggle. With such logic, everybody should say: "might as well stop fighting!", "it is preferable that the U.S. continue to dominate these countries, since there is no possibility for the people to smash it!"

Garces reports that Allende used to make ironical allusions to Mao Tsetung's statement according to which *"imperialism is a paper tiger".* However, it would have been much more useful if, instead of ironically talking about it, he and his advisers had pondered over the significance of this statement. It means that it is impossible to defeat the enemy without having contempt for it from the strategic point of view, that is, if one is not convinced that it can be defeated through struggle. Without such a conviction, it is absurd to undertake any action for liberation and the only thing to do is to sit in resignation. In this way, Vietnam, Cambodia and Cuba would still be under the domination of U.S. imperialism. But according to Mao Tsetung Thought, the complement of strategic contempt for the enemy and of the will to defeat it is the tactical concept of dealing with it very seriously and developing the most clever and powerful struggle in order to win victory. However, a defeatist strategy such as that of the Allende government inevitably led to defeatist tactics that could only bring about total failure. But these remarks do not make much sense when they are addressed to the Popular Unity, whose leadership was dominated by reformists, opportunists and distorters of Marxism.

It is all the more correct to say that if consistent revolutionary anti-imperialist ideas had asserted themselves in the people's movement, the Popular Unity's electoral victory would have been a most timely occasion for a vigorous struggle against U.S. imperialism. The latter was suffering great defeats in the countries where it had intervened militarily, leading Kissinger to say: "I am about to believe that the introduction of American military forces is the worst method of confrontation, because it implies the presence of a foreign element. If we want to assist, it is preferable for us to stay outside and to strengthen the resistance capability of our allies and to assist them without sending in U.S. forces." *(91)* This tactic, however, also failed in Vietnam, Cambodia and Cuba. Furthermore, at the time of Allende's victory, the international situation was also favourable because of the fact that the United States had taken aggressive measures against the countries of the capitalist world to defend itself against their economic competition; and in Latin America, the chain of military dictatorships had not yet been formed. In September 1971, at a meeting of the Special Coordination Commission for Latin America, Chile had obtained the unanimous agreement of all the member countries to "energetically and unanimously" demand the abolition of the 10 percent surcharge imposed by the U.S. on imported manufactured goods. With a staunch anti-imperialist policy and by relying on the masses of the people, Chile could have played a leading role in Latin America. The solidarity of the peoples and even of some government circles with its positions would have been strengthened. Moreover, the first symptoms of the conflict (that was to break out in 1973) between the imperialist countries and the oil-producing countries had already started to show up, and Chile had a very good occasion to exercise strong pressure and play a leading role within the Organization of Copper Exporting Countries (OCEC), of which it was a member.

On the contrary, instead of vigorously promoting the struggle against U.S. imperialism, the UP government adopted the same attitude of impotence and conciliation as it took towards the forces leading the subversion inside the country. Hopes were placed (this refers only to those who did not have any hidden intentions) on the absolutely idealist notion of "moral solvency", conferred by the fact that the UP was acting within the framework of the law, and it was believed that this would be enough to have the reforms accepted by those whom they hit. A tactic of appeasement was followed, similar to that with which some individuals vainly tried to hold back Hitler in Europe. Important U.S. monopolies were permitted to operate in the manufacturing sector, and joint ventures were even undertaken with them. New investments were encouraged. Aggression was tolerated and no significant protest was organized. The blockade was not used as an occasion to suspend or cancel the payment of the Chilean external debt to the U.S., a debt which represented funds "lent" to the Chilean governments out of the fabulous profits accumulated for decades with a ridiculously small original capital outlay. Even the U.S. government itself was expecting and fearing such a suspension. The U.S. Senate Report says on this matter: "A February 1971 Intelligence Memorandum noted that Chile was not immediately vulnerable to investment, trade or monetary sanctions imposed by the United States. In fact, the imposition of sanctions, while it would hurt Chile eventually, was seen to carry one possible short-run benefit — it would have given Chile a justification for renouncing nearly a billion dollars of debt to the United States." (92) Later on, as there was no decision by the Chilean government to fight back, all the measures of the blockade were intensified.

On the other hand, while the Chilean government was conciliating with U.S. imperialism, its mortal enemy from the beginning, it did not take advantage of the measures that were taken against the U.S. in order to develop a broad anti-imperialist mobilization and to strengthen its own position. Even the highly important and serious measure (not only in itself, but also because it was a precedent for the entire world) of declaring "excessive" all profits of the nationalized copper companies greater than 14 percent, refusing to pay them compensation and, on top of this, declaring that they owed Chile $700 million, even such a measure was adopted almost in secrecy, unnoticed by the Chilean people. Thus, imperialism was outraged and there was no response from the people.

In conclusion, it can only be added that the appeasement tactic followed by the Chilean government towards imperialism had absolutely no effect in stopping or reducing the violence of the very efficient actions taken by the U.S. to overthrow it. Not only that, but it spared the U.S. government the serious problem of publicly being seen as committing aggression against Chile. It made it easier for the U.S. to hide behind their official "cool but correct" policy. The weaker the reaction of the Chilean government, the more intense were the economic aggression and the secret interference aimed at preparing a coup d'état. This is precisely the "paradox" that the members of the Church Commission noticed in their investigation. However, it was not the U.S. government which was mistaken, but, as the facts have shown, it was the Chilean government, with its ever more conciliatory attitude. The CIA itself realized this. The internal and external conciliation led to where it only could lead: to the fascist coup d'état, with the people completely unable to defend themselves or fight back. With a powerful anti-imperialist mass mobilization and with an openly hostile attitude from the U.S. government, the situation would have been the opposite: even the putschist manoeuvres of the Army would have run into serious difficulties, because it would have been clear that they were in support of foreign interests. This is precisely what various reactionary circles were fearing when they warned the U.S. government about the reprisals of the Export-Import Bank. In the extreme case, direct aggression by imperialism, even though it might have succeeded temporarily, would have generated a powerful people's movement and allowed the creation of a broad anti-imperialist front not only in Chile, but in large portions of Latin America as well. Fronts of this type in response to imperialist aggression are precisely what have permitted China, Vietnam, Cambodia and so many other countries not only to win national independence but also to develop the revolutionary process further. Let us insist once again, however, that such considerations are not put forward as a strategy that could have been adopted by the Popular Unity, since it is ridiculous to expect "blood from a stone". Our purpose is simply to highlight the contrast between the work of this opportunist leadership and what must be the genuine revolutionary anti-imperialist leadership of the struggles of the Chilean people.

The U.S. government, conscious that the official policy in Chile was not to oppose its actions through a strong anti-imperialist mobilization and concrete measures of retaliation against its activities in Chile concentrated all its means of clandestine propaganda against the only solution left for those who had given up the line of open opposition to imperialism. This solution was compromise with the imperialist agents in Chile. The U.S. imperialists were able to apply all their funds (since they did not have to defend themselves against any attack) to the financing of political or professional groups and to tne development of propaganda aimed at polarizing the forces so that a political compromise would become impossible. (Such compromise would have permitted the Popular Unity to survive, even if it would have been at the cost of decisive aspects of its programme.) According to the U.S. Senate Report on the CIA's activities in Chile, the only investments that had to be made in the Chilean Army were the $20,000 for Viaux and the $50,000 put at the disposal of General Valenzuela. The Army's great "constitutionalist" spirit assured the U.S. imperialists that it would work for a coup d'état without having to be paid, on condition, of course, that it remain in power afterwards.

On March 25, 1970, the 40 Committee approved a grant of $135,000 to oppose the candidacy of Allende and to block any possibility of agreement with the Christian Democrats that could have led to the presentation of a common candidate.

On June 18, Ambassador Kerry made two proposals: intensify the propaganda against Allende and organize his rejection by Parliament in case he was elected. For these two plans, he proposed $500,000, but only $300,000 were approved for the first one. As for the second one, it was decided to wait for the results of the elections, since it was still believed that Alessandri could win.

Later, the multinationals added their contributions. ITT granted $350,000 and the other interested companies sent as much to prevent Allende from being elected. The CIA told them the proper channels through which these funds were to be sent to

Alessandri and the National Party.

With these funds, the CIA organized half a dozen projects involving support for civilian anti-communist groups, campaigns of terror, etc. Also, it supported the anti-UP wing of the Radical Party and made efforts to create dissensions between the SP and the "C"P in order to check the tendency of the latter to make overtures to the Christian Democrats. Funds were also used to support the daily *El Mercurio.*

After the election of Allende through universal suffrage, on September 9, ITT offered one million dollars (at least that, since they talked about an amount "reaching seven digits") to prevent Allende from being elected in Congress.

On September 15, the various putschist solutions already began to take shape for either before the election in Congress (Track I, with its two alternatives) or for after Allende's appointment by Congress (Track II). On November 14, $250,000 were sent for "whatever Frei and his associates think is necessary" to prevent Allende's nomination by Congress. The report of the Church Commission, concerned for the reputation of Mr. Frei, claims that he did not use these funds. The CIA, for its part, undertook a campaign calling upon Frei to "put on his pants", as Kerry advised, and to endorse the plan for a coup d'état.

On September 28, journalists who were CIA agents were sent into Chile from ten different countries in order to assist those from eight other countries who were also under CIA influence. At the same time, $38,500 were given to *"Patria y Libertad"* to be used for provocation to facilitate the coup d'état.

Small amounts were also spent in relation to the plan to kidnap Schneider. Allende's nomination by the Congress marked the failure of Track I.

To avert the dangerous precedent established by Allende's acceptance of the "constitutional guarantees" imposed by the Christian Democrats (this is how Allende won the support of the CDP members of the Congress), the 40 Committee approved, for the first time in this entire campaign against Allende, a grant of $25,000 for the Christian Democratic Party.

In January 1971, concerned by the development of the struggle of the masses and convinced of the failure of the strategy based on the easy, short-term organization of a coup d'état, the 40 Committee granted, on January 28, $1,240,000 for a long-term plan aimed at overthrowing Allende. One month later, on February 25, Nixon inaugurated the official "cool but correct" cover-up policy of his government: "We are prepared to have the kind of relationship with the Chilean government that it is prepared to have with us." On February 11, the committee of the multinationals was formed against Allende.

On March 22, 1971, the 40 Committee, concerned about the possible willingness of the CDP to unite, approved a grant of $185,000 for the wing of the Party led by Frei. On May 10, $77,000 were approved for the CDP press, which was controlled by Frei. According to the U.S. Senate Report, the pro-U.S. lackeys within the CDP were not satisfied with this and they asked for and received $250,000 for "short-term debts" between May 20 and May 26. (93) In April 1971, the Popular Unity had reached almost 50 percent of the vote.

In June 1971, a terrorist group, probably infiltrated by the CIA, assassinated the former Minister of the Interior in the Frei government, Edmundo Perez Zujovic. This criminal act was to serve Frei's wing by taking away from the Popular Unity those sections of the CDP which were flirting with the government and by facilitating an alliance between the CDP and the most rightist sections of the opposition. The first concrete manifestation of this alliance was the support given by the right-wing parties to the CDP candidate during the Valparaiso by-election of July 18. On July 6, the CDP had received $150,000 from the U.S. in order to make a success out of this election, which had great political importance even though it was not going to change the relations of forces within Parliament.

On September 9, the Minister of the Interior, Jose Toha, revealed the existence of right-wing plots to overthrow the government. On the very same day, the 40 Committee allocated $700,000 for financial support to *El Mercurio.* On September 15, the CUT held a meeting in opposition to the persistent rumours about the existence of a conspiracy. The CIA admitted that it had established the first contacts with the putschist group having the "highest probability of success" and that it was in contact with the leader of this group. There were rumours of a coup d'état on the occasion of the traditional military parade for the National Day. The ultra-rightist paper *La Tribuna* came out on that day (September 19) with an editorial denouncing the Christian Democrats for "once again" having lacked courage and patriotic spirit.

In October 1971, ITT submitted to the White House its 18-point programme for the removal of Allende from power within the next six months. In November 1971, the United States granted $815,000 to the opposition parties and to split a party from the Popular Unity (the PIR). A dangerous (for the U.S.) drift of the CDP towards the government had taken place. Nevertheless, on December 1, a united opposition held a march against the government. During this demonstration, a series of provocations took place which, after their suppression, were to be used as a motive for the constitutional charges against the Minister of the Interior. For the first time, it was the CDP which took the initiative to lay these charges. On December 17, however, a private conversation took place between Allende and Tomic, with no concrete results. On December 15, the CIA had received a contribution of $160,000 to support the united opposition candidates who were to run in the January 1972 by-elections in two provinces.

On January 19, although not directly mentioning Chile, Nixon declared that he hoped compensation to the U.S. firms that had been expropriated would be "prompt, adequate and effective". He added that if such were not the case, he might stop the aid to the expropriating country as well as suspend the support given through international development banks.

On February 19, the Plenary Session of the Congress approved the constitutional reform of the three sectors of the economy *(see Chapter 9)* proposed by the Christian Democrats. This reform was to become a major element in the conflict that was to break out later on between the Executive and the Parliament. This conflict was used as one of the pretexts for the coup d'état.

In March 1972, a plot against the government involving the Temuco regiment was exposed. At the beginning of this month, some efforts aimed at getting the government and the more progressive section of the CDP together were noted, but these efforts failed. At the same time, a meeting was held by leaders of the opposition from both the political and business circles in order to plan an offensive against the government. "Because of a subversive plan that was to be implemented during the night of the 24th to the 25th of March by the opposition forces", the Executive refused authorization for two demonstrations to be held by these forces during the month.

On April 11, the 40 Committee approved a grant of $965,000 to strengthen *El Mercurio* for the offensive launched by the opposition against the government. On April 5, the opposition majority in the House adopted a resolution against the government to put on the agenda of the extraordinary session of the Parliament an Arms Control Act. This legislation was later to become a vital element in the preparation of the coup d'état. On April 24, the CIA received $50,000 to split the PIR (Party of the Radical Left) from the Popular Unity and the government, in which it had two ministers. During the same month, the PIR ministers resigned and their party moved over to the opposition. After the coup d'état, Pinochet was to declare to a *Reuter* journalist: "On April 13, 1972, at the Army General Staff, we analyzed the possibilities, and on that day we reached the conclusion that the conflict between the legislative and executive powers had no constitutional solution . . . " In other words, the legal pretext for the coup d'état had already been found. On April 12, the opposition organized a demonstration that it called "the March for Democracy".

In June, a new contribution of $46,500 was made by the 40 Committee to assist the opposition in getting a member of Parliament elected. During the same month, an Intelligence Memorandum to the U.S. government noted that the UP government was probably going to try to make an arrangement with the opposition and to preserve its achievements by taking a more moderate course of action. The government and the Popular Unity agreed with the thesis of the "C"P leaders that important concessions should be made on the programme for reforms in order to reach an agreement with the Christian Democrats. On June 29, after 15 days, the talks between the government and the CDP, mainly on the issue of the constitutional reform of the three sectors of the economy, came to a dead end.

In July and August, according to what Pinochet said later, the Armed Forces were already considering, in their memoranda, "the possibility of taking control over the nation". On August 21 a strike of merchants began which caused severe disorders and forced the government to declare the "state of emergency"

On September 21, the U.S. approved a grant of $24,000 to a Chilean businessmen's organization. Still in September, the military conspiracy headed by General Canales aborted; the latter, along with General Hiriarte, were forced to retire.

On October 10, the truck drivers began their national strike, which was later joined by the merchants and many professional organizations. Opposition political leaders started issuing statements on the "illegality" of the government. The 40 Committee, in order to support the offensive of the opposition, approved a grant of $1,500,000 on October 26. Even though the strike was crushed by the workers (as we have shown several times in this book), the government made important concessions to the opposition and integrated the military into the cabinet. After the strike, the government's members of Parliament had to vote for the Arms Control Act demanded by the Army and the opposition.

At the end of 1972, 15 generals (five for each branch of the military) got together to concretely plan the coup d'état against the government. By the end of January 1973, the Minister of the Economy, a member of the "C"P Secretariat, created a commission to hold negotiations with the CDP on the government-controlled companies and proposed to reduce by half the number of firms that were to be integrated into the public sector. On February 12, the 40 Committee approved a grant of $200,000 to support the opposition parties in the March legislative elections.

In the middle of May 1973, Frei's wing officially took control of the CDP by winning an internal election. On May 30, the Constitutional Court declared that it had no jurisdiction to act as an arbitrator in the conflict between the Executive and Parliament on the question of the constitutional reform of the three economic sectors. Another strike, to be waged in the transportation and other professional sectors controlled by the opposition, was being organized to assist the coup d'état. According to what Pinochet told the magazine *Vea*, "on May 28, an internal security order was issued on a new basis. We were moving from the defensive to the offensive."

On June 6, the time limit stipulated in the constitution for the government to hold a referendum on the issue of the constitutional reform of the three economic sectors expired. On June 20, the copper miners of El Teniente were in their sixty-third day on strike. On June 29, the "tancazo" occurred, the attempted coup d'état by the Santiago Second Tank Regiment. On July 26, the truck drivers' strike resumed. At that time, implementing the Arms Control Act, the Army had already started raiding private houses, trade union offices, factories and various estates. On July 30, as an ultimate desperate attempt, the government was able to resume dialogue, thanks to the Cardinal of Santiago, with the CDP President, Senator Patricio Aylwin. The representative of the government was the President of the Republic.

On August 2, over 10,000 buses and taxis joined the strike. On August 20, the 40 Committee approved a grant of $1 million to support the opposition parties and private organizations in their final attack against the government. On August 23, Prats was forced to resign as Commander-in-Chief of the Armed Forces and Augusto Pinochet took over his functions. On August 27, the trade sector joined the strike, together with several professional corporations. At the beginning of August, the talks between the government and the CDP leadership were already seen as a failure and the parliamentary majority decided to declare the government "unconstitutional" and "illegal". The Army therefore had the legal pretext to take action.

Finally, after Ruiz Danyau's unsuccessful attempted coup d'état in mid-August 1973, President Allende was overthrown on September 11, by a coup d'état.

Therefore, in Chile, there were not only two internal blocs confronting each other (that of the opposition and that of the government), but two international policies: that of U.S. imperialism and that of Soviet social-imperialism. U.S. imperialism admits having spent $8 million between 1970 and 1973 in order to overthrow the Allende government. This sum (which represents only a fraction of the U.S. spending), exchanged through the black market, corresponds to an amount between five and ten times greater than calculated according to the official dollar exchange rate. All this money and the activities of the CIA and DIA agents that were operating in Chile served to promote sabotage, criminal acts, strikes, stockpiling and blackmarketeering so as to speed up the decision of the Armed Forces and the civilian opposition to stage a coup d'état. The U.S. imperialist strategy was not only to prevent all possible consolidation of state capitalism, but also to firmly oppose the intentions of the "C"P leadership to impose its "historic compromise" with the CDP and thus achieve its goals in a roundabout manner, by adapting its strategy of infiltration to the conditions of a country located within the U.S. sphere of influence.

On the other hand, the Soviet strategy was to firmly oppose any significant development of the people's struggles and the hegemony of a proletarian line which would have led to the destruction of the bourgeois state. Every effort was made to achieve a pact with the pro-U.S. populist sectors, even at the cost of openly opposing the organization of the people's resistance against fascist putschism. In this way, the Soviets hoped that a sort of hybrid government would be created, a government that would block any revolutionary solution and allow them to infiltrate themselves within the state apparatus in order to impose on the U.S. imperialists a joint exploitation of the Chilean people. As we will see later, this strategy of social-imperialism implemented in our country through the "C"P leaders is still being promoted today, since the coup d'état, as a "solution" to get rid of the military regime.

Part III
Economic Policy of the Popular Unity Government

Chapter VI
Whose Interests Did the Popular Unity Programme Attack?

The Popular Unity, with its victory in the presidential elections of 1970, only won a small margin of manoeuvre from the hands of the traditional reactionary ruling circles. It had won a part of the Executive power. Only a part of it, since many prerogatives of the Executive were restricted by the constitution and the various laws as well as by the prerogatives of the legislative and judicial powers. Furthermore, within the various departments and government enterprises and public administrations, a large number of officials who had been appointed by the previous governments and who were hostile to the UP enjoyed legal rights of tenure. Many of them, later on, even went so far as to sabotage the decisions of the government, but they could not be fired. In some sectors, a parallel management had to be appointed beside the one appointed by the previous governments. This resulted in enormous expenses, since these officials inherited from the previous governments were maintained in almost complete inactivity and could not be removed.

All other sections of the state apparatus were dominated by the representatives of the U.S. monopolies operating in Chile as well as of the most powerful internal exploiters: the industrial, commercial and financial monopolist bourgeoisie and the landed oligarchy. This state apparatus, apart from the Executive, comprised the legal system in the service of the ruling classes; the Parliament in which the majority opposed the government; the courts of justice which were bastions of the most reactionary circles; the powerful instruments of propaganda (with the opposition accounting for 80 percent of the daily press circulation, 50 percent of the daily radio ratings and 60 percent of the daily television ratings); the Contraloria of the Republic, also led by the opposition, with important rights of inspection over the legal decisions of the government; and finally and most decisively, the Armed Forces and police, in the service of U.S. imperialism and the most reactionary circles in the country.

Even if a large number of rank-and-file activists within the "C"P and other parties comprising the Popular Unity, as well as some honest leaders of these organizations, wanted to build socialism in Chile, without having any clear idea about the real content of such a socialism, this is not, objectively, what the pro-Soviet "C"P leaders wanted. For them, "socialism" was what exists in the Soviet Union, in Poland, in Czechoslovakia and in other countries of the Warsaw Pact with which they totally identify themselves. Starting from a dependent capitalism, they hoped to achieve in Chile what had been achieved in these Eastern European countries through the degeneration of socialism. In other words, they wanted a sort of state capitalism in which a new bureaucratic bourgeoisie, with interests opposed to those of the people, is in command of state power and public enterprises, replacing the old capitalists. The idea of linking this state capitalism to the dominant interests of Soviet social-imperialism was in no way alien to their plans.

Nevertheless, the programme put forward by the Popular Unity (even if it was not to bring about socialism) represented a heavy blow to the interests of the landlords, to certain U.S. monopolies operating in Chile, and to the most powerful sections of the industrial, commercial and financial bourgeoisie. It was precisely at the expense of these interests that the Popular Unity hoped to develop state capitalism and establish the new bureaucratic bourgeoisie. Therefore, even though the UP programme and strategy were nothing but reformism (because the aim was not to thoroughly liquidate the economic power of the ruling classes, nor was it to seize power from them by destroying the state apparatus in a revolutionary manner, nor to put the expropriated means of production or political power into the hands of the people), they came out, given the context, as an "ultra-left" adventurist programme and strategy. Economic and social measures were taken *as though* the prerequisite political power had been seized, while only a portion of the Executive power was under control.

In essence, the three-year experiment of the UP government was an attempt to take advantage of (or to outwit using "legal expedients") laws and institutions that had been designed to serve the most reactionary interests. It was an attempt to limit and overthrow these interests by respecting the rules established precisely in order to consolidate and develop them. In short, it was an effort, with all imaginable shortcomings, to "peacefully" transform a social system that used the mask of bourgeois democracy for the sole purpose of concealing the armed violence that was its real foundation. It was the failure of an attempt to exercise power without having won it and without even the intention of using what had been acquired through the electoral victory in 1970 in a revolutionary way in order to develop a fighting mass movement capable of really seizing such power by smashing the armed reactionary apparatus. This last possibility was in fact — and this is the basic thesis of the present book — absolutely incompatible with the plan for a society based on centralized state exploitation of the people, as was the aim of the pro-Soviet "C"P leaders and some of their followers within the Popular Unity. For a people mobilized in a revolutionary way, it would have been easy to *"turn the guns against the new exploiters",* as Frederick Engels used to say.

To realize the absurdity of this "peaceful road" to state capitalism (under socialist disguise) and to grasp the origins of this failure, which was absolutely inevitable in the eyes of anyone who had analyzed this experience from a genuine Marxist standpoint, we have to begin these chapters on the analysis of the economic policy of the UP government with a survey of the reactionary interests that were hit or threatened by the programme of this government.

1. The Interests of U.S. Imperialism in Chile

The U.S. imperialist domination of Chile was and is exercised in numerous and highly diversified forms. When the Allende government took over, the U.S. monopolies controlled the main Chilean mining resources: copper, saltpetre and iron. They also controlled certain public utility companies, such as the Telephone Company, owned by ITT. They monopolized a decisive portion of Chile's international trade, buying its raw or semi-manufactured products at very low prices and selling it back manufactured goods at exorbitant prices. They were either owners or major shareholders of a large number of firms in the manufacturing sector (the most profitable ones). Finally, they exploited the whole of industry through financial loans, selling or leasing technology, machinery, raw materials, spare parts and fuel, etc.

An important item in the tribute extorted by U.S. imperialism from the Chilean economy is represented by the short-term and long-term interest-bearing loans granted by various institutions dependent on the U.S. government. These loans were linked to various demands for the implementation of a policy favourable to the interests of the U.S. monopolies. In general, they were "tied" loans, in the sense that they had to be invested in the purchase of capital goods or other types of commodities from the United States itself. The investments and loans were always lower than the profits made in the country by those who were granting them, and therefore, they were coming from the very profits extorted from Chile. At the same time, because of their conditional character, the loans contributed to the further swelling of these profits, to the distortion of economic development and to the intensification of the crisis and dependence of the economy. As a consequence, the final result was the necessity of ever bigger loans. It was a continuously developing spiral, a vicious circle strangling the economy of the country. During the Allende government, this external debt reached almost $4 billion, considering both the loans inherited from the previous governments and the new ones. The annual amortization and interest payments on this fabulous debt absorbed over half of the foreign currency inflow. Over 70 percent of these debts represented loans made by the United States.

In 1964, Chile ranked seventh in the world in terms of the volume of U.S. investments, which at that time, reached over $1 billion. In 1970, there were 110 U.S. companies operating in Chile and a large number of others having U.S. capital but with their main office in other countries.

In order to grasp the importance of the capitalist interests hit or threatened by the expropriations carried out by the Allende government, it is essential to say a few words about the large Chilean copper-mining industry. There are three major copper mines in Chile: Chuquicamata, El Salvador and El Teniente. The first two were owned by the giant trust Anaconda Copper Mining and the third one by Kennecott Copper. Chuquicamata and El Teniente are respectively the biggest open-pit and the biggest underground copper mines in the world. Eighty percent of Chile's total copper production comes from these three big mines expropriated during the first year of the Allende government. Throughout the history of its dependence, it is estimated that Chile has exported around 22 billion tons of copper. In 1970, the year of Allende's election, Chile accounted for 11 percent of the world's copper production, that is, over 6.2 million tons. The total value of Chilean exports for the same year amounted to $1.123 billion, $700 million of which represented copper exports. It is estimated that between 1911 and 1970, the big U.S. companies exploiting Chilean copper have made over $4.6 billion of "declared" profits. Analyzing the statistics accumulated up to 1960, the Christian Democratic Senator Radomiro Tomic declared to the Parliament on July 18, 1961: "Throughout these 40 years, these companies *(referring to the U.S. monopolies exploiting Chilean copper)* have withdrawn $3 billion from the country. They started with an initial investment of $3.5 million. Thus, it has been a lucrative business. This sum of $3 billion represents one-third of Chile's physical assets, amassed not in 40 years, but in 400 years." Later on, during the government of his colleague Eduardo Frei, the U.S. companies were to extract in only four years (1965-1968) over $1 billion in "declared" profits.

However, as we have already indicated, copper was not the only source of profit for the U.S. investors. Bethlehem Steel Corporation, a monopoly involved in the exploitation of Chilean iron ore, made $400 million in profits between 1911 and 1970. Anglo Lantaro, also American and owner of the huge saltpetre reserves in the northern part of the country, made $500 million during the same period. ITT, with its investments in the telephone and other services and which was colluding with the CIA in the plans to "destabilize" the Allende government, made some $200 million between 1931 and 1970. Its investments in Chile reached about $100 million in 1970. Finally, Chilectra, through which the U.S. investors controlled electric energy distribution in Chile, made some $120 million in profits between 1928 and 1969. All these companies, except the last one, were expropriated by the Popular Unity government.

We have only mentioned the profits made by the large mining and public utility companies, over which there is relative control. It is extremely difficult to assess the profits made by the U.S. investors in manufacturing industry, in the wholesale trade companies and in other enterprises. It is clear, however, that Chile represented an important prey for the U.S. monopolies, not only because of the large investments in the country, but also because of the high rate of profit on these investments. In 1968, with a capital outlay of some $1.4 billion, foreign investments in Chile generated a net profit (that is, taking into account the interest paid and the devaluation of capital) of over $320 million, or 23 percent of the capital invested. President Allende himself, speaking to the United Nations in November 1972, denounced the fact that the U.S. corporations alone had reaped a profit of almost $4 billion between 1955 and 1970 in Chile.

In addition, as we have already pointed out, right at the time the Alliance for Progress was inaugurated by Kennedy there were concrete plans for the U.S. monopolies and investors to take over manufacturing industry during the Frei administration. Investments in this sector, even though they were threatened under the Allende government, were not substantially hit. The Rockefeller Report recommending the replacement of political parties with the Army in Latin American countries had precisely this goal: to continue the policy of attempting to take over the most profitable manufacturing industries on the continent. The U.S. "aid" to these countries is itself inspired by this objective. The Foreign Affairs Committee of the U.S. House of Representatives said on this question: "The most important reason *(for this economic "aid")* is that these *(developing)* countries are determined to develop. And it is only by participating in this process that we will have the opportunity to direct this development in the manner that best suits our interests."

We think that these brief comments on the U.S. monopolies' interests in Chile are more than sufficient to conclude that it was absurd to suppose that the United States would "peacefully" accept expropriation and the long-term threat posed to their plans for the Chilean economy. Moreover, there was the risk — because of the dominant influence of a pro-Soviet "C"P within the Popular Unity — of an increasing penetration of Soviet social-imperialism in the country. In the past the U.S. government had interfered to overthrow various governments and embroiled itself in expensive protracted wars to defend economic, political and strategic interests of much less importance than those at stake in Chile. Therefore, even if we do not take into account the internal class enemies within the country and if we just consider the presence of U.S. imperialism in Chile, the plan of "peaceful transition to socialism" (or what the Soviets and their followers always refer to as "socialism") was an absolutely adventurist plan.

2. The Landed Oligrachy

Another powerful section of the reactionary ruling classes of Chile that the Popular Unity confronted with its programme for reforms was the landed oligarchy. Historically, the power of this class was built through the ownership of huge latifundia expropriated by the landlords' ancestors from the native population of the country. In this way, a monopoly over the best lands of the country was created. The Fourth National Census on Farming (1965) gives the distribution of landholdings according to their size:

STRUCTURE OF LAND OWNERSHIP IN CHILE
1965

Size of holding	Number	Area	% of total no. of holdings	% of total area
Less than 10 ha	156,708	437,300	61.8	1.4
10 to 99 ha	74,120	2,348,200	29.3	7.7
100 to 999 ha	19,333	5,572,400	7.6	18.7
Over 1,000 ha	3,331	22,290,800	1.3	72.2
Total	**253,492**	**30,648,700**	**100**	**100**

If we consider as latifundia the holdings of 200 hectares and more, we can see that these landlords, with less than 5 percent of the number of holdings, own more than 85 percent of all the agricultural land in the country. On the other hand, 90 percent of the landlords (more than 200,000) own less than 15 percent of the agricultural land. To this we must add 750,000 farmworkers owning no land at all and living in severe poverty.

Traditionally, the policy of the big landlords has been to cultivate only a small portion of their huge estates, ignoring technical progress and brutally exploiting the agricultural workers. Also, through various means, they reduced the small and middle farmers to poverty. In fact, the Chilean landlords took advantage of their "rights" over large stretches of the best lands in order to enrich themselves not through production, but by sabotaging agricultural production and cattle-raising. Protected by their "sacred" property rights, they kept most of the land under their monopolistic control out of production. In this manner, a chronic shortage of agricultural products (increasing in relation to the population) was created. Since it is impossible to go without these products (food products in particular), this sabotage resulted on the one hand in the obligation to import them at high prices from the international market, and on the other hand in the necessity to bring into the market products cultivated at a very high cost, on lands of poor quality located far away from the consumer centres. Any increase in the country's population aggravated the agricultural crisis created by the latifundists and necessitated ever-increasing imports of farm products, as well as the meeting of the demand for these products with very expensive local goods. Because of this situation that they themselves had created, the latifundists had only to bring their products to market (with very low costs of production), and to sell them at the very high prices resulting from their sabotage, in order to get huge surplus profits (differential rent), over and above the average profit in agriculture.

This extremely retrogressive policy, linked until not too long ago with the semi-feudal forms of exploitation of large sections of the peasantry (payment in kind, personal allowances, share-cropping, etc.), allowed the big landlords to accumulate huge profits with minimal investments. At the same time, because of their dominant role within the state apparatus and its institutions, they obtained important credits on the basis of their agricultural estates, the value of which constantly rose because of the ever increasing prices of farm products. But this never stopped them from refusing any audit of their accounts or allowing their estates to be estimated at their real value for taxation purposes.

On the other hand, since their plans were precisely not to make big investments in agricultural production, they channelled their fortunes into speculative and financial operations or used them for investments in import/export enterprises as well as in lucrative industrial, commercial or service businesses. In this way, many members of the landed oligarchy became members of the financial, industrial or commercial monopolist bourgeoisie or gradually merged their interests with those of these classes.

This many-faceted economic power of the landed oligarchy is the reason why it was not completely liquidated, as a social class, by the agrarian reform carried out by the Frei and Allende governments, which expropriated almost 6,000 latifundia, for a total of almost 5 million hectares of irrigated and non-irrigated cultivable land. At the time Allende took office, the big landlords in particular were still extremely powerful. During the UP government, they maintained this powerful position, despite the expropriation of most of their lands. This was the case because the bourgeois state in which they had (and still have) a tremendous influence was preserved, because the agrarian reform provided high compensation payments for the lands expropriated as well as the legal obligation to pay cash for their machinery, cattle, seed, buildings, forests, etc. Also, the agrarian reform required that important reserves of the best lands be left to the landlords upon their expropriation. Finally, the landlords remained powerful because of the strong economic influence they had in the banking, industrial and commercial sectors. Therefore, their political aggressivity doubled when part of their economic interests were hit by the reforms, which did not completely smash them as a class and which did not seize political power from their hands, political power that they controlled along with U.S. imperialism and the monopolist bourgeoisie to which, as we have seen, they were closely linked through various interests. To this, we must add the aggravating circumstance that the target hit was their agricultural estates, on the ownership of which they based their aristocratic pride and their sentiment of social superiority over those who were "only" merchants, bankers or industrialists.

It is no accident, therefore, that the Popular Unity and its government found in the landlords some of their fiercest and most powerful enemies, even though they had quite naively thought that they had more or less been politically and economically eliminated following two agrarian reforms. The landlords never accepted any compromise and fought ceaselessly until the overthrow of the government.

3. The Monopolist and Financial Bourgeoisie

The other section of the class dominating the Chilean state is the monopolist bourgeoisie (industrial, commercial and financial), which is closely linked with U.S. imperialism and the landed oligarchy.

Within the context of the Third World, Chile is a country which has achieved relative industrial development. The world crisis of the 1930's and the Second World War created difficulties for Chilean imports and exports. As a consequence, the capital previously accumulated by the landlords and by those previously involved in the import/export business was largely channelled into manufacturing industry. Before the world crisis, Chile was the only possessor of natural saltpetre. This fact, in addition to the ownership of coal, copper, silver and other minerals, as well as the advantage (until the construction of the Panama Canal) that the Strait of Magellan was the only passage between the Pacific and Atlantic Oceans, resulted in the accumulation of immense fortunes and in the very strong habit of consuming imported goods. Thus, the development of Chilean manufacturing industry was linked to the need for substitutes for previously imported goods once international trade was blocked because of the above-mentioned events. Because of the narrowness of the internal market, this manufacturing industry right from the beginning had a highly monopolistic structure.

At the beginning of the first year of the Popular Unity government, in 1971, the Office of Planning (ODEPLAN) recorded in its annual plan the following structure of the industrial sector:

STRUCTURE OF THE INDUSTRIAL SECTOR

	% of total no. of establish-ments	% of the total labour force	% of total capital	% of total value added
Large-scale industry (more than 200 workers)	3	44	58	51
Medium industry (20 to 200 workers)	30	40	35	38
Small industry (5 to 20 workers)	67	16	7	11

To briefly show how manufacturing industry was highly monopolized when Allende became President of the Republic, we can say that 130 industrial firms, representing only 1.2 percent of the "controlled" factories (thus called in the census because they hire five workers or more) reaped some 35 percent of the total value added in each industrial sector, accounted for 40 percent of the fixed capital and appropriated some 38 percent of the gross returns.

Moreover, the concentration of capital in large-scale industry was very high in comparison with other industry. CORFO statistics indicate that until 1970, large-scale industry was 180 percent more capital intensive than small industry and 50 percent more capital intensive than medium industry. The latter, for its part, was 85 percent more capital intensive than small industry. Within large-scale industry, nine units accounted for 45 percent of the total capital invested in large-scale enterprises, or 25 percent of the total capital in manufacturing industry. As for fixed capital (machinery, equipment, buildings and facilities), 86 percent of it was concentrated in the "controlled" manufacturing industry, and 14 percent only in the small craft units, almost twice as numerous.

In commerce, 12 wholesale trading enterprises (0.5 percent of them) made 44 percent of the total direct sales in the wholesale business. As far as retail trade is concerned, 54 percent of the firms effected 74 percent of the sales.

Bank credit was also strongly controlled by the monopolistic sections of industry, land and trade, since the banks' boards of directors were closely tied to the big corporations. 1968 data indicate that 2.7 percent of the private banks' debtors obtained 58 percent of all credits granted, while 0.4 percent of debtors obtained almost 30 percent. On the other hand, during the same period, 28 percent of the borrowers received barely 2.6 percent of the total loans.

The monopolistic sections of industry, land, bank and trade, closely linked with the interests of the imperialist monopolies, were in full solidarity in their resolute opposition to the Allende government. The links among them result in the entire Chilean economy being exclusively dominated by 12 powerful clans with extensive branches in monopoly industry, banking and trade, as well as in the latifundia and external trade. Studies carried out by the Popular Unity's Ministry of the Economy stated: "In 1966, 17 percent of the enterprises controlled 75 percent of all shares in the limited companies; 28 limited companies controlled practically every sector and branch of the economy. Furthermore, among the 160 biggest corporations, 81 included foreign holdings (of which one-third represented controlling interests)." *(94)*

It is against these 12 clans which controlled (and still control) the economy and political power of Chile jointly with U.S. imperialism that the main reforms contained in the Popular Unity's programme were aimed. In one of its points, this programme states: "The first step in the economic transformation process is the implementation of a policy aimed at establishing a dominant public sector including the enterprises presently owned by the state as well as those which will be expropriated. First, there will be the nationalization of the basic resources controlled by foreign capital and internal monopolies, such as the large mines of copper, iron, saltpetre and other minerals. Thus, the following will be integrated into the nationalized sector of activity:

1. The large-scale industries involved in copper, saltpetre, iodine, iron and coal mining;

2. The financial system of the country, in particular the private banks and the insurance companies;

3. External trade;

4. The large distribution enterprises and monopolies;

5. The strategic industrial monopolies;

6. In general, activities that are decisive for the economic development of the country, such as the production and distribution of electric energy; railways, airlines and water transportation; communications; production, refining and distribution of oil and its by-products, including liquefied gas; the steel industry; cement, petro-chemicals and chemicals, cellulose and paper."

It is clear, then, that the reforms planned by the Popular Unity in order to broaden state capitalism hit the interests of the powerful clans holding power in Chile. Therefore, it was perfectly possible to foresee that they would respond with deep class hatred and would fight by every means possible (legal and illegal, constitutional and subversive) against those threatening their privileges and their very control of power. It was completely illusory to hope that they would commit a "peaceful suicide" and to suppose that their respect for their own laws and institutions was greater than their love for their wealth and their traditional control of Chilean politics.

Chapter VII
Origins of the Shortages
and the Black Market

Salvador Allende was elected President of the Republic on September 4, 1970. He had 1,075,000 votes, 36.3 percent of the total vote cast, beating his nearest opponent, Jorge Alessandri, by 39,000 votes. Since there was no absolute majority (half of the votes plus one), the congress had to hold a plenary session (in accordance with Chilean law) in order to elect the President of the Republic from among the two candidates who had obtained the highest number of votes.

Right from the moment Allende won the largest number of votes through universal suffrage, the Chilean ultra-right and U.S. imperialism began their manoeuvres aimed at preventing him from fulfilling his mandate. In the US. Congress itself it was proved that the CIA had actively participated in these shady manoeuvres aimed at preventing Allende from becoming President and later at overthrowing him. The CIA offered large sums of money to corrupt parliamentarians and to obtain a vote against Allende during the plenary session of the congress. Later, before Allende even took office, his presidency was jeopardized by the assassination of the Commander-in-Chief of the Armed Forces, perpetrated in order to arouse a military rebellion that would prevent Allende's accession to office.

The manoeuvre aimed at preventing Allende's appointment as President by the congress was to get this body to elect Jorge Alessandri, who had come in in second position. The latter would have resigned after having served a short while as President of the Republic and would have called a new election. Eduardo Frei would then have been the sole candidate for the Christian Democratic Party and for the ultra-right forces. For the rightist supporters of Alessandri, Frei offered more guarantees than Radomiro Tomic, who had opposed Allende during the 1970 presidential elections with a programme more or less similar to that of the Popular Unity. With such a manoeuvre, the constitutional provision forbidding the same person to be President for two terms in a row would be circumvented. Between Frei's mandate that had ended in 1970 and his re-election, there would have been the short presidential interlude of Alessandri. The latter, pressed by his supporters, publicly agreed with this manoeuvre and promised to resign, despite the fact that during his presidential campaign one of his slogans was: "Whoever wins a one-vote majority must be President." This political intrigue aimed at preventing Allende from taking office was perfectly legal and constitutional and it was assumed that the Army agreed with it and supported it. One of the parties most interested in such a dismissal of the electoral winner was Eduardo Frei, an extremely reactionary, ambitious and hypocritical politician who was outraged at being called "the Chilean Kerensky" and at going down in history as the one after whom "communism" was to be established.

However, after a sharp struggle, the forces opposed to the constitutional intrigue predominated within the Christian Democrats. The right wing had tenaciously opposed the reforms implemented by Frei and his government at the request of the United States. There was also the fear of the discontent that would have been caused among the rank-and-file Christian Democrats if the congress had violated this old Chilean tradition of electing the one who had obtained the greatest number of votes, even if it was not an absolute majority. On the other hand, a President imposed through parliamentary intrigue would have had to face a popular opposition free of all illusions about the electoral process, in other words, an opposition ready to embark on a revolutionary road for the seizure of power. It was for this reason that Allende's opponent during the 1970 elections, Radomiro Tomic, was one of the first to congratulate him on his victory. This gesture by Tomic provoked a violent altercation between him and Frei.

However, the Christian Democrats took advantage of their decisive influence in the congress to attach conditions to their vote in favour of Allende in the two Houses: they forced him to agree to a so-called "Statute of Constitutional Guarantees". Right from the beginning of his mandate, this statute tied

Allende even more to the narrow frame of bourgeois legality and institutions; later, it became a key element in accusing him of violating his commitments and in openly undertaking to overthrow him under this pretext. Among other things, the statute forbade restrictive measures against the opposition parties and their means of propaganda, even if their activities were openly subversive, as they actually became later. It expressly stated that the only armed forces were to be the ones already in existence and that their Commanders-in-Chief alone were entitled to appoint their subordinates, blocking the way to any democratization within the body of commanders and officers. It forbade any change, on the part of the government, of the class content of education, etc.

1. The "Strike" of Investments in Private Industry

One of the major projects of the Popular Unity government was to reactivate industrial production and trade, which had dropped considerably during the last year of the Frei government. Industrial growth, which had reached 7 percent during the first two years of the Christian Democratic government, fell under 2 percent in 1967, causing the growth indices of the national product to fall as well.

The Allende government, in order to achieve vigorous growth in industrial production and trade, planned to strongly stimulate the people's demand for industrial goods. For this, the plan was to drastically reduce unemployment, to have a redistribution of national income that would substantially increase the portion received by the workers, and to subsidize current consumer goods so as to keep them at official prices that would make widespread consumption possible. The government also thought of using bank credits (which would almost entirely come under state control after the expropriation of the private banks) to stimulate the development of small and medium industries. It was assumed that cheap credit for private industry, together with the development of a powerful and massive demand for industrial products, would be a decisive stimulant of investments in private enterprise.

An important part of these plans to broaden the internal market and to democratize credit was implemented during the first year of the Popular Unity government. Unemployment, which had reached 8 percent of the active population in 1970, dropped to 4 percent, a rate which on the average remained steady during the three years of this government. In 1971, almost 200,000 jobs were created. In 1972, 98,000 other persons were given employment.

Moreover, during the first year of the government, on the basis of a quite significant readjustment of wages, workers' share of the national income increased from 51 percent to 60 percent. In one year, the purchasing power of the workers increased by 20 percent. All this had positive political consequences for the Popular Unity: In the municipal election of April 1971, it won 44 percent of the votes, while in the presidential elections the percentage has been 36.3 percent. After the coup d'état, the military junta took upon itself to brutally reverse this redistribution in favour of the workers that the Allende government had implemented during its first year. As the Christian Democratic leader Radomiro Tomic pointed out in an interview with the Texas University paper *Right On* (November 15, 1974), the free price system and the imposition of low wages and salaries through decrees, as implemented by Pinochet and his cronies, have resulted in "the share of the workers in the GNP falling from 55 percent (the average of the 1970-72 period) to 37 percent." This, Tomic adds, "has meant the transfer of over $1 billion in escudos, from the hands of three million Chilean wage earners (Army and Carabineros included) to those of a few thousand businessmen."

In addition to the stimulation of demand created by the increase in the purchasing power of the workers, light industry also benefited from the breach of the credit monopoly held by the most powerful economic sectors. It has to be considered that already by the middle of 1971, the state controlled 57.2 percent of the shares in private banks, and that in 1973, it held 90 percent of the bank credit. This allowed the issuing of a decree, in February 1971, to reduce the bank rate of interest from 24 percent to 18 percent and for the small and medium enterprises to only 12 percent.

Following these measures taken in the first year of the Allende government, the growth rate of the GNP increased to between 8 to 9 percent. Industrial growth increased to a level between 12 and 14 percent. Inflation, from a high of 36 percent in 1970, fell to 22 percent in 1971.

However, the "expansion" of private industrial production was more apparent than real. The private businesses did bring more goods to the market in 1971, but basically, this was achieved through the mobilization of the unused production capacity of their factories which in 1969-1970, were functioning on the average at only 68 percent of their capacity. Enormous stocks of commodities accumulated in 1970 were also put on the market. Also, in most of the factories, including those that had been acquired by the state, an increase in the volume of goods put up for sale was recorded. This was often taken for an increase in production, but in fact the reason for this was that tighter controls prevented the traditional sales without invoices for tax evasion purposes. In Sumar, for example, one of the largest textile factories of the country, it was discovered when the Directorate of Industry and Commerce (DIRINCO) took over that some 40 percent of the production had not been invoiced by the former owners. All these factors contributed, in the beginning, to the "optical illusion" that the Popular Unity government had succeeded in interesting the private manufacturers in investing in their businesses as a result of the vigorous development of demand and the credit facilities provided for them.

Even though the private manufacturers made tremendous profits because of the intensified demand promoted by the government, the truth is that the net investment in their businesses was nil. They preferred to take their profits abroad and invest them in strong currencies or speculate on the foreign exchange market or in other types of businesses, rather than investing them in their own enterprises. In 1971, Chile's balance of payments suffered a deficit of $320 million, of which $270 million corresponded to the official export of private capital. The private investors not only refused to enlarge or modernize their factories, but in many cases they sold equipment in order to convert it into dollars; they seriously reduced their purchases of raw materials, and in some cases they even distributed the reserves of the enterprises to the shareholders.

Therefore, the policy of encouraging investment in private industry which was implemented by the Allende government even at the risk (as we will see) of creating serious problems in the overall economy of the country, was one of the first and most serious downfalls in the Popular Unity's economic plans. It should be noted that this downfall was of a highly political origin. Even though the stimulative measures had worked out well economically, the Allende government had been unable to rally the medium manufacturers around a policy of expanding and investing in their businesses, despite all the credit and sales facilities that were offered. On the contrary, the most ferocious enemies of the government (the domestic monopolist groups and the U.S. corporations affected by the reforms) were successful in winning over these middle businessmen to a stubborn and uncompromising policy against the government and its plans. The opposition also won over most of the tradesmen. Thus, the manufacturers engaged in a real "strike" of investments, often sabotaging their own factories and paralyzing them in collusion with the transportation and trading sectors. This sabotage by the owners of the non-nationalized factories was extremely serious, since these people controlled over three-fifths of the industrial production, even after all the expropriations that the Allende government was able to carry out.

2. Weakness Leads to Isolation

The failure to win over the middle section of manufacturers and tradesmen to support the development of production, which the UP had thought could be achieved through the expropriation of the big national and foreign monopolies, was also the failure of the very strategy for the seizure of state power into which the "C"P leaders had led the Popular Unity. These middle strata of manufacturers and tradesmen were always conscious that the real control of political power remained in the hands of the monopolist industrial and commercial sectors, of the large U.S. firms and of the landed oligarchy. They knew that these sectors retained a dominant influence over the basic institutions of the state apparatus (including the Armed Forces) as well as on the economic, political and ideological fronts. After all, the Popular

Unity, with its victory in the presidential elections, had only seized a portion of the Executive power, which moreover was tied up by the other components of the bourgeois state and entirely infiltrated in its bureaucratic apparatus by the forces of the opposition. Furthermore, this portion of Executive power had been conquered through a very precarious electoral majority, made possible by the division in the ranks of the opposition.

The economic blows that the expropriations dealt to a few powerful national and foreign monopolies as well as to the big landlords also did not contribute to the image of the Allende government or to making it more convincing in the eyes of the middle strata. Until the very downfall of the government, the state-controlled or expropriated enterprises remained the object of bitter claims on the part of their former owners. Their management by the state was continuously interfered with by the Contraloria of the Republic, by the courts and by the Parliament. Also, as we will see later, these enterprises, instead of being an important source of income and a lever for the overall economy, became the cause of huge deficits and a ball-and-chain tied to the feet of the government.

A later demonstration that the monopolist sectors, despite the expropriations and interference, always maintained their dominant power and never gave up their intentions of getting back their enterprises, was the fact that almost all of these reverted to them after the coup d'état. The expropriations were not irreversible, as the leaders of the Popular Unity had thought. Moreover, those manufacturers who had agreed to sell their firms to the government were subjected to trial by the Military Junta.

Consequently, the Popular Unity and the Allende government did not have a real influence on the middle sections. Such an influence can only be won by a people's movement able to mobilize the broad masses in the fight to seize political power in a revolutionary way, and not only through elections. Such an influence doubles when state power is actually seized and controlled and when the means and strength to defend it actually exist. Only such a control of power, acquired through a genuine revolution led by the proletariat and capable of smashing the bourgeois state, can permit demands to be made on the middle sections and offers of advantages and guarantees for them to be made at the expense of the expropriated monopolist and imperialist interests.

The failure to win over the middle sections of manufacturers, tradesmen, professionals, handicraftsmen and petty-bourgeois involved in service activities as well as numerous sections of white and blue collar workers, the fact that they joined the opposition because of the crisis and the evident weakness of the government, cannot be explained exclusively or simply by some errors made in dealing with these strata. This thesis of explaining the attitude of the middle sections on the basis of some "tactical mistakes" in the relations with them is still defended today by some leaders of the Popular Unity who refuse to draw correct conclusions from the events in Chile and who obstinately persist in advocating the bogus strategy of "peaceful road" to power. Basically, they are hard-core opportunists who refuse to recognize the failure brought about by the implementation in Chile of the line pushed by Khrushchov and his followers and who try to blame some so-called "ultra-left" trends which allegedly infiltrated the Popular Unity for that failure. In fact, even if some tactical mistakes in the relations with the middle sections were made, their moving over to the uncompromising oppositional stand pushed by the most reactionary forces was basically the result of a problem concerning the *power* held by the Popular Unity and its government, or, more precisely, concerning the very weak control of power with which the Popular Unity attempted to impose its reforms. This weakness of political power was the result of the wrong strategy pushed by the "C"P leaders for its seizure and accepted, in the main, by the leaders of the Popular Unity. The best tactics in regard to the middle sections would not have changed anything in their conviction that the Popular Unity and its government had a base of support which was too weak to allow the destruction of the most powerful political and economic forces in the country. No tactical juggling could make them forget the decisive power that the ruling forces still had within the state apparatus, power that made itself irresistibly and increasingly felt during Allende's administration and even before Allende took office. In short, despite the contradictions that the middle sections had with the monopoly and financial bourgeoisie and the landed oligarchy as well as with U.S. imperialism, it is with the latter forces that they had (and still have) the most solid economic links. Consequently, for these wavering sections, it would have been a stab in the dark to turn themselves against the ruling sections in order to support, for immediate advantages only, a government committed to destroying these ruling sections with very low probabilities of success.

On the other hand, the middle sections not only did not believe that the Popular Unity government would succeed, but they also feared for their own interests if the nationalization plans were to continue. Moreover, the fears of the small and middle bourgeoisie were cleverly exploited by the propaganda of the right-wing opposition. This opposition developed audacious and fraudulent campaigns on that front, going so far as to hire phony inspectors who went around visiting large numbers of houses "on behalf of the government" to make a survey of available rooms for "homeless people to be housed in the future". However, we insist on the fact that what influenced the middle sections more than the fear of the government was the glaringly overwhelming power of the reactionary camp: the middle sections feared for their future after the downfall of the Popular Unity if they collaborated with the government. In the face of the (real or imaginary) threats to private property that made them fear for their own interests, the middle sections had only two choices: either attempt to preserve their interests and even gain more liberties by supporting the policy of the Allende government aimed at liquidating the large monopolies, or unite with the threatened monopolies and make a common front with them against the government. There is no doubt that it is this latter solution that the middle and even small manufacturers and tradesmen chose, despite the freedom for expansion that they had gained. The events showed once again how the fears and hesitations of the middle sections can express themselves in a contradictory manner either for or against anti-imperialist or anti-monopolist social changes. If these changes are led by a really strong and powerful revolutionary movement capable of seizing political power, the fear that the offensive of the proletariat inspires in the middle sections (together with the concessions made to them by the revolutionary movement) pushes them to give up and adapt themselves to revolutionary change and even to oppose big capital. On the contrary, if the most reactionary forces keep the advantage, if they have solid control over political power, the middle sections submit to them and the fear of change pushes them to act as the social basis of the fascist aims of big capital. In essence, the problem is posed in this manner: is the United Front led by the proletariat with a Marxist-Leninist line consistent with its interests, or is it led by opportunists, reformists and revisionists, as was the case in Chile?

3. The Gap Between Supply and Demand and the Crisis in the Balance of Payments

The *political* failure of the economic measures aimed at promoting the expansion of private industry was one of the main causes of the shortages engineered by the opposition and later used in order to bring about the downfall of the Allende government. These shortages, accompanied with wild speculation, were one of the basic factors used by the ultra-right forces to develop the social basis necessary for the coup d'état and the setting up of fascism. With the absolute refusal of the private manufacturers to invest in their enterprises and with their increasing participation in the campaigns to sabotage production and distribution, the state policy of vigorously strengthening demand could only lead to a serious shortage of goods on the market. This shortage was to be felt as soon as the manufacturers had finished filling their pockets by mobilizing the unused productive capacities and by depleting the stocks of goods accumulated in their warehouses in 1970. It became worse with the drop recorded in the balance of payments at the end of 1971.

It has to be realized that the steep decline of unemployment, the important rise in the workers' purchasing power in 1971 and the price freeze were not the only reasons for the expansion of demand. There was also a vigorous demand for goods originating from the capitalists, precisely because they were refusing to invest their profits in production and were using them for speculation. They were buying goods in order to sell them on the black market. Moreover, the available profits of the manufacturers were increased by the fact that the government was artificially maintaining the prices of raw materials and energy produced by the state-controlled firms at very low levels (naively hoping that this would stimulate the development of private enterprise). These profits also went into the pockets of the speculators when they were not used to swell dollar accounts in the foreign banks.

When considering this strong increase in demand, we must also take into account the unbridled expenses of the bureaucratic bourgeoisie which developed within the leading sections and intermediate cadres of the Popular Unity. This new bureaucratic bourgeoisie took roots and strengthened itself in the high posts of the public administration and, basically, at the head of the enterprises which in one way or another came under state control: banks, large factories, mines, public utility services, wholesale trade businesses, etc. Of course, these managers of a fully developing state capitalism could have a "top" revenue of 20 times the basic wage of a worker (considering as basic wage what is necessary for subsistence), but it is no less certain that the said top corresponded to almost 30 times the minimum wage of a worker. On the other hand, this legal "top" of 20 times the basic wage was considerably increased in January 1971, when it was decided that it was the "net" top salary (that is, what is left after all tax deductions) that would equal 20 times the basic wage. In the middle of 1971, such a "net" revenue was equal to the monthly income of a businessman with a capital of around one million escudos, which means, in the context of Chile, of a quite powerful middle-size capitalist. But this "top" salary was not the only income. These state officials could have other revenue not restricted by the "top" of 20 times the basic wage in the form of travel and other expenses as well as definite privileges such as housing, food, cars and fuel, etc. This "top" was somewhat like the "ceiling" of the airplanes, depending on the power and "motors" of those having to cope with it. On the other hand, this "top" only referred to their income as state officials, but these people could enjoy other important revenues from enterprises or private functions.

As we have pointed out, this only refers to the legal,

"legitimate" incomes of the state bureaucrats who were in office during the Allende government. It has to be added, however, that many of these officials and business managers or public servants, to various degrees, also enriched themselves by illegal means, such as demanding bribes for definite services, receiving commissions, often in dollars, before they would give authorization for imports or exports, engaging in black market dealings or barter of various goods that they could get at artificially low prices, demanding a supplement from tradesmen before selling them goods at the official prices, and so on. The Minister of the Economy himself, Orlando Millas, an important leader of the "C"P, was forced to admit to the Plenum of the Central Committee of his party that there were "those who fraudulently enrich themselves by climbing 15 promotion grades at a time, by continuing to receive fabulous salaries in certain enterprises, by living in the houses of the former managers and by using the state vehicles for private purposes." On his part, Orlando Munoz, sales manager of the Distribuidora Nacional (DINAC), a state wholesale trade business, wrote in a circular to the staff of this firm: "Recently, some severe disciplinary actions had to be taken against certain comrades for embezzlement of funds, organization of parties in the stores, misuse of the firm's vehicles, accidents, conclusion of sales for their own benefit, falsification of customers' names on the documents, preferred sales, speculation, counterfeit of vouchers, giving the keys of stores to unauthorized persons, and selling to private individuals while it is strictly forbidden to do so."

The formation of a bureaucratic bourgeoisie, relatively strong in numbers compared to the expropriated capitalists, considerably multiplied the demand for goods and the resulting shortages, since industry was not expanding and the imports were severely restricted by various factors. The new bureaucratic bourgeoisie had an enormous appetite for consumption, well-being, and even luxury. Those who never had cars, refrigerators, television sets and abundant clothes and food were suddenly given the possibility to acquire all these things. Many of them left the apartments that they used to rent in the proletarian or middle-class areas to buy houses in the areas where the big bourgeoisie used to live. This *parvenu* attitude of improving one's standard of living in such an accelerated manner became intensified to the extreme after the opposition began its offensive to overthrow the government, when uncertainty and demoralization had set in concerning their future. In such circumstances, many state officials, already despairing of their ability to do something about the overall problems of the country, adopted the mentality of *après moi le déluge* and scrambled to enrich themselves before it was too late. From that moment, despite the calls for honesty given by President Allende, the cases of corruption and illegal gains multiplied. All this had repercussions on consumption and generated a strong pressure on a very tight market. The consumption capacity of 10 or more officials with their families is undoubtedly higher than that of a capitalist who already owns the essentials in terms of durable goods and whose consumption capacity in terms of perishable goods is limited by the number of members of his family. This is true even when these officials taken together have revenues equal to that of the capitalist.

The vigorous increase in demand not only had to cope with an industrial expansion deliberately "frozen" by the manufacturers, but also with an agriculture that had been stagnating since the 1950's and regressing compared to the natural growth of population. In 1947, the contribution of agriculture to the gross national product was 17 percent, while in 1969 it had dropped to a little over 7 percent. During the 1965-1970 five-year period, however, with the agrarian reform initiated by the Christian Democratic Party, an average annual increase of 3 percent was registered, while for the 30 years before, the average annual increase had been only 1.8 percent. When Allende took office, however, the increase of the last decade was still lower than the natural growth of population.

To this backwardness of farm production, inherited from the previous regimes, we must add the refusal on the part of numerous middle-size farmers to sow or to invest in their estates as well as the sabotage perpetrated by the big landlords. The latter engaged in burning crops and slaughtered some 120,000 sheep (for the Magallanes region alone). They exported 200,000 head of cattle and created a strong purchasing power in the rural areas which was used to sabotage the remittance of the goods produced on the expropriated lands to the government, thus stimulating the development of the black market.

Furthermore, the peasants who remained in the countryside to work on the large expropriated estates in most cases only enjoyed the moral satisfaction of being liberated from the all-powerful and despotic arbitrariness of the big landlords. They fell into the hands of a much more demagogic state bureaucracy against which it was much harder to fight since it had the support of the political activists within the very ranks of the workers. In fact, on the estates affected by the reforms, the work was much heavier than before and was motivated by a hypothetical profit that would allow the improvement of the minimum wage of the peasants. This anticipated profit could only be obtained after the amounts advanced by the State Bank to finance the year's production had been paid back with an annual interest of 12 percent. Moreover, 50 percent of this profit went to the Agrarian Reform Centres for the creation of a common fund used to meet the debts of the expropriated estates unable to pay back the sums loaned by the State Bank for the year's production, 25 percent went into capital accumulation, and only 25 percent could be distributed to the peasants. A study carried out in January 1972 in the Talca Province by students of the Agronomy Department of the University of Chile doing their practical probation period in settlements of this region revealed that *all* the Agrarian Reform Centres of the region, far from making profits, ended the year with debts to the State Bank. Among broad sections of the farm workers on the expropriated estates, who were doing more intensive work without getting anything more than the minimum peasant wage, there was the sentiment that through struggle, they could have got much better wages from their former landlords. It is not surprising, then, that as soon as the initial illusions disappeared, a large-scale black market developed on the estates affected by the reform on the basis of falsifying production data and refusing to deliver the goods produced to the state bodies. President Allende even had to denounce certain settlements for selling the selected potatoes that had been given to them for sowing on the black market. In this manner, the peasants were defending their standard of living, as they realized that they had just changed masters. On the other hand, many peasants aware of what was going on on the lands reformed by the government preferred to seize the land through direct struggle and to cultivate it without the control of the Agrarian Reform Corporation. (CORA).

One of the consequences of the refusal to invest in the private sector and of the problems briefly explained was the aggravation of the already acute crisis of the balance of payments by the end of 1971. This further deepened the crisis of farm production that already existed when Allende took over. In order to compensate for the insufficient farm and industrial production and to meet the excessive demand that it had created, the government had to increase imports. This took place in extremely disadvantageous conditions, because of the steep drop of the copper price on the international market (the sale of copper accounted for three-quarters of Chile's foreign currency inflow), because of the spectacular rise of food prices on the world market, and because of the credit embargo as well as the obstacles set up by the United States to the renegotiation of the Chilean external debt in reprisal against the expropriation of U.S. firms. In 1971, expenditures on food imports alone had increased by 60 percent compared to the previous year. According to the statistics given in a study carried out by the Industrial Development Corporation and published in 1972: "In 1971, Chile's balance of payments registered a deficit of $225 million, a figure which must be increased to $335 million if we are to consider postponed payments, matured debts and special credits granted by the International Monetary Fund. The net foreign exchange reserves," the study adds, "dropped from $377.6 million in September 1970 to $57.6 million in September 1971." These figures were not denied. In this way, the efforts to offset the shortages by importing goods were to become a new factor in an even worse shortage of even more essential products by generating a severe crisis in the foreign currency reserves. In November 1971, the Central Bank was forced to ban the importation of 300 items that could previously have entered the country.

The deep gap between supply and demand and its consequences and the shortage of goods on the regular markets rapidly turned into one of the major contradictions facing the

Allende government. This contradiction was cleverly used and promoted by the opposition (under CIA advice) for what was euphemistically called the "destabilization" of the Allende government, in other words, to aggravate the crisis, broaden the discontent and prepare conditions for the military coup d'état. Thus, the opposition's propaganda skillfully used the increasing shortage of commodities and was able to generate within the population a real collective shortage "psychosis". Thus, anyone with resources and storage facilities began to stockpile commodities just for the fear that they would be lacking in the future. Then, through the wholesale firms that remained under its control, the opposition began to organize the receiving and concealing of goods to be sold at very high prices on the black market. A large number of individuals who had never even been involved in trade before (including some belonging to government circles) engaged in this lucrative activity. On the other hand, taking advantage of the big difference between the artificially low rate of the dollar and its rate on the black market, Chileans and foreigners took huge quantities of goods out of the country, either for trade or for their personal use. Suffice it to say that in certain periods, it was possible to buy a pair of shoes for less than one dollar on the black market, which dollar had been bought at the official low rate. In November 1971, over 500 tons of commodities were to be exported to Argentina.

Even the official prices fixed by the government for the basic necessities in order to prevent inflation and stimulate demand contributed to promoting stockpiling and speculation. These prices were much lower than what was required by the unsatisfied demand. Just by purchasing a product at the official price from a factory or from a wholesale distributor, it was possible to sell it for 10 times the official price or more on the black market. Consequently, it was much more lucrative to participate in the plans of the opposition to sabotage the economy through speculation than to engage in a normal productive or commercial activity. Moreover, thanks to the "magic" virtues of the reactionary propaganda, this form of theft (unbridled speculation, receiving and concealing of commodities and, in general, anything that contributed to make the living conditions of the people more intolerable and to intensify the discontent), while filling the pockets of the speculators, became a "meritorious" activity in opposition to "communism", a "noble", "patriotic" and "democratic" activity. The ladies of the aristocracy who had filled their basements with concealed commodities and who were using vans and even trucks to temporarily stock merchandise for speculation pushed their cynicism to the point of demonstrating in the streets banging on empty cooking pans. In this way, they influenced broad sections of the middle class and workers who were the actual victims of the shortage and speculation, intensified the discontent and prepared public opinion for the coup d'état. During the short period from January 5 to January 25, 1973, the government press (with photographs of the places, names and addresses of the culprits) denounced the stockpiling of 150,000 litres of wine, 133,000 kilos of meat, 3,000,000 kilos of rice, 9,350 litres of oil, 20,500 kilos of flour, 3,400 bags of cement, 57,000 food cans, 83,000 kilos of sugar and many other articles that were denied to the public because they were "unavailable" on the market or that could be bought at the official price only in small quantities and after repeated attempts, after hours and hours of intolerable waiting in line-ups. An additional proof of the complicity of most of the tradesmen and merchants in this stockpiling and black market is that the day after the coup d'état, as if by miracle, the stores started selling all the goods previously denied to the public because they were "unavailable".

The measures that the government attempted to take against stockpiling and speculation had to be implemented without any legal support because the opposition, despite its hypocritical outcries against shortage and speculation, persistently refused in Parliament to approve legislation against economic crime tabled by the government. These government measures, moreover, were applied in a weak manner and did not stop speculation. On the contrary, they were used by the opposition to further arouse the hostility of the tradesmen against the government.

4. Failure of an Attempt to Control Distribution

In the middle of 1971, the government undertook to set up the Boards of Supply and Prices (Juntas de Abastecimientos y Precios — JAP), basic organs that were supposed to fight against speculation and stockpiling of goods as well as to ensure their distribution at the official prices. Right from the beginning, however, they were handicapped by the typical ambiguity deriving from the dominant opportunist line in the Popular Unity. They were neither organs of "people's power" (as defined by the Minister of the Economy Pedro Vuskovic at the first provincial assembly of the Santiago JAP's, held in June 1972), nor legal bodies recognized by the law and having legal prerogatives. The only resemblance to bodies having legal prerogatives was the possibility for each JAP tó appoint *ad honorem* price inspectors recognized by the Ministry of the Economy. As soon as the JAP's were set up, the opposition parties declared war against them. They decided not to join such "illegal" organizations and revived the Boards of Citizens, fully recognized by the law, in opposition to the JAP's. In this manner, an acute sectarian fight concerning the distribution of goods to the population was generated between the Boards of Citizens, controlled by the opposition, and the Boards of Supply and Prices, controlled by the government parties. Through the State Central for Wholesale Distribution, the government parties controlled some 33 percent of wholesale trade, and through the JAP's, they favoured those merchants and sections of the population supporting them. The opposition parties did the same with the assistance of the Boards of Citizens with the two-thirds of the wholesale trade that they controlled. Thus, as speculation and shortages intensified, ever larger sections of the population polarized around the two warring blocs out of their need for basic necessities in terms of food and subsistence.

In October 1972, the opposition dealt one of its heaviest blows to the economy in general: the employers' strike, which particularly aggravated the already severe problems of shortages and speculation. This strike lasted from the beginning of October to the beginning of November 1972. It involved the merchants (only 36 percent of them did not respect the strike order), the owners of the trucks used in the transportation of goods (some 12,000), the public transportation system and numerous professional corporations. The manufacturers also tried to impose a lock-out in the industrial sector. The CIA actively participated in this strike (providing strategic leadership as well as financial support), as it later publicly admitted during the investigation of the U.S. Congress. The strike not only intensified the shortages and speculation to the point that they became intolerable for the population, it also dealt a severe blow to agricultural production. Huge quantities of milk, fruit and vegetables were lost (precisely the types of foodstuff that could not be stockpiled). The transportation of seeds, fuel and fertilizer for the just begun spring sowing was stopped. Because of this, the crops of rice, wheat, oil seeds, sugar beets, etc. were seriously damaged. According to President Allende himself, some 132 million escudos were lost in freight, transportation and toll fares. Three billion escudos were wasted in food products that became inedible due to the closing down of stores, and 364 million were lost as uncollected taxes. In conclusion, the President estimated the damages caused by the strike, two weeks before it ended, at $100 million. The second strike organized by the opposition on the eve of the coup d'état (August 1973) was to cause a loss of more than 200 million escudos per day, ruining 50 percent of the vegetable crops by blocking transportation to the consumer centres. These strikes, accompanied by open sabotage, had the effect of dynamite placed by the opposition into the severe breach in the economy that had been created by the shortages resulting from the blockade, difficulties of importing, the sabotage and stockpiling, the "strike" of private investments in industry and the failure in managing the state enterprises.

The government, instead of developing the important counter-offensive launched by the people and the working class in particular to defeat the first strike organized by the opposition, restrained this counter-offensive (as we will see later) and attempted to solve the problem through timid administrative and legal measures. In January 1973, the government tabled in Parliament legislation against economic crime and attempted, through the Ministry of Finance, to take control of the distribution of goods.

The legislation against economic crime was discussed by Parliament in the beginning of 1973. The National Party (ultra-rightist) simply voted against putting this legislation on the agenda. The Christian Democratic Party and the Party of the Radical Left (Partido de la Izquierda Radical — PIR) resorted to an even worse manoeuvre: they voted for including the legislation on the agenda but with the intent, as Senator Carmona of the CDP put it, of "turning it into its opposite", which they actually did. The legislation of the Executive proposed jail penalties "for those who make false declarations or give wrong information about their economic activities, for those who destroy or withdraw from the market items of basic necessity with the intent of creating shortages, subverting public order or disturbing security, administration, national health and economy." Penalties were also provided for those who "destroy or do not use the plants and machinery, the plantations and other means of industrial, mining, agricultural or commercial production, those who accumulate raw materials or goods in quantities greater than those required by the enterprises or for their personal consumption." Once the agenda was approved, the National Party was appointed to present a counter-bill opposed to the one tabled by the government. In this counter-bill, of course, no mention at all was made of those engaging in stockpiling, black market, sabotage and other criminal activitities of this kind. Instead, there were penalties provided for public servants exceeding their rights, as well as provisions against the state taking control of enterprises for a period exceeding 30 days. Another clause stipulated penalties if the Executive did not take a stand within 30 days on any application submitted by an enterprise to raise its prices. The issuing of currency (which, in Chile, is a prerogative of the Executive) was made conditional on prior approval by the Senate; the expropriated manufacturers could submit their cases to the Supreme Court of Appeal, which would be empowered to nullify the resolutions of the government; and so on. In short, the opposition's majority in Parliament reduced to pieces the law proposed by the government against economic crime and set up another one exclusively aimed at blocking the implementation of the government's programme.

The administrative measures parallel to the bill against economic crime also demonstrated the utter impotency of the Popular Unity government which had no actual control of power or legal prerogatives within a bourgeois society that it wanted to transform into state capitalism. On January 11, 1973, the

Minister of Finance, Fernando Flores (member of the Movement for United Popular Action — MAPU) created the National Secretariat for Distribution, which would enter into exclusive contracts with the private industrial firms producing consumer goods of basic necessity and would organize the marketing of such goods. However, these contracts were not binding and in order to make them effective, it only provided that "the government will take into account how the enterprises have respected and fulfilled the provisions of the marketing contracts." This was absolutely ridiculous, given the now openly subversive and resolute character of the offensive launched by the opposition to overthrow the government. In the public sector, on the other hand, the remittance of all production to the state distribution firms was compulsory. It should be noted, by the way, that the point referring to the state enterprises includes provisions showing to what extent they were also using sectarian privileges and engaging in black market. It provided that they should stop "direct trade with and sales to the public." It pointed out that "payments in kind" and "preferred sales" would not be tolerated. Concerning the countryside, the Finance Minister's document simply proposed to "channel the bulk of farm production into the state marketing mechanisms." The farm workers were called upon to "prevent agricultural products from going to the black market." Concerning the wholesale trade, the document provided that "the National Secretariat for Distribution will exercise authority on the firms distributing groceries and food products . . . The private wholesale trade enterprises will be regularized and integrated into the programmed system and they will have to account for the source of their basic necessity products." It also pointed out that "the government will not tolerate the maintenance of any private monopoly over the distribution of any goods". Finally, concerning the retail trade, while reiterating the role of the JAP's in exposing and taking *"direct actions"* against stockpiling and speculation, the document listed 30 basic items to be distributed to each family through an agreement between the JAP's and the merchants in each area.

In fact, as was shown by the short period it was circulated, the document of cabinet minister Flores was not a decision applicable through the actual mobilization of the people; neither was it a policy statement which would be applied by force of law; nor did it reflect the views of all sections of the Popular Unity, (considering what is implied by the measures it proposed). It seems that it was just an attempt by Flores' party to confront the government with a *fait accompli* and mobilize it to control distribution and make a first step towards the rationing of necessities. However, as it originated from a government having no absolute control on political power and which, because of the opportunist nature of those exercising hegemony over the Popular Unity, was unwilling to mobilize the masses in order to impose its decisions, the document, in the final analysis, was nothing more than a statement of intent which further outraged the opposition and further revealed the weakness of the government. The response of the opposition was not long in coming. "This is a clear and definite measure for totalitarian control over the country . . . The Chilean people cannot tolerate being submitted to such an irreversible dictatorship," declared Eduardo Frei, the Christian Democrat leader. "Chileans have the obligation and the duty to resist these dictatorial measures that the Popular Unity's Marxist government has decided to implement in our fatherland . . . We will not tolerate the establishment of 'Chekas' on every street which will investigate every family before delivering a piece of fish, a little salt or oil . . . At this point, the people must refuse to provide information, they must set up defence committees on a street basis," said the Christian Democratic Senator Rafael Moreno. "In Chile," said the National Party Senator Francisco Bulnes, "the establishment of a regime similar to that of Cuba is just about to be achieved . . . Castroism took advantage of the hunger of the people to impose ration cards and up to now, it continues to control the reactions and will of all Cubans." The Christian Democratic Senator Juan Hamilton declared: "This is a monstrous and sinister speech *(that of Flores)*. Whoever does not comply with the JAP's and the UP is not going to eat." Moreover, the Corporate Action Command, which led the October 1972 strike, declared: "Conscious of their duty to lead the strug-gle for their freedom, the Chilean corporations advise the government that they will not accept the establishment of a rationing system." The Confederation for Democracy (CODE), regrouping the opposition parties, also pointed out: "Given the arbitrariness and the threats issued by the Minister of Finance as well as the anti-constitutionality of these measures, we call upon the people to energetically, but peacefully, resist all pressures, to oppose any census in their houses or areas."

The measures announced by Flores were also vehemently opposed by the leading organizations of tradesmen. Most of them, committed to the opposition, were participating in the "patriotic" activity of stockpiling commodities in order to sell them on the black market which they were promoting. Therefore, they absolutely refused to hear or talk about any control of distribution, let alone rationing. On January 12, the Confederation of Trade Institutions, the Chilean Central Chamber of Commerce and the United National Confederation of Small Industry and Handicraft issued a joint document. They stated: "The imposition of a quota on the necessities allocated to each family, as announced by the Minister, Flores, is nothing but pure and simple rationing." The document also analyzes so-called violations of the Constitutional Guarantees (the compromise signed by Salvador Allende with the Christian Democrats as a condition for the latter to vote for the former's designation as President of the Republic by Parliament) allegedly contained in the document tabled by Flores. Finally, these leading bodies, "because of the seriousness of the situation", ordered their rank and file, among other things "not to join, or, as the case may be, to withdraw from the JAP's, because these organizations have become real 'storm troopers' seeking and calling for the destruction of trade and commerce without solving any problems the country is faced with in terms of supply, not to accept any procedure which would imply the implementation of what is actually a rationing system, as proposed by the government" (95).

Faced with this counter-offensive, the government, because of its precarious power base and its refusal to mobilize the masses to solve the basic problems, took refuge in a defensive position. President Allende wrote a letter to El Mercurio to deny its allegations according to which rationing was to be imposed. He wrote: "There will be no food rationing, but a genuinely equitable and humane distribution of goods essential for the subsistence of the family." The editor of *El Mercurio* replied in this way: "The sentence that we quote taken from a speech by Mr. Allende at the May 1971 demonstration *('Chile is not used to and does not want rationing'),* is no lie and it has been interpreted as the President's declaration of faith in democracy! The enormous lie, which the country will not tolerate, is that Marxism, as time went by, deprived this declaration of its force and rapidly moved outside the law to organize the system of Boards of Supply and Prices (JAP), which is now complemented with actual rationing, deciding what one can consume and the conditions to obtain it . . . We have to rely on the actual statements of the Minister of Finance, as published in the magazine *Chile Hoy* (Chile Today) . . . The author of these statements, Mr. Fernando Flores, said: 'The problem of rationing, of considering the necessity to put quotas on consumption and not to let the market operate freely, could have been politically shocking three or four years ago; it could have been seen as an extremist measure. Not today.' " *(96)*

On January 22, in a vain attempt to calm the opposition attacks, President Allende decreed the formation of the National Secretariat for Marketing and Distribution, with its National Council. To head it, he named a regular Army general, Alberto Bachelet; the nomination would cost Bachelet death in prison after the coup d'état.

Meanwhile, the director of the nationalized wholesale marketing firm Agencias Graham, Luis Inostroza, who apparently had taken the statements of cabinet minister Flores seriously, took a census in a few districts and issued provisions cards to each family, immediately beginning the distribution of 15,000 to 20,000 "people's baskets" containing 20 to 30 items. The National Secretariat for Marketing and Distribution quickly rejected this initiative and asked the government to dismiss the director of the Agencias Graham, which it did shortly after. This dismissal created a major incident: more than 500 residents who had received "people's baskets" held a meeting in the offices of the Agencias Graham. They obtained the dismissal of Inostroza's replacement, but failed to have Inostroza restored to his post. Later, in order to head off initiatives of this kind, General Bachelet, with the permission of the government, asked for the resignation of all the directors and deputy directors of the public distribution companies, naming military men and "technicians" to replace them. For his part, Minister of the Economy Orlando Millas, a member of the "C"P Secretariat, publicly reaffirmed that the "rationalization" (not rationing) of product distribution was the exclusive responsibility of the National Secretariat for Marketing and Distribution. In addition, President Allende spoke to the country on the radio and television networks at the beginning of April to state that there existed "a campaign, not one of rumours, but which responds to the determination of a section of citizens or workers to carry on an escalation aimed at taking over certain factories, certain companies, basically the state and private distribution companies". He declared in this regard: "On several occasions I have spoken to the workers to make them understand that their rights are one thing (and no one is going to teach me to respect them), but the commitment I have made with my conscience to implement the Popular Unity programme has nothing to do with the precipitancy, demagogic attitudes, improvization or spontaneity into which some sections of the workers have thought best to fall." *(97)* This was to throw a bucket of cold water on the popular mobilization to fight speculation that cabinet minister Flores' speech had given rise to, and on initiatives that had been taken in certain sectors to distribute essential commodities directly to the population.

However, the government's attitude of capitulation in the face of the protests aroused by the modest and timid attempt to control distribution in no way appeased this attack. In mid-May, the National Party presented Parliament with a charge under the constitution aimed at impeaching the Minister of the Economy, whom they accused of illegally creating the JAP's and the National Secretariat for Distribution and Supply. At the beginning of June, the Christian Democratic Party joined in this accusation. On June 20, the minister was suspended from his post by Parliament, and was finally dismissed on July 5.

Thus the government floundered, reduced to utter impotence because of its reformist nature, in the face of the speculation and shortages that cruelly hit the workers and middle sections. Thus, even before the uncontrollable inflation was unleashed, the opposition succeeded in cancelling out the effects of the income redistribution which had been implemented during the first year of the government for the benefit of the workers. The workers were earning nominally more money, but it was only with luck and at great sacrifice that they could buy essential goods at the official prices. In general they were forced to pay the high black market prices. This affected in an even more widespread and intensive way the "white collar" workers and the middle sections in general, who were at the mercy of the speculators, for they did not live in the camps or in the "emergency" housing estates *(callampas)* which were organized so as to be able to defend themselves up to a point against speculation and to collectively demand supplies.

In this way, large sections of the population underwent great sacrifices, which in the case of the workers were added to exploitation, to satisfy even their vital needs: fuel for cooking and heating, bread, milk, fruit and vegetables, clothing. Some commodities, meat for example, practically disappeared from the diets of the workers and even of large middle sections. At certain times things got to the point of replacing sugar with saccharine in the restaurants and tea parlors.

Furthermore, beginning in 1972, to this acute shortage was added an intensified inflation that became virtually uncontrollable in the last months of the UP government, with price increases reaching more than 1 percent per day. In addition, public transport, which was absolutely inadequate and half paralyzed due to the difficulty of importing spare parts, was literally assaulted at each station by avalanches of people, some of whom hung onto the windows like human bunches of grapes. Transportation from the workplace to home thus became another hardship, added to that of the food queue. All this, seasoned with the opposition's propaganda blaming the government for everything and showing that "this is socialism for you", gave rise to much discontent against the government. Even amongst the sections which were sympathetic to the government, the idea spread that "whatever might put an end to this unbearable situation would be better than what we are going through". This state of mind was just what the putschists needed to carry out their plans; it is what the CIA itself admitted having encouraged and financed in order to "destabilize" the Allende government, although of course the CIA did not limit itself to creating a current of opinion in favour of the fascist coup d'état.

Chapter VIII
The Development of
State Capitalism

One of the fundamental aspects of the Popular Unity programme, precisely the one it used to pass off its state capitalism as "socialism", was the nationalization of the key sectors of the economy. Essentially, these sectors were: industrial monopolies, some wholesale trading companies, private national and foreign banks, as well as some mining and public utility companies that were in the hands of U.S. corporations.

1. Procedures for the Nationalization of Companies

The procedures for state control of these companies were of two kinds: the purchase of shares from their owners by the state, or requisition or intervention. Given the legalistic spirit that pervaded the Popular Unity, buying shares from the owners of these companies could only be done if the latter agreed to sell them. In some cases (such as that of the big paper industry monopoly), the opposition waged a campaign to block the sale of shares and even raised funds to offer a better price than the government for shares belonging to the people who might be tempted to accept official offers. In general, in order to set promotional precedents which would encourage other shareholders to sell, the government paid high prices for the shares it bought, and thus took a step down the steep slope leading to the exhaustion of its financial resources. Simple arithmetic sets the expenditures for buying the banks, mines and other companies in U.S. hands at some $100 million up to December 1971, without counting the debt of the big copper industry which the government took over on expropriation. The same source (cf. *Causa Magazine,* No. 22, December 1971-January 1972) estimates the amount paid in 1971 to expropriate domestic banks and factories and to indemnify expropriated landlords at some $200 million.

As for the companies whose owners had no intention of selling, "legal expedients" permitting requisition or control of them were used to subject them to state management. These "legal expedients" consisted of applying an old decree (number 520) brought down by a *de facto* government which had existed in 1932. This decree allowed the state to take over management of a company paralyzed by a labour conflict and have it operate under the management of a government delegate. It also allowed the state to requisition basic industries which were not adequately supplying the consumer market. However, neither requisition nor managerial control made the state the owner of the company.

Up to the coup d'état, the government succeeded in nationalizing some 90 companies and most banks through the procedure of buying shares. In the same period, it requisitioned about 170 companies and took control of 155. In this fashion, the state went from 40 percent control of the national product through 43 state enterprises before Allende's victory, to 60 percent control of the national product on the basis of 415 companies bought, requisitioned or controlled.

In 1971, before the crisis was unleashed, the Popular Unity government made its most spectacular progress in state control of enterprises. By one or another of the procedures mentioned, about 70 industrial enterprises were brought under state control or ownership. Amongst them were the big textile firms, the beer and cement monopolies, the copper and steel smelting companies, and several electronic firms. In addition, 16 domestic and foreign private banks were bought out, with the result that 90 percent of banking credits came under state control. Through these measures, the government controlled 85 percent of the country's exports and 45 percent of its imports at the end of 1971.

By vigorously expanding the public sector, the Popular Unity government thought it could get hold of a decisive lever in the economic (and political) development of Chile; it also thought it was obtaining the means to plan and guide this development. One of these means was control of the major part of the surpluses, which could be invested in the country. ODEPLAN refers to "the extraordinary responsibility incumbent on enterprises in the social ownership sector, for they must generate savings equivalent to about 10 percent of their product. This goal," ODEPLAN adds, "may seem exaggerated, but we must remember that it is in this sector that the biggest and most productive enterprises and industrial complexes are concentrated. However, this implies an extraordinary responsibility for the workers and managers in this sector: they must realize that on their ability to create surpluses depends the chance for the whole country, once freed from the bonds of imperialism and the monopolies, to make major, sustained progress in its level of production." *(98)*

In a veritable medieval alchemist's dream, the UP tried to transform a capitalist society dependent on imperialism, one which moreover had a low level of economic development, into a state capitalism headed by a new bureaucratic bourgeoisie. All this without first taking power away from the old exploiters. Like a winner in an honest poker game claiming what is owed to him, the UP tried to expropriate the enterprises of the old exploiters following its electoral victory. It attempted to take away the wealth of the sections that were really dominant, using its own legal and institutional instruments and through the classical economic mechanisms at work in capitalist society, that is, without making the radical rupture with these institutions and economic mechanisms that a real political conquest of power would imply. The UP thus forgot (amongst other things) the influence possessed by those who exercise their class dictatorship through the control of power, when they use these laws and institutions as well as their economic strength. It was this strength and this influence over the whole of society, conferred by the conquest of power, that made it possible in China, for example, to dry up one of the most acute inflationary situations ever seen in the entire world within a few months after the victory of the revolution. However in Chile, this influence conferred by power worked in the opposite way, for it was held precisely by the forces that the UP wanted to wipe out.

Such a plan by the UP could only have been born out of the convergence of the Machiavellism of some with the utopianism of others: of the Machiavellism of those who knew, like the pro-Soviet "communist" leaders, that they could not mobilize the people in a revolutionary way for their plan of state capitalism; and of the utopianism of those who honestly (as seems to have been the case with President Allende himself) let themselves be fooled by the former and by their own social-democratic training and who thought it was possible to advance in this manner towards socialism.

However, Chile is a country with a poorly developed economy, distorted by imperialist domination. Therefore, it is possible to advance towards socialism only by first expropriating the means of production held by imperialism, the big bourgeoisie of the cities and the big landlords of the countryside. In order to do this, it is essential to seize political power and smash the bourgeois state apparatus as well as the ferocious armed and unarmed resistance of the reactionaries. This can only be achieved by winning over the petty and middle bourgeoisie, by putting them under the leadership of the proletariat, and by neutralizing those who cannot be mobilized against the main enemies. The united front around the proletariat can only be built on the basis of the strength and power acquired by the proletariat and peasantry in their revolutionary struggle. This strength and power will enable the proletariat, while exercising firm control over the non-expropriated bourgeoisie and imposing its own conditions on it, to offer it reliable guarantees of survival and development. Finally, the march towards socialism is only possible by making serious efforts and sacrifices, on the basis of developing the political consciousness of the broad masses, in order to move forward by relying on one's own forces. Only people who have gone through such experiences of struggle and who do not have any doubts that they have seized power and really control it (since they fought for it) will be ready to make every sacrifice to develop the economy of the country and consolidate its independence.

As nothing like this had taken place in Chile and as political power (after Allende's election) still remained in the hands of the long-time reactionaries, it was decided to take a demagogic attitude towards the workers and the middle sections of manufacturers, tradesmen and farmers. Since the Popular Unity government's base of support was precarious and was not derived from the fact that the people had fought for power and seized it, the government continued to provide incentives "from the outside", as is traditionally done with an electoral clientele. From there stem, during the first year of the government, the largely artificial promotion of full employment, the accelerated redistribution in favour of the workers, the equally artificial curbing of inflation through the administrative control of prices and the subsidies for basic necessities, and later on, in order to cope with the unsatisfied demand stimulated in this manner, the intensification of consumer goods imports at the expense of foreign exchange reserves. This is not to suggest that such measures (amongst others) for the benefit of the population would not be just and necessary after the victory of a genuine revolution, but that they would have been taken in a completely different context. They would have been implemented by means of an implacable expropriation, without compensation, of the means of production held by the most powerful internal reactionaries and imperialists, thus paralyzing their capacity to sabotage the economy, which had devastating effects in Chile. They would have been accompanied (thanks to the efficient mechanisms made available by political power) by the control and recuperation of the huge profits made by the private firms following the expansion of the people's consumption. They would have been accomplished by making compulsory the reinvestment of most of these profits, by preventing the exodus of capital abroad, by restricting imports to what is strictly necessary, and by fiercely opposing speculation and hoarding. This could have been done by ensuring a genuinely productive use of the credits granted, which in large proportion were used for speculation. They would have been implemented by preventing the growth of a new voracious bureaucratic bourgeoisie which was snatching up an important portion of the surplus-value produced by the workers. All this is given as an example of what could have been achieved with a policy apparently similar to that of the Allende government if political power had really been seized. However, none of this was possible within the framework of the reformist and legalist logic based on fictitious political power which was characteristic of the opportunist plan tried out by the "C"P leaders through the Popular Unity.

On the other hand, a genuine seizure of political power would have allowed the development, from within the people themselves, of a political consciousness sufficiently high to permit the implementation of measures benefiting the people, in accordance with the economic development of the country, ensuring its solidity and continuity. One should not forget that in Chile, the per capita income was $792 a year in 1972, and that the problem of raising the general standard of living of the people could therefore not be solved by a simple redistribution of income. Even an imaginary egalitarian redistribution of income among the 10 million Chileans (with the absurd assumption that no deductions would be made for capital accumulation and other productive expenditures), would barely give every Chilean some $66 a month. While expropriating the means of production held by the main internal and foreign exploiters, it is also absolutely necessary to make tremendous efforts in order to promote accelerated and all-sided economic development. Such a development can only be achieved when the people spend maximum energy, when they are absolutely certain that this is done in their own interest, that is, only after they have seized and actually control political power. In such a case, which has certainly nothing to do with the phony "socialism" of the USSR and its satellites, the "spirit of initiative" lauded by the sycophants of capitalism as the motive force of progress is not exhibited by only a tiny handful of exploiters but by millions of people making up the broad masses. It is not the consequence of egoist profit-making aspirations, but is inspired by the concern for the collective interests of society.

However, when the Popular Unity and its government launched its campaign for redistribution of incomes, full employment, price control, consumer goods imports, loosening credit for manufacturers, broadening the public sector and agrarian reform (together with the purchase of shares and the compensations that followed), they did so without any real power for controlling the backlash that these measures were to generate on the part of the bourgeoisie, the petty-bourgeoisie and even large sections of the workers. Relying on electoralist political methods, which are very similar to the advertising methods of the consumer society, they believed that their stuff would be bought. Subjectively, they thought that the facilities granted would induce the non-monopolistic bourgeoisie to invest in their businesses, that the expansion of consumption would get the merchants interested in vigorous normal development of their activities, in harmony with the official policy, and finally that the full employment and redistribution of income policies would make the workers the most solid bulwark of the government. According to this idyllic theory, the entire huge initial expenditure incurred by the government in the implementation of the policy was supposed to be recovered through the development of powerful state and private industry, trade and productivity.

However, as we have already pointed out, the non-monopolistic bourgeoisie, which the government hoped to influence by means of simple economic incentives, basically behaved according to a political criterion (a reactionary political criterion) and moved over, right from the beginning, to those who actually controlled political power. Worse, it took advantage of all the facilities granted by the government as well as the serious shortage problems which appeared later, without in any way responding to the illusory expectations of the government. Finally, incapable of realizing its reformist pipe dreams, the government was forced to pay out of its pocket (i.e. out of the workers' pockets) for the efforts it had made to offset its lack of real political power with economic incentives. It was forced to break into the funds allocated for investments, into the money reserves and even into the profits of the state enterprises, sacrificing the savings, surpluses and investments of the state which were supposed to play a leading role in the economy. Later, when these resources were depleted, the government stubbornly stuck to this policy, which had failed to mobilize anyone, and began to print money in order to continue these incentives. Inflation was thus generated on a scale never before seen in the history of Chile (the Military Junta has done much worse since it took over).

In this manner, faced with an excessive demand, not only could the government not rely on private investments and the stimulation of industry necessary for coping with it, but it also largely paralyzed public investments, which in Chile, accounted for over 75 percent of total investments in the country. Chilean state investments depended on foreign credits, most of which, as we have seen, had been blocked. They also depended on the profits derived from exports, which had been seriously affected by the drop of the copper price, by declining production in the mines and by the skyrocketing prices of everything Chile imported. Finally, they depended on tax revenues, also affected by the parliamentary sabotage of laws on finance by the employers' strikes and by the uncontrollable speculation which gripped the economy. To illustrate the only one of these three aspects which it is possible to quantify, we can point out that the 1971 Act to Readjust Remunerations, because of Parliament's rejection of the financing proposed by the government, only obtained some 18.4 percent of the necessary financing. The 1972 legislation got 22.4 percent. Tax revenues decreased from 83.7 percent (of the total budget) in 1970, to 69.7 percent in 1971 and 58.3 percent in 1972. It was therefore useless to dream about the initial plan of playing a leading role in the economy through an important policy of state investments. The latter, which represented 26.9 percent of the total in 1964-1970, dropped to 22.4 percent in 1971 and to 17 percent in 1972. The previously accumulated reserves and (later) the printing of money hardly succeeded in preventing a more rapid decline of the economy and in supporting a system of gratuities which was believed to be an instrument for controlling political power that had not been won.

In addition, the enterprises taken over by the state were either bought at high prices, or requisitioned or controlled through the "legal channels", with all the obstacles and difficulties that these questioned procedures implied: restricted rights over the enterprises, constant legal disputes with the owners, and, finally, ever more acute contradictions with the Contraloria, with the Parliament and with the courts. These state organs, not satisfied with verbal opposition to the use of these nationalization procedures, took stiff measures to block their administration. They ordered that enterprises be restored to their former owners and went so far as to imprison managers or government representatives who opposed police intervention for such restitution. In this manner, instead of increasing the strength of the government-controlled sector and helping to solve problems, every new extension of the public sector resulted in bigger deficits, additional unchecked issues of currency, and more conflicts with the organs of power controlled by the reactionaries, further revealing the weakness of the government and the failure of its policy.

2. Some Data Concerning the Fiscal Crisis

Because of the extremely acute struggle that existed between the opposition and the Popular Unity government, and because of the plan of the former to discredit the latter so as to "destabilize" it, the data provided by the opposition forces about the crisis affecting the Allende government are generally exaggerations of reality. On the other hand, the data supplied by the government for purposes of defending itself tend to hide the reality and to belittle the crisis. Despite this, the crisis reached such proportions that it was hardly necessary to exaggerate it and impossible to hide it from public opinion. Since the very experience of the Popular Unity and its government is a highly controversial matter, we have chosen to report both the data of the opposition and the official figures concerning this crisis. These data will give an idea of the torrential drain of financial resources that resulted from this attempt (bound to fail) at overthrowing the ruling classes by following a reformist road.

Let us first deal with the fiscal deficit. In one of its bulletins, the Central Bank, the state body responsible for regulating finances, talks about a 2 percent decrease in the 1971 tax revenue, accompanied with a rise of 47 percent in expenditures for a total gross fiscal deficit of 9,330 million escudos for the year. *(99)* In the middle of 1972, the Industrial Development Society, an opposition organization comprised of the main manufacturers, forecasted a total deficit of 18 billion escudos by the end of the year. In mid-December 1972, José Musalem, Christian Democratic opposition parliamentarian, spoke of a fiscal deficit of 12 billion escudos in 1972 and claimed that the 1973 deficit would reach 50 billion escudos. *(100)* Finally, the Minister of Finance imposed by the Military Junta, Lorenzo Gotuzzo, said in October 1973 that the deficit for that year could be calculated at 148.4 billion escudos. *(101)*

Concerning the balance of payments deficit, the Central Bank recognized as early as in the middle of 1971 that reserves had fallen by $156 million between September 1970 and April 1971. *(102)* In December 1971, the Christian Democratic parliamentarian Andrés Zaldivar, former Minister of Finance in Frei's government (a position that he used to launch an alarmist campaign orchestrated by the CIA just before Allende took over in order to intensify the crisis), declared that: "the balance of payments deficit is $350 million, one of the highest that Chile has ever recorded." He claimed that "the government has eaten up $450 million from the reserves". *(103)* In general, the observers of both the opposition and the Popular Unity recognize that the 1971 deficit was a little over $300 million. As for 1972, Alfonso Inostroza, Chairman of the Central Bank, reported that the year-end balance of payments deficit would reach $350 million. *(104)* Finally in February 1973, a leak of information (for which a section of MAPU, a member party of the UP, has since claimed responsibility) revealed that on January 3, 1973, the foreign exchange reserve reached zero and that President Allende, during his visit to the USSR, had obtained dollars for four additional months only.

As for the expansion of the money supply caused by the uncontrolled issues made by the government, Juan Dios de Carmona and José Musalem, rabid Christian Democrat opposition leaders, spoke in July 1971 of an issue of 6.1 billion escudos for the public sector between October 30, 1970 and April 1971. *(105)* At the end of 1971, *El Mercurio* mentioned some "international monetary experts" who allegedly claimed that Chile had doubled its money supply during the 1970-1971 fiscal year, raising it from 7,561 million escudos to 15,253 million. *(106)* The Central Bank bulletin, for its part, recognized in February 1972 that a daily increase of 11.2 million escudos had taken place in 1971. *(107)* Later in September 1972, Alberto Baltra, Senator of the Party of the Radical Left (PIR), an organization which the CIA admitted having financed and which left the UP for the opposition, claimed that the currency issues reached 8 billion escudos in 1970 and more than 28 billion on June 20, 1972, an increase of 250 percent. *(108)* Shortly after, the Central Bank, at the request of the upper house officially announced that the 1972 issues amounted to 36,367 million escudos, representing an increase of 171.4 percent compared to the 1971 issues. *(109)* Finally, the spokesmen of the Military Junta responsible for discrediting the Allende government talk about 20 billion escudos being issued in 1971 ($200 million at that time) and 216 billion during the eight months Allende was in power in 1973. *(110)*

As for the drop in production and the losses in the state enterprises, the data, interpretations and sources are most varied. We report here some data published in the press and some aggregate figures.

In January 1972, David Silberman, general manager of the state firm Cobre Chuqui, who was assassinated by the Military Junta, admitted that a 9 percent fall in production had taken place in 1971 at Chuquicamata, El Teniente and El Salvador. For these three copper mines, the biggest in the country, production fell from 553,000 tons to 483,000 tons. *(111)* At the same time, the opposition press reported that 3,000 workers had been hired, bringing their total to 9,500. In June 1972, the executive vice-president of El Teniente mining corporation, Armando Arancibia, spoke of a deficit of $18,339,240.45 in 1971. In January 1973, the Copper Corporation (CODELCO) announced a loss of $500 million in its 1971-72 income. *(112)*

As for the Chilean Chemical Mining Corporation (SOQUIMICH), involved in saltpetre extraction and bought from the U.S. for $11 million, they talk about a loss of 12 million escudos in 1971, a loss that the opposition estimates at 42 million escudos. From November 1970 to March 1973, 732 additional workers were hired. *(113)*

In June 1972, William Jalaf, president of the Chilean Textile Institute, claimed that the Sumar textile factory (one of the biggest in the country) alone lost some 7 to 8 million escudos a month. *(114)* In February 1973, the CORFO Textile Committee secretary Andrés Van Lacker claimed that the total loss of the nationalized factories reached one billion escudos in 1972. *(115)*

On November 20 1972, the opposition press reported that as of October of that year, losses of 133 million escudos had been registered by FENSA, a large steel factory manufacturing home electrical appliances. Almost half of these losses ($63 million) were allegedly due to a mistake by one of the government managers, who had signed sales contracts at old prices for a two-and-a-half month period. A fall of 35 percent in the production capacity of this firm was also mentioned. Its total capital was 180 million escudos. *(116)*

As for the state wholesale trade corporation DINAC, its balance sheet of June 1972 reports losses of over 20 million escudos and debts (including for taxes and social allowances) of 172 million escudos. Its authorized capital reached 50 million escudos. (117)

In February 1973, Guillermo Gacitua, president of the labour union at CHILECTRA, the state corporation for the distribution of electrical energy, stated that this firm lost 60 million escudos in 1971 and 150 million in 1972. *(118)*

In the middle of 1972, a special commission appointed by the Chamber of Deputies to study the situation in the state-owned or -controlled companies published a report. It said, among other things, that there were 263 state-controlled enterprises and that 47 percent of all factories were already in the hands of the state. It also said that the losses accumulated until then by these factories amounted to 23 billion escudos. *(119)*

The state organization responsible for planning (ODEPLAN) admitted that the public sector of the economy had recorded losses of 21,871 million escudos in 1972. *(120)*

For 1973, we only have the statistics of the Military Junta, which is interested in discrediting the Allende government to the maximum in order to justify its arbitrary measures and the intensification of the crisis and superexploitation under its yoke, as well as the data provided by politicians such as Alberto Baltra, a supporter of the junta. Baltra talks about losses of 21 billion escudos in 1973 in four companies of the public sector (The United Breweries, the Pacific Steel Corporation, the National Mining Company and the Chilean Chemical Corporation). *(121)* He also mentions losses of 2.149 billion in eight state textile firms. The Military Junta estimates the total 1973 losses of the firms under state dependence at 175.809 billion escudos, some 27 billion more than total fiscal deficits, which amounted to 148.400 billion escudos. *(122)*

The causes for the deficits of the state-controlled enterprises are of various types. First of all, these losses are linked with the general crisis of the economy, which forced the government to break into its funds to cover its deficits instead of using them to promote new investments. They are also related to the fact that the government introduced extremely low official prices for the goods produced by these enterprises in order to artificially slow down inflation and to promote the expansion of consumption together with investments in the private sector. They are also due to factors of a social nature, such as the lack of experience of the state officials in the management of these enterprises; the absence of a genuine political commitment by the workers to the process, which often gave rise to open indiscipline; the sabotage or resignations of many reactionary technicians; speculation and black marketeering engaged in by many top sections of the bureaucracy; and the fall in productivity caused by excessive hiring aimed at reducing unemployment. CORFO itself said in its 1972 annual report on the nationalized firms that: "The productivity per man decreased because of excessive employment last year."

Finally, the crisis of imports also affected the deficit in the public sector: it prevented the timely renewal of machinery, the importation of spare parts and raw materials essential for some enterprises.

The deficits of the state enterprises (which were supposed to bring a surplus) and of the budget in general were met by the government with uncontrolled issues of currency, which by the end of 1971 unleashed increasingly uncontrollable inflation. According to the National Institute of Statistics, a 22.7 percent rate of inflation was registered for the month of August 1972, the highest monthly rate in 20 years. (123) During the first eight months of the same year, inflation reached 63.5 percent. In August 1972, the opposition in the Chamber of Deputies spoke of 243 percent inflation in the first 20 months of the UP government. (124) In November 1972, the opposition press spoke of 130.2 percent inflation for the first 10 months of the year, the highest inflation ever known until then in Chile. (125) For the previous 12 months, the press estimated that the cost of living had gone up by 195.5 percent. (126) Finally, the National Institute of Statistics reported in July 1973 a 283.4 percent increase in the cost of living during the previous 12 months. *(127)* Therefore, according to the official indices, which as is well known, tend to hide the real extent of the cost-of-living increase, the cost of living rose by almost 1 percent per day in 1973. In any case, this inflation rate was far surpassed by the Military Junta, whose official 1973 index for the rise in the cost of living was 508 percent, and whose real inflation rate as everyone knows, exceeds 2 percent per day.

Part IV
The Bourgeois Institutions Confronted by the Allende Government

Chapter IX
The Opposition by Parliament, the Contraloria and the Courts

Parliament was another bastion of the ruling classes that the Popular Unity and its government had to confront. Following the parliamentary elections of 1969, the composition of Parliament, at the time Salvador Allende took over the Presidency of the Republic, was as follows: Out of a total of 150 members, the opposition had 89 (34 National Party and 55 Christian Democrats), the government controlled 61 members (24 Radical Party, 15 Socialist Party and 22 "Communist" Party). The government was also in the minority in the Senate; out of a total of 50 senators it had only 21. In 1971, before the economic crisis made itself felt, the government succeeded in increasing its parliamentary representation by winning the support of some Christian Democratic senators and members of Parliament who broke with their party and joined the government forces, followed by a group of party members. In this way the government came to have 90 representatives out of a total of 200 in the two houses. In 1972, its parliamentary representation dropped again to one-third of the total, as 22 Radical Party representatives went over to the opposition. Finally, in the March 1973 elections, the government received 44 percent of the vote, thanks to a determined electoral fight that gobbled up tens of millions of dollars and on the basis of artificially maintaining the fiction of nearly full employment. This was done at the price of aggravating the economic crisis and the budgetary deficit to the utmost. Nevertheless, the government's representation in the two houses fell to 83 representatives (7 Radicals, 7 Independents, 35 Socialists and 34 "Communists"). The opposition, on the other hand, although it did not obtain the two-thirds majority that it had its eye on in order to legally impeach President Allende, elected 117 representatives (69 Christian Democrats, 42 National Party and

6 Radical Party).

Taking advantage of its majority, the opposition systematically and implacably used Parliament, as well as all the other institutions of bourgeois rule that it controlled, as instruments to obstruct all the government's plans. It used and interpreted to its convenience the prerogatives of Parliament and the existing laws in order to intensify the economic crisis, to prevent the government from finding a legal way out of its problems, and to discredit it with a view to overthrowing it. Thus the opposition spoke constantly and with the most thorough cynicism of the so-called "illegal acts" of a government that was completely attached to legalism, while at the same time it backed all sorts of illegal activities conducive to its overthrow: employers' strikes, sabotage, arms trafficking, assassinations, the hoarding of products and, as the culmination of all this, the execution of the fascist coup d'état, which completely cancelled all the legal guarantees in the name of which it supposedly was fighting the Popular Unity government. It was a really disgusting spectacle to see all the bourgeois politicians speak in emphatic and solemn tones of the necessity of respecting the law and the constitution (which they alone were violating) while they feverishly prepared the advent of the fascist hangmen who would establish as a system of government, with the complicity of these bourgeois politicians and in their filthy interests, torture, massacres, imprisonment and the abolition of all legal and constitutional guarantees.

1. Parliamentary Obstruction

One of the procedures (perhaps the least injurious) used by the opposition majority in Parliament to combat the government was the launching of bills designed to restrict the traditional prerogatives of the Executive, or other propositions which forced the government to use its right of veto. This right consisted in the ability of the President of the Republic to cancel, add to or modify certain aspects of laws approved by a simple majority in Parliament. To overrule the veto, Parliament had to obtain a two-thirds majority on the original proposition. If a two-thirds vote was not obtained, the President's decision stood. Although the opposition knew in advance that the Executive would veto propositions that were reactionary or contrary to its policy, it forced it to use its right of veto. This served the opposition's propaganda, which pictured the government as being against the legislative work of Parliament, as fighting against the so-called "civic majority" represented by the parliamentary majority.

On August 20, 1971, for example, the government was forced to veto a bill from the Chamber of Deputies by means of which the opposition intended to deprive the President of the Republic of his power to determine the characteristics of the coin and bank notes printed in Chile. In September 1971, the government had to veto an opposition bill which would set up national television networks at the expense of the public treasury, with the goal of extending the influence of one of the opposition's most powerful means of anti-government propaganda, channel 13' television, throughout the country. Presented as "an attack on freedom of expression", the veto against this bill was intensively used by the opposition during the entire term of the Allende government to develop protests by students and other sections of the population.

With respect to bills proposed to Parliament by the Executive, the opposition's tactic was to oppose their inclusion on the agenda, to indefinitely postpone voting on them by means of delaying tactics, or to completely change their content during article-by-article discussion. Thus, for example, the budgetary bills were systematically modified as to their financing. Every time the government tried to fight inflation in financing the budget and to readjust wages and salaries by taxing the highest-paid groups, the parliamentary majority passed these bills with inflationary financing based on taxation of everyday consumer goods. In the same way, Executive proposals (contained in budgetary or other bills) increasing taxes on the richest groups and on luxury goods were cancelled. Parliament also rejected a law against tax fraud, which in 1971 was greater than the total budgetary deficit for the same year. On another occasion, the budget of the state railway was cut, fitting in with the employers' strikes aimed at sabotaging transportation; funds for literacy work were withdrawn; and the budget of the Production Development Corporation (CORFO), a key organization for economic development in the public sector, was cut by two billion escudos.

In June 1971, a government budgetary provision for the hiring of a thousand uniformed carabineros was rejected. The pretext used was that the government had to first "dissolve and disarm the armed groups (?) acting outside the Constitution". Thus the Executive's timid attempt to get reliable men into the police force through hiring failed.

The list of the various forms of obstruction against all the propositions tabled in Parliament by the government would be lengthy: this obstruction went to the extent of refusing to authorize ministers to travel abroad. Here we will merely cite some of the main bills rejected in Parliament by the opposition majority or changed in their essential content. It is not necessary to refer again to the bill against economic crime, mentioned in an earlier chapter, which was substantially changed into an anti-government bill, its original purpose having been completely transformed. On the other hand there was the Executive bill designed to reform the Political Constitution in order to create a unicameral Parliament: the Executive never even succeeded in having it voted on. A bill presented in December 1971, aimed at regulating the distribution of paper to newspapers by creating a National Paper Institute, met the same fate. In addition, the government's educational reform plan, called the "National Unified School" bill, was so furiously attacked by the opposition circles, not only through their propaganda instruments but also through mass street demonstrations of anti-government students, parents' associations and teachers, that the government was forced to completely bury it. Although the government backed down on this reform, the issue was used until the collapse of the government to bring large numbers of people in the field of education into the corporate and employers' movements to overthrow it. Lastly, a conciliatory bill which was presented by the "C"P leader and Minister of the Economy, Orlando Millas, without consulting the other Popular Unity parties, a bill considerably reducing the number of firms to be incorporated into the social sector of the economy, was also rejected by Parliament.

All this blind and rigid obstruction in Parliament exposed the illusions of those who believed in the lies spread by the "C"P leaders that it was possible to take advantage of these bourgeois institutions to advance toward "socialism", rather than destroying them as Marxism teaches. In no way was Parliament playing its accustomed role as a place where the interests of the various sections of the bourgeoisie were harmonized and conciliated in a fairly flexible manner. Because the plan for state capitalism disguised as socialism, advocated by the Popular Unity, threatened the interests of the most reactionary groups, which were in control of power, Parliament became a brick wall, indeed, a war machine against all the government's initiatives. In this stubborn and implacable opposition, it did not matter that the government measures were for the people or were designed to alleviate the acute economic crisis; it did not matter that these initiatives coincided with some points in the electoral programmes of the opposition parties. Only the goal of demolishing, obstructing, and condemning any solution to failure was taken into account, for this was necessary in order to overthrow the government.

2. Constitutional Indictments

Another method used by the opposition parliamentary majority to discredit the Allende government and upset the implementation of its plans was that of constitutional indictments against ministers of state and other trusted officials of the Executive. The opposition took advantage of the power given the Chamber of Deputies by Article 39 of the Constitution, to "Declare to be founded or unfounded indictments drawn up by at least ten of its members against the following officials: **a)** the President of the Republic . . . **b)** Minister of State, for the offences of: treason, extortion (abuse of power), misappropriation of public funds, corruption, infraction of the Constitution, violation of the laws, failure to apply the laws, and grave breach of the security and honour of the nation." If the indictments were approved, the Chamber had the prerogative of suspending the minister in question, after which the Senate had the power of removing him from office. These powers could be exercised independently of subsequent action by the courts against the accused. This procedure had the additional advantage of being not a complex system of indictment such as the one used in the courts but a mere judgement "in their soul and conscience" by the members of Parliament as to the infraction of Article 39 of the Constitution, a judgement made by a simple majority vote. The only reason the procedure was not used to impeach the President of the Republic was that in his case a two-thirds vote was required, something the opposition could never put together.

The procedure of constitutional indictments, extremely unusual in Chilean political practice (it was used only on rare occasions after the 1925 Constitution), became a powerful weapon against the Allende government. The indictments became progressively more numerous, in full coordination with the development of the legal and illegal offensive aimed at overthrowing the government. It was a question not only of hindering any stable and coherent government policy but also of showing clearly, alongside the likeminded activity of the Contraloria and the courts, *who* really controlled power in Chile. This trial of strength was of decisive importance in showing the extreme weakness and lack of real power on which the Popular Unity experiment was based and in encouraging the hesitant middle sections to unite with the subversive opposition led by the most reactionary forces (which they did).

The constitutional indictments began with the one presented on February 2, 1971 by the National Party against the Minister of Justice, Lizandro Cruz Ponce, alleging that certain amnesties granted to leftists imprisoned by the previous government were illegal and unconstitutional. This indictment failed because the Christian Democrats abstained from voting, maintaining that these amnesties came under the sole responsibility of the President of the Republic. Later, on March 10, the National Party presented another charge, this time against Labour Minister José Oyarce, "for abuse of power and violation of constitutional order". Oyarce had invoked the "legal loopholes" mentioned above to name administrators for certain factories. This charge also failed. However, on May 12, the intendant of Colchagua province was relieved of his duties for "abuse of power"; the pretext was the accidental death of a landlord who suffered a heart attack when his lands were expropriated.

The National Party, still alone in taking these initiatives, launched a constitutional indictment on September 8, 1971 against the Minister of the Economy, Pedro Vuskovic, for "abuse of power, violation of the laws and failure to apply the laws". As examples of these so-called violations of the law (which in reality were examples of the arbitrary class interpretation which the reactionaries put on the law), the National Party named the nationalization of the banks by direct purchase of their shares and the requisitioning of enterprises. This charge against Vuskovic (which failed for want of support by the Christian Democrats) was reiterated in December 1971 by the National Party, the hardest hit by the expropriations.

In December 1971, when the first symptoms of economic crisis under the Popular Unity administration made themselves felt, the Christian Democrats abandoned their previous position of abstaining on constitutional indictments. On December 2, 1971, it was the CDP that presented an indictment against Interior Minister José Toha, under the pretext that he was responsible for not having dissolved what were alleged to be armed groups affiliated with the government. These groups, according to the CDP, had assaulted participants in a demonstration organized by the opposition to protest against shortages. As might have been expected, the National Party joined in this charge on the following day. Finally, with the support of the CDP, this method of opposition initiated by the National Party won out, obtaining the majority vote in Parliament necessary to make the charges stick. Thus on January 6, 1972, the Chamber of Deputies approved the indictment against Toha by 80 votes to 59. Toha was immediately suspended from his duties under Article 39 of the Constitution, as interpreted, of course, according to the interests of the rightist opposition. On January 22, the Senate brought the procedure of constitutional indictment to its culmination, removing the Minister of the Interior from office for so-called "infractions of the Constitution, violation of the laws, failure to apply the laws, and grave breach of the security of the nation (?)". On January 3, a spontaneous mass demonstration was held outside the Presidential Palace in protest against the suspension of Toha. The participants in the demonstration wanted to march on Parliament and take it. The President of the Republic calmed them down, declaring: "Our strength is political consciousness . . . When the time comes for the people to adopt a different attitude, I will be the one to give the call and to take on all the responsibility." However, as we know, this call never came; the only calls that were heard were for conciliation, always aimed at holding back the fighting spirit of the people. In the end, President Allende only responded to the dismissal of his minister with another equally artificial manoeuvre, naming him Minister of National Defence in a timid attempt to salvage the government's prestige. The weakness of the official response allowed the opposition to turn its tactic of bringing down government ministers into a real sport, like a game of bowling.

On June 21, 1972, a Commission of Inquiry, named by the Chamber of Deputies in regard to a few pieces of baggage sent from Cuba that did not go through customs, charged the new Minister of the Interior, Hernan del Canto, with "offences and irregularities". On June 23, the National Party laid a constitutional charge against del Canto, adding on the accusation of "responsibility in common law offences of smuggling and tax fraud" and of "failure to apply the provisions for public order in the face of the illegal occupations". The document mentioned the occupation of land by the peasants and of factories by workers in labour disputes. In other words, this indictment was designed to clearly establish the government's "obligation" to repress any mass movement considered a threat to the interests of the ruling classes. On July 5, 1972, the Chamber of Deputies approved the charges against the Interior Minister for "having gravely compromised the security of the nation, infringed the Political Constitution of the state, violated the laws, failed to apply the laws and gravely abused his power". On July 27, with the ratification of the indictment by Senate, del Canto was removed from office. As can be seen, the essence of the charge was that he had not used the legal system to repress the people, a legal system designed to defend the interests of those who own the means of production. Thus the very policy of the government was labelled "illegal" to the extent that it did not repress certain forms of people's struggle. In this way, the Popular Unity government began to confront not only a number of institutions of bourgeois rule controlled by the most reactionary strata, but also a legislative system created to serve the interests of these strata. President Allende faced the dismissal of another of his ministers by transferring him to the position of Secretary General of the government. In the same stride and as part of the charges against the Interior Minister, Senate discharged the Intendant of Santiago from his post at the request of a special investigator appointed by the Court of Appeal, for having failed to repress the occupation of the court of Melipilla (a district near Santiago) by a group of peasants protesting against the arbitrary actions of the judge of the court. Shouting "Judges, sellouts, thieves, corrupt!", a crowd of workers and peasants assembled opposite the Parliament and court buildings to protest the dismissal of the Intendant and the Minister of the Interior. Fully expressing the sentiment of the people, a peasant leader said: "We have to unite to destroy the bastion of the 'momios', *(128)* the Parliament and bourgeois justice. To the swine in Parliament — with the respect due to swine, comrades — we say that they will be held accountable to the people for everything they do against us." The President of the Supreme Court, Enrique Urrutia Manzano, sent a protest to the President of the Republic regarding the demonstration held in front of the courts, and the latter replied by assuring him that such actions would not be repeated. Urrutia Manzano nonetheless insisted to the President: "Your Excellency states that Mr. President has forbidden the holding of public demonstrations in the area where this one took place, and in some cases has given the order that the workers not parade in these places. This Court is gratified that such is the case; but our satisfaction would be greater if the orders of Mr. President had actually been implemented in the specific case which concerns us. We hope", he warned in conclusion, "that in future there can be no infringement of orders coming from such a high place, even if such infringement is spontaneous or by surprise." *(129)* Urrutia Manzano and his confederates in what the peasant leader justly called the "bastion of the 'momios' ", the Supreme Court, made maximum use of this court to block any reform affecting reactionary interests and to offer judicial protection with impunity to fascist saboteurs and assassins. All this was done, of course, in the name of so-called "sacrosanct respect" for the existing laws. Their real "respect" for the constitution and the law was demonstrated after the coup d'état: they unconditionally upheld all the arbitrary, illegal and unconstitutional measures of the Military Junta. Urrutia Manzano exposed the real motives for all their actions when, immediately after the coup d'état, he had the supreme impudence to demand that the military restore to him his two large expropriated estates; he went by helicopter to take charge of his former properties, as payment for his services.

In August 1972, the National Party tried to use nothing less than the agricultural crisis as cause for a constitutional indictment against the minister concerned. This charge did not succeed at that time because of its crude pretext, but it was successfully repeated later on, as part of a collective indictment against several ministers. However in mid-October, as though not to lose the initiative, the opposition charged the Intendant of Bio-Bio province under the Constitution for having ordered the temporary closing of a radio station that was encouraging its listeners to join the illegal strike in transportation, commerce and other corporations, a strike being waged that month by the opposition with the express aim of overthrowing the government. The pretext for this charge was offered to Parliament by the Contraloria, which ruled that this order to close did not "conform to the law". On October 25, the Intendant of Bio-Bio was removed from office. It is obvious that Parliament, the Contraloria and the courts joined forces, raising a hundred and one legal quibbles to prevent the government from using the existing laws to defend itself, while they themselves actively used this legal system to serve their subversive plans to overthrow the government.

On the day the Intendant of Bio-Bio was removed from office, the Chamber of Deputies passed a resolution of protest because the government had forced the radio transmitters to broadcast a national programme dealing with the opposition strike. "The government", the resolution stated, "has constantly and repeatedly violated the provisions of the Constitution, even in matters so fundamental to a democracy as freedom of expression, thus placing itself outside the law. Such a situation of illegality alters and upsets the rule of law, compromises the security of the nation and threatens the social peace." *(130)* It would be difficult to imagine a more cynical and hypocritical statement. The opposition was invoking the Constitution, the laws, the rule of law and social peace to protest against a few timid measures, quite usual under all previous governments, which were designed to head off an openly subversive, putschist movement, a movement aimed (as events have shown) at completely destroying the entire legal and constitutional system!

On October 28, during the employers' strike, the opposition, united in the so-called Democratic Confederation (CODE), decided to indict under the Constitution no less than four ministers: the Ministers of the Economy, of the Interior, of Agriculture and of Education. The impeachment of these ministers was not carried through because the whole cabinet resigned on October 31. The opposition did not stop there, however, and on November 2, Senate removed the Intendant of Santiago from office for the alleged offences of "arbitrary detainment, prohibiting a demonstration, and threatening to occupy certain districts of Santiago".

The year 1972 closed with a constitutional indictment presented on December 13 by the National Party and the Radical Democratic Party against the Minister of Finance and member of the "C"P secretariat, Orlando Millas. He was accused of having taken reprisals against participants in the October 1972 strike. On December 28, which is celebrated as "Holy Innocents' Day" in Chile, the Chamber of Deputies suspended Millas from his duties by a vote of 75 to 42. President Allende, "castling" as usual when faced with constitutional indictments, named Millas Minister of the Economy and Fernando Flores, the leader of MAPU, Minister of Finance. On January 10, Senate ratified the constitutional charge against Orlando Millas, but his dismissal was inapplicable because he had been relieved of his duties as Minister of Finance.

On March 28, 1973, it was the Christian Democrats' turn to present a constitutional indictment against the new Intendant of Santiago, Jaime Faivovic, "for failure to fulfill his obligation to maintain the peace and public order". But the peace and public order were being disturbed basically by the fascist armed groups and by opposition students. On April 15, the Chamber of Deputies suspended Faivovic, and ten days later Senate removed him from office by a vote of 28 to 0. The government members no longer participated in debate on the indictments, since their arguments counted for nothing, the opposition's majority voting machine being the only factor at work.

On June 7, the Christian Democratic Party presented another constitutional indictment against Orlando Millas, this time as Minister of the Economy, "for unconstitutionally granting powers to the Boards of Supply and Prices (JAP's)". Millas, incidentally, was one of the champions in the "C"P leadership of the theory that it is possible to build "socialism" in Chile using the laws and institutions of the bourgeois society. On July 5, Senate removed him from office.

But that was not all. In May 1973, the opposition unleashed another offensive of strikes and violence designed to overthrow the government. The opposition's plan to disrupt the functioning of the government by impeaching minister after minister was part of this offensive. Thus, alongside the constitutional indictment against Millas, the Christian Democrats laid charges against the ministers of Labour and of Mines on May 24. Furthermore, as though all this was not enough, the National Party and CDP members presented a constitutional indictment on the same day against Interior Minister Gerardo Espinoza for having authorized a search of the Channel 6 television station of the University of Chile. On July 3, he was suspended by the Chamber of Deputies.

On August 2, the ministerial impeachment offensive continued in full coordination with the general offensive which one month later would overthrow the government: the Minister of the Interior, Carlos Briones, was indicted under the Constitution. The pretext, this time, was the "poor treatment" which some had allegedly inflicted on certain opposition members of Parliament by some carabineros.

Finally, on September 4, 1973, only one week before the coup d'état, the Christian Democratic Party presented a constitutional indictment against *all* the ministers of state, holding them responsible for not having put an end "to the unconstitutional and illegal acts" of which the opposition majority in the Chamber of Deputies had accused the government. The sole purpose of this indictment was to supply Pinochet and his fascist clique with a legal excuse to carry out the coup d'état.

3. The Christian Democrats' Constitutional Reform

Because of the decisive role it played as "legal" cover for the coup d'état, we have left to last our analysis of the plan for constitutional reform of the three economic sectors (public, mixed and private) which was put forward by Christian Democratic senators Hamilton and Fuentealba. In fact, the constitutional reform bill was supposed to be a veritable "act of surrender" imposed on the Popular Unity and its government. The bill transferred to Parliament, that is, to the opposition majority, the power to decide which companies could be incorporated into the public or mixed (partnership of state and private capital) sectors of the economy, and which had to remain in the private sector. This was supposing that the parliamentary majority was in the mood to enlarge the public and mixed sectors at all, for the bill was an obstacle that the opposition put in the way of any nationalization or transfer to the mixed sector of a private company. Moreover, the methods the Executive used to oppose this reform bill led to a serious jurisdictional conflict between the Executive and Parliament, the Contraloria and the Constitutional Court. This conflict was to serve as a pretext to declare the government "illegal" and "illegitimate" and to "justify" openly calling on the Armed Forces to overthrow it.

The constitutional reform bill was introduced on October 20, 1971 and approved by Congress in plenary session on February 19, 1972. In essence, the bill changed Article 10 of the Political Constitution, which guaranteed the right of property and established the procedure for nationalization of an asset in cases where it was considered to be "in the public interest". According to this article of the Constitution, no one could be deprived of his property except by virtue of a law and with compensation. But the article left the government the power to decide in each case, in accordance with the development of the country, the question of which assets, companies or means of distribution, production or financing it considered appropriate to expropriate for reasons of public interest; although such nationalization ultimately depended on the passage of a law, that is, on a parliamentary majority. The Christian Democrats' constitutional reform, however, was intended to "freeze" the procedures for nationalization once and for all. It required that a definition be given in law of the assets and means of production which *would be possible* to bring into the social sector of the economy and make state property, and of those assets which would constitute the mixed sector and be the joint property of the state and private owners; the rest would remain in the private sector.

Furthermore, taking away the ability of the state to nationalize private companies by buying their shares, the bill established that it was only through legislation that the state, municipalities and public sector bodies and companies could be authorized to purchase shares or titles belonging to private persons in order to nationalize their assets or means. Thus, even with respect to the companies defined by law under the reform as liable to be transferred into the state sector, the opposition blocked the procedure that the government had used to nationalize companies, that of buying their shares through financial bodies such as CORFO. With this provision, not only did the opposition annul the procedure that CORFO had used under different governments since its founding, but it also deprived the Executive of a right that every citizen in Chile enjoyed. What is more, once the state sector were defined, the approval of the opposition would be necessary for the transfer of each company, since the passage of a law, dependent on the majority in Parliament, was required.

In another point, the reform abolished all the provisions which directly or indirectly allowed for the nationalization of distribution, financial or other enterprises, assets or means of production. This was an attempt to void the government's application of what were called the "legal loopholes" to control certain companies by requisition or takeover. These loopholes had been furnished by the old Decree-Law 520 from 1932, which authorized the government to act if for various reasons a company was unable to supply the market.

Lastly, the Hamilton-Fuentealba reform retroactively annulled the nationalizations that the government had carried out by buying shares over a period of nearly six months. It declared "void and without effect the acts or agreements carried out or honoured by the state or by the bodies or entities which make up the state or which are under its control or dependent on it, from October 14, 1971 onward, to buy shares or bonds from private persons for the purpose of nationalizing or bringing under state control goods — or service-producing companies, without the express authorization of a law enacted in accordance with the stipulations of paragraph 16 of Article 44 of the Political Constitution of the state." This provision voided the nationalization of the cement monopolies, the numerous textile firms, the banks and many other companies that had been brought into the state sector through the purchase of shares. Not only did this violate the right already exercised by the Executive of buying shares in a company on the same terms as any citizen; but it also violated the right of the shareholders who had agreed to sell the state their shares.

In sum, we can say that this constitutional reform not only struck at the heart of the plans for the development of state capitalism that the Popular Unity and its government were making and implementing, but also represented a declared return from the presidential system to the parliamentary system, which had long ago been abolished in Chile. From this point of view, the reform would act as a real provocation by taking away a number of exclusive prerogatives of the Executive. Its acceptance by the government would have meant unconditional surrender. Apparently, therefore, the opposition was expecting the Executive to reject it. Given the ambiguity of the provisions of the Constitution as to the quorum required for Parliament to override an Executive veto, the rejection of the reform by the Executive would then lead to a confrontation between Parliament and the government, which is just what happened. This gave the opposition the opportunity to accuse the Executive of violating the Constitution. While the 1925 Constitution expressly required a two-thirds majority in Parliament to override a veto, the constitutional reform approved in January 1970 left the necessary proportion ambiguous. The opposition used this as grounds to maintain that, since the Constitution did not expressly require a two-thirds vote to override the veto of the original reform bill, "it must be understood" that a simple majority was enough. Amongst other arguments it gave in maintaining that a two-thirds majority was necessary, the government pointed to Article 108 of the Constitution, which stated in its first paragraph that "the reform of provisions of the Constitution will be governed by the same rules as a bill", these rules requiring a two-thirds majority in Parliament to cancel an Executive veto. However, it would be useless to try to determine whether the government or the opposition was in the right in this polemic on constitutional law, since the essence of the struggle clearly did not lie for either side in a problem of legal purism. What counted was the struggle for power, a confrontation between classes, and the legal arguments were only a pretext. The proof of this was that none of the opposition's "pure experts" in legal matters agreed with the government's thesis, and none of the government's experts shared the opinion of its opponents. The interpretation of this problem depended on concrete political interests.

The other "way out" remaining to the government under the Constitution in case of disagreement between the Executive and Parliament on constitutional reform was to call a referendum so that the citizens could decide the disputed points. However, when this possibility actually came up in 1972, 22 Radical Party members of Parliament who had supported the government had just gone over to the opposition, precisely because of the government's veto of the constitutional reform bill, thus reducing the government's representation in Parliament to one-third of the total. Because of this, the government, which was already on the defensive on many fronts, became even more fearful of defeat in a referendum, which it judged would be even worse than a defeat in Parliament. Incidentally, this refusal of the Executive to resort to a referendum in a matter concerning one of the fundamental aspects of the government's programme confirms our thesis on the weak base of support it had in its control of power and its resulting growing isolation from the masses and in particular from the middle strata.

On February 21, President Allende declared: "By virtue of the power conferred on me by the Constitution, I propose to Congress that it delete or alter all the provisions of the bill which entail denial of the prerogatives that no one has ever previously attempted to deny the Executive power." At the same time, he rejected the idea of calling a referendum and declared that he would resort to the arbitration of the Constitutional Court. The next day, the opposition members of Parliament rejected the idea that the Constitutional Court should solve a dispute between the majority in Parliament and the government, for this would imply recognition of a "superior authority" over and above the three branches of state power.

On April 6, 1972, the two ministers of the Radical Left Party (RLP), resigned and its members of Parliament went over to the opposition. The president of the RLP, Luis Bossay, said: "The problem of interpeting the Constitution, arising out of the veto of this kind of bill (referring to the CDP constitutional reform), has resulted in a jurisdictional conflict with unforeseeable consequences." Showing his agreement with the reform, he added: if the veto "was approved as it stands, this would mean that the small and middle producers would continue to be put in a position of total uncertainty and insecurity." Of course, the jurisdictional conflict that he saw coming had very "foreseeable" consequences for this sector and he wanted to join the reactionary opposition camp while there was time.

In June, President Allende began discussions with the Christian Democratic Party leadership with a view to reaching an agreement on the delimitation of the three sectors of the economy and thus avoiding the conflict that was looming. However, the only effect of the discussions was a two-week postponement of the vote in Parliament which was to reject the presidential vetoes of the reform bill. The discussions broke off at the end of June without reaching agreement on which enterprises would be amalgamated into the social sector, nor the executive prerogatives that were taken away in the reform bill. The truth is that the President of the Republic, trusting in the "constitutionalist" and "apolitical" nature of the Army High Command (a trust promoted by the "C"P leaders), still believed that he could count on enough room to manoeuvre to refuse a compromise with the Christian Democrats. Such a compromise would have meant giving up a number of aspects of the development of state capitalism or sharing it with the CDP.

At the beginning of July, the Executive vetoes were overturned by Parliament. In October 1972, the merchants, transport corporations, liberal professions and others who were staging a strike designed to overthrow the government, included in the demands they presented to the government the full promulgation of the constitutional reform, or, failing this, the calling of a referendum.

In May 1973, President Allende stated in a speech broadcast on the radio: "I am speaking to the country to inform you that yesterday I requested the involvement of the Constitutional Court. I asked it for a judgement on the position of Congress regarding the vetoes I used against the bill drawn up by two members of Parliament to change the Constitution. Congress' move is an obstacle to the formation of the social sector and consolidates the capitalist system. The procedure followed by the present majority in the two Houses holds a serious threat to the very essence of our institutions. Congress is attempting to ignore the stipulation of the Constitution which establishes that the will of the majority in Congress cannot take precedence over that of the head of state without a two-thirds vote of its members." President Allende then said clearly — and in this he was completely right — that for the Executive to accept a reform of the Constitution that it could only block if it had a parliamentary majority (since its vetoes could be overturned by a simply majority vote) would effectively mean turning over the government of the country to the opposition majority in Parliament. *And this was obvious, because all the powers of the Executive were determined by the Political Constitution of the state and could be taken away by constitutional reform. This included the stipulation that a two-thirds majority was needed to impeach and remove the President of the Republic.* While denying that the Constitutional Court was qualified to deal with this kind of problem, the opposition stated that to solve this sort of jurisdictional conflict, the Executive could call a referendum, which the President of the Republic was refusing to do "because he knows very well that he is governing against the will of the majority of the people".

On May 15, President Allende promulgated those articles of the constitutional reform with which the government agreed and sent the others, on which there was no agreement with the opposition, to the Constitutional Court. Two days later, the

Senate and Chamber of Deputies, through the opposition majority, declared the Constitutional Court unqualified to pronounce judgement on the disagreements between the Executive and Congress on matters of constitutional reform, and gave notice that any decision of this Court in the matter would be null, void and without effect.

At the end of May, the Constitutional Court declared itself unqualified to decide on the voting procedure for constitutional reform in Parliament. Previously, the government had stated: "In this event, neither of the powers involved in establishing the laws being able to impose its criterion of interpretation of the constitutional norms of procedure for bills reforming the Political Constitution, it is the sole responsibility of the President of the Republic to promulgate that part of the bill on which there is no disagreement with Congress, that is, to proceed with promulgation leaving aside the provisions which, although they were vetoed, were not reaffirmed by the two houses of Congress." In answer to this, the speaker of the Senate, Eduardo Frei, and the speaker of the House, Luis Pareto, jointly sent the text of the constitutional reform to the Controller General of the Republic, stating that a partial promulgation of the reform "would violate the clear and express provisions of the constitution", which established that if the government did not hold a referendum within a specified time, "the bill approved by Congress will be promulgated". However, this argument did not overcome the disagreement, since from the government's point of view the vetoed part of the bill had not been passed, as the vote to overrule the veto had not won a two-thirds majority.

The intransigence of the two sides in interpreting the powers of congress and the Executive, the two branches in which the opposition and the government respectively had concentrated the formal aspect of their struggle, moved the conflict onto the ground where power struggles are always settled in the last resort: onto the ground of force. This was just what the opposition wanted, because it was ready to settle the issue in its favour on this ground. On the other side, the government and the coalition supporting it were materially, politically and ideologically disarmed by the opportunist, pacifist and legalist sermons of the "C"P leaders, and continued to embroil itself in useless legal arguments, to foster hope that the Army would not take sides in the oncoming confrontation and indeed would prevent it, and to believe in a negotiated solution to the conflict. The demands of the opposition, however, always were more in the nature of an ultimatum based on force. The president of the Christian Democratic Party, Patricio Aylwin, stated in June 1973 that: "If President Allende is seeking social peace and wants to avoid civil war, he has the means to do so: to go to the people in the democratic manner to clear up the questions at issue." The basis of these threats was obviously not that the Christian Democrats or their allies in the opposition were prepared as civilian political forces to lead a civil war against the government, but that they were assured of the support of those who gave the orders to those who had the guns, the Armed Forces. Thus, the traitorous, tearful slogan given at that time by the "C"P leaders — "No to civil war" — neither moved nor frightened the civilian political forces of the opposition, who had men ready to take up arms for them; it only demobilized and tried to frighten the people, who could have fought against the military coup d'état.

On June 6, 1973, the constitutional time limit for the government to call a referendum expired. The final opposition offensive had already been unleashed, through strikes, sabotage, violence, street demonstrations, and finally, at the end of June, an attempted coup d'état by a tank regiment. On July 2, the Contraloria made its contribution to what served as a pretext to show that the government had "violated the Constitution": it rejected the Executive's partial promulgation of the constitutional reform. A National Party member of Parliament, Sergio Diez, declared: "This government is running out of legal loopholes. First it tried to use the Constitutional Court to keep itself afloat. When that body recognized it was unqualified, the government resorted to the Contraloria, which said that the attempt to partially promulgate the three sectors bill was unconstitutional ... The only thing left for it to do is to promulgate the reform completely or to place itself outside the Constitution." Juan Hamilton, the Christian Democratic senator, went even further than Diez, stating on July 5 that: "The government is incurring the charge of failure to apply the

Constitution by not having fully promulgated the constitutional amendment as soon as the Contraloria rejected its intention of promulgating it in part."

In fact, these were not the first statements tending to prepare public opinion for the removal of the government by the Armed Forces or for its resignation. There was a sustained campaign. This offensive began in April 1973, after the long summer vacation. Sergio Onofrio Jarpa, president of the National Party and an ex-Nazi, fired the first shot by declaring that: "The political immorality of the Popular Unity has shaken the Rule of Law in Chile . . . the time has come for Congress to analyze the consequences of the continual arbitrary, illegal and anti-democratic conduct of the government, and for it to declare that the latter *has irreversibly lost its authority and the legitimacy of its mandate."* (Our emphasis) Three days later, Jarpa's National Party colleague, Senator Francisco Bulnes, followed suit by stating: "Since the first centuries of the Christian era, jurists have maintained that a government of legitimate origin becomes illegitimate if it continually abuses power, violating the basic norms that it must obey. This is called 'illegitimate exercise', and unfortunately it is what is affecting Mr. Allende's government. We, citizens who want to live in a democracy, cannot continue to ignore *the illegitimacy of the government* or to consider it only academically. Against an illegitimate government which is heading straight toward the abolition of democracy and moreover is destroying Chile's economic heritage, we are forced to use all the means at our disposal that would not lead to a greater evil." (Our emphasis)

On May 28, the Supreme Court took after the government by declaring: "For the 9th time, this Supreme Court must inform Your Excellency of the illegal attitude of the administrative branch, which is illicitly intervening in judicial affairs, as well as of the obstruction by the Carabineros of orders emanating from the Criminal Court, which according to the law the Carabineros must execute without hindrance. All of this indicates open, obstinate rebellion against judicial decisions, heedless of the changes which such attitudes or omissions produce in the legal order; which means, moreover, that there is no longer merely a crisis in the Rule of Law, as we represented to Y.E. in our previous communication, *but an impending or imminent breach in the legal order of the country."* (Our emphasis) On the same day, the Corps of Generals and Admirals in Retirement from National Defence sent a letter to the President of the Republic, stating: "If the Constitution is interpreted in a tendentious manner or is not respected, *the resulting actions would be illegitimate,* which would amount to breaking the existing link between the authorities and the Armed Forces." (Our emphasis) "One can no longer maintain a detached attitude toward events in Chile, all the more so if one has worn the uniform of the homeland, for each must assume his responsibility before the severe judgement of history," the letter concluded.

In mid-June, the National Party published a statement in which it maintained that: "Legally and morally, *no one is obliged to respect nor to obey a government which is no longer legitimate."* (Our emphasis) It added: "Those who still believe that Mr. Allende's presidential mandate has not been vitiated by illegitimate exercise now have final proof that the validity of his mandate has come to an end: the President's refusal to fully promulgate the bill on the three sectors of the economy. Mr. Allende has deliberately and systematically violated his solemn promise to respect and apply the Constitution and the laws. It was this promise that enabled him to be elected President of Chile by the majority in the National Contress." The government replied to the National Party statement, which was published under the title "Mr. Allende Is No Longer the Constitutional President of Chile", by declaring that such a statement "constituted criminal subversion" and by ordering ministers, deputy ministers and intendants not to grant hearings to representatives of this party — as a response to such a seditious attitude.

The Christian Democratic Party maintained a slightly more cautious attitude at this time, even hoping for a government surrender in its favour. This political nuance was reflected in the agreement reached on July 12 by the Chamber of Deputies, which stated: "Whereas: H.E. the President of the Republic has given the order to occupy the factories in order to 'defend the government', and this order has been carried out by the Popular Unity parties . . . Faced with this position of open illegality in which the President of the Republic himself and all the members and parties of the government have put themselves, the Chamber of Deputies resolves to remind H.E. the President of the Republic *that he is putting himself in a position of open illegality* and that his attitude is leading the country to the brink of armed conflict . . ." This order to occupy the factories was given because of the spread of another strike of the employers and certain professional corporations in the framework of the final offensive to facilitate the military coup d'état. As a reproach to the weakness of the Christian Democrats' position, Senator Bulnes of the National Party maintained that: "Toward a government that has fallen into *unquestionable illegitimate exercise,* we, members of Parliament, cannot just gather up the legislative crumbs that the Executive throws us, while behind our backs it deals with very serious matters that should be the subject of legislation and violates the provisions of the law and the constitution on a daily basis . . . If we do not adopt in time all the positions that the constitution and the law authorize us to, we will be as guilty as those who are impelling this process forward." (Our emphasis)

However, on August 14, 1973, the Christian Democrats insisted only on denouncing the so-called "illegality" of the government's action. They stated: "The Popular Unity government *is maintaining a position of illegality and open violation of the Political Constitution* by not promulgating the reform approved by Congress that requires the formation of the social sector to be subject to legislation . . ." (Our emphasis) On August 23, the Chamber of Deputies made another decision, one which openly incited the Armed Forces to stage a coup d'état. (The Commanders-in-Chief of the Armed Forces were part of the Cabinet, President Allende having forced them to participate in it in order to head off the final offensive of strikes, sabotage and violence aimed at overthrowing the government.) The Chamber decided to point out to the ministers from the Armed Forces and the Carabineros that *"in the face of the serious disturbance of the constitutional and legal order of the Republic,"* it was not suitable for them to endorse a partisan policy through their presence in the Cabinet. The resolution of the majority in Parliament stated that the presence of ministers from the military in the government seriously compromised the professional character of the Armed Forces and the Carabineros, "openly infringing the provisions of Article 22 of the Political Constitution and seriously harming their prestige as an institution".

On the eve of the coup d'état there appeared many statements from corporations controlled by the opposition forces (such as the College of Physicians, the College of Lawyers, the Federation of Students of the Catholic University, etc.), declaring the government to be illegal and demanding its resignation.

As is apparent from all we have explained, Chile's "institutionalist" and "legalist" tradition, far from allowing reforms affecting the interests of the ruling circles to be made through the "legal", "peaceful" and "institutional" road, as the phony communists proclaimed, at most merely made the arch-reactionary circles feel obliged to dress up their subversive plans for a coup in hypocritical legal pretexts. This tradition probably also made the repression more brutal and the elimination of all legal guarantees more complete, for it was necessary to radically extirpate the habits of legality, institutionality and exercise of certain democratic freedoms in order to establish fascist dictatorship. In this manner, class interests wiped out this superstructure about which revisionism propagated so many illusions; with the stroke of a pen they obliterated the "originality" and "exceptional character of the Chilean process" ("the England of Latin America") on which the "C"P leaders based their anti-Marxist theories. Once again, practice was to confirm Lenin's words: *". . . the very idea of the capitalists peacefully submitting to the will of the majority of the exploited, the very idea of a peaceful, reformist transition to socialism, is not merely sheer philistine stupidity but also downright deception of the workers, embellishment of capitalist wage-slavery, and concealment of the truth. That truth consists in the bourgeoisie, even the most enlightened and democratic, no longer hesitating at any fraud or crime, even the massacre of millions of workers and peasants, so as to preserve private ownership of the means of production." (4)* This also happened with the experiment of the Popular Unity and its government, even though their expropriation of the big bourgeoisie and of certain imperialist monopolies was intended only to develop state capitalism and not genuine socialism. All the more reason why the people must prepare to actually seize power for themselves!

4. The Government's "Guerrilla Warfare" Against the Contraloria and the Courts

As we have already pointed out, management of the companies that had been confiscated or controlled by means of the "legal loopholes" was perpetually being disputed by their owners. In this the owners could count on the unqualified support of the Contraloria (which was responsible for "watching over the legality" of the government's decisions) and on the complicity of the Courts. These two bodies, which showed their "legalist zeal" for everything that would hinder the government's plans, are today clearly revealing both their reactionary class nature and the hypocrisy of their former pretension of defending the existing institutions and laws: they have accepted all the illegal, arbitrary, anti-constitutional and genocidal acts of the Military Junta and have openly collaborated with it. But they are not the only guilty ones: also guilty are those who called themselves Marxists and who promoted respect for the institutions of bourgeois rule and for the Armed Forces, preventing the people from destroying these lairs of the most reactionary forces.

To get around the opposition of the Contraloria, the government continually had to resort to a measure that the Constitution enabled it to take in urgent and exceptional cases: the decree of insistence, which had to be signed by the President of the Republic and all his ministers. In addition to the obstruction and interference of the Contraloria, designed to intensify the administrative crisis in the public sector, there was the systematic rejection of the decisions of the Executive by the Courts.

In this manner, the management of enterprises confiscated or taken over was continually hindered, the Executive was shown before public opinion to be governing outside the law, and the constitutional indictments presented by the majority in Parliament with a view to removing ministers of state for alleged violations of the law or for other reasons were legitimated. All this guerrilla warfare waged against the government by Parliament, the Courts, the Contraloria and other ruling institutions controlled by the opposition finally created the image of an "illegitimate" government "outside the law". When the time came, this image enabled the opposition to replace guerrilla warfare against the government with open war, waged by the Army, in order to overthrow it through violence.

This process, this systematic offensive, like almost all of the experience of the Popular Unity government in a wide variety of fields, illustrates the basic thesis of this book: the failure of the "peaceful road", of the legalist and reformist road, to seize power from the ruling circles in Chile. A failure which occurred even though what was at stake was not in the least the building of socialism or a genuine people's anti-imperialist, anti-oligarchic and anti-monopolist revolution, but merely the replacement of the old system of exploitation by a new one: state capitalism.

Let us look at a few examples of this institutional struggle, which was, of course, only one aspect of the many-sided offensive that the opposition unleashed and continuously escalated until the overthrow of the government.

In June 1971, the Contraloria issued a warning that: "The occupation of a factory, if it constitutes an illegal act, neither authorizes nor makes feasible the requisitioning of the establishments in question." In the same period, without holding a hearing, the Contraloria rejected the decision of the Industry and Commerce Administration (DIRINCO) to order the requisitioning of the big "Manufacturas Yarun" textile mills. The following month, without holding a hearing, it rejected DIRINCO's decisions to requisition the Progreso, Panos Oveja Tomé, Rayon Said, Lanera Austral and Algodones Hirmas textile mills. In August, the Contraloria reaffirmed its judgements, telling DIRINCO that "the Contraloria finds it legally necessary to warn you that it is not possible in law to uphold the implementation of the decisions" bringing the various textile plants under state control.

At the end of August, the workers of the National Tire Industry (INSA) occupied the offices of the factory, declaring that "the Production Development Corporation (CORFO) must take over the company". On September 3, the government decided to requisition the nine plants of the United Breweries Company monopoly. Pedro Vuskovic, Minister of the Economy, justified this requisition on the grounds that there was a shortage of beer due to conflicts between the workers and the company. Five days later, the National Party presented a constitutional indictment against Vuskovic. It accused him of abuse of power, violation of the laws and failure to apply the laws, and stated that the nationalization of the banks without enabling legislation was contrary to the constitution and that the requisitioning of enterprises "is illegal and represents a flagrant violation of the Constitution and existing legislation". During the debate, a National Party member of Parliament stated: "Almost all the requisitions ordered to date have been based on illegal strikes provoked by the government, which is the first to refuse the requests of private individuals and to asphyxiate industry economically by denying it price increases and credits." On September 10, the Contraloria reaffirmed that the "occupation" of an enterprise does not authorize "the enactment of unilateral measures such as back-to-work orders (for the purpose of establishing state control) when such occupation is illegal." The warning referred to the back-to-work order at the INSA (tire) and NYLINSA plants. Finally, on September 13, the Contraloria categorically refused to give effect to the requisitioning of and control over several factories, including the big Rayonhil and Manufacturas Sumar textile mills, and ordered these firms restored to their owners. On September 28, the Contraloria rejected DIRINCO's latest decisions to requisition certain fish and textile plants, stating that the reasons given by DIRINCO to justify such measures did not correspond to the conditions required by law. The government finally decided to requisition the eight largest textile mills in the country by means of a decree of insistence, so as to allow no appeal. On October 1, Victor Garcia, a National Party senator, denounced the illegal nationalization of a number of companies and banks that the government had bought, confiscated or brought under its control. Another rightist member of Parliament, Mario Arnello, asserted that the decree of insistence used by the government to requisition companies was "absolutely illegal". In December

1971, the National Party presented another constitutional indictment against Minister of the Economy Pedro Vuskovic, stating that "during his entire term as a minister he has constantly demonstrated arbitrariness, illegality, violation of the Constitution and the law, and abuse and misuse of power." In the same month, the Society for Industrial Development stated: "Thus the nationalization of enterprises by means of a procedure considered illegal by the Contraloria is reinstated and imposed through decrees of insistence." This referred to the requisitioning of the "El Volcan" factory by the government.

Disregarding the warnings of the Contraloria and the opposition, the government requisitioned the CALAF plant in Talca province and the FANALOZA plant in Penco district, Concepcion province. The CALAF requisition was to be rejected by the Contraloria on February 9, 1972. But before that, in January 1972, the courts would join the Contraloria in its work of obstruction. On January 4, the Supreme Court upheld a suit filed by the Yarur textile firm against a DIRINCO requisition. On the same day, the courts restored the daily newspaper *La Manana* to its owners. The paper had been occupied by its workers, who demanded the government take over the enterprise.

On January 18, the Contraloria refused to validate a back-to-work order at the GASCO company, which had been on strike since January 15. A few days later the government was forced to order a return to work by means of a decree of insistence. At the end of January, the Controller reaffirmed, in regard to this gas-manufacturing and distributing company, that: "the illegal act of occupying offices is not sufficient grounds to prove paralysis of activities vital to the national economy", which condition would have justified the requisition.

When it was brought into the government with two ministers at the beginning of 1972, the Radical Left Party (RLP) published a statement on the attitude the UP government should adopt, stating in part that: "We believe that in no case can labour disputes be used to transfer companies which do not satisfy the conditions required by law into the public or mixed sector . . ." Failure to respect this demand would later be one of the pretexts used by this party to withdraw from the government and join the opposition at the instigation of the CIA (as the U.S. Senate report on CIA involvement shows).

Referring to a decision by the Executive Council of CORFO to allocate funds for the purchase of the shares of 91 companies that the government wanted to nationalize, a spokesman for the Society for Industrial Development stated: "This declaration by CORFO did not surprise us: it shows once again that the government plans to use illegal means to build up the public sector of the economy." All this pressure was designed to force the government to submit its nationalization plans to Parliament, where the opposition could use its majority to scuttle them. It was for the same purpose that the Christian Democrats later presented their constitutional reform aimed at delimiting the three sectors of the economy. The reform was a key part of the opposition's plan to prove the "illegality" and "illegitimacy" of the government and justify the open appeals for its overthrow by the Army.

On February 14, 1972, without holding a hearing, the Contraloria rejected DIRINCO's decision to requisition the El Volcan plant. The reasons given in the whereases of the Contraloria's ruling were that it could not accept either the legality of the measure or the pretext for it (shortage of vulcanite, gypsum and insulating material), and that the illegal strike against the company was provoked expressly to bring about its requisition.

At the end of February 1972, the leaders of the Society for Industrial Development (SOFOFA) sent a letter to President Allende stating that "the method of transferring companies using the loophole of an offer to purchase by CORFO and negotiations between CORFO and the shareholders is irrational and intrinsically unjust". In short, they wanted to deny the government the right enjoyed by any individual to buy the shares of companies registered with the Stock Exchange. This prohibition, a harsh and unjust restriction on the government's activities, was part of the constitutional reform of the three economic sectors presented by the CDP. Parliament's pressure against the system of requisitions and control intensified in March. The leader of the Christian Democratic parliamentarians, Luis Pareto, stated: "I believe that the requisitioning of factories which the constitutional reform stipulates may only be expropriated by means of a law of the Republic is a challenge to Congress and an additional demonstration of Mr. Vuskovic's abuse of power and lack of respect" (referring to the Minister of the Economy). Domingo Godoy, a National Party representative, added that: "The President of the Republic has the floor: if he disagrees with the actions of his Secretary of State, the latter should hand in his resignation. Otherwise, one must conclude that he has been overwhelmed by the communists or that he really agrees with the minister's arbitrary policy, despite his statements to the contrary." Meanwhile, SOFOFA, through its president Orlando Saenz, again insisted that: "The government is not following legal and democratic methods for the transfer of factories to the public sector. It is using requisitions with a view to expropriation, and that is illegal." Carrying on this campaign to create in the public mind the image of illegal activities by the government, which in fact was scrupulously staying within its legal prerogatives, the opposition Radical Democratic Party stated: "While the constitutional reform bill (concerning the three sectors of the economy) is binding on the government, cabinet minister Vuskovic is grotesquely ridiculing Parliament by persisting in his attitude of violating the laws, putting the legislative branch in a ridiculous position both nationally and internationally." The president of the National Confederation of Retail Trade Establishments and Small Industry, Rafael Cumsille, one of the ringleaders of the two strikes organized by the opposition to overthrow the government, stated: "The transfer of a company to the public sector must be done for really well-founded reasons, by means of specific laws and not by methods unknown in Chile, as the Minister of the Economy personally is doing, trying to make the population believe that the independent workers in industry and commerce are responsible for the critical situation of shortages that the country finds itself in."

In the midst of this public relations offensive to discredit the legal conduct of the government, the Contraloria returned to the attack. On March 17, 1972, it again rejected the requisiton of the big Madeco copper-refining company. On March 23, without a hearing, it rejected the decision to requisition the Ceresita plant. On April 19, it declared DIRINCO's decisions to requisition the "Cachantun Mineral Water" plant and the non-alcoholic beverage plants of the United Breweries Company to be illegal. At the beginning of May, the Fourth Superior Court of Santiago joined the offensive against the government by rendering a judgement ordering DIRINCO to restore the requisitioned Rayon Said plant to its owners within five days and to compensate them for damages. The judgement stated that DIRINCO did not have the authority to requisition factories. For its part, the Insurance and Corporate Supervisory Board published a report stating that the government-appointed administrator at the CALAF plant "is completely incompetent to exercise any function whatsoever, because the order or decision by virtue of which he was appointed has been rejected by the Contraloria". Stepping up its attack against the government, the Contraloria finally suspended from office the director of DIRINCO, Patricio Palma, for having failed to reply to three official letters demanding that he justify takeovers of enterprises.

However, the government continued to use the procedures condemned by the opposition. On June 13, 1972, it used a decree of insistence signed by the President and all his ministers to order a return to work at the FENSA electrical appliance company and to take over the company. The Controller immediately reported this to the Supreme Court, because the hearing into the offences of occupation and violation of the right to work committed at FENSA was still going on in the Seventh Superior Criminal Court. Later, the President of the Republic himself asked the Supreme Court that the judge of the Seventh Criminal Court cease his judicial activities in regard to FENSA, which were hindering the activities of the government administrator. The Supreme Court unanimously decided to turn down the President's request. The judge conducting the FENSA trial launched proceedings against the administrator for having taken charge of the plant when it was at the disposal of the court. On June 26, the government administrator of FENSA was judged guilty of "preventing the execution of a court order". In early July, the directors of the FENSA plant, encouraged by the judicial support of the Contraloria, launched a suit against ex-

Minister of the Economy, Pedro Vuskovic (foreseeing a constitutional indictment against him, the government had discreetly relieved Vuskovic of his duties) and against the administrator of the company "for prejudicial acts which to date have resulted in losses of 15 million escudos". Finally, on November 8, without holding a hearing, the Contraloria rejected a DIRINCO decision attempting to legalize the FENSA requisition. At that time, the opposition press wrote of losses of more than 70 million escudos for the company.

On June 29, 1972, the Contraloria attacked the government's plan to establish norms for the operation of the Automotive Corporation, rejecting an Executive order as "not in conformity with the law". At the beginning of July, after having turned down two previous Executive orders, the Contraloria launched proceedings against a government decree of insistence aimed at regulating the Automotive Corporation.

At the end of June, the courts ordered the forcible evacuation of the Perlak plant, which had been occupied by workers demanding the takeover of the plant. The following month, the government was forced to use another decree of insistence to requisition a number of factories which were the object of constant litigation with their owners. Amongst these were some we have already mentioned: Madeco, Cachantun, CALAF, and two United Breweries plants.

In October 1972 came the strike in transport, commerce, public transportation and other employers' and professional corporations led by the opposition. These corporations presented a set of demands to the government. One of the demands presented as a condition to end the strike was "restitution of assets that have been requisitioned or taken over . . . with appropriate compensation".

Already putting forward his plan to declare the government "illegal" and "illegitimate", Supreme Court President Enrique Urrutia Manzano, in his speech to open the 1973 judicial year, described the decrees of insistence used by the Executive as "legal loopholes" and stated: "Because of the various problems posed by social movements in recent years, and with respect to cases which this Court has had the opportunity to review, as a result either of complaints or of other proceedings, we have established that there is a sort of inefficacy in the work of verifying the legality of orders issued by the Executive, which is the responsibility of the Contraloria. This is due to the fact that the representations made by the Contraloria to the Executive are bypassed by a mere decree of insistence issued by the Executive itself with the signatures of all the members of the cabinet, who, in general, are of a political nature; thus *the illegal order ends up being implemented."* (Our emphasis)

In March, a polemic developed between the Contraloria and the Minister of the Economy following the Contraloria's rejection of a government order requisitioning the "Bio-Bio" cement factory. The minister accused the Controller of "constantly changing his views . . . and issuing judgements that tend to weaken the administrative actions of DIRINCO". The Controller replied: The Political Constitution of the state and complementary legislation clearly define the area of jurisdiction of the Executive branch and of the Contraloria is to oversee this responsible for the administration of the country, which must be done *within the framework of the Constitution and the law.* The responsibility of the Contraloria is to oversee this administration, precisely so that it is carried out within the constitutional and legal framework; the Contraloria has a duty to point out actions which go beyond this framework. This is exactly what the Contraloria has done, and what on this occasion has drawn the attention of the minister. On the other hand," he concluded, "neither the Political Constitution nor any law gives the Minister of the Economy, Development and Reconstruction the power to oversee the acts of the Contraloria." (Our emphasis)

Despite these problems, the government sent the Contraloria another decree of insistence on April 10, 1973, in order to implement the requisition orders that the Contraloria had rejected. This seems to have been the last decree of insistence before the coup d'état.

All this guerrilla warfare against the government was not waged in an isolated manner. It was coordinated more and more closely with the offensive launched in Parliament; with the courts, which systematically opposed the government on many points besides the requisitioning of companies; with all the activity to develop speculation and shortages; and finally, with a political offensive that went from attacks in the press and large-scale protests to the stoppage of vital activities and violence and sabotage against the vital centres of the economy. Even during the two big road transport strikes, the Contraloria rejected the government orders requisitioning the means of transportation that had been illegally paralyzed under the pretext that "large-scale requsitions lack specific itemization of the object requisitioned". It must be borne in mind that the Contraloria had never felt these legalistic scruples under other bourgeois governments.

There is no doubt that the reason the Contraloria and other institutions were able to obstruct the government's plans was precisely the ambiguity and feebleness of its reformist politics, which were in contradiction with its ambitious plans to deprive the ruling classes of their means of production. The government's practical actions (for example, inciting factory occupations and labour disputes as pretexts for requisitions) were always feeble and halfway, if not hypocritical; they allowed the opposition, through its instruments of propaganda, to show that the government was inconsistent with respect ot the strict legalism it claimed to profess. The government did not create an open, vigorous mass movement to smash the manoeuvres of the reactionary circles that were taking advantage of the laws and institutions in their service and under their control, except for a few limited and timid mobilizations designed to serve as pretexts for the use of the "legal loopholes". On the other hand, the laws and institutions created by the exploiters to serve their interests and manipulated by them were virtually useless as instruments to dispossess them, and as a result, acting within the law, the government was forced to show its weakness by using inadequate and anachronistic decrees and resorting to emergency measures such as decrees of insistence. Thus at the beginning of the government's term, the Contraloria let a few requisition orders pass without raising any objection, for fear of a real mobilization of the people. But, "once the initial moment of surprise and confusion had passed" (as the Military Junta was to say in its writings against the Allende government), the Contraloria began systematically to turn down the requisition orders and, in conjunction with the courts, to obstruct their implementation.

Chapter X
The Chilean Police and
Armed Forces

The Chilean Army has a strong internal discipline. It was organized some one hundred years ago on the model of the Prussian army. Even today the uniform reminds one of the Nazi army. The Chilean Navy has traditionally been influenced by the British Navy. As for the Air Force, which is of more recent vintage, it was modeled after the U.S. Air Force. Since the end of the Second World War, the decisive influence on the Chilean Armed Forces has come from the United States.

1. The U.S. Plans for the Militarization of Latin America

The investigation carried out by Roy Hansen established that as early as 1965, 55 percent of the high-ranking officers of the Chilean Army had spent an average of one year in the United States or in the Panama Canal Zone, where the anti-guerilla training is provided. This percentage has increased considerably since then. Between 1950 and 1965, over 2,000 officers of the Chilean Armed Forces received training in various places under U.S. control. Between 1966 and 1973, 1,182 officers were trained in Panama alone.

With regard to military aid and arms sales between 1953 and 1966, Chile holds second place in total volume of military supplies, next to Brazil, a country with a population of over 100 million. Tables III and IV, reproduced from the Church Commission Report, gives some idea of the magnitude of these military sales. *(132)*

Neither the aid nor the sales of arms to the Chilean Armed Forces were stopped during the Allende administration, despite the threats issued by Ambassador Kerry, which shows how the U.S. government trusted the Chilean High Command.

The U.S. government's concern for the Latin American armed

Table III MILITARY AID

Fiscal year	Planned	Accorded
1966	$8,806,000	$8,366,000
1967	4,143,000	4,766,000
1968	1,801,000	7,507,000
1969	784,000	2,662,000
1970	852,000	1,966,000
1971	698,000	1,033,000
1972	870,000	2,227,000
1973	941,000	918,000
1974	912,000	619,000

Table IV MILITARY SALES

Fiscal year	Orders	Delivered
1966	$ 1,057,000	$1,490,000
1967	2,559,000	1,690,000
1968	4,077,000	2,100,000
1969	1,676,000	2,147,000
1970	7,503,000	9,145,000
1971	2,886,000	2,958,000
1972	6,238,000	4,583,000
1973	14,972,000	2,242,000
1974	76,120,000	4,860,000

* Figures are from a Department of Defense response to a Senate Select Committee document request and are unclassified.

forces has increased considerably since Rockefeller declared that they were the most secure substitute for the political parties of these countries. As early as 1964 General Robert J. Wood, Director of Military Assistance for the U.S. Department of Defence, pointed out: "There is a Security Programme being implemented for the Alliance for Progress . . . the basic aim of which is a Latin American military leadership." *(133)* Such views were already in the document worked out in 1963 by the U.S. Department of Defence stating the aims of the Military Aid Pact

(MAP): "The MAP also enhances the *political aims* of the United States through the training programmes which bring many foreign military leaders to this country . . . It serves not only to improve the technical capacity of the military personnel, but also to familiarize them with the requirements of a responsible military leadership in contemporary society." *(134)* And what is the motive behind this desire of the U.S. government to develop a "military leadership" in Latin America? The U.S. Secretary of Defence, Melvin R. Laird, put it this way before the U.S. Congress, on June 3, 1969: "The MAP will make every effort to ensure that every dollar invested as aid will be used in the most effective manner possible to support the external policy and the security of the United States."

The contacts between the Chilean Armed Forces and the Pentagon, far from diminishing, were stepped up under the Allende government. All of the 21 logistic flights carried out by the Chilean Air Force outside the country took place in the United States. By May 25 of the same year, the High Commands of the Chilean Armed Forces were visited by an Admiral and a Rear-Admiral as well as by two U.S. generals, one from the Army and the other from the Air Force, representing the Southern Command. Members of the U.S. Military Mission also participated as "guest professors" in anti-communist courses given by the Military School and the Naval Academy of Playa Anucha, in Valparaiso. These are just a few examples illustrating the close and uninterrupted links that exist between the Pentagon and the Latin American High Commands. The centre of this influence is the Southern Command of the U.S. Armed Forces, whose headquarters are at the Panama Canal. A feature story published by *Le Nouvel Observateur* in October 1973 gives some idea of these links. It says: "The Panamanians call it the wall of shame. It is a barrier of barbed wires and iron bars separating the South American universe from the Canal Zone, which is under U.S. jurisdiction. Behind this wire curtain, the American Way of Life reigns supreme. Huge buildings house the various departments of an organization which today makes Latin America tremble: The Southern Command. Its latest victory: Chile . . . The Southern Command is at once an information centre, a multidisciplinary 'military university', and an operational base. In the anti-guerilla school, thousands of Latin American officers and sub-officers are getting trained for the war against subversion. These officers receive full technical training in the various military schools scattered throughout the Canal Zone: a telecommunications school, a staff school, an aviation school, etc. Underground buildings, quarters carved out of the rock house the nerve centre of a communications system that covers the entire continent . . . Here, the U.S. officers are in direct contact, by telephone and teletype, with their correspondents established in all the South American capitals, where their role is more important than that of the "official" U.S. ambassadors. An air network is superimposed on the telecommunications system. In order to transport themselves to Rio, Santiago or Montevideo, the civilian agents and the military 'pupils' of the Southern Command have their own airplanes, their own airports . . . The creation of the centre dates back to the beginning of the 60's. It reflects the strategic option adopted by Washington after the failure of the Alliance for Progress. Kennedy's generous programme, whose aim was to aid those countries which would carry out social and agrarian reforms, collapsed in the face of resistance by the Latin American ruling cliques. In order to stem the Castroite advancement and 'subversion', the United States decided to play its military card . . . In the Military Schools of the Panama Canal Zone, a myth is being generated of 'solidarity' amongst South American soldiers. This psychological action has had great success. Here is its central theme: 'We all have the same concerns, we are patriots, we want reforms and we have a common enemy: communism'. For the Catholic officers of the Southern armies who generally come from the middle classes, these simplistic formulas have most often sufficed to ingrain a rudimentary political consciousness. Thirty-five thousand of them received the teachings of the Southern Command. They were the cadres of the armies that took over in Brazil, in Bolivia, in Uruguay and in Chile. And the solidarity between the 'gorilles' is not just empty talk." To corroborate this with a single example among many, let us just point out that Pinochet was in Fort Leavenworth in 1955, at the Southern Command in 1956, and, during the same year, he participated in the Military Mission of the Chilean Armed

Forces to Washington.

It is easy to imagine the impact and the influence of these contacts and links of the Chilean military with the U.S. Armed Forces as well as their role in what took place if one takes into account the relative neglect of the ruling circles towards the Armed Forces in Chile. In fact, the governments prior to that of Allende took for granted the loyalty of the Army to their interests and relied on the solidity of the professional spirit with which it defended them. Moreover, because of the strong influence of a conciliatory and legalist "communist" party, the Army did not have to face a powerful mass upsurge, and therefore these governments were not so worried about increasing the military budget. Normally, the union bureaucrats and the political opportunists provided better service that the Army in suppressing the popular masses. In difficult periods of very sharp struggle, it was generally enough to call upon the Carabineros, an organization sufficiently well armed to carry out its functions and highly disciplined. The salaries of the military personnel corresponded to this secondary role which was assigned to them by the ruling classes. The contempt generally exhibited toward them by the Chilean society was yet another source of the soldiers' resentment which explains, although in a partial and a secondary manner, their brutality after the seizure of political power as well as their inclination to control it completely. Men in uniform were looked at scornfully, especially in the upper classes. The military career itself was synonymous with academic failure or inability to get a professional title. A large number of youth were sent to the military school as punishment for misbehaviour in the civilian institutions or for poor academic performance. In addition to all this, there was the frustration of those who have pursued the military career and who have not used their guns for almost 100 years, except on those occasions when the police forces alone were not sufficient to massacre the workers.

The study by Roy Hansen, sponsored by the CIA in 1965, correctly points out: "It has been proven that the Chilean Army is an organization in decline. This decline was not only reflected in the budget allocated to it, in its rate of growth and its technical deterioration, but also in the decreasing prestige of the (military) career and the consequent broadening of its social base of recruitment. We have also demonstrated," he adds, "that the officers are highly conscious of this decline and its implications for themselves, their profession and their institutional goals." Hansen then comments: "The decline of the military necessarily generates hostility and resentment, especially against the political institutions, and in this way, it acts as an incentive to participate in politics." *(135)*

The attitude of the ruling circles of rejecting any participation by the military in the state apparatus, together with the fact that they considered them incapable of exercising these functions, not only intensified this incapability, which was very real, but also fed the resentment of those wearing the uniform. Frei himself gave as one of the reasons for the reluctance of the Armed Forces to intervene in the early period of the Allende government, the fact that "the military (as opposed to that of other South American countries) has no training whatsoever in public administration, and they are very conscious of this." This was in fact one of the reasons why the military coup was postponed for three years: the military wanted to prepare themselves for governing and they did not want to remain simple puppets of civilian politicians, even rightist ones.

Not too many years were necessary to confirm the predictions of the previously mentioned CIA study concerning the frustrated appetites of the military. In 1969, during the latter part of Frei's term, the movement led by Viaux (the *Tacnazo*) erupted. No doubt, the accuracy of the CIA's predictions was due, not only to its having all the facilities needed for its investigation, but also to the fact that it was already working as actively as the Pentagon to ensure that the Chilean Armed Forces, like those of other countries, would begin to play a leading role in Chilean politics, in line with the recommendations of the Rockefeller Report. "We are here," said Viaux, remaining in the Tacna Regiment after he had been ordered to retire, "to try to prevent the Army from collapsing as an institution . . . if the Armed Forces collapse, motherland collapses." Major Arturo Marshall, who was later to play an important role in the organization of the fascist groups during Allende's administration, had refused to attend the *Te Deum* of the National Holiday with his unit, for reasons similar to those which Viaux was to give a few days later. After being dismissed from his position for carrying out this activity, he wrote a letter to the Commander-in-Chief "exonerating" himself for his action. He wrote among other things that the members of the Armed Forces "no longer enjoy the respect they rightly deserve, despite the hypocritical protestations of affection by way of medals and decorations on the part of those who at bottom always consider us as just a necessary evil and not a guarantee of the solidity of the nation". He called for the "necessity of real career opportunities for all those who correctly fulfil their duty, the necessity for justice in terms of salaries which must be brought into line with those paid in the other public services, and the necessity to find a solution to the inadequacy of training facilities, of equipment, armaments, etc." He added: "We must draw attention to the fact that all levels of military personnel are fed up with the knowledge that, as an institution, we are not up to the level of the sacred mission entrusted to us; we are fed up with broken promises, we are tired of the administrative inefficiency caused by the system which everyone is confronted with." Concerning the political parties, he pointed out: "Like the majority of the population, we have absolutely no trust in them. The mental blindness which has stricken them forbids any one of us to rely on them for our aspirations. Several times, however, in the course of the formation of the movement, we have been urged from various sides to deviate in one way or the other."

Obviously, the CIA and the Pentagon worked actively to intensify this resentment within the Army: the aid, the improvement and the training which it received from the U.S. assumed all the more importance for it, compared to that which it received from the Chilean government. When it came to the repressive plans of the U.S., aimed at maintaining firm domination over Latin America, after the failure of the reformist plans of the Alliance for Progress, the Chilean military felt that it was accorded the importance that it truly deserved. The military coup, therefore, forms part of imperialism's overall strategy of militarizing the governments of the continent (and on this point it seems that even the rightist politicians were mistaken, even though the coup was executed to serve their reactionary interests). The resentment of the Chilean military provided an excellent breeding ground for carrying out these plans which today manifest themselves also in Peru, Bolivia, Argentina, Uruguay, Ecuador, Brazil and Paraguay. It is possible that some of these countries will return to civilian governments, but the Armed Forces, if they are not destroyed by the people, will not be an instrument of the civilian politicians, but on the contrary, the latter will be a provisional instrument of the Armed Forces.

The installation of this new policy of U.S. imperialism in Latin America explains many of the features of the coup d'état in Chile, which are surprising even to its civilian organizers. It explains why, despite Nixon's initial haste, the Armed Forces were reluctant to be dragged into the adventures of the civilian politicians and decided to act as an obedient body receiving orders from the highest levels. It explains the decision to use all the opportunities offered by the Allende government to train cadres in the factories and state institutions, including the state department, themselves, despite the suspicions of the right-wing forces. It explains the elimination from Chilean political life of all the political parties and the tendency to put active or retired Army people in all the key positions. It explains the active campaign waged by the Military Junta in all spheres of activity, from the schools to the mass media, to create a public opinion for the importance of the Armed Forces. Finally, it explains to a large extent the brutality of the repression aimed at imposing a long period of military rule by making every effort to suppress all seeds of resistance.

The reactionary nature of the High Commands of the Chilean Armed Forces, and their willingness to unite with those who always flattered them, supported them and indoctrinated them while the dominant political forces despised them, i.e., their willingness to serve the plans of U.S. imperialism for the domination of the whole continent, also explains the inability of the Allende government to win over not even one single important section of the Armed Forces. The many efforts which it made in this direction came too late, despite the obvious advantage that none of its predecessors had done anything of the sort before. There were those who had been working for decades within the Armed Forces and who offered more than a simple participation in a civilian government — they held out the prospect of direct seizure of the government. Furthermore, the Allende government appeared to be in open opposition to their long-time protectors in the Pentagon. Because of this, the spectacular increases of salaries granted to the Armed Forces were of no use, nor were the increase of the military budget, the housing projects for the soldiers, the important participation that they were granted in the enterprises, in public administration and in the ministries, nor were the flattering words of public praise — all of this was to no avail. The bets had already been placed with the failure of the Alliance for Progress, the greatest effort undertaken to deceive the masses of the people Lenin pointed out that the ruling classes use "the carrot and the stick" against the people, that is, deception and repression. It seemed that for Latin America, the time of the "carrot" was over and the only thing left was the "stick" brandished by the military.

2. Short History of the Repressive Role Played by the Chilean Armed Forces

Only the armed people can oppose the reactionary armed forces. The essential role of the Armed Forces in the bourgeois state is to prevent the people from ridding themselves of their exploitation through the only "argument" that the oppressors understand, that is, revolutionary violence. It is not the people who seek or love violence. The people are subjected to violence on a permanent and daily basis. Lenin points out: *"The necessity of systematically educating the masses in this and precisely this view of violent revolution lies at the root of* the entire *teachings of Marx and Engels." (136)*

The fact that the sham "Communist" leaders of the "C"P have given up this basic principle of Marxism should be enough even for the most ignorant to grasp that those individuals do not desire the liberation of the people, but rather want to ally with, or substitute themselves for the old exploiters. As a consequence of these unavowed aims, they cannot agree with the smashing up of the bourgeois army and they can only aspire to take it over by convincing its commanders that they, as phony "Communists" are nothing but the partners or the successors of the old reactionaries. Therefore, the praise that the leadership of the "C"P has for the Armed Forces is no proof of naivete on their part. It is we who would be naive to believe such a thing. Such praise is just as sincere as that coming from all other reactionaries and as a result, it takes no account of the suffering of the people under their oppression. It is for this reason that even today, despite the terrible extermination carried out by the Armed Forces against our people, they continue to praise them. More than that, the leadership of the "C"P actually prepared this extermination, predicted by the genuine Marxists, by systematically advocating blind confidence in the Army.

On September 19, 1970, two weeks after Allende's election, the daily *El Siglo,* official organ of the "C"P, stated: "Throughout our history, there is not a single fact which seriously contradicts the idea that the Armed Forces are in the service of freedom, democracy, and self-determination of the Chilean people . . . The Army founded by O'Higgins can never direct its fire against the people. This would be to negate itself. On the contrary, its *raison d'être* is to guarantee that the will of the people will prevail over the base interests, anti-patriotism, and meanness of those who mix up the interests of the fatherland with their own." Declarations of this type, which are neither accidental nor sporadic, but rather systematic, uttered almost daily before, during and even now after the fall of Allende's government, are not only a complete abjuration of the basic principles of Marxism (we are already used to that), but they are also, as far as Chile is concerned, a cruel farce and an insult to the thousands and thousands of workers who have been slaughtered by the Armed Forces since our country existed as an independent nation. Such a cynical and shameless distortion of the history of our country cannot be explained by the simple desire to adulate the military, who know very well what they have done, as they were simply fulfilling their role. It can only be explained by the urge to demonstrate to the Army, and to the reactionaries protected by it, their willingness to collaborate by ideologically disarming the people in order to facilitate the task of repression.

A brief account of the activities of the Army and the police from the turn of the century until the period just preceding the coup of September 11, 1973, will be enough to show to what extent the pro-Soviet phony "Communists" of Chile have falsified history with the intention of being admitted as partners in the present system of exploitation.

At the turn of the century, in 1903, 40 dockworkers of Valparaiso were slaughtered by the troops in the course of a strike struggle of over one month over economic demands.

In 1905, a large number of workers holding a meeting were murdered with bullets and swords, many were wounded.

In 1906, the marines of the warship *Blanco Encalada,* in collaboration with the reactionary white guard called *Guardia de Honor,* killed scores of workers in the port of Antofagasta (in the northern part of the country) for the "crime" of holding a meeting.

In 1907, in the yard of the Santa Maria school in the northern city of Iquique, there occurred one of the most brutal massacres (at least up until then) in the history of the Chilean proletariat (tens of thousands of native people were exterminated by the Spanish conquerors). The workers of the saltpetre enterprises were not only exploited to the maximum by the imperialist mines, but they were also swindled by them. They were not paid in money, but instead, they were given tokens issued by the companies. These tokens had to be spent in stores owned by the same imperialist firms. In these stores, not only were the prices charged very high, but the workers were also cheated on the weight or measure of the items that they had to buy there. In order to protest against such extreme forms of despotism, the saltpetre workers organized a march to Iquique. Their only demands were the right for other merchants to establish themselves in the area and for the company to use uniform weights and measures. Once the marchers had gathered in the Santa Maria school, the troops started shooting at the crowd of workers and their families with machine-guns. The cannons of three warships were pointed towards the city which was patrolled by the Marines, and the local regiments were strengthened with others brought from Copiapo, Antofagasta, Tacna and Talca. The report of General Silva Renard himself, who was in charge of the massacre, constituted a most eloquent testimony. This report was published in *El Mercurio* of Antofagasta on December 22, 1907. It said: "Convinced that it was not possible to wait any longer without compromising the respect for and the prestige of the authorities and the public forces, and realizing that it was also necessary to overcome the rebellion before the day was over, at 3:45 p.m., I ordered a volley from the O'Higgins Regiment towards the roof already mentioned and another volley from a marine squad located on Lautaro Street towards the door of the school, where the most rebellious and agitated strikers were to be found.

"This volley was responded to with revolver and even rifle shots, which wounded three soldiers and two marines and killed two grenadiers' horses. I therefore ordered two other volleys and a machine-gun fire in the direction of the roof where the Committee was shouting in the midst of flags and sound of bugles. After this, that is at most thirty seconds later, the crowd surrendered." During these "thirty seconds", 3,500 workers were assassinated and thousands and thousands of others were wounded.

In 1919, the Armed Forces murdered a large number of workers of the refrigerating plants in the southern province of Magallanes, during a demonstration held in the city of Puerto Natales. One year after, in the same area, the regional authorities set the premises of the Workers' Federation of Chile on fire while a meeting was being held inside. Not satisfied with this, they shot at the workers who were able to escape from the flames.

In 1921, the scene of the massacre was again the saltpetre plains. That year around 8,000 workers were unemployed in the area. Despite this fact, the saltpetre companies took the decision to close down the saltpetre plant of San Gregorio, which employed more than 3,000 workers. The President of the Republic himself, Arturo Alessandri, was one of the shareholders of this firm. Faced with the threat of unemployment, the workers of San Gregorio mobilized themselves with the support of the Workers' Federation of Chile. They wanted nothing more than compensation for the layoffs that had been announced, money to return south to their families while awaiting new work and for the re-opening of the businesses which had been closed down to force them to leave. In order to discuss these demands with the employers, they decided to march to the offices of the company. When they got near there, 100 workers were murdered. The next day, the Esmaralda Regiment was transferred to San Gregorio. The troops broke into the hospital where the wounded were and smashed their heads with their rifle butts. Afterwards, they formed an actual hunting party against those who had escaped and killed another 100 persons. Many others were taken, bound with barbed wire, to the Antofagasta barracks to be tortured.

Things did not change over the next 20 years. In 1925, the workers of the saltpetre plants of Pontevedra and La Coruna were forced to raise demands similar to those that had caused the massacre of 1907. In June 1925, the government of Arturo Alessandri and the saltpetre firms, which had already attracted U.S. capital, took various repressive measures against the workers. Their newspapers were banned, their homes were searched, their leaders put in jail and sent to the south and the right of assembly was suppressed. In order to protest against this, the workers of some 100 saltpetre enterprises went on strike. Immediately, the troops were sent to suppress the workers with machine-guns and even cannons. A landing was made by the cruiser *O'Higgins* and the destroyer *Lynch*. The slaughter began in the workshops of Alto San Antonio. The unarmed crowd fled towards the saltpetre plant of La Coruna, leaving numerous wounded on the road. In the meantime, the massacre had also begun at the Pontevedra plant. At La Coruna, where the bulk of the workers were, the buildings were shelled with the heavy artillery of the Racangua Batallion and assaulted by the marines of the cruiser *O'Higgins*. Some 600 workers were killed in that place alone. The rest of them surrendered when they were promised that their lives would be spared. Nevertheless, the slaughter continued in the plains against the unarmed workers. They were forced to dig their own graves before being cowardly assassinated. Many others were taken aboard the cruiser *O'Higgins* and dumped into the high sea. Finally, others were assassinated in the Cavancha velodrome where they had taken refuge. This systematic slaughter lasted for over two months, with a final toll of many thousands of people killed.

In 1928, the Minister of War, Colonel Carlos Ibanez, who had led the massacres of La Coruna and Pontevedra, became President of the Republic as reward for his "merits" in the service of the reactionaries. In Copiapo, he had over 100 miners killed. Many opponents of the government were thrown into the high sea.

In 1934, under the second presidency of Arturo Alessandri, the peasants of the Bio-Bio highlands began to be expelled from their lands to enrich the big landlords. The problem had originated in 1929, when the government had recognized a big landlord's right of ownership over 175,000 hectares of land on which a large number of settlers were living. As the peasants refused to leave the lands on which they had been living for generations, they were attacked by the military and police forces. Some 500 rebel peasants were made prisoners. They were tied to the cinches of horses and taken to Temuco and Concepcion, cities located hundreds of kilometers away. Out of the total, only 23 arrived at Temuco alive. And the prisoners were only the survivors among those who had been killed on their lands.

Under the presidency of Gonzalez Videla (1946-1952), the murders of workers continued and a legal dictatorship was set up. With the participation of the repressive forces, tens of thousands of people were jailed, tortured, thrown out of work, sent to concentration camps and deprived of their civil rights.

Under the second presidency of Ibanez (1952-1958), the repressive laws of the previous government continued to be applied. On April 7, 1957 the Carabineros and later the Armed Forces were used against the sustained demonstrations of the workers and students organized against the price increases and the wage freeze imposed by the U.S. controlled International Monetary Fund. The government went so far as to release hoodlums from the jails so that their misdeeds could be used to justify the massacre. Several hundred people were killed by the troops.

Under the presidency of Jorge Alessandri (1958-1964), son of the butcher of workers of San Gregorio, La Coruna, Ranquil and Lonquimay in the Bio-Bio highlands, two workers were killed and dozens suffered bullet wounds during a national strike. Later on, in 1962, the Air Force shelled the residents of the shanty-town of Jose Maria Caro, killing eight and wounding over forty.

During the term of the Christian-Democrat Eduardo Frei (1964-1970), who had promised a "Revolution in Liberty", the troops attacked the striking workers of the copper mines of El Salvador in order to defend the imperialist interests. Not only workers, but also women and children were killed during the attack. In 1969, the armed police attacked a hundred families in the city of Puerto Montt for the "crime" of occupying a vacant area where they had built some miserable dwellings with planks, tin sheets and cardboard. Eight townspeople were killed and some 30 others were wounded with bullets. Their modest homes, together with all their belongings, were doused with fuel and set ablaze.

Even under the Allende government, before the coup d'état, workers, students and peasants fell under the blows of the repression, murdered either by the police forces or the big landlords. Some sailors who had dared to oppose the preachings of their officers in favour of the coup d'etat were tortured in the most bestial manner, without opposition from the government, as a prelude to what tens of thousands of people would have to suffer later on. In preparation for the coup d'etat, brutal searches were carried out in working class areas, trade unions, factories and in the countryside, causing one death and numerous injuries. The civilian police themselves, under the command of a socialist and with a member of the "C"P as assistant chief, arrested and savagely tortured some activists of a faction of the Socialist Party itself who were advocating the preparation of armed struggle against the military coup.

This brief report of the massacres culminating in the bloodbath of September 11, 1973, only includes those slaughters which marked an epoch and does not account for the thousands of workers or students whose deaths were not given significant coverage by the news media because they had been murdered individually during demonstrations. Nevertheless, it can be said that from the turn of the century until the last coup d'etat, over ten thousand people, mainly workers and peasants, have been murdered by the Chilean Armed Forces and police. This is in a country where the population reached 10 million only recently. If we add to these the thirty or forty thousand people who were killed during the barbaric massacre that began on September 11, 1973, we arrive at a total of some fifty thousand persons. From this short account of the handiwork of the Chilean repressive forces, we can see that since the Second World War, because of the more efficient police control and preventive legal repression, together with the ever increasing influence of the traditional left-wing parties and their leaders whose role was to put a brake on the people's struggles, there tended to be less of the large-scale massacres of workers which were frequent in the past. However, considering the end result of this process whereby deception took precedence over bloody repression, that is, the brutal slaughter carried out by Pinochet and his cronies which claimed four times as many victims as had fallen in more than half a century, it can be seen that the repressive role of the Armed Forces and police in the service of the exploiters has not changed at all.

In order to have a proper idea of the repressive role of the Chilean Armed Forces and police, it is necessary to keep in mind that we have only listed some of the main massacres carried out against the workers. We would have to add the hundreds and hundreds of thousands of people wounded during these massacres as well as those who have been tortured, jailed, thrown out of their jobs, sent to concentration camps and relegated to inhospitable regions, deprived of all rights or victims of "justice" of an openly class nature. All this has also been done with the direct support and assistance of the armed and police apparatus through which the ruling classes exercise their dictatorship.

The repression that followed September 11, 1973, was not only characterized by the ferocity of those who fear the people and want to teach them a lesson they will remember for a long time. It was also an expression of the reactionary class rage of the High Command and officers of the Armed Forces and the police who wanted to take revenge in the most cruel manner against those who had dared to call them "progressive" and supporters of the anti-imperialist and anti-oligarchic reforms. Obviously, they did not want to leave a shadow of doubt concerning which side they stood on; and when they felt used by those whom they hated, they ferociously took revenge. The number is not small of those who have been brutally tortured while having to listen to the slogan of the Popular Unity repeated to them mockingly by their sadist torturers: *"Soldado amigo, el pueblo esta contigo."* (Soldier, my friend, the people are with you. — *Ed.).*

Here, then, is an example of the "constitutionalist" Armed Forces and police who, according to some people, never did anything "throughout our history, to seriously contradict the idea of an army in the service of freedom, democracy and self-determination of the Chilean people." . . . There you have "the Army founded by O'Higgins" which "could never aim its guns against the people", for, in doing so, it "would have to negate itself". Is it possible to imagine more shameless falsifiers of the history of the Chilean people? Is any greater insult possible to the thousands and thousands who have been massacred by the repressive forces?

Another example of the unscrupulousness and unbelievable cynicism of the leaders of the "C"P which culminated in their flattery of the Chilean Armed Forces and police, is the fact that all these massacres received full publicity in the "C"P's own press before Allende became President. How, then, are we to explain their subsequent amnesia? By the very simple fact that in the past, before they became part of the government, they had to propagate stories about these massacres in order to frighten the workers and to bind them to their peaceful and parliamentary road. On the other hand, once they had achieved their electoral goal, they had to flatter the Armed Forces and prettify them in the eyes of the people to make them forget this record of repressive activities. Once in power, the reminder of these massacres would have put them in a very uncomfortable position, before both the Armed Forces and the people.

But there is still more to it. Even today, after the monstrous carnage carried out by the Chilean Army and police which has horrified the entire world, the leaders of the "C"P, in an "open letter" sent to the Chilean military, persist in claiming that the right has succeeded in destroying "the glorious traditions of the Armed Forces", to "tear the Armymen away from their professional tasks and put them in the service of a minority", as well as to "convert many of them into hangmen, torturers and jailers". We can then ask: If recently, on September 11, 1973, the Armed Forces were "put" in the service of a minority, "torn away" from their noble professional tasks and "converted" into hangmen, torturers and jailers, who then was responsible for the massacres of the Santa Maria school, of La Coruna, Ranquil and Lonquimay, El Salvador, Puerto Montt and so many others? Who were those who acted as the torturers and jailers under the successive Chilean governments to serve the ruling minority? Who forced the workers, the overwhelming majority of the country, to endure the exploitation and the poverty to which they were submitted by a tiny minority? Can we ignore at will, with Olympian serenity, all these historical facts, while crawling before the Armed Forces to obtain their pardon?

3. The Opportunist Campaign of Praise for the Armed Forces and Police

The sham "communists" ' prolonged campaign to flatter the Armed Forces is a basic pillar of their plan to advance towards state capitalism in alliance with the pro-U.S. populist forces. Only this plan could have a remote chance of being accepted by the latter Forces and imposed as a *fait accompli* on the U.S. government, but in any case, the traditional repressive forces had to be preserved and all revolutionary mobilization of the people had to be suppressed. The result of this policy is well known: it led to a massacre even more brutal then the usual ones, the worst massacre in Chile's history, against a people which was disarmed, both materially and ideologically.

This campaign of falsification began quite early. On September 19, 1970, a few days after the presidential election, the editorial of the "C"P in *El Siglo* said: "Those who wanted to lead our Armed Forces into adventures aimed at serving the anti-patriotic interests of a privileged minority class ran into the firm will of our soldiers of never being Pretorian forces, but professional armed forces with a very clear sense of their mission and their role in the common work for the progress, the sovereignty and the integrity of our homeland . . . On more than one occasion, the Armed Forces have shown their reluctance and their opposition to being used for repressive tasks in the service of a status quo which the most progressive forces have taken and take upon themselves to smash . . ." The editorial concluded: "The people have no doubts about the patriotism of the Army as well as its respect for and loyalty to the constitution, and they will continue to applaud them as they march through the streets, today and tomorrow as well."

One month later, *El Siglo* continued its clamour in another editorial: "Chile has confidence in its Armed Forces, and it has every reason and right to do so. For many reasons, they are the guardians of our independence and the normality of our constitutional life. Without participating in politics, they are the guarantee of the normal functioning of our people's institutes. On the other hand, it is the sons of the people who make up the solid base of the Armed Forces and the people themselves consider them as their own. This is the correct assessment which the key events of our history confirm so brilliantly." *(137)*

The following day, *El Siglo* persisted: "At this moment when the people are preparing to take power, to be the executor of its programme as well as the architects of their destiny and that of their fatherland, such identification between the armed institutions and the people's forces is all the stronger and more timely.

"The Armed Forces of Chile are destined to be a guarantee that the people can tranquilly get on with the noble tasks with which they are entrusted. These guardians of a professional spirit and a profound respect for the civic tasks of the people constitute an insurmountable obstacle for those who would divert the Chilean political life from its normal democratic course." *(138)* Some obstacle!

In March 1971, when the Allende government was already set up, the "C"P daily stated: "The government is invincible . . . because it relies on the disciplined support of the armed institutions of the country."

In September 1971, a little more than one year after Allende's election, *El Siglo* wrote in its editorial page: "Today, thanks to the government elected by the people and the programme of the Popular Unity, the Armed Forces have the opportunity to play an outstanding role in the quest for a happy future for all Chileans and thus for the fatherland.

"The Armed Forces are not some small section of citizens alien to the historical development and the struggle that all the people are waging today to win their future . . . The Government of

President Allende, the political parties forming the Popular Unity and the other groups of citizens constituting the base of political support for the government are conscious of this fact. The glorious professional character of the Armed Forces of the country does not escape their notice. The Chilean working class, tempered through thousands of fierce battles and represented in the action of the government, has stretched out its hand to the soldier and it has done so with the assurance of finding a loyal friend. The entire people have taken up the great task of building the national homeland because they know that their sons, their brothers, their friends in uniform also participate in building the future society and will also share in its benefits.

"The Armed Forces uphold the glorious banner of respect for the political development of the country. And today, they are part and parcel of this process. The Chilean people, the workers and peasants, know this. For this reason, the applause of today will be more resounding. And when an ordinary worker shouts 'Long live Chile!' as the troops march by, he will be expressing the salute of the Chilean masses to their Armed Forces." *(139)* Let us recall, in this regard, what the U.S. Senate Report on CIA intervention in Chile said concerning the same month when *El Siglo* was making such declarations: "By September 1971 a new network of agents was in place and the Station (of the CIA — *J.P.)* was receiving almost daily reports of new putschist conspiracies." Here you have the "loyal friends" to whom the people should have "stretched out their hand", according to the advice of the "C"P leaders!

Throughout 1972, when the putschist plots were coming one after the other and the opposition was undertaking large-scale offensives to overthrow the government, the flatteries by the "C"P leaders and their followers in the UP for the Armed Forces continued without interruption. We will not include them here for lack of space. Instead we will reproduce what they said in 1973, during the last months of the government at a time when everyone was aware that the Army was feverishly preparing a coup d'état.

On March 21, 1973, on the occasion of the 41st Anniversary of the Chilean Air Force, the branch of the Armed Forces most closely linked with U.S. imperialism and distinguished by its cruelty during the massacres and tortures that followed the coup d'état, *El Siglo* editorialized: "Firmly dedicated to its professional tasks, the Chilean Air Force has deservedly won the affection of all the citizens, who respect its traditions, who applaud as its units and officers pass by because it is wholly at the service of Chile and all Chileans." The editorial concluded: "With its Air Force, its Army and its Navy, Chile advances towards the future with full confidence. The people and the Armed Forces of Chile want a new motherland with no Chileans left on the sidelines, with all of them completely happy with their new life." Some happiness!

At the end of March, this paper carried an article signed by Marcel Garcés, who speculated on the "love" that the Armed Forces felt for the achievements made under the UP programme. He wrote: "Outside the ministerial cabinet of the people's government, there is no doubt that the Armed Forces will continue to be vigilant in accomplishing their fundamental mission: the defence of national sovereignty and the strict protection of security. At the same time, in keeping with our modern times, they will continue to play a salient role in the policy of economic and social development, working together with the workers and the most progressive sections of society. Such is the understanding of the people's government and it is no accident that it has been this government and not those of the bourgeoisie which has understood that the Armed Forces are not a decorative element of the national community but have the right and duty to participate in the great national upsurge to rescue the country from under-development and dependence, for the redemption and defence of the national wealth, for state control of strategic industries and for the liberation of the productive forces caught in the cobweb of the latifundium, the monopolies and the private banking and financial oligarchies.

"The Armed Forces and the people", concluded the editorial, "are not opposing sections of the national community. They are deeply united in the historic challenge of progress and genuine national liberation." *(140)* Today it is clear to everyone that far from the realization of these lying prophecies and illusions, the High Command of the Armed Forces have, since the coup d'état, done nothing but return to "the cobweb of the latifundium, the monopolies and the banking and financial oligarchies" whatever had been expropriated by the previous government and intensified the dependence of the country on U.S. imperialism.

On April 20, 1973, *El Siglo* carried an editorial stating that: "A great reactionary conspiracy is in progress against the Chilean people, their social, trade union and political organizations, against their government and in short, against the country itself and its basic institutions. With new ingredients and new recipes, the same national and foreign promoters of the events of last October are again trying to sow chaos and to push the Chileans towards civil war." And, unable to close their eyes any further to the military conspiracies, they added: "The secret leaders of reaction have long paid close attention to the Armed Forces. They have resorted to numerous manoeuvres of every kind to divert them from their professional tasks and to drag them into partisan politics." However, no denunciation was intended here, since, the editorial carried on: "The Armed Forces of Chile have a strictly professional training as well as a deep sense of responsibility, honour and patriotism which is all to their glory . . . Today, when the fascist beast rears its filthy head again, the attack against the armed institutions would increase their worth. The people are vigilant and alert. Once again the Armed Forces will prove the solidity of their institutional principles and professional morals."

On April 17, Volodia Teitelboim, a member of the Secretariat of the "C"P, wrote an article in *El Siglo,* in which he approved the praise addressed to the Armed Forces by Orlando Millas, himself a member of the "C"P Secretariat and Minister of Economy, praise which he uttered in Parliament when defending himself against the constitutional charges raised against him by the opposition in order to have him removed from office. Teitelboim wrote: "We highly appreciate the correct, firm and reasoned language used by Comrade Orlando Millas to expose the philistine and putschist 'momios' who raised a dishonest constitutional accusation against the Minister of Economy. These dandies of the right who launch out into attacks against the Armed Forces," he added, "received the scathing reply that they deserved." He went on to quote the shameful and servile flatteries addressed to the Armed Forces by Millas: "I most energetically protest against the procedure used in the text of the charges, of launching insults against the leaders of the Armed Forces of the Republic who carry out their duties with self-denial and lend their cooperation for the resolution of the problems of the nation."

Then, donning a theatrical air, he offers himself up as a victim in order to preserve the honour of the Armed Forces: "I am a political person, honourable Members of Parliament. You can attack me and I fully assume my responsibilities. But no one has the right to use the hatred of some parliamentarians and the methods of cheap politics to attack the honour of the members of the Armed Forces." Vain and servile demagogy! At the end of 1972, five generals from each branch got together to make concrete preparations for the coup d'état.

On July 6, Marcel Garces returned to the charge in *El Siglo:* "The Armed Forces of the nation are not strangers to the effervescent social process spearheaded by the people, the builders of the new society. They are part of the national community and consequently, they cherish all that is happening in the field of economy, culture and other aspects of social life. Chile has set an example for the world and has written a page of history which is full of teachings as to how the people can succeed in recovering their basic resources, organizing the economy with a just distribution of income and ending the exploitation of man by man. They set an example as to how this process can be democratically carried out and defended by relying on the constitutionalist Armed Forces who are loyal to their institutional doctrine and who also participate in what Allende called the 'great policy' of National Economic Sovereignty." Thus, this "lucid" observer, this real swindler, portrayed the Armed Forces, which were festering with putschist groups scrambling with one another, not only as strictly "professional" and "constitutionalist", but as enthusiastically taking part in nothing less than a policy supposedly aimed at "ending the exploitation of man by man". There you have declarations worthy of a medieval alchemist!

Two days later, still in the pages of *El Siglo*, the "C"P leader Jorge Insunsa, continued to sow illusions about the Armed Forces, a section of which had already organized, at the end of the previous month, one of the first open putschist attempts, the *Tacnazo*. He stated: "The calls of the United Workers' Central to oppose the subversive actions of the domestic and foreign reactionaries who want to unleash a civil war can in no way be interpreted as measures tending to arouse the people against the armed institutions, which are faithful to their traditions of respect for the constitutional government. The people are getting organized to defend their livelihood, to guarantee the democratic development of Chile, to carry the process of revolutionary change through to the end by averting the armed confrontation sought by the reactionaries, and to oppose the reactionary subversion by preventing it from causing our country irreparable damage in terms of lives and wealth . . . It is therefore absurd to pretend that the trade union or 'poblacion' organizations are 'insurrectional forces' when the organizational measures taken are aimed precisely at averting reactionary subversion, and when such an attitude links them closely with the Armed Forces, which guarantee the democratic development of our country's political process . . . The efforts to create a gap between the Armed Forces and the people will fail. The very fact that the defeat of the coup d'état of June 29 was the result of the resolute action of the Armed Forces, Carabineros and the police together with the mobilization of the masses served to weld thousands of soldiers with the people. It is not in vain that during the demonstration, the people were shouting in unison: *'Soldado, amigo, el pueblo esta contigo!'* (Soldier, friend, the people are with you!)." We have already seen how the torturers of the Armed Forces, after the coup d'état, used this stupid and treacherous slogan put forward by the "C"P leadership.

4. "Constitutionalist" and Purely "Professional" Armed Forces?

There is a serious mistake made by the analysts of the UP experience (such as Garces, the advisor of Allende), who suggested and still suggest that the coup d'état in Chile took three years to come about because of a so-called "legalist", purely "professional" and "constitutionalist" spirit of the Armed Forces, which had prevailed over the class interests upheld by the High Commands. The truth is that until the victory of the Popular Unity, it was not such doctrinaire and moralist considerations that determined the behaviour of the Armed Forces, but the fact that the constitution and the prevailing laws and institutions were fully serving the interests of the reactionary ruling classes of Chile and U.S. imperialism. The Armed Forces, therefore, were not "legalist", "constitutionalist" and "professionalist" because they were apolitical, but because such legality and institutionality were sufficient until that time to defend the ruling classes. If they supported the groups controlling the government, it was not because they respected these institutions and laws (Allende respected them scrupulously), but on the contrary, they supported these laws and institutions to the extent that they served the big internal and external exploiters. It is precisely for this reason that their repressive "professionalism" made them the most effective instrument of oppression of the people, whereas they were content to carry out this task in a disciplined fashion, without interfering in the rivalries between the various bourgeois circles contending for the government or the Parliament. This was the case, of course, only as long as it was only the traditional bourgeois groups which were taking turn in managing the existing system of exploitation and oppression. In this repressive professional role, the Chilean Armed Forces have given excellent and abundant proof of their effectiveness and class orientation throughout the history of Chile, We have already given examples of their repressive activity, always against the people and in support of the exploiters, which show their true reactionary political position. As additional evidence of the fact that their loyalty is not to some abstract legal or institutional precepts, as some suggest, there are various examples of the contempt of the High Commands and officers of the Armed Forces towards the civilian politicians, the very managers of all this legality and institutionality of bourgeois democracy. With their professionalism the commanders and officers of the Armed Forces saw themselves as better defenders of the capitalist order than these civilian politicians, even though the latter were part of the legality and institutionality and were its official administrators.

As it happens, when Allende was elected (legally and constitutionally), a serious incompatibility surfaced between the legalist and professionalist habits of the Armed Forces and the outright reactionary spirit of their High Commands and the majority of their officers: the professionalism and legalism that they practiced had changed its label and no longer served the usual reactionary interests. Allende, under the "Marxist" slogan of building "socialism", was planning (and seriously began) to nationalize the means of production. Furthermore, he was planning to expropriate possessions of the United States, the main supplier of arms, credits, grants and professional as well as ideological training for the Armed Forces. All this, besides, was, according to the U.S., threatening the balance of forces with the most powerful enemy of the Western Christian World, to which Chile belongs: the Soviet Union, represented in the government by the "C"P. Finally, Allende was not suppressing the mobilization of the people with the same energy as his predecessors and there was the serious danger of paramilitary popular leftist armed groups being formed (those of the right were encouraged and supported by the U.S. themselves).

It is easy to imagine the reaction of the High Commands and officers of the Armed Forces in the face of all this. Since 1968, they were in the habit of sending all their Military School graduates to the Panama Canal Zone for a two month anti-guerilla training course organized by the United States. According to U.S. sociologist Roy Hansen, (141) in his study in 1964-65 sponsored by the Rand Corporation, the University of California and the Ford Foundation (three institutions closely linked with the CIA), the Chilean Army sent 55 percent of its elite members to the United States for an average period of 14 months. Furthermore, the same study included a survey of 37 recently retired generals and it was revealed that 73 percent of them had parents who were professionals, businessmen and company directors; 81.6 percent of their best civilian friends were directors and professionals, 8.3 percent landlords, 2.8 percent politicians and 2.8 percent businessmen. Employees and workers: 0.0 percent. Also, it said that all four armymen who reached the rank of general in 1964 came from the upper class.

It is therefore perfectly natural that despite their constitutionalist and professionalist habits, because they were loyal to their class position, they felt absolutely no obligation towards the Allende government despite all its efforts to win their sympathy. In fact, Allende during his rule treated the Armed Forces in a way that they had never been treated by the previous governments, which, assured of the class loyalty of the Armed Forces, had left them poorly equipped with meagre salaries and with no participation in the civilian institutions and enterprises of the state. It was precisely this neglect which served as a pretext for General Viaux in his attempt to overthrow the Frei government by a coup d'état in 1969. Allende, on the other hand, began by substantially improving the differential scale of salaries, particularly favouring the generals, whose salary went from 12 times the minimum wage in 1970 to 21 times in 1972, thus attaining a 75 percent improvement as compared with the workers' incomes. The budget of the Department of Defence was considerably increased. By the end of 1971, over 265 positions in the state economic apparatus were occupied by active military people. All the links of the Armed Forces with the United States were maintained: the training visits, the U.S. Military Mission in Chile, Operation *Unitas*, etc. Finally, on various occasions, Allende included high-ranking officers of the Armed Forces in his Cabinet. Nevertheless, the class spirit of the High Commands and officers of the Armed Forces was so solid that the government obtained very little influence by this move. All the estimates of President Allende and his advisors concerning the ascendancy they thought they had were, until the end, absolutely wrong and subjective. Shortly before his death, Allende spoke of "three traitors", even when the few supporters the Popular Unity had in the Armed Forces (basically in the troop and the recruitment contingent) had already been annihilated right in their barracks. Only very small groups were able to offer a certain resistance. The leaders of the Armed Forces deceived Allende so skillfully that an individual like Colonel Washington Carrasco (one of those who escorted the Chancellor to Cuba in 1971 and who later became Commander-in-Chief of the Third Division) was considered a "progressive": on the morning of September 11 he ordered the murder of 250 trade union leaders, workers and peasants. Even General Torres de la Cruz — one of the most fanatical military fascists — was considered, almost to the end, by Allende and other UP leaders, as an "Allendist". We also know what Pinochet said to Allende on the very eve of the coup that he led: "You can always count on my unconditional loyalty, Mr. President."

From the real events which took place in the Armed Forces (covered up by the campaign of praise directed at them by the government and in particular by the "C"P leadership in the vain hope of seducing them) the following emerges: the fact that the coup d'état took three years to come about is due not to the "constitutionalist" spirit or still less to the "democratic" or even "progressive" spirit of the Armed Forces, as some have suggested, but rather to the *excessive number of putschist tendencies, whether of internal or external origin, which were fighting to have their say within the Armed Forces.* These putschist tendencies, deriving from pressures from the U.S. CIA and DIA, the National Party, the Christian-Democratic Party and the fascist group *Patria y Libertad* as well as from the personal ambitions of certain militarists, endangered the unity and "professionalism" of the Armed Forces as a repressive force as they weakened their *esprit de corps.* These tendencies naturally provoked many premature attempts at a coup d'état which endangered the effectiveness of the army. The need to discipline all these putschist tendencies and to place them under a single high-level command which would not threaten the unity of the Army and which would choose the most opportune moment was one of the conditions which delayed the carrying out of the coup d'état.

If the Chilean "constitutionalism" and "institutionalism" played any role at all in delaying the coup, it was not because of the scruples of the military and their "loyalty" to these principles, but because of the difficulty of smashing at one blow the democratic guarantees and legal rights that had prevailed for decades in Chile. The presence of General Prats as Commander-in-Chief of the Armed Forces was another factor which delayed the plans of the putschists, at least until such time as they could remove him from office. Prats was one of those extremely rare generals on whom President Allende and the "C"P leadership seemed to have a certain influence. It was a mere accident, in the government's favour, which brought him to this post as he happened to be second in seniority to General Schneider, who was murdered during one of the first attempted coups.

The highest ranking armymen (including apparently General Schneider) were demanding certain minimal conditions before involving themselves in a coup d'état. One of these conditions was the "destabilization" of the Allende government by means of intensifying the economic crisis which would create a powerful movement of public opinion against the regime. They also demanded that the coup be led by the highest level hierarchy (and not by some two-bit adventurer) so as to preserve the unity of the Armed Forces and thus be in a position to confront the risks entailed by brutal suppression of the long tradition of bourgeois democracy in Chile. This last demand meant (although not necessarily) the removal of Prats.

The U.S. government, however, and Nixon in particular, paying no attention to the Chilean situation, carried on as if dealing with a country used to coups d'état. In this manner, they created a serious situation within the Armed Forces by applying excessive pressures to provoke a military uprising before Allende took office. Nixon had personal reasons for acting in this fashion, which were brought to light by the comments of a high-ranking official of the White House, contained in the U.S. Senate's documents of inquiry on the ITT intervention in Chile. He stated: "This memo from the White House may give you some hint of the depth of the President's concern over the situation in Chile. In my view, Nixon believes that the Chilean situation can hurt his election chances in 1972 for many reasons, including the establishment of a Havana-Santiago communist axis. He thinks he would be blamed for the substantial advances the communists have made in the hemisphere under his administration." *(142)*

This tactical haste which Nixon superimposed onto the strategic decision of overthrowing Allende and the resulting desire to organize the coup between the time of Allende's election and his assumption of office created serious difficulties for the CIA and DIA. The CIA reported: "A military operation is impossible; the Army is neither able nor willing to seize power. We are not in a position to provoke or to unleash a coup d'état." *(143)* But the orders given by Nixon during the meeting of September 15, 1970, were categorical. Richard Helms, director of the CIA, commented on this meeting: "I left the meeting with the distinct impression that we had been asked to do the impossible and that it would be a tremendous task to get him to understand this." *(144)* The head of the group of intervention in Chile, for his part, commented: "I had the feeling that the unforeseen was immense, that things would not work and that we would burn ourselves if we allowed ourselves to be dragged into such an adventure . . . What chances did we have to successfully carry out a coup d'état or, at the least, to prevent Allende from becoming President? . . . The chances were not even one in ten . . . I can assure you that the general sentiment of the people I was in contact with in the Agency was: 'My God, why were we given this mission?' " *(145)* Nevertheless, the White House pressures continued, practically forcing the CIA and DIA agents into adventure.

As the President of the Republic, Frei did everything possible over the course of a few weeks to create the economic chaos which would provide the Armed Forces with their pretext. But, aş we have seen, he himself stopped short of calling for a coup d'état. While the opposition forces and the multinationals were actively sabotaging the economy, Frei's Minister of Finance, Andres Zaldivar, told the radio and television networks on September 23 that "the fear of an Allende electoral victory" had been enough to produce a severe economic crisis. His obvious intention was to sow panic and to aggravate the crisis. The panic generated by these declarations combined with systematic sabotage provoked the withdrawal of some 600 million escudos (about $50 million) from the State Bank: 54 million escudos from the savings deposits; some 11 million from the readjustable savings funds; and some 322 million from the savings and mortgage accounts. Thus, the State Bank was forced to remit $80 million to the private banks (one fifth of its total currency reserves) so as to cope with the "money rush" of their depositors. Meanwhile, the refusal of the large national and foreign enterprises to sell on credit to the smaller and medium-sized enterprises and the commercial sector seriously harmed the latters' economic activity.

However, the short period available to cause economic catastrophe (and satisfy Nixon's haste) as well as the failure to deceive public opinion by casting all the blame on Allende, who had not even taken office yet, resulted in the impossibility of creating a significant mass movement in support of the putschists. Faced with this situation, Schneider, Commander-in-Chief of the Armed Forces, demanded at least a legal pretext to unleash the coup. He himself suggested such a pretext when he declared that he would respect "the verdict of the polls or of the National Congress". The problem, therefore, became to get the Parliament to reject Allende's nomination. If this gave rise to disorders, all the better. The Armed Forces would crush them, defending the legal prerogative of the Parliament to name whichever candidate had received the most votes. But Frei did not succeed in involving his party in this manoeuvre and everyone knew in advance that the Congress would appoint Allende.

In these circumstances, the CIA and the DIA, still subject to the imperative pressures of their government, had to lend their support to the adventurers within the Armed Forces, who were offering to kidnap Schneider. In this manner, they killed two birds with one stone: they neutralized the man who was hesitating to launch a coup without a legal pretext, and they accused the left of having kidnapped him with the aim of inciting an armed uprising. Consequently, they did not hesitate to try to divide the Armed Forces. In a telegram dated September 23, 1970, the Santiago Station of the CIA reported to its headquarters: "We have good reasons to believe that neither Frei nor Schneider will take action in the present conditions. Every scenario in which one or the other might play some active role seems for the present to be totally unrealistic. They might, of course, try some adventures in the direction of the lower-ranking officers (Valenzuela, for example). This means that we will have to provoke a split within the Armed Forces." (146) On October 6, after various people had been sounded out, a telegram from the Santiago Station reached the CIA headquarters. It said that Viaux (the general who had been retired after an unsuccessful putschist attempt in 1969) "was ready to unleash a coup d'état on the evening of October 9 or in the morning of October 10." Moreover, the CIA, according to the Senate Report on its activities in Chile, "knew that the plans of all groups of plotters began with the abduction of the constitutionalist Commander-in-Chief of the Chilean Armed Forces, René Schneider." "It quickly became obvious to both White House and CIA representatives that a military coup was the only way to prevent Allende's accession to power", that is, the only way to meet Nixon's categorical demands. "To achieve this end," the Report added, "the CIA established contact with several groups of military plotters and provided weapons and tear gas to one group." Some contacts had been made which led to a kind of pact between the group headed by Viaux and the one led by Camilo Valenzuela, Commander of the Santiago Garrison, who distrusted Viaux's real contacts.

The Santiago Station of the CIA, however, continued to send reports which were pessimistic about Nixon's obstinate decisions. The headquarters was even forced to draw their attention to the fact that: "Reports should not engage in analysis and arguments, but should be confined to reporting on actions undertaken." *(147)* On October 8, the CIA's intervention group in Chile had reported: ". . . At the highest level, the Armed Forces are incapable of coming to an agreement to block Allende." *(148)* According to the deposition of Karamessines before the U.S. Senate, meetings were held between October 10 and October 22, and "the President made remarkable efforts to convince all the people present of the absolute necessity to thwart Allende's election to the Presidency." *(149)* On October 10, a telegram reached Santiago from the headquarters: "We want to encourage Viaux and improve his plans for a coup d'état. Try to influence him." *(150)* The issue was thus to encourage him but at the same time, to prevent him from launching some adventure. The "encouragement" for this "honourable" general of the Republic consisted of $20,000 and a life insurance of $250,000 for his partners.

On October 15, two Chilean generals made one last attempt to convince Schneider to join the coup d'état. He refused. Undoubtedly, this refusal cannot be attributed to Schneider's constitutionalist spirit, as it has repeatedly been suggested, for in this case he would have taken action against the putschists. Furthermore, Schneider was one of those militarists closely linked with the United States. In fact, it was he who had authorized Roy Hansen to investigate the Chilean Armed

Forces, even giving him access to documents of the General Staff, which were forbidden to Chilean civilians. All this, however, did not mean that he (any more than Frei) was ready to follow Nixon's whims and embark on a dangerous adventure, a battle involving a high risk of defeat. The proof that Scneider's attitude was at the very least reasonable, is that the U.S. government itself and the CIA Central changed their mind, even though too late, and tried (at least according to what they say) to restrain Viaux until his plans were improved.

The CIA Central finished by describing Viaux's attempt as "having very little chances of success and likely to damage any subsequent and more serious action". (151) On October 15, Kissinger met in the White House with his assistant General Alexander Haig (later to become commander of the NATO forces) and Thomas Karamessines, Chief of the CIA's Secret Services. Nixon was apparently absent. From this meeting, a telegram was sent to the Santiago Station of the CIA for General Viaux. It said: "We have studied your plan. Based on your information and our own, we have concluded that your plan for a coup d'état cannot succeed for the time being. If you fail, it may reduce the chances of success in the future. Keep your cards in your hand. We will keep in touch. The time will come when you and your friends can do something. You still have our support." (152) The decision to postpone Viaux's coup was transmitted on October 17 to one of his partners who replied that what he was being told was of little importance since it had been decided to proceed with the coup d'état no matter what happened. The result of Viaux's adventure are well known: Schneider was murdered during the kidnapping and the civilian commandos who took part in the action were so clumsy that they were caught a few days later.

The whole story of this abortive attempt clearly illustrates the two basic reasons which we have pointed out as the cause of the delay in the coup d'état to overthrow Allende. On the one hand, the High Commands of the Armed Forces had opted for united action and decided not to be led by any two-bit adventurer. On the other hand, they wanted to wait for more favourable conditions, that is, for some legal pretexts and a more evident attrition of the UP government, so as to be able to rely on a social base favourable to the coup.

In order to prepare for united action as the material conditions for the coup were developing, it was necessary for the highest ranking putschist group to contain and bring under their leadership the innumerable sections which wanted to launch into anarchistic actions. As we shall show further, no less than six attempted coups came to public attention before the final successful one. The analysis of these attempts and the reports of the CIA itself on the proliferation of these groups confirm our thesis that the really decisive factor was the reactionary class nature of the High Command and officers of the Armed Forces, and not their so-called staunch "constitutionalist" and "professionalist" spirit. This latter thesis is nothing but the continuation of the shameful and treacherous campaign waged by the "C"P leaders during the period of the Allende government, the campaign to flatter and praise the Armed Forces so as to disarm the people against them. Even today, these leaders maintain the same position and they present what happened as the work of a few "traitorous generals" who sought to "divert" the Armed Forces from their "legalist" and "apolitical" traditions. Their obvious aim is to refurbish the bankrupt policy of alliance with the CDP and to get the approval of the Armed Forces to go back to Chile and resume legal activities in Chile one day and thus continue to deceive the people.

The truth is that the putschists began organizing against Allende as far back as 1964, when there was just a remote possibility that he might win the presidential elections. The Senate Commission headed by Church established, in its Report, that on June 19, 1964, "the Chilean Defence Council (the organization responsible for coordinating the Armed Forces — J.P.) . . . went to President Alessandri to propose a coup d'état if Allende won. This offer", the report continues, "was transmitted to the head of the CIA Station, who told the Chilean Defence Council through an intermediary that the United States was absolutely opposed to a coup." This answer was only natural, since the U.S. had invested over $3 million to get Frei elected and the surveys predicted that he would garner over 50 percent of the vote, which is what actually happened. But there is more to it: "On July 20," says the Report, "the Deputy Chief of Mission at the U.S. embassy was approached by a Chilean Air Force general who threatened a coup if Allende won. The DCM reproached him for proposing a coup d'état and there was no further mention of it." Finally, the Report stated: "The CIA knew in advance that the Radical candidate for the election, several other Chileans, and some ex-politicians from another Latin American country had met on June 2 to organize a rightist group called the Legion of Liberty. They said this group would stage a coup d'état if Allende won, or if Frei won and set up a coalition government with the Communist Party. Two of the Chileans at the meeting reported that some military officers wanted to stage a coup d'état before the election if the United States Government would promise to support it. Those approaches were rebuffed by the CIA." *(153)* Such are the "constitutionalist" and "professionalist" Armed Forces which the "C"P leaders and their supporters talk about! Concerning these above-mentioned officers of a coup d'état, we must keep in mind that they were practically spontaneous and within the "professional" norms of the Armed Forces, since at that time, the far right, the CDP and the U.S. government, certain that Frei would be elected, had absolutely no interest in promoting a coup d'état. One can therefore imagine what the situation was in these same Armed Forces during the period of the Allende government, while all these groups were striving to provoke a coup.

Later, shortly before the 1970 presidential elections, the CIA started to prepare for the eventual necessity of a coup d'état in Chile. "In July 1969", the Report of the Church Commission discloses, "the CIA Station in Santiago requested and received Headquarters' approval for a covert programme to establish intelligence agents in the Chilean Armed Forces for the purpose of guiding a coup d'état. The programme lasted for four years. It involved agents drawn from all three branches of the Chilean military."

The Report continued: "During August, September and October 1969, it became increasingly clear from the agents' reports that the growing dissatisfaction and unrest within the Armed Forces was leading to an unstable situation. The events culminated in the abortive military revolt of October 1969 — the *Tacnazo,* named after the Tacna Regiment of Santiago. How close the 'amateurish *Tacnazo'* came to success was a lesson to remember, particularly in light of the upcoming presidential election of 1970 and the strong probability that Salvador Allende would emerge victorious." *(154)* With this attempt, which only raised certain economic demands for the Armed Forces (demands which were met by the government), Viaux began in actual fact to offer his services to the United States who would need them in case Allende won.

The Report of the Church Commission goes on to describe the facilities that the CIA had for finding Chilean military groups willing to stage a coup (and as we shall see later on, it was not the only one to seek out such groups). About the period which was to culminate with Viaux's second attempt, which we have already described, the Report writes: "Between October 5 and October 20, 1970, the CIA made 21 contacts with high-ranking Army and Carabinero officers in Chile. Those Chileans who were inclined to stage a coup were given assurances of strong support at the highest levels of the U.S. Government both before and after the coup. *(155)*

Further, the Senate Report states: "By September 1971 a new network of agents was in place and the Station (of the CIA — *J.P.)* was receiving almost daily reports of new putschist conspiracies." Doubtless inspired by the "constitutionalist" spirit of the Armed Forces! The Report then proceeds: "The Station and Headquarters began to explore ways to use this network." *(156)* The Report then reveals a fact which shows that the CIA had learned from its error of encouraging Viaux and had understood that it had to wait for the Armed Forces themselves to designate the leader of the coup and unite behind him. In October 1971, the CIA opted "in favour of passing 'verifiable' information to the leader of the putschist group which Headquarters and the Station perceived as having the highest probability of success." And further: "During 1972, the Station continued to monitor the group which could mount a successful coup, and it spent a significantly greater amount of time and effort penetrating this group than it had on previous groups. This group had originally come to the Station's attention in October

1971. By January 1972, the Station had successfully penetrated it and was in contact through an intermediary with its leader." *(157)* As we can see, the group with "the highest probability of success" did not come out of the blue as a result of a last minute "treason", as the supporters of the thesis on "constitutionalist" Armed Forces try to pretend, but it had already been detected among various other putschist groups in 1971.

If the CIA had such success in finding putschist groups within the Chilean Armed Forces, it is easy to imagine what occurred there when we consider that the various opposition parties were also acting with the very same perspective about the Allende government. Even the tiny fascist group *Patria y Libertad* was able to provoke an attempt at a coup d'état: the unsuccessful *Tacnazo* of June 29! But furthermore, with respect to the United States (by far the most influential "stimulator" of the putschists), one has to realize that it was not only the CIA which was involved. The Report of the Senate Commission says: "Ambassador Kerry . . . was authorized to encourage a military coup, provided Frei concurred in that solution. At the meeting of the 40 Committee on September 14, he and other 'appropriate members of the diplomatic mission' were authorized to step up their contacts with the Chilean military officers to assess their willingness to support the 'Frei gambit'." *(158)* The so-called "Frei gambit", in which Frei himself later refused to get compromised, consisted in his transferring power to a Military Junta under the pretext of averting a civil war. This junta would then call an election in which Frei himself would run. In order to organize the coup, the U.S. Ambassador was even authorized to lie to the Armed Forces and threaten them that if Allende was inaugurated as President, all military aid and sales of arms would be stopped. To lend a semblance of credibility to this threat, "Kerry was authorized to inform the Chilean military that the whole MAP (Military Aid Pact — *J.P.*) and all military sales would be suspended pending the outcome of the Congressional election on October 24, *(159)* that is, until the Congress decides whether or not to name Allende to the Presidency. The threat of cutting supplies did not only fail to materialize, but on the contrary these supplies increased significantly once Allende took office, which shows how much the U.S. government trusted the putschists within the Armed Forces.

Apart from the intervention of the U.S. Ambassador to promote a coup, the Pentagon was also very active through the Defence Intelligence Agency (DIA). Despite the fact that this participation was zealously kept secret (even in the Senate Report) because it compromised the U.S. Armed Forces in low calibre putschist intrigues, there are many testimonies of the DIA's involvement in both the preparation and the execution of the coup d'état. There are even some who think that the DIA played a more effective role than the CIA itself because of its extensive contacts with the Chilean military. It is undoubtedly to the DIA that the Senate Report is referring in veiled fashion when it alludes, in quotes, to "other appropriate members of the diplomatic mission". Who would be more appropriate than the U.S. military, with their extensive and flexible contacts with the Chilean military?

Concerning the participation, so secret and hidden, of the DIA in the coup, it is necessary to point out that under Frei's administration, tensions occurred between the Chilean and the U.S. Executives because of a fact that caused a real scandal shortly before the presidential elections. Some 100 members of the U.S. Navy had entered the country by passing themselves off as the "naval band" of Operation *Unitas* (cancelled that year because of the Chilean elections). It was later discovered that these were no innocent musicians but high-ranking officers. Significantly, later on, the date of the coup d'état was chosen to coincide with the precise moment when the U.S. Navy was displaying a large number of ships in the Chilean territorial waters under the pretext of Operation *Unitas*.

Besides, the Church Report cannot help but recognize that "U.S. military attachés maintained contacts with the Chilean military for the purpose of collecting intelligence." It then comments: "Whether these contacts encouraged the Chilean military to oppose Allende; or whether the Chilean military — already goaded toward a coup during Track II — took encouragement to act against the President from those contacts even though this was not the intention of the U.S. officers — this is one of the major questions surrounding the clandestine activities of the U.S. in the period of the Allende government." *(160)* Most subtle considerations, on the part of those who did not hesitate to invade the Dominican Republic, Vietnam, Cambodia and so many other countries! It is obvious, however, that the DIA's intervention acquired particular importance after the failure of the first attempt to stage a coup d'état through Viaux — that is, when it was stated that it would be awkward to try to divide the Armed Forces through contacts "from below" with the putschists and that only a command of the highest level would be able to discipline all the putschist groups and act effectively. However, even before Viaux's failure, Thomas Karamessines, the CIA Director of Operations and chief liaison officer with the U.S. government, had already sought coordination with the DIA, as he said before the Senate Inquiry Commission: "We also had to contact the broadest sections of the Chilean Armed Forces, especially the high-ranking officers with whom we had no regular liaison, not having foreseen such a necessity. But we were sure that our military representatives in Chile knew them well . . . To make sure that this attaché would collaborate with our efforts to get information, we still needed the agreement of the DIA." This rather belated proposal for coordination between the two agencies does not mean that the DIA was not already active on its own, as were the embassy and the multinationals. The CIA, then, approached Jamie N. Philpott, Assistant Director of the DIA, who sent the following message on September 28, 1970, to the U.S. military attaché in Chile: " . . . you should work in close coordination with the Chief of the CIA, or, in his absence, with his assistant and advise him as to the leading military figures who might play a decisive role in any movement that could eventually deny the Presidency to Allende." *(161)* The second part of the message shows how carefully the Pentagon's activity was covered up, to the extent that the U.S. Senate itself, as it seems, did not have the right to expose it: "Do not inform the Ambassador or the Defence attaché of this message and do not give them any clue about its content. In your routine activities, follow the instructions of the Ambassador. At the same time, I want, and I now order, you to act in concert with the Chief of the CIA. This message is for you only. You should not discuss it with anyone other than the CIA agents who will be recognizable. The CIA will identify them to you." Typically, both Kissinger and Bennet, Director of the DIA, in their depositions before the Senate Commission denied any knowledge of these arrangements which, nonetheless, appear in the declarations by the CIA officers before the same Commission. The persistent denials by the U.S. ruling circles of the Pentagon's participation in the coup d'état against Allende are just as ingenuous as the efforts of Senator Church to save Frei's reputation. The latter is the only Chilean politician referred to by name in the Report and every time the name comes up, it is said that "he knew nothing about this operation", or "he refused to participate in that operation", etc. This obviously proves the exact opposite.

To complete the list of the anti-constitutionalist and reactionary putschist tendencies which fought to have their say within the Chilean Armed Forces, we have at our disposal not only the facts admitted by the CIA officers before the U.S. Senate, but also the account of the frustrated coup d'état attempts that took place from the time Allende took office to the coup that overthrew him on September 11, 1973. If we include Viaux's, which we have already analyzed, we can count six attempted coups d'état before September 11. And these are just the ones that were brought to public attention. How many were stifled right within the Armed Forces before even coming to light?!

In March 1972, Colonel Julio Canessa Roberts from the Temuco Regiment was caught organizing a network to sabotage agricultural production together with the landlords of the region. Later, he tried to confine his regiment to its barracks, at a time when it was to join the Valdivia and Osorno Regiments. He had close connections with the fascist organization *Patria y Libertad* in the area as well as with the *Rolando Matus* commando group from the National Party, and he provided all of them with para-military training and assisted them in smuggling weapons from Argentina. It was later discovered that these military had links with General Alfredo Canales, of the Santiago Garrison. When he heard about these facts, Allende exposed them to General Prats who, in consultation with the junta, decided to transfer Canessa to the Military School in Santiago to restrain his premature putschist urge.

In September 1972, during a celebration in Vina del Mar in which the high-ranking military leaders participated, General Alfredo Canales, quite drunk, started talking loosely and confidentially told Rear-Admiral Horacio Justiniano that a coup was being prepared to overthrow Allende, about whom he spoke in abusive terms. Justiniano, who was not yet aware of this putschist manoeuvre, consulted with General Prats in the capital. Prats, for his part, consulted with the generals of the Santiago Garrison, Canales included. Considering the danger represented by Canales' disloyalty and the fact that the President of the Republic would probably be informed by Prats, the generals agreed to retire Canales. At the same time, in order not to arouse the suspicion of the government, they decided to make the plot appear as if it had been discovered and denounced by the Military Intelligence Service. Canales was known for his stubbornness (for which he had been given the nickname *El Macho*) and he had already declared: "They can't throw *me* out that way. I am not Viaux. I've got half the Army behind me." The necessity to organize the coup d'état in a hierarchic and constitutional manner prevailed (at the time, the CIA and the U.S. government had clearly understood this necessity) and Canales was retired. His putschist attempt was denounced by President Allende on September 14, 1972, as the "September Plan".

The putschist plan to be organized from the highest level included, however, a number of tactical measures to facilitate its execution. From the point of view of looking for a legal pretext, the plotters awaited the expiry of the constitutional delay during which the President of the Republic could call a referendum on the Constitutional Reform of the three sectors of the economy. Allende would then be at the mercy of the Parliamentary opposition. This is what happened on June 6, 1973. Shortly after, on July 2, the Contraloria rejected the proposal of the government to enact on its own those Articles of the Reform which had not been vetoed by the Executive. This was what the majority Parliamentary opposition had been waiting for. It could now declare the "illegality" of the government for having "violated" the constitution thus providing the Armed Forces with the legal pretext they required. On July 2, the Christian

Democratic Senator Juan Hamilton (a *confidant* of Frei, in politics as well as in "unofficial" affairs), declared: "the government had already violated the constitution in not enacting the full amendments to the constitution reform of the three sectors) as soon as the Contraloria had rejected its intention of enacting it in partial form." The Armed Forces were also waiting for the upcoming truck drivers' strike which was to begin on July 25 and which the taxi drivers and other professionals were supposed to join. Furthermore, from the operational point of view and by way of sounding out the possibility of popular resistance, they had planned to raid a number of factories, trade union offices and working class homes within the framework of the Arms Control Act, which had been approved by both the opposition and the government. Meanwhile, within the Armed Forces, a fierce repression was initiated against all those suspected of having sympathy for the government or even some scruples of a legalist or constitutionalist type. Finally, it had been planned to obtain Prats' resignation by means of a series of provocations. One of the officers involved in the coup declared to the *New York Times* on September 27: "We would have taken action even if Allende had called a referendum or had been able to reach a compromise with public opinion. Nothing could stop the coup after Prats' resignation. We were just putting the last touches on the plan."

On the morning of June 26, the military plotters together with the CIA and certain sections of the opposition began open provocations against Prats. As the latter was going to his office, Virginia Cox, a virago of the ruling class, blocked his way with her car and started insulting him. Prats, thinking that the person was a man, intercepted her car and walked out of his own, revolver in hand. At this exact moment, a number of cars surrounded the general and groups of people mobilized for the provocation came out to abuse him. Prats had to flee in a passing taxi. His car was completely covered with slogans such as: "General Chicken", "Prats the queer" . . . As if by some "miracle", there happened to be a large number of journalists on the spot. The next day, Prats was portrayed as insulting and threatening "a woman" with his gun and trying to assault her. This was just the beginning of a campaign to force Prats to resign so that the coup could be led from the top level and without splitting the Armed Forces. These provocations finally achieved their purpose. On August 23, Prats handed his resignation to Allende following a demonstration held against him at the door of his home by a group of women including wives of various Armed Forces officers. On August 22, Prats met with 22 generals to draft a resolution exonerating him. Only four generals accepted his demand and 18 opposed it. Among those who had agreed to "exonerate" him was General Augusto Pinochet.

However, before the conditions foreseen in the plan of the putschist high command could materialize, there was another military group, incited by the fascist organization *Patria y Libertad,* which tried to hasten them. The day following the initial provocation against Prats, a captain of the 2nd Armoured Regiment was arrested for inciting his armymen to rise against the government and the Commander-in-Chief of the Armed Forces. The next day, the commander of the unit, Lieutenant-Colonel Roberto Souper, was relieved of his duties. On the 29th, the Armoured Regiment rebelled and sent six tanks to shell the *Moneda* and freed their captain who was held at the Ministry of Defence. Aware of the putschist activities which were developing throughout the Armed Forces, these military were trying to rush things and take the leadership of the putschist movement. However, the most important leaders of the coup d'état, in close contact with the CIA, were waiting for various conditions to be met (such as those enumerated above) in order to ensure the success of the operation. The rebels were urged to surrender and they did after they realized that no other unit had followed them. The leaders of *Patria y Libertad* immediately sought asylum at the Embassy of Ecuador.

President Allende had been informed, however (probably by Prats himself before his resignation), that the following generals were also involved in a plot to overthrow him: Bonilla (CDP supporter who was to die in an "accident" after the coup), Nuno, Baeza, Arellano, Javier Palacios and Torres de la Cruz. It was on this occasion which we have already described that Allende was prepared to retire them and was opposed by the "C"P leadership, which he had consulted between August 21st and 23rd. On his part, Pinochet, the leader of this plot, did his utmost to convince the President that it was preferable to dismiss them after the formation of the Armed Forces Qualification Council, which was to meet in mid-September. Meanwhile, Allende and the UP leaders decided to set up a coordinating body between the United Workers' Central and the Armed Forces and to elaborate a plan to oppose any putschist attempt. The liaison officer between the Armed Forces, the Central and the government was none other than . . . Augusto Pinochet.

But before the final coup, there was still another attempt led this time by General Cesar Ruiz Danyau, Commander-in-Chief of the Air Force. Taking advantage of his close links with the United States, this general tried to advance the coup by a few days so as to acquire a leading role among the plotters. Because of the extremely serious political crisis, President Allende had appointed a Cabinet comprising the four Commanders-in-Chief of the three branches of the Armed Forces and the Carabineros. Ruiz wanted to use this fact in order to provoke an Air Force mutiny and unleash the coup. To this end he resigned from his position as Minister of Public Works. Given the desire of the President to have the Commanders-in-Chief of the Armed Forces in his Cabinet, this meant that Ruiz also had to resign as Commander-in-Chief of the Air Force. But he had made prior arrangements with the officers of the Air Force so that they would not accept his resignation as Commander and would use it as a pretext to mutiny and drag the rest of the Armed Forces with them. On Saturday, August 18, Allende met with Prats, with the Commander-in-Chief of the Navy Admiral Raul Montero, and with the most senior Air Force general next to Ruiz Danyau: General Gustavo Leigh, today a member of the Military Junta. Allende informed them of the plot prepared by Ruiz Danyau and brought evidence of his participation in putschist plans as well as his links with the CIA. He then threatened to release all information publicly, which would have been extremely damaging to the general plan for a coup d'état. Right after this, he asked them that General Ruiz be dismissed and replaced by Gustavo Leigh as Commander of the Air Force. General Ruiz was thus forced to resign from his position in the Air Force. Nevertheless, he never gave up his intentions. While Leigh had already been appointed to replace him, he went to the Channel 13 television programme "Now Let's Improvise" and appeared on the air wearing his Air Force Commander's uniform. I personally participated in this programme and when I got out, I met the journalist Frida Modak, director of the Information and Broadcasting Office of the Presidency of the Republic. At the request of President Allende, she had unsuccessfully tried to pass a message to me asking me to reveal that Ruiz Danyau was no longer Commander of the Air Force. The officials of Channel 13, however, absolutely refused to let the message go through. Meanwhile, in the programme, the fascist Jaime Guzman, leading member of *Opus Dei* and presently acting as ideologue and advisor to the Military Junta, was collaborating with Ruiz Danyau's provocation: "We are facing the most serious event that ever occurred under the present administration . . . The President of the Republic, according to what you're saying (talking to Ruiz — *J.P.*) puts as a condition for being Commander-in-Chief of any branch of the Armed Forces that the person be a minister in his Cabinet, in a government which is highly politicized. In other words, Mr. Allende thinks that the Armed Forces are a sort of Pretorian guard of his own . . . Nothing like this ever happened before . . . I maintain that this is deception. I say so because if the President told you, Mr. General, that you had to give up the post of Commander-in-Chief if you no longer wanted to carry on as Minister because he wanted to have all three Commanders-in-Chief in his Cabinet, he was fooling you . . .But much more serious is the fact that the President could come to such considerations and demand that a Commander-in-Chief became part of his Cabinet as a condition of retaining his position in the Armed Forces." *(162)* The next day, the Air Force remained in its barracks and the Joint General Staff of the National Defence, already under the control of the leading putschist group, sent emissaries to convince the members of the Air Force that they should stop and wait. Thus, because of his personal ambition, Ruiz Danyau missed the opportunity of becoming a member of the Military Junta and since the coup, he has had to be satisfied with the position of Rector of the University of Chile.

Now that the High Command of the Armed Forces was in the hands of the putschists and that their leader was in close contact and full agreement with the CIA and the DIA, the only thing left was to wait for the most appropriate time. In other words, certain favourable conditions which we briefly described above had to be met before fixing the date of the coup d'état. This date had to be advanced a few days in order to prevent Allende from announcing, on September 12, his intention to present the Parliament with the plans on which he had come to an agreement with the CDP, then led by Fuentealba. If there was no majority to support them, President Allende was willing to enact the constitutional reforms approved by the opposition or call a referundum in case of disagreement. The leadership of the "C"P had sent him a letter in which it accepted such a referundum and gave him full powers *to come to an agreement with the CDP*, even at the cost of a practically unconditional surrender. Therefore, despite the extreme polarization brought about by the opposition and the U.S. government, the latter was faced with the danger of "the Chilean predilection for political compromise" asserting itself. This is precisely what the Soviets wanted.

The moment of the coup had been long awaited and actively prepared for. Pinochet, in an interview with a *Reuters* journalist on December 29, 1973 said: "Look, I have here a memorandum dated August 1972. Here is another one dated July, which says that it is possible to seize control of the nation. In 1972, in the vicinity of the capital, we started to train units for the fight against extremist groups." The CIA, for its part, reported that it had detected the most important putschist group in October 1971. It also said that in January 1972, a few months before the decision Pinochet talks about, this group had been penetrated and contacts had been established with its leaders. One of the tasks to carry out during this waiting period was to hold back the numerous and uncoordinated putschist groups stirred up by the greedy ambitions aroused by the CIA, the DIA and the various opposition forces. This had to be done while keeping the high command of the coup under absolute secrecy. Another reason for this delay and possibly the most important one considering what happened since September 11, was the desire of the Armed Forces to ensure their *autonomy* vis-a-vis the political parties, to establish direct contacts with the U.S. government which would permit them to stay in power after the coup. This was fully consistent with the new line presented by Rockefeller to replace the Latin American political parties with the Armed Forces. Thus, the putschist command used the opposition parties and made them believe that they would inherit the government after the coup, to install themselves in the government and force the parliamentarians to resign. In this sense, the decision of Allende to have the participation of the Armed Forces in the ministerial departments, public utility companies and other sections of the state was skilfully used to train members of the Armed Forces for the future tasks of governing. The number of civilian advisors presently required is indeed very small. This is another reason why the putschists cultivated the confidence of the UP government in their constitutionalist spirit and refused to precipitate a coup d'état which otherwise would have served only the civilian politicians.

This organizational set-up of the coup and the necessity to wait for certain objective conditions before taking over the government and then actually governing without needing political tutelage, is what the ideologues of the government (including the advisor of Allende, Joan E. Garces) "mixed up" or "pretended" to mix up with the so-called "constitutionalist" and purely "professionalist" spirit of the Armed Forces. During the period of the Allende government, Garces (we mention him because of the great confidence Allende had in his advice) became a party to the "C"P leaders' public praise of the "progressive" and "democratic" spirit of the Armed Forces. In his analyses since the coup, he portrays the Armed Forces as above class struggle, as highly legalist and professionalist spectators willing to support the government as long as it is capable of ensuring the good functioning of the economy and the institutions. Since this was not possible due to the aggressiveness of the opposition and the interference of the CIA, on top of which came the disagreements and the "ultra-left" trends within the Popular Unity, the Armed Forces, according to Garces, were "dragged" into intervention by some of their members. This was probably Allende's opinion as well towards the end of his government, when even the most naive politician could no longer ignore the existence of putschist movements within the Armed

Forces.

In a book published after the coup, for example, Garces writes: "This attitude of Allende (of separating politics and the Armed Forces) was not unilateral, but was shared by the Army itself which, as an institution over and above its internal rival groups, adopted during this period a professional role which was clearly distinguishable from the centres of political decision-making within the state." In another instance, he claims: "To the extent that Allende succeeded in showing that his government and person meant the possibility of preserving social peace and the state political institutions, the professional armed apparatus supported him, and in the process reduced to impotency those small groups which wanted to overthrow him." *(163)* For Garces to continue to demonstrate such political naivete after all that has happened (not only before, but also after September 11), is either to conceal some ulterior motives — like the "C"P leaders who would like to depict the coup as being the work of a few traitors "who diverted the Army from its apolitical role" in the hope of being allowed to return to legal political activity in Chile — or else it is an attempt to conceal his wish to absolve himself of his responsibility for Allende's errors. Garces dares to say all these things after the testimony of the CIA itself about the innumerable putschist groups operating within the Army, after the coming to light of the many unsuccessful coup attempts and after Garces himself had recognized that "in a deliberate and systematic fashion, the Latin American military institutions have been indoctrinated to confront a so-called 'internal enemy' (the anti-oligarchic or pro-socialist popular social organizations) who they fear will take up insurrectionary forms of struggle." *(164)* And Garces was posing as Allende's "Marxist" advisor! Today, he is trying to lend some coherence to the hodge-podge of reformist measures which he inspired by claiming: "The fact that the putschist forces succeeded in September, 1973 cannot obliterate the fact that for three years they went from failure to failure." In order to corroborate this brilliant assessment, he quotes the CIA, which stated before the Senate Commission: "We were informed that it (the coup — *J.P.*) was going to take place thirty-odd times before it actually did." And Garces concludes: "Despite the wishes of the putschists, no matter how paradoxical it may seem at present, the obvious role of the Armed Forces during this period is to be the armed support for the policy of the UP." *(165)* This boils down to saying: this man has unsuccessfully tried to steal my money 30 times, thus proving how disinterested and honest he is! What a brilliant conclusion! The reasoning of Garces could make a little bit of sense if there had existed in the Armed Forces a High Command which was actually more constitutionalist than reactionary   as he and the government thought — and which had been subordinated and bypassed by lower-ranking officers with fewer legalist scruples. In fact, Garces claims: "It is among the latter *(those of lower rank)* that the putschist pressure took hold more readily." But (how paradoxical!), after Prats was removed it was the Commanders-in-Chief of the Armed Forces who led the coup with the support of almost the entire General Staff. Even Garces himself cannot name more than three or four generals who abstained from the coup d'état and prudently left the service when it was about to materialize for the sake of preserving the "unity" of the Army, that is, of course, the putschist unity. Evidently, the necessity to suppress the wild and untimely putschist ambitions of the lower-rank officers is transformed by Garcés into a so-called "anti-putschist" spirit on the part of those who stopped them in order to prepare the coup in its most effective form. The CIA, as we have seen, only made a mistake in the initial stages and it was very quick to understand with whom it had to link itself. The political circles opposing the Allende government were also absolutely convinced of the reactionary class nature of the Armed Forces and their High Commands in particular. Only the government did not see this or refused to see it. According to the ITT document examined by the U.S. Senate, Arturo Matte, the liaison between the armed forces and the multinational corporations, claimed right in September, 1970: "The Armed Forces realize the great danger that Allende's accession to power represents for democracy. They agree that he must be stopped. However, the General Staff of the Armed Forces and Frei would prefer a constitutional solution (that is, nomination of Alessandri by the Congress). This does not exclude violence, whether spontaneous or provoked." *(166)* The CIA, despite Nixon's impatience, had also realized quite early that what the leaders of the Armed Forces wanted was *just a legal pretext.* On October 14, 1970, the CIA Headquarters sent instructions to the Santiago Station, pointing out: "It seems that the coup does not have a pretext or a justification sufficient to make it acceptable in Chile or in Latin America. Therefore, it seems that it is necessary to create one in order to back it up . . . you can include various themes that the military might use to justify the coup." *(167)*

The three year delay in carrying out the coup was due, first and foremost, to fear in the face of the popular masses, secondly to the burning desire of the military to leave aside the political parties, and finally to the division of the Armed Forces into various subversive factions created, especially at the beginning, by the putschist pressures exerted by the U.S. government. The constitutional pretext, in any case, was in no way a crucial requirement, but merely a compensating factor required, in the beginning, for united action in the absence of sufficient conditions on other fronts: intensification of the crisis, social movement against the government, etc. This is evidenced by the fact that the coup was unleashed without being motivated by a violation of the Constitution by the government, with highly questionable "constitutionalist" arguments. Furthermore, the date was advanced precisely at the moment when the High Commands of the Armed Forces learned that Allende was ready to yield and fall into the legal traps which the opposition had set for him.

For anyone not yet convinced of the arch-reactionary spirit and anti-constitutionalist mentality of the military leaders, it is enough to look at their conduct since the coup d'état. What is left of the Constitution? What is left of the laws that existed in Chile? What remains of the institutions that were functioning before? Which political parties and trade union organizations can operate? What remains of the freedom of the press and other civil rights? Even the electoral lists have been burnt in order to avoid temptations . . .

Before such irrefutable facts, which cannot be explained by a sudden change of mentality, the only thing that can be said is: "God save us from such constitutionalist military forces!"

5. The Implementation of the Arms Control Act

In March 1973, the Armed Forces went on to prepare the coup by using the weapon generously given to them by the government parties when they passed the Arms Control Act. This law was unanimously approved by the parliamentarians of both the government and the opposition. It was presented before the Senate by the CDP deputy, Juan de Dios Carmona in the beginning of 1972. On April 5 of the same year, the Chamber of Deputies held a special session to discuss the issue created by the discovery of army weapons in a small truck. The opposition press had falsely declared that it was a government truck and that its occupants were members of some security apparatus of the President of the Republic. Later, it was established that one of those travelling in the truck, Osvaldo Delgado, was an "ex-commando" of the Army, where he had "specialized" as "parachutist, commando and frogman". The other person arrested, also a suspiciously "ex"-soldier, confessed that he had stolen the weapons when he was at the Parachutists' School. In short, it was a provocation mounted by the Military Intelligence Service and the CIA as a pretext to accelerate the adoption of the Arms Control Act. During the session of the Chambers held to deal with this matter, a draft resolution was approved asking the government to add to the agenda of the special session of Parliament the arms control plan then being discussed in the Senate. Later, after the compromise reached with the opposition to resolve the strike of October 1972 with the aim of suppressing the popular offensive, and after a joint discussion between the Armed Forces and the government, Carmona's bill on arms control was accepted in the main by the government and unanimously approved by Parliament. It was published as the Arms Control Act in the October 21, 1972 issue of the *Diario Oficial (Official Daily — Ed.)*. The passing of the law had been demanded in point no. 5 of the so-called "Chile Report" presented to the government by the corporations of the opposition during the strike of October 1972. Joan E. Garces himself, Allende's advisor, recognizes that this law was the result of an agreement between the government and the Armed Forces. In the book he wrote after the coup, he points out that the final draft of this law (which was made even more severe by the opposition's majority in Parliament), "was — according to Minister Toha — prepared jointly by the government and the High Commands of the Armed Forces". This is an absolute refutation of the evasive hints of the Popular Unity leaders since the coup d'état, that this law was the result of some "technical error" on the part of the government members.

The Arms Control Act gave the Armed Forces the right to carry out investigations and raids following any report (even by an individual) of the possession of arms by civilians. Anyone caught in possession of arms was declared liable to ten years in prison and "arms" were defined to include not only firearms but also many kinds of sharp or blunt instruments. The Act even provided for life imprisonment and the death penalty for "anyone who, by deed, mistreats a member of the Armed Forces". It also moved directly into the field of political repression and condemned "those who want . . . to rise against the state power".

The raids carried out under the Arms Control Act not only served to find out any potential focus of resistance to the coup d'état that was being prepared, but were also used to intimidate the workers and discourage, in advance, any possibility of resistance. The victims of these raids were treated with extreme brutality, as foretaste of what awaited them after the coup d'état. One of the first such raids was carried out at the Metropolitan Cemetery, where a large number of graves were violated and where the caretakers were forced to kneel in the rain for hours. On August 12, 200 soldiers of the Mountain Regiment N° 19 of Colchagua raided a state organization in the town of San Fernando: the Agricultural Mechanization Centre. They destroyed furniture and other material and arrested 40 workers. In Santiago, Group 10 of the Chilean Air Force raided the Cobre Cerillos factory with five busloads of soldiers (or 150), causing damage estimated at over two million escudos. During the same month, General Torres de la Cruz (known as "Allendist", as we have seen), at the head of the Fifth Army Division, organized a joint land, air and sea operation of two thousand men to raid the industrial district of the city of Puntas Arenas. For this, he used tanks, recoilless rifles, helicopters and airplanes, in an obvious attempt at a military coup. The workers were forced to lie on the ground in below-zero temperatures without moving for six hours and were beaten and insulted by the troops. One worker was shot in the back and killed. In all of this operation, the only thing seized was a .22 calibre revolver belonging to the watchman of the Lanera Austral textile factory.

During April, May and June of 1973, there was an average of three raids a week. The following month, the raids averaged almost one a day and in August, over 45 were carried out. Of the 24 raids in July, 10 were against factories, 3 against government offices, 4 against UP offices, 3 against trade union offices and only 2 against organizations of the opposition — for the sake of appearances.

With these actions, the Armed Forces were initiating the offensive to overthrow the government. Let us recall the declaration of Pinochet (after the coup) in the *Vea* magazine: "On May 28, an internal security order was issued concerning changing the basis of our action. From the defensive, we passed over to the offensive." On July 26 the truck drivers went on strike. In August, they were joined by the tradesmen, the public transportation, the professionals, etc.

While the Armed Forces were brutally raiding the centres of the people, the fascist groups, under the advice of the Armed Forces and the CIA, unleashed a series of outrages and acts of sabotage with impunity. There were no raids against them, even though they were publicly boasting that they were armed. Even the *El Siglo* issue of August 28, 1973, in drawing up the balance sheet of these atrocities from the beginning of the truck drivers' strike until August 15, reports 250 terrorist actions of the opposition: 71 against non-striking trucks (often with dynamite), 80 against buses and minibuses carrying passengers, 40 against railroads, 10 against bridges, 6 against pipelines (one of which killed 6 persons and wounded 12), 31 against factories, public service enterprises, commercial centres, etc. As of August 15, five murders had been perpetrated. Between January and May of 1973, over 200 atrocities of various sorts were carried out by the opposition. Only 100 of them were investigated by the courts of "justice" and the 83 persons accused were acquitted because of "lack of evidence".

Despite the passive attitude of the Armed Forces towards the real authors of the criminal atrocities and acts of sabotage and in fact, despite their active terrorism against the popular forces, the "C"P leaders were unable to get rid of their deliberate "naivete" concerning the collaboration of the military and the opposition to prepare a coup d'état. They merely expressed their "astonishment" about the anti-people character of these raids and begged the military to direct them against the fascist groups. The whole thing was described as a "manoeuvre by the right" to "split" the Armed Forces from the people.

On July 23, *El Siglo* commented on a statement by the United Workers' Central written in the same vein by the "C"P bureaucrats who led this organization: "Until now, the raids have been carried out against people's organizations, against the workers. The large majority of them gave no result, such as those reported by the Osorno local of the United Central and the Channel 9 of the University of Chile. None of them has affected the real promoters of violence, those who openly work for the overthrow of the government and those who call upon the Armed Forces to overthrow the constitutional President of the Republic." The article continues: "The United Workers' Central issued a note vigorously protesting against those trying to oppose the Armed Forces to the workers." The article then quotes a portion of this "vigorous" statement of the Central saying: "We are astonished that it is only the factories and the working people's areas that are raided, while it is other organizations, such as the *Patria y Libertad,* that have publicly stated their decision of arming themselves organizing criminal acts and carrying out subversion." The "vigorous" statement goes on: "It is no mystery to anyone that the United Workers' Central is not an organization conspiring against social order . . . Once again, some people are trying to create problems between the workers and the Armed Forces. All this is being done with the underhanded intent of weakening the positions of those who support the goverment and oppose putschism."

To supplement the foregoing and establish beyond doubt that it maintained its slavishness before the Armed Forces, *El Siglo* pointed out in its editorial of the same day: "The statement of the United Workers' Central says that some people are once again trying to create problems between the Armed Forces and the workers. The facts prove that these intrigues are serious and have to be exposed and clarified once and for all. The Armed Forces have all the respect and affection of the people — nobody can do anything against this."

On August 4, the most brutal of all the raids took place — the one against the industrial centre of Puerto Natales which we have already reported. On this day, another statement of the United Workers' Central appeared in *El Siglo*. It said, among other things: "Through our trade union organization, we, the workers, are willing to collaborate with the forces of law and order (i.e., the Army and police —*J.P.)* to make sure that the fanatics will not achieve their aims." How the Army putschists must have laughed at such servile and stupid proposals!

On August 8, one month before the coup d'état, a statement of the Central Committee of the "C"P appeared, which timidly said: "We do not conceal that we are deeply concerned by the manner in which the Arms Control Act has been implemented in various places." Yet, the editorial of the same day says: "Today, the Armed Forces are exhorted by reality and by the confidence placed in them by the government to carry out important tasks in terms of economic development, national defence and national sovereignty. The workers cannot understand these sorts of operations and the deployment of tanks and cannons. The workers do not want the manoeuvres of the putschists to succeed in developing hatred between the Armed Forces and the people."

Showing the opposition between the line of the phony "communists" and the line of the genuine communists, the next day, the arch-reactionary *Mercurio* reproduced one of the numerous leaflets of the Revolutionary Communist Party in order to whip up a scandal and attack it. The leaflet reads in part: "No more illusions! While the reactionaries are raiding, blasting and killing workers, what are we doing? People's power . . . Yes But not with empty hands . . . In order to seize power, the people can only rely on their own strength, not on the Armed Forces created by the bourgeoisie. Fight for a people's army! . . . Arm the people politically, ideologically and militarily!"

But *El Siglo* persisted in its line of deception until the end. It kept presenting the raids of the Armed Forces as the result of some "irresponsible accusations" by the opposition for the purpose of "setting the Armed Forces and the people at loggerheads". For example, concerning the raid of Puerto Natales, the worst of all, *El Siglo* wrote: "This action of the Chilean Air Force is the result of irresponsible accusations brought before the Armed Forces by rightist elements with the intention of opposing them to the workers through the implementation of the Arms Control Act." The official organ of the "C"P had no concern for the workers being raided or for the lot of the people in case the Armed Forces seized power. It was only concerned that incidents of this kind might tear up the phony image which they had created for the Armed Forces and that the people might begin to organize in order to fight them. The other parties of the Popular Unity were also paralysed by the same praising attitude towards the Armed Forces into which they had been dragged. Even the General Secretary of MIR, in his speech to a meeting of the Revolutionary Workers' Front at the Caupolican Theatre of Santiago in May 1972, said: "With the Carmona draft *(the Arms Control Act — J.P.),* they want to draw the Armed Forces into the police and repressive tasks of internal government, tasks that they have only taken up in dictatorial countries such as Brazil, Uruguay, Greece and Indonesia. They want to set the Armed Forces against the people. They want to put them in the service of the hatred, bitterness and rivalries of the reactionary parliamentarians."

6. Opposition to Any Preparation of the People for Armed Confrontation

The lavish praise for the reactionary Armed Forces, as we have already shown, is part and parcel of the plan of the "C"P to impose a system of exploitation under a "socialist" disguise, a system of state capitalism to be set up in alliance with the pro-imperialist forces. Because of this plan, what they fear most is that the people be won over by the revolutionary currents and start organizing for armed struggle. This effort to disarm the people ideologically and physically continued during the UP government, during the coup d'ètat and is maintained even now, against any resistance aimed at defeating fascism.

The positions of the RCP and other anti-reformist groups

which were part of the Popular Unity, or close to it, were ridiculed and described as "ultra-left provocations" or "adventurist" stands. Any attempt to create armed groups among the people was categorically condemned and suppressed. As early as October 10, 1970, Daniel Quintana wrote in *El Siglo*, in a paternalistic and smug tone: "In the small ultra-leftist groups, there may be and there must be a lot of honest people, misled children or thrill-seekers who may be, at the very bottom of their heart, well-intentioned persons." Orlando Millas, for his part, claimed in the June 13, 1971 issue of the same paper: "The theses advocating armed confrontation and the irresponsible calls for violence must be ended once and for all. If they carry on, they must be thoroughly denounced as being against the people's government."

President Allende was easily won over to these positions of the pro-Soviet "Communists", thanks to his social-democratic background and the influence of freemasonry. On September 15, 1971, the United Workers' Central organized a meeting to oppose putschist manoeuvres that had been uncovered. A large section of the masses were shouting and demanding arms to oppose the subversion. Allende said, however: "Demagogically asking for arms is not the issue, because the arms are our political beliefs and our resolution to win. The Chilean Armed Forces and Carabineros are institutions which display their professional sense and obedience to the constitution and the law. It is because of this that I am President of Chile." The following month, in a press conference, Allende declared: "In our country, there are no other armed forces than those established by the constitution, that is the Army, the Navy and the Air Force. Therefore, any armed group wanting to take action is creating problems for the government." He then said: "We have given strict instructions that these armed groups, as soon as they are discovered, be prosecuted under the Internal Security Law of the State. I add that the government will act implacably, no matter what the name or political affiliation of the individuals involved in such manoeuvres may be." *(168)*

This position was not only put forward in the initial period of his government. It was maintained until the end. In the critical month of August 1973, on the 11th, *El Siglo* published Allende's declarations on the appointment of the military cabinet. He said: "In this country, there will be no Armed Forces other than those established by the constitution and the law. In this country, there will be no parallel army. In this country, the chain of command will be preserved. In this country, the Armed Forces, Carabineros and Investigaciones have written their loyalty and obedience to the civilian power in the history of the democratic evolution. For this reason, the government will reject any attempt at subversive infiltration of the Armed Forces, Carabineros and Investigaciones." However, a month earlier, on July 8, *El Siglo* had published an interview in which Allende let his doubts show through and declared his willingness (although weak and hesitant) to call upon the people to oppose the attempts to overthrow the government. Let us recall that Allende at least had the intention of setting up, through the Civilian Defence Law, unarmed civilian groups which could be armed in due time and be capable, in the eventuality of a coup, to assist the "loyal" sections of the Armed Forces in crushing the fascist groups and putschist sections of the military. In this interview, he said: "We did have confidence, we do have confidence and we will continue to have confidence in the Armed Forces, in the Chilean forces of law and order. The Popular Unity's programme states that there will be no other armed forces other than those established by the constitution and the laws. We have repeated this time and again. But if a civil war breaks out, programmes disappear, the constitution disappears, and I suppose that a government has the right and obligation to defend itself by every means possible . . . When I was telling the people that I believed in people's power, I conceived such a power and agreed with it only as a form of people's organization allowing them to participate in the government. Therefore, I feel quite indignant when the same elements who were hoping yesterday that the subversive attempt would bear fruit are today underhandedly looking for a way to claim that it is the parties of the Popular Unity, the United Workers' Central and the government who are going to arm the people and who are setting up a people's power alongside the government itself . . . To me, it is evident and certain that the vast majority of the Chilean soldiers will never accept the role that some are trying to assign to the Armed Forces. The possibility that they get transformed into satraps crushing the workers and people is not consistent with their history and tradition."

The correct conclusion (obviously not for the plan promoted by the "C"P of Chile) was drawn by the widow of Salvador Allende after the coup d'état and the murder of her husband by the military. In an interview published by the Mexican newspaper *Excelsior*, on September 20, 1973, she pointed out: "It is not enough to take power through elections. The people should have been armed or should have had an army of their own." Just to what extent these initial spontaneous declarations expressed the conclusions Allende was about to reach (although too late), it is hard to tell. Very quickly, his widow was dragged into the international campaign orchestrated by the "C"P leaders and the Soviet Union in order to hide their own responsibility in what took place in Chile and give their own interpretation of the facts. Such declarations were never heard again.

The policy of the "C"P leadership and their followers in the Popular Unity towards the increasing and irrevocable involvement of the Armed Forces in the putschist plans of the Pentagon, the CIA and the internal reactionary opposition groups was one of bravado and threats, and finally, of desertion, sabotage and liquidation of any attempt to resist the coup. The bravado and threats were mainly characteristic of the first period of the Allende government, although they continued to a certain extent in the latter period. In the final analysis, since they were nothing but bravado and threats, they contributed in making the repression of the people more brutal.

One of the most notorious for these blusters about "what will be done" in case the opposition tries to overthrow the government was Luis Corvalan, the General Secretary of the "C"P. On September 6, 1971, on the Anniversary of the Communist Youth, he said: "some say that life is highly unsettled . . . Whether or not the Chilean situation is so unsettled, that's what we'll see. But in the meantime, we can declare that nobody will negate what we've achieved. We're going to fight against any attempt to take us backward, and from now on, there are things which are irreversible . . . We know that there are problems and even germs of dissatisfaction amongst the people because of this or that problem which has not been solved or properly solved. But at the same time, we know what immense strength and reserves the Chilean revolution possesses and these will all be mobilized against those trying to roll the wheel of history backward. These last few weeks, the reactionaries feel encouraged in their dreams of taking back the government. The coup of the Bolivian 'gorillas' has been most timely for them. But they are plucking up their courage to no avail. We will not back down even in the face of guns. They better keep this in mind and not complain if the people let them have it." *(169)* On December 4th of the same year, Corvalan said over the radio: "This week, a series of important events brought to light the sinister intention of a reactionary sector to cause chaos and overthrow the government. On this, the first thing to be said, so that the plotters don't have the shadow of a doubt concerning our attitude, is that they won't be given the green light for subversion and those who come looking for trouble will get their fill . . . The working class and people of Chile won't permit fascist gangs to come out in the streets again. We won't allow another demonstration like the one of Wednesday. And this is no empty talk. This is the will of millions of sons and daughters of the people, a will which is fully shared by the 150,000 militants of our party and the 50,000 war-tempered members of the Communist Youth. The fascists will be stopped! They will have to prove their mettle in combat!" *(170)*

The fascist gangs took over the streets almost without any resistance and contrary to what Corvalan had announced, his words were just "empty talk". On the same day he was talking, the premises of the "war-tempered Communist Youth" were assaulted with total impunity. While this was taking place, he was insisting: "They want to overthrow the People's Government by creating a chaotic climate in order to launch a coup d'état. But they will have to face a people which is mobilized, a working class ready for anything in order to defend its victories. This colossal human wall will stop any reactionary putschist attempt with the same energy and violence as used by the right wing. If the 'momios' keep conspiring, the people will let them have it." *(171)*

In October 1971, Orlando Millas, Isidoro Carrillo, director of the Lota mine and member of the CC of the "C"P, and Victor

Diaz, also a CC member, took the floor at the National Conference of the "C"P. Millas said: "For this reason, it is appropriate to point out that the people will not tolerate treason against Chile. If the reactionaries want a fight, they will have it, and any attempt to raise a hand against the Government of President Allende will be crushed in an exemplary manner." Victor Diaz repeated what Millas said: "The people will not tolerate treason against Chile. Any attempt to rise against the people's government will be crushed by the full force of the law and the fighting and united mobilization of the masses." Isidoro Carrillo, for his part, said: "The Conference will serve to undertake the mobilization of the people, to defend our victories and at the same time to warn the enemies of the people that nobody can stop the revolution, even if U.S. imperialism gets angry." *(172)* Right after the coup, Carrillo and other leaders were found by the military in their trade union office and they were shot to death. They were waiting for instructions from their party as to what to do about the coup d'état . . .

In 1972, Corvalan still held similar views (at least in words). During an interview which was later published in the form of a pamphlet entitled "Corvalan, 27 Hours", he said: "If the reactionary forces, or a portion of them, decide tomorrow to embark on the road of subversion and if the latter breaks out, the Government, all the parties of the Popular Unity and the working class and people will bar their way and use whatever means possible to smash them resolutely and rapidly. Such is our will. Such is the will of the people and the Government. This is also our obligation. This is our duty to the fatherland and the revolution."

Further, answering the journalist who was pointing out to him the fact that "the Chilean popular forces are unarmed would facilitate the victory of a rightist insurrection", Corvalan said: "The working class have their own arms, and one of the most powerful is the general strike. There is no doubt that in the case of such a hairbrained attempt — and this is the directive the United Central has given — the workers of the country would completely stop all activity throughout the country and occupy the factories. This alone would have a very strong impact. I would say decisive. But in addition to that, the proletariat and people could use — and I think they will use — other elements as well. They could use whatever their hand can fetch and turn even working tools into combat weapons." This is the man calling "adventurist" those who advocated arming and seriously preparing the people for an armed confrontation!

In January 1973, right in the midst of the electoral campaign for the renewal of Parliament, Corvalan was still carrying on with his empty threats: "They have absolutely no concern for the lot of the people nor for the destiny of Chile," he said at a meeting held in front of the Government Palace. "They know that their revanchist designs and any attempt to topple the government, whether through subversion or constitutional trickery, such as accusing and dismissing the President of the Republic, would purely and simply bring about a bloodbath. When they write on the walls 'Jakarta' — the name of the Indonesian capital where a coup d'état resulted in the murder of 400,000 patriots in less than 24 hours — they are showing to what extremes their bloodthirstiness can take them. Once again, we say that we do not want a confrontation and that we will do everything possible to avoid one. But if they ask for it, they will get it. If the reactionaries embark on this road, they will get what they deserve." *(173)*

All this bluster, however, came to an end after the March 1973 election, more precisely, at the Plenum of the Central Committee of the "C"P held at the end of May. The purely defeatist slogan "no to civil war" was then formally adopted after it had been raised during the snivelling campaign of Volodia Teitelboim for the Senate. And what brought about this sudden change? The failure of Prats' trip to the Soviet Union during the same month? This may have had some influence, but the decisive factor was that the "C"P leadership then realized that all their efforts to build up a base of support within the Armed Forces had been in vain. Prats was more and more isolated. In his absence, the High Commands of the Armed Forces had finally united and adopted the plan for a coup to be led from the top. They moved from planning to action. As Pinochet pointed out during his interview after the coup: "On May 28, an internal security order was issued concerning changing the basis of our action. From the defensive, we passed over to the offensive." It was also in May that the hopes of the "C"P leadership for an alliance with the CDP went down the drain. Through an internal election, the leadership of the CDP was taken over by the section led by Frei which had opposed any compromise.

For the first time, the "C"P leaders and those under their influence in the Popular Unity began to face the glaring fact that a coup d'état for the benefit of imperialism and the worst internal reactionaries was being prepared within the Armed Forces. Prior to that, as a result of their subjectivism and tailism to their Soviet ideologues and their sustained efforts to mystify the role of the Armed Forces, they had ended up being themselves convinced that these would act as more or less impartial arbitrators if a violent confrontation ever broke out between the government and opposition forces. They needed the Armed Forces in order to establish their state capitalism and with this in mind, they praised them to the skies and ended up believing that there existed a real possibility of relying on them in case of an armed rebellion by some sections of the opposition. The Popular Unity leaders ended up believing that the potential armed confrontation between the opposition and the government could be reduced into a clash between civilian forces. They also believed that a large-scale propaganda campaign against civil war coupled with the timely intervention of the military to stop a confrontation of this type would ensure the latter's short duration and pave the way for imposing the so-eagerly desired compromise. It is for this reason that Corvalan, in the already quoted interview of 1972, said: "I already talked about a situation of force, an extra-constitutional situation in which the reactionaries or a part of them would jump out of the limits set by the constitution and resort to arms to take back the government. In the worst case, such a situation could lead to a civil war, fulfilling the desire of a minority which has gone out of its mind. I think that even a situation of this type, at this time, would be more or less short-lived. To me, it seems difficult that such a struggle will last for very long." Then, answering a question by the journalist, he added: "Why? Because I don't think that this country would tolerate a long struggle of this nature. For this, it seems to me that the situation would settle down in a few days or in a few weeks . . . I am relying on the fact that 90 percent of the country rejects civil war."

Then came the period when the "C"P leadership, while carrying on its campaign to adulate the Armed Forces and drawing highly dramatic pictures of what a civil war would mean, made stern threats and claimed that "even the stones would be turned into weapons" in order to smash to smithereens those who would try to overthrow the government. Of course, this was understood to apply only if the "minority which has gone out of its mind" was composed of civilians only.

In May, 1973, however, the on-going "no to civil war" campaign which was formally approved by the Plenum of the Central Committee took up a new content and significance. As we have pointed out, it had become obvious by then that leading sections of the Armed Forces were involved in the subversive plans of the opposition. But neither the "C"P nor its followers in the Popular Unity could say this openly. An open call to stop a military coup meant the mobilization of the people to confront the Armed Forces and we have already seen why the "C"P leadership would never take such a road. Against this background, the campaign based on the slogan "no to civil war" took on really grotesque features. Since the "C"P leaders knew that those preparing the coup were not a mere civilian "minority which had gone out of its mind" and that any threat to fight "with fire and blood" against those unleashing a civil war (let alone a coup d'état) would turn against the Armed Forces, they completely stopped bragging and threatening as they used to do. Consequently, the whole "no to civil war" became a "humanist" campaign à la Mahatma Gandhi. Furthermore, this campaign became completely out of place, since nobody in the civilian opposition had a civil war in mind. The mission of the opposition was only to create the conditions and pretext for the military coup being prepared. The slogan of Corvalan and his cronies thus became nothing more than a laughing matter in the ranks of the opposition. In fact, the role of the opposition, at that time, was to promote the Constitutional Reform of the "three sectors" and bring about an irreconcilable conflict between the Executive and the other public powers, to start a campaign to accuse the government of electoral fraud in the March 1973 elections, to promote the strike of the truck drivers, tradesmen and others, to systematically dismiss the government ministers, to facilitate the implementation of the Arms Control Act, to organize various provocations to get Prats' resignation, etc., etc. Thus, the opposition only had the mission of creating the social conditions and concocting the legal pretexts for the military to proceed and topple the government. It is quite natural, then, that it cynically joked and sneered at the hue and cry of the "C"P drawing an apocalyptic picture of the civil war's atrocities. For example, Jorge Navarrete, the representative of Frei and his team in the most widely broadcast political television programme, "Now Let's Improvise", dared to say on the air: "It is precisely to avoid the atrocities of a civil war that we believe that the best solution is that the Armed Forces stop a government which has violated the constitution and legality and which has led the country into an irreversible economic and political crisis." Afterwards, when he was asked whether this statement meant that he supported the idea of a coup d'état, he replied that he, "personally", preferred a coup d'état to the "atrocities" of a civil war.

At this point, Corvalan and his friends were no longer talking about a confrontation that would last a few days only because "90 percent of the country rejects civil war". On the contrary, Corvalan declared in the May 28 issue of *El Siglo*: "The authors of escalation are trying to belittle the importance and the truth of the denunciations made by the popular sections and the CP in particular (about the danger of civil war). For this reason, they want to discredit a campaign which has grown tremendously . . . Some believe that we are exaggerating the danger, or that it simply does not exist. In order to have a civil war, they say, there has to be a division within the Armed Forces, but these stand united. The facts show that the Chilean society is in the process of being divided in two, that we are within a hair's breadth of a trial of forces and that the political atmosphere is being loaded with hatred. In other words, the main factors conducive to a fratricidal war exist or are developing. To a certain extent, it is possible that such a war would involve civilians only." Then, in order to counter the jests and jeers that the latter assertion would cause in the opposition circles, which were fully aware that a coup d'état was being prepared, he added the veiled threat that this "division" might also extend to the

Armed Forces: "On the other hand, it is clear that the Armed Forces stand united in the fulfilment of their professional duties and it is in the country's interest that it continues to be so. But when the Chilean society reaches the point where the norms of social order get violently smashed and there are those who want the class struggle to be transformed into armed confrontation, even the unity of the military institutions can suffer a breakdown, since no institution or person can be completely detached from the fighting trends."

In essence, the ultimate line of the "C"P leadership was completely dishonest and equivocal and had nothing to do with what was happening. It was deliberately ambiguous and consisted in irresponsible threats (especially in the beginning) coupled with pathetic appeals to the "humanitarianism" of those who wanted to smash the government and unconditional surrender to them. The threats gradually fizzled away and were replaced with an attitude of snivelling and increasingly begging the reactionaries. This was a line of demobilization of the people and it was consistent (in its extreme inconsistency) with the usual politics of all opportunists who place their hopes in appeals addressed to their opponents. They raised the slogan of "no to civil war" as the central issue precisely at the time when both they themselves and their opponents were certain that *there would be no civil war* because the people were disarmed and the Armed Forces were united for a coup d'état. Under the circumstances, then, this was a line of getting the people to accept complete surrender as long as it was to avoid the "atrocities of a civil war", or, more concretely, of a coup d'état, since they did not dare to call a spade a spade.

Such a policy of cowardly appeasement corresponded to the line already taken up in 1972 and presented in the long interview of Corvalan. This line was officially reiterated as the tactics to be followed during the May 1973 Plenum of the "C"P Central Committee. In this interview, Corvalan said: "What we are saying today is, first of all, that in times of serious difficulty, the reactionary forces are trying to destroy the present government by extra-constitutional or supposedly constitutional means. If they fail — and our duty is to make every effort to ensure that they fail — or, in other words, if we are capable of binding the hands of the enemy, stopping the coup d'état, preventing subversion and keeping the country on the constitutional path, and if, therefore, we succeed in helping the Allende Government complete its mandate and accomplish at least the basic points of its programme, we will be able to win over those sections of the people who don't stand with us at the present time or who are filled with doubts and misunderstandings. In such an eventuality, I don't see how it would be possible for the adversary to so easily recuperate its lost positions through the 1976 elections."

In May 1973, these purely defensive tactics and the eagerness to have an alliance at all costs with the CDP were strengthened by the already quite concrete threat of a coup d'état as well as by the certainty that even if the Popular Unity could make it until 1976, it had absolutely no chance whatsoever of winning another election. According to the opportunist logic of those exercising hegemony over the Popular Unity, the most important thing was therefore to make sure that they would last until 1976 without being swept away by a coup d'état. With this, there was a remote chance of achieving the alliance with pro-U.S. populism so much dreamed about. Thus, Corvalan put the tactical line this way before the May 1973 Plenum: "Carry on until the 1976 elections and ensure the victory of a new people's government", evidently by convincing those who "don't stand with us" or who are "filled with doubts and misunderstandings".

In the meantime, since they refused to really mobilize the people to defend the government (contrary to what they had boasted they would do), the only thing left for them was to beg the reactionaries. They could only make horrifying descriptions of a civil war in order to deter the reactionaries from staging a coup d'état or, in the extreme, to prevent any resistance if it took place anyway, since such resistance would make their alliance with the CDP more difficult (because of the necessity of having the agreement of the Armed Forces for this alliance). By saying "no to civil war" and rejecting by word and deed any intention to organize resistance against the coup, they were drawing in advance a demarcation line between themselves and anyone who would try to oppose this coup. They were telling the putschists: "We will not be the ones standing in your way. Be kind enough to remember it." Actually, they were only continuing their policy of slavishness and praise towards the Armed Forces, b··t this time with the very concrete threat of a coup d'état. The aim was to get the Armed Forces to tolerate their existence so that they could continue deceiving the people. This was merely a logical attitude on the part of those who had to win over the Armed Forces in order to convert themselves into exploiters. Consequently, this line of "no to civil war" was the quintessence oɪ the same policy of betrayal and capitulation that they had foll: wed throughout the Popular Unity administration.

On July 8, 1973, during a meeting organized by his party in the Santiago Caupolican Theatre, Corvalan implored again: "We have always upheld — and we still do so despite the recent events — that in the conditions of Chile, it is actually possible to wage the anti-imperialist and anti-oligarchic revolution and march to socialism without civil war, despite all the necessary fierceness of class struggle."

"The enemy," Corvalan added, "is trying to block this possibility completely. We have to do the opposite. While this road is not completely blocked, we have to work to keep it open and broaden it. This is in the interest of the people, in the interest of the present and future generations, in the interest of the security of the fatherland. Civil war would not only bring about untold sufferings, deaths and irremediable material losses, but it would also leave the country defenseless in front of the 'gorillas' of the highland who are dreaming to invade our northern territory with the help of very powerful countries." *(174)* The latter part of this argument is also obviously intended to convince the Armed Forces of the dangers involved in a situation of violence.

The entire subsequent practice of the "C"P leaders was consistent with this policy of capitulation to the putschists. A few weeks before the coup, they asked their militants to turn in the few weapons which might have been in their possession. In 1974, I happened to meet some of these militants in Peru. They used to work in the large nationalized "Hirmas" textile industry. With great naivete they praised the "foresight" of the leaders of the party in forcing them to turn in their guns shortly before the coup. "Imagine what would have happened if they had found them on us," they commented. On their part, the leaders of the United Workers' Central, led by a leading member of the "C"P, ordered the workers to stay at their workplaces. This is exactly what the putschists were demanding when they established a day and night curfew for a number of days. They wanted to immobilize the workers while the armed troops would take control of the key centres and surround the workplaces in order to kill or jail those who were on their black lists. Joan E. Garces reports the following conversation which he had in the morning of September 11 at the Government Palace with Jorge Godoy, Minister of Labour, former president of the United Workers' Central and member of the Political Bureau of the "C"P. "Comrade Minister," Garces said, "it seems that this time, the coup involves the Navy as well as the Air Force and the Army . . . Every passing minute is precious . . . I wonder if it would not be better for the workers to deploy themselves for certain concrete objectives, including the centre of the city, instead of remaining concentrated in the factories." And Godoy answered: "No. The workers are better off in their workplaces. There, they know what to do." Garces comments, recollecting his thoughts of the moment: "The answer is scathing. I don't think I should insist. But still, I don't understand. The rebel forces are beginning to deploy throughout the city while the workers, on the other hand, are immobilized in their factories. Faced with mobile enemy forces which are centrally coordinated and disposing of offensive means and resources infinitely superior compared to the few hundred guns and sub-machine-guns to which the workers have access, the workers are waiting at fixed points, practically isolated from one another. I don't see how such a combat plan can suit the present situation. It rather seems that this is a plan for non-combat." *(175)* This is precisely what it was: "a plan for non-combat". Capitulation to the coup was what was advocated by the "C"P leadership since they had formally adopted the line of "no to civil war" which, obviously, could only demobilize the workers predominantly under the influence of the Popular Unity. It was precisely in order to disarm those who were not willing to follow this capitulationist orientation, that the Arms Control Act had been passed and implemented. Shortly after his conversation with Garces, the same Jorge

Godoy was compelled by the Military Junta to appear on radio and television to call upon the workers to cease all resistance and obey the new government. Until now, we have not heard a single word from the "C"P leadership denouncing or even criticizing such betrayal by a member of their Political Bureau. This means that Godoy was implementing a treacherous decision of the entire leadership of his party. Such is the manner, then, in which Corvalan's promises of "letting them have it" were "fulfilled". This is what all his bluster about forcing them to "prove their mettle in combat" boiled down to. This is how his militant declarations of "stopping any reactionary putschist attempt with the same energy and violence" . . . was put into practice. Such were his "obligation" and "duty to the fatherland and the revolution."

On the other hand, the "150,000 members of our party and the 50,000 war-tempered members of the Communist Youth" who, according to Corvalan, would make sure that "the fascists will be stopped", were led into unconditional surrender by their leaders. Large numbers of them were killed or put in jail for a long time without even having tried to oppose the reactionary Armed Forces.

The other leaders of the Popular Unity were led into the same position of capitulation to the putschists. According to Garces, "while Allende and his personal guard were deciding to refuse any surrender and continue to resist, another meeting was taking place at the Sumar factory. It was the meeting of the Political Committee of the Popular Unity. After half an hour of deliberations, the leaders of the political parties arrived at a decision: no resistance." *(176)*

This is how the U.S. government reaped the fruits of patient and protracted work within the Armed Forces aimed at implementing the policy recommended by Rockefeller as early as 1969: to replace the Latin American political parties with the military. It had an easy victory in Chile. With trivial opposition, it was able to annihilate tens of thousands of Chileans who opposed imperialism. Over 100,000 were put in jail and several hundred thousand were forced to emigrate. In this manner, U.S. imperialism added one more country, one more link, to its chain of military dictatorships it had planned to establish in Latin

America to defend its interests.

Until now, no self-criticism has ever been heard from those who, two days before the coup, were writing in *El Siglo*: "There is and there can be no antagonism whatsoever between the people, their government and the armed institutions." On the contrary, with their utter cynicism they are using the thousands and thousands of people killed, tortured, jailed or exiled as well as the millions of Chileans dying a slow death because of the ferocious exploitation and pauperism introduced by the military dictatorship in order to deploy, throughout the world and with the millionaire support of the Soviet Union and its accomplices, a campaign to resurrect the policy which brought the Chilean people into a tragedy beyond description. When they publicize the sufferings of the Chilean people (for which they are responsible to a decisive extent), they only want to create an international pressure on the U.S. government so that it will deign to install less bloodthirsty military in command of Chile, military who would tolerate the gradual resumption of their usual activities of deceiving the people and promoting phony socialism with joint exploitation by the two superpowers. For this reason, today as always, they oppose the organization of any armed resistance aimed at overthrowing the fascist junta. They are desperately looking for "progressive" militarists to flatter; and they seek to form an alliance with the Frei section of the CDP. In short, they continue to implement the line dictated by the Soviet Union as if nothing had happened in Chile.

Part V
Contradictions within the Forces of the Opposition and of the Government

Chapter XI
Struggles Within the Putschist
and Anti-Putschist Forces

The development of state capitalism by the "peaceful road", which the Popular Unity government, at the instigation of the "C"P leadership, attempted to promote, had the "virtue" of gradually uniting the different classes affected by the government's reforms. This led, from the middle of 1971 onwards, to an increasingly systematic offensive to overthrow it. In this offensive, the most retrograde internal groups and the most reactionary forces of U.S. imperialism finally won the leadership of the opposition movement and imposed their openly putschist, subversive strategy on it. Thus they blocked any possibility of conciliation or transaction between the government and the CDP, which would have made the coup d'état unnecessary.

1. The Forces of the Reactionary Opposition

At the beginning, there were in fact certain rather pronounced differences in style between the opposition to the Allende government led by the National Party and that led by the Christian Democrats. We mention only these parties because they were the two main opposition political forces, with other less important forces grouped around them.

The differences in tactics between the CDP and the NP (as well as the links between them as opposition forces) reflected the class interests (internal or foreign) represented by the leading groups of the two parties.

As far as its leadership is concerned, the Christian Democratic Party is the representative of the relatively developed sections of the non-monopoly bourgeoisie in Chile, although it also reflects the interests of a few isolated monopolies. In addition, it represents the desire of fairly large sections of the middle bourgeoisie for development in alliance with U.S. imperialism, as well as the aspirations of a developing bureaucratic bourgeoisie, in that there was some development of state capitalism under the Frei government. In addition, judging by the substantial investments that the CIA admits having made to launch it and by the advance of U.S. imperialism in Chile under the Frei government, the CDP particularly represents certain U.S. monopoly and financial circles. These are the circles that have an interest in promoting certain reforms in order to develop capitalism and expand consumption, with a view to taking over the most profitable part of Chilean manufacturing industry. This is why the Frei government, inspired by the "Alliance for Progress" policy inaugurated by Kennedy, undertook reforms which hit at the interests of the financial oligarchy. The reforms, which included moderate agrarian reform, setting a minimum wage for peasants, and legislation for the unionization of agricultural workers, were part of the Frei government's plan to develop capitalism in the countryside and thus to enlarge the internal consumer market for industries, notably those financed by U.S. investment. This plan to expand consumption was expressed on the international level by the economic integration of a number of Latin American countries through regional agreements (such as the Andes Pact), which were promoted by the Frei government. These pro-U.S. reforms that went against the interests of the landed oligarchy and of some sections of the monopolist bourgeoisie made a joint candidacy by the CDP and the NP in the 1970 presidential elections impossible, thus allowing Allende to win with a percentage vote lower than he had received in the 1964 election (39 percent of the vote in 1964 as against 36.3 percent in 1970).

The reforms against the monopolies and landed oligarchy, combined with an intensive campaign of demagogic propaganda generously funded by U.S.-dependent financial bodies and by the CIA, were used to develop a popular movement in support of the CDP. The Christian Democrats, as the majority party in Chilean politics, could count amongst their members and amongst their vast electoral clientele not affiliated with the party, large numbers of small producers and tradesmen, professionals, handicraftsmen, white-collar employees, and even a considerable number of agricultural as well as urban workers. It should be remembered that in the middle of the UP government's term (May 1972), at the elections for the leadership of the CUT, the Christian Democrats received nearly the same percentage of the vote as the "C"P and SP ("C"P 29 percent; SP 26.5 percent; CDP 26 percent) and won the presidency of the most important district council of the CUT, the Santiago Council.

Besides the demagogy that went with their reforms, the Christian Democrats took advantage of the anti-communism fomented by those who intentionally presented as a model of "communism" the repressive, exploiter regimes of the USSR and the Warsaw Pact member countries. They also benefited from the dominant influence of Catholicism over the Chilean people and from the support of those circles within the Church which opposed the ultra-reactionary positions of the Opus Dei.

Although the policy of the CDP leadership did not aim at assisting the sections of the people that supported it, it nevertheless needed them and their electoral support. It therefore had to keep them in mind and make concessions to them (even if these were of a formal nature) in order not to lose them. This anti-rightist electoral base was one of the reasons why the methods the CDP used to oppose Allende differed somewhat in the beginning from those used by the extreme right (although certain differences continued to exist until the end). The CDP did not systematically oppose the extension of state capitalism through expropriations. This was why it did not at the outset support the constitutional indictments issued by the National Party against the Allende ministers who were implementing the expropriations. Of course, it did intend to limit the expropriations; to insist they be carried out through legislation voted on in Parliament, where it could tip the balance either towards the opposition or towards the government; and to force the government to negotiate with it so that it might share in the control of the nationalized businesses. There is no doubt that this demand for control corresponded to the U.S. imperialist interests represented by the Christian Democrats. U.S. imperialism did not oppose an expansion of the public sector that would allow it to make deals with and invest in more stable, solid, state-guaranteed businesses. But it could obviously not agree to the control of this sector by a government in which a pro-

Soviet "Communist" Party played a dominant role. The constitutional reform of the three economic sectors presented by the Christian Democrats served this purpose. Later, however, when the CDP was led by the most reactionary forces in the country and by imperialism to participate in subversive opposition, this reform would be used as a legal pretext to justify the overthrow of the government, rather than as a negotiating instrument. The reform was in fact first presented as a basic condition for CDP-government agreement; but later, when Allende wrote the Christian Democrats that "If an agreement were reached, I would be willing to promulgate the constitutional reform in order to clear away the formal obstacle so that we could move on to discuss the essential concerns of the workers and of all Chileans" *(177)*, his offer was rejected.

The CDP tried to make its style of opposition appear different from the National Party's in order to maintain its electoral popularity: it did not wish to be seen to be publicly associated with putschist or subversive plans, nor with the extreme-right or fascist circles which were more or less openly behind these plans. It preferred to use the law and the corporations to lead a longer-term offensive and to intensify the economic crisis in order to force the government either to capitulate (so that it could control it) or to resign (so that it could succeed it). The Christian Democrats thought that if they were unable to achieve these goals in the middle term, their work would in any event create conditions for the defeat of the Popular Unity in the presidential elections that were to take place in 1976. A sort of intermediate plan was put forward for a time during the parliamentary elections of March 1973: the idea was to win an opposition majority big enough to legally impeach the President of the Republic. The Christian Democrats really feared an openly illegal coup d'état, for they did not know whether they would take over from the government after its overthrow, nor how long it would be before the return of elections, in which they could bring their entire weight as largest party (28.5 percent of the vote in the 1973 parliamentary elections) into play. "We know when the military will take over the government, but we don't know when they will leave", was what the more moderate elements in the CDP repeatedly stressed to the impatient ones. Time showed they were right: the Military Junta had the electoral lists burned so that the "politicos" would not get any ideas about a quick return to elections.

Although these reasons help to explain the reticence of the Christian Democratic leaders to join in the coup d'état preparations with the same vehemence as the NP, their influence on the CDP's practical position was gradually reduced by the pressure of events, and in the end they only accounted for subtle differences between the two opposition groups. The rapid political and economic decline of the government (which from 1972 on could no longer risk calling a referendum) and the impatience of the oligarchy and U.S. imperialism to overthrow it made the Christian Democrats fear the execution of a coup d'état over which they would not have decisive influence. This was why they were led to adopt a policy less and less distinct from that of the putschists and to join in their attacks designed to overthrow the government. In the end, the CDP leaders could be distinguished only by their eagerness to be the spokesmen for the ultimatums that accompanied each anti-government offensive and the eventual recipients of a possible government surrender. Often they were criticized in the extreme-right press for these "weaknesses" and for their tendency to conciliate with "Marxism". This increasing convergence between the CDP leadership (of which the most reactionary, pro-U.S. wing, led by Frei, took control in the final months of the Allende government) and the putschist circles became more and more apparent after the March 1973 elections. The results of these elections — a draw between the government and opposition forces — destroyed the hope of legally removing the government through a constitutional indictment against the President, a solution which was also acceptable to the least fascist wing of the National Party.

The National Party (with 21.2 percent of the vote in March 1973), some minor opposition parties that followed it, the fascist *Patria y Libertad* group, and an important section of the High Commands of the Armed Forces and Carabineros with close links to the Pentagon and the CIA, aimed to create conditions to overthrow the government as soon as possible. These groups represented the interests of the most economically influential ruling forces in the country: the landlords, the monopoly and financial bourgeoisie, and, with respect to the United States, the military interests of the Pentagon in Latin America. Furthermore, the U.S. Senate investigation of CIA activity in Chile against the Allende government showed that the U.S. government (especially Nixon and Kissinger) supported the policy of quick and implacable overthrow of the Chilean government using all necessary means short of direct invasion by U.S. military forces. It did so despite the moderating influence of those who tried to mediate so as to treat the Chilean government less harshly and attempt to conciliate with it through the CDP.

Feeling the effects of a serious economic crisis and of the loss of prestige resulting from its defeats in Vietnam, Cambodia and other countries, the U.S. government preferred a Draconian solution to the Chilean problem and resolutely organized the coup d'état. Thus, as in other Latin American countries, it reaffirmed its refusal to allow Soviet-influenced movements to threaten its hegemony over the continent. A UP defeat in the 1976 presidential elections would have allowed it to organize an intensive propaganda campaign demonstrating the failure of the alleged experiment with "socialism" through the peaceful road and showing that the U.S. had been "tolerant" towards it; but the traditional left forces united in the UP would have remained intact, ready to return more vigorously to the attack by taking advantage of the mistakes of their successors and by having self-criticism of their own errors. Moreover, the State Department wanted to prevent certain sections of the CDP, inspired by more liberal forces in the U.S., from seeking an agreement with the Allende government. This sort of agreement, even if it represented a government surrender to the CDP, would have implied a deal between the hegemonic interests of Soviet social-imperialism and U.S. imperialism in a region clearly located within the U.S. sphere of influence; as a result, it would have been a clear victory for the USSR and a "bad" example for more distant countries such as those of Europe.

But the decisive factor that prevented an agreement of this kind and made the U.S. government decide to speed up the coup d'état project that it had been backing since President Allende's election was the exceptional growth of the struggle of the masses under the Popular Unity government and the growing inability of the latter to control this struggle and keep it in check. The mass struggle had already caused the defeat of Frei's pro-U.S. reform plans and his efforts to create a tame populism, and it had also been an important factor in Allende's 1970 electoral victory. Even if the UP and CDP leaders were to reach an agreement, the mass struggle threatened to create an uncontrollable situation if genuinely revolutionary ideas were taken up by the mass movement. The growth of the people's struggle also accounted for the brutality and extent of the repression following the coup d'état, something that many find inexplicable given the fact that the UP did not put up a strong resistance to the coup. The fascist terror was designed to punish the people, to check their struggles in Draconian fashion, to terrorise them and wipe out what they had won by fighting, and especially to prevent the fusion of the mass movement with genuine Marxism-Leninism, prevent it from turning its back on revisionism. Because of the UP's close links with Soviet social-imperialism, its plan for state capitalism threatened the hegemony of the U.S. in its contention with the other superpower. But the victory of a genuine revolutionary movement represented an even greater danger.

As far as the landlords and Chilean monopoly and financial bourgeoisie affected by the Popular Unity reforms were concerned, a coup d'état would guarantee them repressive power and an influence on the future government (which they could not gain electorally or in the event of a CDP-UP compromise) that would allow them to abolish the reforms affecting their interests — the very ones the UP leaders considered "irreversible". At the same time, the coup would allow them to brutally wipe out what the workers had won and to drastically check their fighting spirit. It would also permit them to attack the middle manufacturers and tradesmen, whom they had used as allies to overthrow the government, not only so as not to have to make further concessions to them, but also so as to drive them to bankruptcy and thus increase the concentration of economic and political power in their own hands. Of course, none of this would come about if the CDP and the Allende government were to reach an agreement.

In fact, as we pointed out at the beginning of this chapter, the trend was for the opposition increasingly to unite around the plans and methods of action leading to the coup d'état. Beginning in mid-1971, the opposition forces not only ran jointly in various by-elections (parliamentary, professional, student, etc.) to beat the government, but also formed a unitary opposition organization, the Democratic Confederation (CODE), on the eve of the first big general offensive against the government (the October 1972 strike). This body united the Christian Democrats, the National Party, the National Democratic Party (PADENA), the Radical Democratic Party and very soon the Radical Left Party (RLP), which left the government at a critical moment at the instigation of its CIA backers. Through CODE, the opposition put up a united front not only in the March 1973 parliamentary elections but in the entire legal and illegal offensive destined to overthrow the government.

During almost the entire term of the Allende government, a current within the CDP led by Tomic, Leighton and Fuentealba was attracted by the government's appeals for unity. But although it held the leadership of the CDP until May 1973, this current did not succeed in counteracting the strong influence within the party of the Frei wing, which opposed any agreement with the Allende government. In June 1972, after the government and the UP leadership made major concessions, the CDP and the UP were on the verge of signing an agreement, but the Frei wing torpedoed it. The conciliatory nature of the Tomic-Leighton-Fuentealba current in the CDP did not mean that its members did not participate in the many-faceted offensive against the government. On the contrary, they hoped that this offensive would force a surrender and a compromise fully favourable to the interests represented by the CDP. To mention just one example, it should not be forgotten that Fuentealba, today in exile and one of the leaders of the sections of the CDP openly opposed to the Military Junta, was a co-author of the bill for constitutional reform of the three economic sectors, which would be a key legal pretext for the overthrow of the Allende government.

2. Differences Within the Popular Unity and With MIR

As to the Popular Unity forces (or more generally, the anti-putschist forces, whether linked with the government or not), the analysis of their contradictions under the Allende government is quite complicated. Looked at superficially, the overall politics of this period seems to have been simplified in form by the sharp confrontation between two powerful political blocs (the opposition bloc and the government bloc), but in fact the problem was far more complex, especially with respect to the forces opposing the coup d'état. Many books and almost all the films on the events in Chile tend only to show this schematic, superficial division: on one side, the "people's" government, and on the other, a reactionary and subversive opposition that finally wins over the middle sections. The government forces are depicted through mass meetings and demonstrations, factory occupations, volunteer work, propaganda campaigns, etc., as being firmly committed to the policy of the government. This schematic representation prevents people from understanding the role played by all the forces which supposedly supported the government without reservation, in the criticial stages of the coup, and how the opposition and the CIA were able to mount an offensive of such destructive efficiency. Naturally, the only "explanation" given by the "C"P leaders and their ideological mentors (the Soviet leaders) is the "treason" of certain leaders of the Armed Forces and the brutality of the repression that accompanied the coup d'état. Although it does not exonerate these leaders, who until the very day of the coup d'état continued to promote trust in the Armed Forces and to demobilize the people, such an "explanation" at the same time serves to hide the essential aspect of their treason: their opportunist and anti-Marxist politics. The truth is that the forces which should have stood up to the putschists, although great in number (even if we subtract those the opposition won over or neutralized), were completely ineffective in face of the fascist coup because of the opportunist politics predominant within the UP. In addition, they were ineffective because they were in fact divided and were only allowed to unite around harmless, showy actions that the phony communists used to try to frighten the bourgeoisie so as to then negotiate with it, getting various concessions in exchange for their ability to demobilize the masses and emasculate their revolutionary fighting spirit. Thus the bulk of the anti-putschist forces were only mobilized for electoral-type meetings and demonstrations; for passive occupations of factories; for adoption of resolutions against putschism, which of course did not allude to the Armed Forces; and finally, for the fatal trap of remaining in the workplace when the military occupied the cities and decreed a curfew for several days. As a result, the government's build-up of strength against putschism was like a blind elephant: unable to counter-attack effectively, giving the enemy a target while failing to terrorize him with its size. Lenin correctly pointed out: *". . . reference to the majority of the people* (and the UP did not even have a majority — J.P.) *decides nothing as far as the specific issues of a revolution are concerned. This reference, made by way of proof, is in itself a specimen of petty-bourgeois illusion. It shows unwillingness to admit that in a revolution the enemy classes must be* defeated, *the state power that defends them must be* overthrown *and that the 'will of the majority of the people' is insufficient to bring this about. What is needed is the* strength *of the revolutionary classes that will and can fight, a strength which at the decisive moment and place will* crush *the enemy's strength."* Lenin then adds: *"How often has it happened during revolutions that the small but well-organized, armed and centralized power of the ruling classes, the landowners and the bourgeoisie, has crushed piecemeal the power of the 'majority of the people', who were poorly organized, poorly armed and lacked unity." (178)*

Amongst the forces we have described as opposed to the putschists, while there were contradictions and divisions both in views and in actions, the dominant trend was the opportunist, reformist, revisionist trend, falsifying Marxism, which was imposed by the leaders of the pro-Soviet "C"P. As we will see further on, all attempts to develop a political line or course of action differing from this trend were frustrated, succeeding neither in winning the leadership of the Popular Unity as a whole nor in determining the conduct of the government. The opportunist line of the "C"P leaders was accepted by the leadership of the Socialist Party (SP) — despite some rank-and-file opposition, and despite statements by the leaders and resolutions that appeared to differ. This line was also supported by several small groups belonging to the UP, such as the Radical Party (RP), the United Popular Action Movement (MAPU) (so long as it was dominated by "C"P infiltrators led by Gazmuri); the Independent Popular Action (IPA); and the Social Democratic Party (SDP). Attempts to advance a line relatively different from the dominant one took place amongst some Socialist Party rank and file (the Cordillera District, for example); in MAPU, with the victory of a trend opposed to Gazmuri following the December 1972 congress; in the Radical Youth, which was to be expelled from the RP at the end of the Allende administration; in the Christian Left (CL); and in the Revolutionary Left Movement (MIR), which, although it was never admitted into the Popular Unity, worked within the general framework of the UP policy. For its part the Revolutionary Communist Party (RCP) was not part of the Popular Unity and had a line different in principle from that which held sway within the UP.

Despite their numerical weakness, most of the political groups belonging to the UP had the right to vote in meetings of the conglomerate, although in the "rationing" of official positions and ministries they were but weakly represented. President Allende, who in general followed the line of the "C"P leaders, though with different motives, also had the right to cast a vote in UP meetings.

The policy imposed on the UP by the "C"P leaders (which we will only outline here because it is analyzed throughout the book), expressed itself in their resolute opposition to any revolutionary mobilization of the people to seize power or even as a means to oppose the putschists; in their flat refusal to denounce the Armed Forces and mobilize the people to destroy them; in their vain efforts to court the Armed Forces command and to infiltrate it in order to make the army serve the government; in their scrupulous respect for the laws and institutions of the bourgeois state; in their setting increased production as the main task of the workers, in opposition to the workers' struggles and demands; and in their constant quest of an alliance with the pro-U.S. faction of the CDP, on the orders of the Soviet rulers. As far as the "C"P leaders were concerned, the essence of this policy, as we have stressed in the present study, was not the result of mere ideological errors, still less of purely tactical mistakes. It was an opportunist and anti-Marxist policy, inseparable in substance from their plan to establish state capitalism disguised as socialism. Since this was only another system of exploitation, they could not establish it except by preserving, in the main, the bourgeois state and its laws and institutions (including the Armed Forces), and by initially checking and later crushing any revolutionary mobilization of the people. Another reason this had to be done was that for the "C"P leaders, the plan for state capitalism was intimately linked to the efforts of Soviet social-imperialism to gain military, economic, political and ideological influence in Latin America using Chile, but without openly confronting U.S. imperialism — that is, by trying to impose joint domination of the two superpowers in Chile through an alliance with the CDP.

The trend in the UP and close to the UP that attempted to oppose this dominant line on certain points was essentially inspired by petty-bourgeois ideology. Although some sections of it were and are receptive to some Marxist-Leninist ideas, the influence of "Castroite" revisionism, Trotskyism, anarchism and other anti-proletarian ideas is very strong within this trend. Very many supporters of this trend had the determination and aspiration to fight for socialism, as many of them demonstrated by sacrificing their own lives. However, this determination and aspiration were defeated because of an ideology that was confused, vacillating and erroneous on basic points, an ideology that prevented them from becoming an alternative destined to lead a revolutionary struggle for power and condemned them to being nothing more than the radicalized wing of revisionist reformism. Their opposition to the dominant opportunist trend in the UP was over secondary aspects unrelated to the essence of this political line. Thus they stopped halfway, short of a break with the opportunists, which was indispensable to winning the broad masses over to a revolutionary line. Often, in opposing the opportunist leaders, they put forward utopian, "leftist" positions, which, combined with the dominant right opportunism, facilitated the collapse of the UP's experiment with state capitalism. However, the role of these utopian positions was very secondary and not decisive, as the "C"P leadership today cynically maintains in an attempt to hide its own fundamental responsibility in the defeat of the Allende government.

The points of difference were: the intention of those opposed to the dominant opportunist line to support UP policy through a more militant mobilization of the masses, to which end they tried to strengthen organizations (such as the "Communal Commandos" and "Industrial Cordons") outside the control of the opportunist bureaucracy in the CUT and the big unions and federations; their promotion of actions that were independent of the bourgeois institutions and legality, which the government and the dominant trend in the UP wanted to respect strictly; their attempt to prepare their members militarily, without, however, preparing the masses for armed confrontation with the putschists and for actual seizure of power; their opposition to the efforts of the "C"P leadership to reach an agreement with the CDP even at the price of important concessions on the UP programme; their desire to advance towards socialism by extending the scope of government nationalizations and expropriations even further than the UP programme provided; and their attempt to build mass organizations, which they labeled "people's power" without having in fact seized power.

The contradictions between these positions and the dominant official line in the UP and the government led to acute crises within the pro-government forces. They did not, however, result in the development of a genuinely independent line, and were usually resolved at the top, through the imposition of the "C"P line. However, these disagreements undoubtedly diminished the coherence and efficiency of the plans of the "C"P leadership; and, added to the disputes over recruitment and command, they contributed to the UP's inability to stand up to its enemies. We will now briefly analyze some of the crises precipitated by the struggle between the two trends within the forces supporting the UP government.

First, however, a few words about the Socialist Party, which, as one of the two most powerful parties in the UP, played a key role in upholding the hegemony of the line of the "C"P leadership within the coalition. The SP has the features more of a heterogeneous front than of a party. It is actually a federation of various groups, from the freemasons and social-democrats to Trotskyist and "Castroite" trends. In addition, it had been infiltrated by various political groups seeking influence or members in its ranks. Of course, infiltrators from the "C"P and even the Soviet KGB (which had agents in almost all parties) were not missing.

Although it had strong reservations about the plan for an alliance with the CDP, the SP leadership in practice generally acquiesced to the "C"P policies. However, in order to hold onto the rather numerous radicalized elements amongst its membership, who harboured strong and ancient grudges against the "C"P, the SP leadership had formally adopted resolutions or made statements disagreeing with the "C"P line. But these statements and resolutions had almost always remained dead letter, resulting in a profound contradiction between words and deeds that was the source of deep resentment and malaise for many members. For example, at the 21st Congress of the SP, held at Linares during the Frei administration, a resolution was passed stating: "Our strategy in fact rules out the electoral road as a means to attain our objective of seizing power." And at its 22nd Congress, held in Chillan in 1967, the SP declared: "Revolutionary violence is inevitable and legitimate. It necessarily results from the repressive, armed nature of the class state. It is the only road leading to the seizure of political and economic power and to its subsequent defense and consolidation. Only through the destruction of the bureaucratic and military apparatus of the bourgeois state can the socialist revolution be consolidated . . ." Further: "The peaceful and legal forms of struggle (ideological, electoral, for demands, etc.) do not by themselves lead to power. The Socialist Party considers them as limited instruments of action, incorporated into the political process that is leading us to armed struggle."

These resolutions did not prevent the SP, during the Allende administration, from calling only on these "limited instruments of action" and doing nothing to destroy "the bureaucratic and military apparatus of the bourgeois state"; on the contrary, the SP joined in the chorus of praise for the Armed Forces and police orchestrated by the "C"P leaders. Furthermore, in 1969, in a statement on Viaux's coup d'état attempt, the SP Central Committee declared: "The position of the Socialist Party on the Armed Forces problem was opportune and clearly demonstrated. We have always defended the just aspirations of an economic, professional and technical nature of our military institutions, while advocating that they be incorporated in the process of radical change that our society categorically demands." Thus there was no longer any question, at that time, of "the destruction of the bureaucratic and military apparatus of the bourgeois state", to quote the resolution of the congress, but of strengthening this apparatus from the "economic, professional and technical" point of view and of integrating it in "the process of radical change". Only a party as heterogeneous as the SP could bear up under such gigantic contradictions in its formulations!

But the contradictions between word and deed were much greater still than those between one statement and another.

One of the first struggles between the dominant line in the UP and its most radicalized section took place at the time of the two parliamentary by-elections of January 1972, in the constituencies of Linares and O'Higgins-Colchagua. The opposition coalition ran a Christian Democrat in O'Higgins-Colchagua and a National Party leader in Linares. In view of this election, in Linares, the Provincial Peasant Council and the Political Committee of the Popular Unity, as well as MIR, signed an agreement in December 1971 to put forward a platform that was more radical than the UP's on the question of agrarian reform. This platform called for "closed-door expropriation of estates" (that is, the expropriation would include all animals, installations, tools, etc.), a measure not included in the agrarian reform then in force, which had been brought in under the Frei government. The platform also called for lowering "the limit for expropriation from 80 to 40 hectares (of irrigated land or the equivalent)", thus increasing the number of estates to be expropriated. Another point in the platform stated that "Expropriated land should not be paid for" and argued against the right granted to owners by the CDP agrarian reform law of keeping a reserve of land after expropriation. In addition, the platform called for "prohibition of the expropriation of any property of less than 40 hectares of irrigated land (or the equivalent)". Other points dealt with the demand for technical assistance on the expropriated estates and with stimulants for the cooperatives and Peasant Councils. Although these were only campaign slogans, the platform was rejected by the Central Committee of the "C"P and therefore also by the national leadership of the Popular Unity. This created contradictions and disputes amongst the various groups working on the election campaign. The platform was rejected despite its concluding statement: "We resolutely give the call to struggle for these slogans, to promote them through each of the battles the peasants wage against the 'momios', to prevent this programme from being bureaucratized in offices . . .", and despite its final call "to fight in the city and in the countryside for the passage of a new agrarian law". For the sake of its coveted alliance with the CDP, the "C"P absolutely refused to fight to change the agrarian reform law approved by the Frei government, and opposed any programme proposing the slightest modification of its restrictions. Let us add only that the two by-elections (in Linares and O'Higgins-Colchagua) were lost by the government.

In late January 1972 (the elections having taken place on January 16), there was a "self-criticism" meeting in the El Arrayan district. However, the discussion at this meeting was only superficial, denouncing sectarianism and bureaucratism and appealing to "the morals of the civil service". The meeting also came out against the occupation of land by the peasants; and, indirectly condemning the struggle of the workers for their demands, it maintained that: "the improvement of the living conditions of the workers . . . can be accomplished through mechanisms other than individual remuneration", that is, through social works.

In March 1972 the opposition mounted a fresh offensive to overthrow the government. On March 6, a meeting took place on an estate belonging to the President of the Confederation of Production and Commerce, Jorge Fontaine, between the President of the Supreme Court, the President of the Senate (a Christian Democrat), the President of the National Agricultural Society (the organization of the big landlords), the President of the Society for Industrial Development (the organization of the industralists), and the assistant editor of *El Mercurio.* Also participating were representatives of Opus Dei and of the opposition political parties. In other words, the participants in this meeting were representatives of the main state, employers' and political institutions through which the most reactionary forces controlled power. Only the Armed Forces remained outside, but they were undoubtedly well informed of the decisions taken, as the coup d'état attempt that took place shortly afterwards proves. It was at the end of the month that Major Marshall made this attempt. The coup was to be carried out on March 28, by means of an opposition march, which the government, aware of the putschists' plans, prohibited. The March 6 meeting of the main opposition leaders was in response to a dialogue that had started up three days earlier between the Minister of Justice (a member of the Radical Left Party) and two CDP members of Parliament. On April 6, the dialogue, which had all the earmarks of a mere diversionary manoeuvre by the right, was broken off, and the RLP, on the orders of the CIA, withdrew from the government to join the opposition. On April 11, the opposition organized the "March for Democracy" and on the 18th, the government responded with a demonstration by its supporters.

In the framework of this offensive, the opposition wanted to organize a demonstration in Concepcion, a bastion of the UP forces, on May 12. It wanted to take to the streets in order to lend a mass character to its subversive plans. The UP forces and in general all anti-putschist elements (including MIR and the RCP) decided to block the way to the reactionary forces and to hold a demonstration in Concepcion on the same day. However, the "C"P Central Committee disavowed the Regional Committee of the province and ordered the Intendant, Vladimir Chavez — a "C"P member — to ban the demonstration by the left. Afterwards he also banned the opposition demonstration. In any case, 15,000 people representing the anti-putschist forces assembled on the campus of the university and began to demonstrate when they learned that right-wing groups were meeting in the central square of the city. Then, on the orders of the "Communist" Intendant, ferocious police repression was unleashed. A sixteen-year old high school student, Eladio

Camano, who was a member of the RCP youth organization "Spartacus", was assassinated. About forty people were injured, some of them seriously.

The Popular Unity of Concepcion and MIR then drew up (without "C"P participation, of course) a statement of principles criticizing the government's attitude and accusing it of "making deals with the enemies of the people". Disavowing its regional committee, the SP leadership made common cause with the "C"P leaders and came out against this manifesto. The manifesto pointed to the existence of the two policies within the political forces supporting the government: "One policy maintains that one can make deals with the enemies of the people, which really means forgetting the existence of the class struggle. This policy basically relies on the state apparatus, not on the power of the people and on the masses, and goes so far as to repress the sections of the left that do not share its policy of conciliation. In practice, this policy seeks to transform the present government into an arbitrator, restricting its activity to the framework of a system of institutions that would give equal guarantees to the people's forces and to the forces of counter-revolution.

"The other policy firmly maintains that conciliation with the enemies of the working class is not possible. It upholds the necessity of relying on the strength and organized mobilization of the masses, rejecting any expression of dogmatism and sectarianism amongst the people and opening the way to discussion within the left on the direction and future of the revolutionary process."

The first response to this "subversion" by small parties in the UP and by MIR and some of the SP rank and file was given at the end of May by the upper bureaucracy of the UP (the SP and "C"P leaders) during the CUT leadership elections. In a closed-door caucus between these leaders and the CDP trade union cadres, which lasted several weeks, they divided up the leading positions in the CUT "by secretariats" and caused many ballots cast for other parties, including the RCP, to disappear, so that the results of the vote would correspond to the fraud planned at the top.

On June 5, 1972, at a UP meeting held in the Lo Curro district, the "C"P leaders launched a big offensive to paralyze the process of nationalizations and to make concessions to the Frei wing of the CDP and to the opposition in general, in order to bring about the desired pact with pro-U.S. populism. Corvalan had called a press conference after the events in Concepcion to state that these events should be considered "extremely serious" and that "a hammerblow" was needed in the government. The newspaper *La Prensa,* belonging to the right wing of the CDP, had already drawn the "C"P leaders' attention by stating: "The growing attitude of uncontrolled revolt in the countryside is today beginning to take over the cities." More concessions were needed in order to renew the dialogue and reach an alliance. The policy formulated by Orlando Millas at Lo Curro included a series of concessions to the monopolist sections of the bourgeoisie, to the imperialist corporations and to the landlords, under the misleading slogan of "present consolidation for future advance". In fact, it was a matter of visibly retreating from the UP programme in order to reach an agreement with the CDP. Millas' proposals essentially consisted of limiting the expropriations of enterprises to a number acceptable to the Christian Democrats, thus obtaining a parliamentary majority for their approval; of freezing the Agrarian Reform; and of submitting to the demands of an instrument of U.S. control called the International Monetary Fund by restricting credit, cutting down the budget, freezing wages and salaries and paying indemnities to expropriated U.S. companies. With the exception of some proposed guarantees for small and medium businesses, Millas' proposals were fundamentally concessions to the monopoly bourgeosie, the landlords and U.S. imperialism, and not a policy designed to win over the middle sections, as he claimed. At the same time, on behalf of the "C"P leadership, Millas described as "pure anarchism" the efforts of the most radicalized section of the UP to mobilize the masses and gain control of production from the base. Clearly showing that the "C"P wanted to establish state capitalism in Chile, Millas defined the "participation" of the workers as mere "respect for the hierarchy", "for democratic central leadership" and as obedience to "iron social discipline".

It was the MAPU representatives who developed the most coherent attack against Millas' position at the Lo Curro meeting.

However, they fell into the trap he had set of conceiving the advance towards "socialism" only on the economic level and not on the level of organizing the broad masses to destroy the bourgeois state and seize power. Thus, they advocated, as an "answer" to the retreat proposed by Millas, an accelerated process of expropriations and takeovers of from 1,500 to 2,000 important production and distribution firms, all this while power was basically in the hands of the most reactionary forces. After a discussion in which the "C"P theses won out, the SP, which had attacked them, albeit weakly, ended up submitting to Millas' policy. Millas was named Minister of Finance, replacing Vuskovic (a supporter of accelerated takeovers and expropriations), and the Socialist Carlos Matus was appointed Minister of the Economy to assist him.

On June 12, CDP president Renan Fuentealba opened up a dialogue with the President of the Republic. Rather than accepting the shameful concessions offered by Millas, Fuentealba presented a real ultimatum, which would involve the almost total abandonment of the Popular Unity programme. The CDP demanded approval of the Hamilton-Fuentealba constitutional reform of the three economic sectors, the implications of which we have already analyzed. Out of the ninety companies remaining on the government's list (down from the 250 it initially wanted to nationalize), the CDP only agreed to fifteen being transferred to the state sector and twenty being organized as "workers' enterprises", with the rest having to become mixed enterprises with contributions from individuals, from the workers and from the state. It categorically demanded that the big monopoly paper industry remain in the private sector and that 160 firms which the government had taken over be restored to their owners. It also demanded that public sector advertising be equally distributed amongst all the communications media, be they government or opposition-controlled. Such was the essence of the agreement which, according to a statement by the "C"P leadership after the coup d'état, the government was on the verge of signing with the CDP leadership and which the Frei wing defeated. On June 29, 1972, another attempt at an agreement with the CDP, started up by the "C"P leaders with the support of a few of their faithful in the UP, also failed, and the discussions ended. On July 5, Parliament refused to suspend debate on the vetoes and that same day a constitutional indictment was presented against the Minister of the Interior.

At the beginning of July, the workers of the Cerrillos Cordon, in the southwest sector of Santiago, blocked the access roads between the capital and the coast. On July 12, they organized a march on Parliament together with peasants from the Maipu region. Police and numerous trade union bureaucrats tried in vain to detour the column of marchers from their objective. The demonstrators opposed the deals Millas was making on the Popular Unity programme and shouted slogans against Parliament and the judiciary. The march provoked a protest from the Supreme Court.

At the end of July, desperate to obtain at any price the agreement with the CDP that the Soviets were demanding of him, Orlando Millas tabled his first bill in Parliament, a bill to establish a Yugoslavian-style National Self-Management System for state enterprises. Millas did this on his own account, without consulting the Popular Unity parties. Besides state-owned enterprises, his National Self-Management System would also include the government-controlled companies in the textile and shoe industries. The bill was rejected by the CDP, which considered it a distortion of its "workers' enterprise" scheme, and by the SP, which described it in its periodical *Ultima Hora* as a "new reformist concoction".

On July 27 in Concepcion, the revolt against the opportunist line of the "C"P and those who supported it in the UP leadership started up again. On MAPU's initiative, the SP, the RP, MAPU, the CL and MIR gave a common call for a "People's Assembly", aimed, according to its promoters, at "assuring that the revolutionary process in the region develops not along a bureaucratic and paternalist road but in accordance with a correct mass line". According to MIR, the Assembly would demonstrate "that the people are beginning to build their own power". The regional leader of the SP stated at a press conference that the People's Assembly was in the UP programme and was "part of the Party's policy". The regional leadership of the RP made similar statements. But the regional leader of the "C"P, on instructions from the national leadership of his party, publicly denounced the Assembly as a "leftist manoeuvre". In reply, the regional secretariat of the SP stated: "We think it is very serious for a Popular Unity party to disavow the People's Assembly in terms that could be used by the National Party." In addition to the various parties, the call for the Assembly was signed by sixty unions (carpenters, steel workers, coal miners, textile workers, metalworkers, construction workers, etc.), 31 settlements, 16 student organizations, 27 centres for mothers, and 5 peasant organizations. On July 31, President Allende himself sent a letter to the leaders of the UP condemning the initiative of the Concepcion regional committees and stating: "The people's power will not be born out of the divisive manoeuvre of those who wish to create a lyrical illusion engendered by political romanticism, an illusion they call, taking leave of all reality, a People's Assembly." In this letter, Allende pins his hopes on the parliamentary elections of March 1973, and concludes: "The system of institutions must be changed in depth . . . but it will change by the will of the majority of the people, expressed by the appropriate means." The reason for President Allende's intervention was not only his faith in the bourgeois institutions, but also the pressure put on him by the "C"P leadership, which spoke of "leftist" manoeuvres to divide the UP and isolate the "C"P, as well as the influence of the furious reaction by the opposition press to the Assembly in Concepcion. The Christian Democratic newspaper *La Prensa* stated: "They are forming a People's Assembly in Concepcion to replace Congress", and went on to declare that this was an "act of sedition". The initiative of calling a People's Assembly did, in fact, represent an attempt to get free of opportunist tutelage and to call on the masses. It was disavowed by those who held hegemony in the UP, and defended in a lukewarm fashion by certain leaders of the parties involved in it. Thus it ended up as nothing more than a lengthy oratorical field-day, leading to no concrete action.

On August 4, as supreme proof of its desire to achieve an alliance with the CDP, the "C"P leadership, through an Undersecretary of the Interior who was a member of theirs, carried out a brutal raid on the Lo Hermida shantytown, ending in one death and several being wounded by bullets. This raid was the precursor of those later carried out by the Armed Forces under the Arms Control Act.

Despite this demonstration of "good faith" towards the right, opposition street demonstrations intensified in late August and early September 1972, in preparation for the employers' strike which was to break out the following month. In Llanquihue province, three peasants were assassinated by a commando group of landlords. In the capital and other major cities, high school students led by the opposition were used with the support of fascist groups to create large-scale street disorders. The government was forced to declare a state of alert in the capital.

As usual, the government's only response was to organize a parade of its supporters, similar to the parades in an election campaign, on the occasion of the anniversary of Allende's electoral victory, September 4.

Following the October 1972 strike, organized by the opposition in coordination with a general offensive (sabotage, violence, etc.) aimed at overthrowing the government, the contradiction between the official UP line and the most advanced sections of the UP came up again. The contradiction was even more patent, of course, with the line and actions put forward by the RCP. The "C"P leaders, as well as the reactionary headquarters of the October strike, were terrorized by the actions that the masses (particularly the working class) were beginning to take, and by their fighting response to the putschist offensive. On all fronts of the mass struggle (I personally witnessed this in the Communal Commando of Nunoa), sharp disputes came up between the trade union or party bureaucrats of the "C"P and the members or middle cadres of the Socialist Party, MAPU, MIR, the CL, etc., over what to do in the face of the reactionary strike and offensive. The "C"P bureaucrats systematically opposed all mass actions supported or led by the more advanced forces to reopen shut-down businesses under mass control, to confiscate immobilized means of transportation, to organize groups to defend the factories against terrorists and saboteurs, to carry out direct distribution of commodities to the shantytowns and of raw materials and fuel to the factories, to get armed in preparation against coup d'état attempts, etc. The "C"P leaders insisted it was necessary to leave it up to the Armed Forces and police to "solve" the strike, and maintained that the Industrial Cordons and Communal Commandos should not give themselves powers not provided for in law. When the government and the opposition finally reached an agreement, it was less to stop a strike that was already coming apart at the seams thanks to the response of the people, than to check the growing counter-offensive of the masses. In this agreement, the government made shameful concessions to the organizers of the strike and appointed a military cabinet with full powers to solve the conflict. At the same time, the government hastened to cancel out all the *de facto* gains that had been won by the most advanced sections of the people, and launched an offensive to demolish the mass organizations (Cordons, Commandos, etc.) that had played a leading role in the struggle, putting pressure on all UP members to leave these organizations and diverting the UP forces into preparations for the March 1973 parliamentary elections. It was at this time, on October 21, 1972, that the government and opposition together passed the Arms Control Act, the fateful role of which in the coup d'état we have already analyzed. The government approved this Act as a guarantee to the opposition and to the Armed Forces that were now part of the government that it was not about to let the masses of the people escape from its control again and threaten to block the road to subversion, either on their own account or under revolutionary or anti-reformist leadership.

Corvalan and company naturally hastened to applaud the military cabinet, and they supported it by naming Luis Figueroa, a leader of their party and President of the CUT, as Minister of Labour. A report quoted Corvalan as stating that the military cabinet "is a step forward, a sign of the strength not just of the UP but of constitutional government, of Chilean democracy. With the formation of this cabinet," he added, "a very important qualitative change has come about, a definite modification in the relations of forces. There is no doubt that a Cabinet in which the three branches of the Armed Forces and the working class are represented constitutes an impassable bulwark against subversion." *(179)*

The SP, for its part, first issued a verbal protest against the "solution" to the strike, stating that "the people are opposed to any policy that would mean freezing the process, even until next March", and that it was necessary to "rely on the strength shown by the people to hit at and smash the subversive forces once and for all". But as usual it ended up reaching a top-level agreement with the "C"P leadership and appointed Rolando Calderon, the Secretary General of the CUT, as Minister of Agriculture. However, the left-wing sections of the SP protested against the government's action, stating that the October crisis "has resulted in raising the class consciousness of and in qualitative progress for the people's organizations, and in a strengthening of class unity". They added: "In this context, the masses were expecting the Socialist Party and the government to respond by forming a cabinet 'to go forward'. However, the political leadership of the process, in accordance with its reformist line, has once again chosen 'social peace with the bourgeoisie'. The entry of the main military leaders into the cabinet actually means checking the revolutionary impetus of the workers. By resolving the October crisis this way, the government has given in to the demands of the bourgeoisie and to pressure from the reformist sections, despite the struggle of the revolutionary trend (in the SP) . . . The presence of CUT representatives in a cabinet of this type, compromising the working class by an alliance in the superstructure with the generals, is another inconsistency of the proletarian parties." They then proposed an eight-point platform: **"1)** Extend the social ownership sector to all large or medium enterprises in which the workers are demanding nationalization. Generalize workers' control in this sector. **2)** Expropriate all latifundia of more than 40 hectares of irrigated land using the 'closed door' method and without any reserve for the landlords. Give the Peasant Communal Councils the power to distribute the resources and to guide the expropriations. **3)** Prevent the institutionalization of the Communal Commandos, which must not be subordinated either to the government or to the UP. **4)** Create Provincial Commandos, and later a People's Assembly, supreme organ of national sovereignty, in which the workers must be represented as a class. **5)** Institute the right to vote for non-commissioned officers and privates, and establish a single ladder of promotion (ending the distinction between commissioned and non-commissioned officers). **6)** Create a state distribution network and give the Communal Commandos control of retail distribution. Generalize the 'family basket' and 'people's stores'. **7)** Give the Communal Commandos and the CUT the right to demand the removal of corrupt officials. **8)** Suspend payment of the external debt." The platform concluded on this note: "On the basis of this programme of transition to socialism, the question of SP-CP relations must be posed afresh. Unity with the communists must serve revolutionary principles, and in no case should we favour unity for the sake of unity, hitching our Party to the reformist wagon." *(180)*

The leadership of MAPU, headed by Gazmuri, unconditionally supported the "C"P position, despite rank-and-file opposition that would result in a leadership change at the December 1972 Congress. The CL publicly expressed its disagreement on the question of the military cabinet, as did the Radical Party youth, while the RP, the IPA and the SDP upheld the position of the "C"P leaders.

On November 8, 1972, MIR called on "the working class and people to reject the formation of this cabinet" and maintained that: "The incorporation of generals into the cabinet has changed the character of the government: — The traditional people's parties are no longer the political axis of the government. They must now give up an important part of this role to the army. — Although it has not properly speaking lost the support of the people, the government has undoubtedly further weakened its already deteriorating links with the workers' drive and will to struggle. Moreover, although it has got the support of the Armed Forces in exchange, it is still subject to pressure from them." The MIR statement concluded: "Today, when the reformists are attempting to block the road to the creation of the People's Power by forming this UP-generals government, the working class and people must more than ever struggle to strengthen and develop the Coordinating Committees, to convert them into embryos of power, into Workers' Communal Councils, which will culminate in a People's Assembly and a Revolutionary Workers' and Peasants' Government . . .

"Struggle to defeat the policy of the new UP-generals government, which will lead to the regulation and paralysis of the people's struggle and to concessions to the bosses!

"The workers and people must exercise vigilance over the new UP-generals government!

"Long live the Coordinating Committees and the Workers' Communal Councils!

"Open up the road to the counter-offensive of the working class and people!

"Open up the road to the People's Power!

"Immediate workers' control of the small and medium enterprises requisitioned or occupied during the employers' strike!

"Final expropriation of the big enterprises requisitioned or occupied during the employers' strike!" *(181)*

However, in the Industrial Cordons and Communal Commandos, instead of concentrating on mobilizing and preparing the masses to face the coup d'état and on organizing the struggle for a real conquest of power, this opposition to the conciliationist solution to the October strike, because of the influence of the radicalized sections of the UP and MIR, was oriented towards propagating the fiction of "parallel power", towards defending some of the powers which had been won *de facto* during the strike by these organizations, and towards opposing the restitution of a number of enterprises occupied by the workers during the employers' strike. Thus, instead of building a broad mass movement against the main enemies and against the Armed Forces that protected them, this opposition was influenced by Trotskyist elements who had infiltrated the traditional left parties and MIR to wage virtual entrenched warfare against small and medium owners whose businesses were still occupied, thus strengthening the reactionary opposition front. In this manner, the dissatisfaction caused by the conciliating posture of the government and of the dominant leading circles in the UP towards the forces that controlled power was diverted against medium and even small enterprises where the unions were influenced by the radicalized wing of the UP and by MIR.

On January 24, 1973, the "C"P leaders took another step in their desperate efforts to reach a pact with the CDP at any cost. That month, the opposition had impeached the Finance

Minister, "C"P leader Orlando Millas. Appointed Minister of the Economy, Millas now issued a bill reducing the number of companies to be transferred to the public sector to only 42, and offered to negotiate the cases of 123 big companies taken over by the government or occupied since the October strike. The bill also provided for co-management of many of these big companies by the state, the employers and the workers. As we have already seen, the SP and the CL came out against the Millas bill. On January 27, MAPU issued a statement through its Political Commission (a statement which would provoke the "C"P agents who had infiltrated MAPU's ranks to split it during the following month) calling for a mobilization to:

"a) Consistently and uncompromisingly implement the policy promised to the people by cabinet minister Flores. Only with the masses can the black market, speculation, inflation and shortages be beaten. The bureaucratic mechanisms must support the mass organizations and subordinate themselves to them.

"b) Create, develop and propagate the organs of people's control and power, particularly the JAP's and the Communal Commandos, in all provinces. Only by building and developing the people's power will the country's fundamental economic problems be solved.

"c) Demand a substantial modification of the recently announced bill on the incorporation of enterprises into the social ownership sector (the Millas bill). The workers do not and will never agree to manage their enterprises jointly with their former exploiters. The workers do not and will never accept the restitution of any major enterprise, large or medium-sized. The workers are demanding the expropriation of all the industrial and commercial monopolies in the country, not just 90 of them." (182)

Meanwhile, on January 25 and 26, the workers of the Cerrillos-Maipu Cordon put up barricades and blocked access to the capital from the coast. The following day, construction workers and several thousand workers mobilized by the Vicuna Mackenna, San Miguel and Nunoa Cordons joined them. Demonstrations were held against the Millas bill in Valparaiso and other major cities. On the 26th, workers from the Santiago

Cordons marched on the centre of the capital and demonstrated in front of the Palace of Government. Corvalan would later complain of the "holding, in front of the Palace of Government, of a demonstration in which Orlando Millas' head was demanded and the Communist Party was attacked, with the participation of sections of the Popular Unity".

In the course of the demonstrations against the Millas bill, certain political groups in the Santiago Cordons put forward a "common" platform:

"We, workers of the industrial cordons, put forward as an immediate programme of class action:

"1. The struggle for the transfer into the hands of the workers, into the socialized sector, of all enterprises producing vital necessities, of the food industry and of the building materials industry.

"2. The struggle for the immediate expropriation of the big private distribution companies.

"3. The expropriation of farms of more than 40 irrigated hectares; confiscation of the land and nationalization of the farms.

"4. Institute people's control of production and people's control of distribution. The workers will decide what will be produced for the people, what use will be made of profits and where food will be stored. For this purpose, we call for the immediate constitution of workers' vigilance committees in all private sector enterprises.

"5. The struggle to establish worker management in all enterprises in the socialized sector.

"6. Let no enterprise — neither those in the construction industry, nor any other enterprise in the hands of the workers — be restored to its owners. Immediate withdrawal of the Millas bill . . .

"7. The JAP's and Communal Commandos must have the power to impose sanctions. Supplies to merchants must be controlled, and those who do not sell, who hoard and speculate must be punished. Their businesses must be closed and commodities sold directly to the settlers. The workers of the industrial cordons will mobilize themselves to make this power effective."

The document states in conclusion: "We believe that to control the means of production and distribution is to consolidate the process and go forward. This is why we oppose any type of concession to the bourgeoisie." *(183)*

Of course, such a platform did not actually come from the rank-and-file workers of the Cordons and the Commandos, but rather from the Trotskyist-leaning political groups in the radicalized wing of the UP and MIR, who conceived the "advance towards socialism" from a purely economist point of view. The real necessity to conquer political power and to struggle to do so was forgotten; these elements had the illusion that economic and political power could be transferred to the workers by asking the government to do it, this government which was living its last months besieged and attacked by the reactionary opposition. In this way, the most important thing about the people's counterattack that had smashed the October strike, that is, the struggle of the masses against the obvious attempts to establish fascism, was dispersed or minimized because of the tacit illusion that one controlled a parallel "power" and that one would consolidate it by defending or demanding new economic powers relating to production or distribution. We say "dispersed" and "minimized" because such slogans in fact led each union to attempt to control the factory it had occupied during the employers' strike or to defend food distribution franchises, while giving up the initiative on the fundamental problem: the preparations of the reactionary opposition for the armed destruction of the government, the Cordons, the Commandos, the unions, etc. The proof of this is that the Arms Control Act, which even the UP members of Parliament voted for along with the opposition, did not arouse any protests in the Cordons and Commandos similar to those we have just described.

In any case, the mobilization of the Cordons and Commandos led to the withdrawal of the Millas bill by the government, and caused the failure of the no less illusory plan of the "C"P leaders to pacify the opposition by abandoning the fundamental aspects of the UP programme.

Later, taking advantage of the relative stability resulting from the unexpected success of the UP in the March 1973 parliamentary elections, the "C"P leaderhsip launched an offensive to get rid of the opposition that it had found in its way right inside the UP. Both the opposition press and the "C"P leadership (albeit for different reasons) tried to "blow up" MIR, attributing more importance to it than it really had in Chilean politics. The opposition did so (going so far as to give MIR credit for actions in which it had not participated) for the purpose of portraying it as the "real leader" of UP policy and presenting the conciliatory, legalist, strictly reformist spirit that dominated the coalition as a "hypocritical mask" hiding its real intentions, which supposedly coincided with the "extremist" line of MIR. After the obstacles that the Millas bill ran into, and after the parliamentary elections, the "C"P leadership adopted this tactic of the opposition. Its purpose was to attack its opponents within the UP as MIR infiltrators or as being influenced by MIR, and to justify the "anti-leftist purge" that it wanted to implement. Three days after the March elections, Corvalan told a meeting at the theatre-circus in Caupolican: "Close ranks around the government, that is the most important political task, the most patriotic and revolutionary task of the moment. This is why we once again condemn the attitude of the leaders of MIR, their desire to create organs of parallel people's power in opposition to the People's Government, their commitment to lead the workers to falsely believe that this government is reformist, their plan aimed at dividing the Popular Unity into two opposing blocs and interfering in one of them.

"It is clear that MIR does not like the Armed Forces presence in the government. On our part, we wish to state that we share the opinion expressed by the President of the Republic in a recent press conference that the Armed Forces have accomplished an historic role in these last months. Together with the working class, they have helped to tie the hands of those who wanted a civil war, a bloodbath. Faithful to the legally constituted government and respecting the constitution, they have not been and are not opposed to the President's duty to carry out his programme of government. The overwhelming majority in the country feels grateful to the Armed Forces for their loyalty to their professional doctrine and their traditional comportment in election campaigns . . .

"The results of these elections favour the consistent implementation of the programme and a more energetic attitude by the government towards right-wing subversion. The people and the government must advance the struggle against the black market. The people and the Armed Forces must continue to constitute the main guarantees of internal security against the fanatics who want fratricidal war." *(184)*

Shortly after the parliamentary elections, the "C"P leadership also launched its conspiracy to divide MAPU, in which a trend of "fanatics" opposed to its line had won victory. The "C"P infiltrators in MAPU sent *El Mercurio* an internal MAPU document in which their opponents severely criticized the attitude of the UP and analyzed the profound economic crisis that then existed. On March 7, using this pretext, these infiltrators who had been expelled from the MAPU leadership occupied the headquarters and other offices of the party, as well as the Sargento Candelaria radio station, which belonged to it. At the same time, they convened a press conference to announce the "expulsion" of the majority of the Central Committee elected at the MAPU Congress in December 1972. They immediately received the support of the "C"P newspaper *El Siglo.* Following this split, it was proved that the "C"P leadership, not content to have infiltrators in the ranks of MAPU, was financing the entire section that supported its positions. Corvalan himself finally gave public support to the splittist faction, stating: "The CP does not interfere in the internal affairs of sister organizations, but it is not at all indifferent to what is happening in MAPU. For we cannot be indifferent when a faction of that party gives *El Mercurio* a document attacking the government, calling it reformist, and vilifying the Communist Party. We have no sympathy for these groups. We say so clearly." *(185)* A few days later, a number of members of the Radical Youth who opposed the subordination of the Radical Party leadership to the "C"P leadership were expelled. For its part, the Socialist Party removed three members of its Political Commission, precisely those who were the most opposed to the line of the "C"P leaders.

The methods used by the "Communist" leadership to smash those who opposed it within the UP, even at the cost of splitting the parties, demonstrates one of the features of revisionism in the present period, when it serves as a "fifth column" of social-imperialism. To its traditional opportunist line are added police methods, infiltration and espionage typical of the Soviet KGB (the social-imperialist CIA), which are used even against its so-called allies. Some months before, the "C"P leaders had tried to split the RCP, using an agent that they had managed to infiltrate into the leadership. Unable to defend their opportunist positions on the ideological level, they resort to secret plots, espionage, provocation, slanders and other devious methods to clear the way for their reactionary, anti-people politics.

Finally, in two plenums held simultaneously on March 28 by the SP and "C"P Central Committees, the "C"P leaders strengthened their hegemony over the "purged" SP leadership. The two organizations made statements stressing the role of "communist"-socialist unity as the backbone of the Popular Unity, thus blocking the attempts made by the more radical sections of the UP and by MIR to establish a new pole around which to unite the forces, one with a different orientation.

At the time of the coup d'état attempt of June 29, 1973 (the Tacnazo), there was an intensive mass mobilization and an upsurge in the activity of the Industrial Cordons and Communal Commandos. The opportunity for a people's counterattack against the putschist circles presented itself once again. But at the anti-putschist meeting held in front of the Palace of Government on the very evening of the 29th, the President of the Republic exercised himself to render homage to the Armed Forces, giving them the credit for smashing the plot. Several generals even appeared on the balcony of the Moneda to be applauded by the people; amongst them were some of the future leaders of the coup d'état, such as Pinochet, Bonilla (who was to be the junta's Minister of the Interior), Cesar Ruiz (who would attempt a coup d'état of his own shortly afterwards), etc. The demands put forward by the masses to arm the people and dissolve Parliament were rejected by President Allende in his speech. Meanwhile, within the Armed Forces, the deliberations continued, as did the pressure on the government. Some wanted to carry out the coup d'état immediately, while Pinochet and his group, already closely linked to the CIA, preferred to wait for a more opportune moment; that is, to rely on legal pretexts, to get rid of Prats, to manage the coup d'état at the highest level, and to make full use (as they began to do), of the Arms Control Act to head off any possibility of popular resistance. On July 8, Luis Corvalan spoke at a meeting of his party and insisted on dialogue with the CDP, then officially controlled by the Frei wing. Like President Allende, who had stated in his speech: "Tomorrow the factories will again send up smoke to hail our free homeland; again at work to make up for the hours lost in Thursday's strike; tomorrow everyone must work more, produce more, make more sacrifices for Chile and for the people", Corvalan demobilized the workers and limited them to concerning themselves with the tasks of production. "We are continuing and will continue", he said, "to hold high the banner of struggle against civil war and to strive to overcome the difficulties the country is experiencing. The tasks relating to production are still the order of the day. To divert our attention from these tasks is to play the game of the enemy. We are not giving, we will not give them that pleasure." *(186)* While all the organizations in the UP (except a few "C"P-financed satellite groups) were for taking the offensive and for arousing the fighting spirit of the masses, President Allende once again let himself be dragged along by the confidence in the Armed Forces promoted by the "C"P leadership and by the myth of a possible alliance with the CDP, and on July 25 made a public call for dialogue with the latter. This was just the respite that the military, alarmed by the mobilization of the masses and "outstripped" by the adventurous coup attempt of the 2nd Armoured Regiment, needed in order to prepare the deathblow against the government and the people.

Beginning in July 1973, the opposition looked forward to the coup d'état with a double tactic: the National Party and *Patria y Libertad,* as well as the CIA and the Pinochet team it was advising, were concerned only with creating favourable conditions for the overthrow of the government through a coup d'état. These groups were partial to a merciless coup, a "Djakarta", as they wrote on the walls, which would paralyze the mass movement for a long time, spreading terror. Without ruling out this alternative, the CDP leadership wanted to take over the government through a military cabinet and obtain an unconditional surrender, which, by completely isolating Allende from his rank and file, would facilitate his resignation in favour of Frei. This was why, while continuing together with the rest of the opposition to promote a ferocious offensive of strikes, street demonstrations, violence and sabotage, the CDP agreed in principle to carry on a dialogue with the government; the demands it put forward, of course, would virtually have meant the cancellation of the reforms carried out by the government over a three-year period. The CDP leaders leaned towards a "white coup", in which the government would capitulate in their favour with the endorsement of the Armed Forces, the administration of the country would change hands, and repression would be limited to the forces that opposed this "solution". This was why they demanded, as a first step to begin the dialogue, the appointment of a cabinet in which the Commanders-in-Chief of the Armed Forces would be included. In this manner, by taking the government from within and laying siege to it by means of the developing offensive, the CDP leaders thought they could force it to surrender; and at the same time they would gain the upper hand over those (such as the NP and other extreme-right forces) who would have preferred a strictly military government and thoroughgoing repression against the entire Popular Unity, even against those, such as the "C"P leaders who had implored an agreement.

The position of the most hard-line groups had already been expressed in February 1973, that is, even before the March elections (in which some opposition groups cherished the idea of winning a parliamentary majority big enough to remove Allende), by the leader of *Patria y Libertad,* Robert Thieme. He stated: "We are heading towards the final exhaustion of the liberal democratic system in Chile. This game of the political parties, be they in the government or the opposition, is coming to an end . . . We know that there is no political solution . . . The liberal democratic system dies for us on March 4; we know that the solution will not be brought about by the traditional methods of the parties . . . It will be brought about by the methods of the Armed Forces . . . Without them all efforts would be in vain and even suicidal."

This solution was precisely the one the CDP was seeking to

avoid: it was a solution outside the usual politics, and would prevent the CDP from imposing "its true right" of succession as the majority force in the opposition and in the country and as the interlocutor earnestly sought after by the "C"P leadership and by those who followed its clumsy policy.

Furthermore, with respect to the anti-putschist forces, Frei and company's promises of a dialogue had the "virtue" of dividing them still more deeply and of assuring the active mobilization of the official government circles, the "C"P leaders and their supporters within the UP against any attempt to organize resistance, to mobilize and arm the masses. Given the opportunist conditioned reflexes of the pro-Soviet "Communists" who exercised hegemony in the UP, these promises of dialogue were an even more important factor in "disarming minds and hands" (in the words of Cardinal Silva, who was used as bait to ensure that the dialogue with the CDP would be swallowed) than the Arms Control Act itself, which was implemented by the Armed Forces. The "C"P went all out on the offensive to liquidate the Industrial Cordons and the Communal Commandos. Although accused of splitting, it went so far as to form organizations parallel to them in certain communes in order to take away their effectiveness. The Minister of the Interior, Carlos Briones, who was named to the post so that his close links with the CDP might facilitate the dialogue, authorized the use of public force for the first time to evacuate the factories occupied during the "tancazo". His actions against the people went so far that the SP had to expel him from its ranks.

Thus the offensive and siege against the government and the military preparation for the coup d'état went on side by side with the exchange of letters and interviews between President Allende and the president of the CDP, Patricio Aylwin. On July 26, the truckers' strike, which had wreaked havoc in October 1972, began afresh. The same day, Aylwin stated: "Publicly, before the Chilean people, from the ranks of my party, and praying God to assist me in fulfilling the trust placed in me by all my comrades, I accept the invitation that the President of the Republic has extended to the national leadership of my party to seek a minimum consensus." At 12:30 p.m. on July 30, the dialogue began. Aylwin laid down the following as non-negotiable prior conditions for any agreement: **(1)** the formation of a cabinet to include the Commanders-in-Chief of the Armed Forces and the Director-General of the Carabineros; **(2)** unreserved submission by the government to the decisions of the judicial branch, Parliament and the Contraloria; **(3)** promulgation of the constitutional reform of the three economic sectors, and recognition of the fact that a simple majority is sufficient to overturn an executive veto; **(4)** restitution of the factories occupied in the wake of the "tancazo"; **(5)** intensification of the campaign to disarm all political, trade union and civil groups; **(6)** an end to the "illegal" activity of the JAP's; irrevocable surrender of Television Stations 9 and 13 to the reactionary administrations of the University of Chile and the Catholic University.

A plenum of the SP Central Committee stated in regard to the discussions that: "If the conditions that the CDP sets for the 'minimum consensus' sought by the Cardinal and other personages involve the acceptance of a deal on the programme or an abandonment of the goals of the revolutionary process, then the SP may go so far as to withdraw from the government." Further on, the statement said: "The Socialist Party will never agree to conciliate with the enemies of Chile, of the people's government, of the workers. At present, any formula for a deal with the Christian Democrats serves only to encourage the factious groups which are at work amongst them and amongst the rest of the reactionaries, whose sole and unalterable goal is the recovery of power and of their privileges."

On August 2, against the backdrop of the buses and taxis joining the strike, the dialogue between President Allende and the CDP continued in the form of letters. Allende offered to promulgate the constitutional reform of the three economic sectors, but he considered that: "To carry out another cabinet change, barely a month after the present cabinet has taken over its duties, would not offer any solution to what the country is demanding of us." The next day, the CDP leadership said it considered the dialogue ended, stating: "It is painful to observe that the President of the Republic and his government have a different perception than the majority of Chileans as to the gravity and urgency of the problems afflicting the country." The same day, all the ministers resigned, giving the President full freedom of action to renew the dialogue. On the 4th, Divisional General Manuel Torres de la Cruz carried out the first coup d'état trial in the southern zone, coordinating all the Armed Forces in the region under his command to stage brutal raids against a number of factories, as we described in a previous chapter.

On August 9, President Allende carried out the Christian Democrats' demand and appointed a new cabinet including the Commanders-in-Chief of the three branches of the Armed Forces and the Director-General of the Carabineros. Two days later, the SP, forgetting the statements issued by the recent plenum of its Central Committee, signed a joint statement with the "C"P (through the Political Commissions of the two parties) approving the military cabinet. The statement listed the subversive activities of the opposition and said: "This clearly shows that there is a most dangerous conspiracy against the Popular Unity government and the working class . . . To deal with this conspiracy is the task of the new cabinet . . . which Comrade Allende has defined as a cabinet of national security." Then, arrogating to themselves without further ado the right to represent the entire Popular Unity, the two parties continued: "While not hiding the difficulty of the task, the Socialists, Communists and the entire Popular Unity express their confidence in the fact that the combination of the invincible strength of the people, their unity of purpose, and the fulfillment by the Armed Forces and the Carabineros of their constitutional duties will discourage right-wing putschism and establish a climate of authority and respect that will allow the development of the creative and productive forces of the workers." *(187)*

The left-wing sections of the SP, the CL, MIR, MAPU and of course the RCP came out against the military cabinet. The Political Commission of MAPU stated: "The policy of conciliation now is expressed in the incorporation of a section of the Armed Forces in the cabinet under conditions that go far beyond what is acceptable to the revolutionary forces . . . MAPU rejects such a measure because it means further weakening and disorienting the working class and people . . . To form a new cabinet that supposedly will establish so-called 'social peace' is to deceive oneself once again. It is to believe that with promises and concessions the right will put aside its plans for a coup, no matter what concrete forms they take. It is also to believe that the loyalty of the constitutionalist sections of the Armed Forces can only be won by offering them positions in the government." In conclusion, MAPU stated: "The choice is: attack or be attacked! With the people's power and by going on the offensive, we will smash and liquidate the fascists!" *(188)*

MIR described the new cabinet as a "cabinet of capitulation" and maintained that "in this cabinet, the workers' parties that formerly held positions in the axis of the government will tend to be displaced by the Armed Forces, which historically constitute the backbone of the bourgeois order of the bosses." MIR stated in conclusion: "To justify his new cabinet, Mr. Allende permitted himself to assert that there was leftist subversion in the Navy and that, once again, the extreme left was hold out its hand to the extreme right and to fascism. In reality, the only person on the left to shake the hand of a reactionary in public was Mr. Allende, when he began his capitulation to Patricio Aylwin." *(189)*

On the other hand, the newspaper *El Siglo* published an article on August 12 by Jorge Insunza, who wrote: "The security of the nation can only really be guaranteed by the fusion of the people and the army . . . Leftist elements are trying to spread mistrust amongst the people, particularly amongst the working class, regarding the significance of the cabinet for the development of the revolutionary process . . . The formation of the new cabinet creates conditions to bridge the gap between the Armed Forces and the people that had been created by the reactionary offensive. Thus it blocks the road to coup d'état and civil war."

In late August, a coup d'état attempt by Ruiz Danyau took place and General Prats resigned his post as Commander-in-Chief of the Armed Forces. Concerning the appointment of Augusto Pinochet as Prats' successor, Victor Diaz, a member of the "C"P Political Commission, commented in a statement to the Argentinian newspaper *Nuestra Palabra:* "The appointment of General Augusto Pinochet is being interpreted as a victory for the constitutionalist line." This was only thirteen days before Pinochet personally led the final coup d'état. On the same day, the Chamber of Deputies published a statement containing the "legal" pretext the putschists were waiting for to act. It declared: ". . . the government is guilty not of isolated violations of the constitution and the law; it has made such violations a permanent pattern of behaviour".

The military cabinet, the last cabinet of the Allende government, was also the expression of a fresh disagreement between the most radicalized sections of the UP and the dominant trend controlled by the "C"P leadership. Eduardo Aquevedo, undersecretary of MAPU, gives this account of the meeting which, rather than resisting, made the decision to form a cabinet including the Armed Forces as a final attempt to reach agreement with the CDP: "Through what had already been said, the military uprising was anticipated. The resignation of Prats from the cabinet and as head of the army and the letter in which reference was made to the misconduct of officers were in themselves a clear warning of the future behaviour of the army. Moreover, there was concrete information to this effect. But we did not know exactly how and when this uprising would be carried out. Our information was substantial, but our confusion even more so. A few days before, on Friday the 7th and Saturday the 8th of September, I participated in a meeting of the party leaders with Allende. The question of the coup d'état was directly stated, and distinct positions were put forward. For our part, in accord with other parties having similar ideas — the SP, the Christian Left and MIR, which was not participating in the meeting — we advocated preparing for armed confrontation, insurrection and civil war, which would divide the Armed Forces in our favour, as the only way out of the situation. The military coup was knocking at the door.

"Another group, consisting of the CP, the right wing of the SP, the Gazmuri group — a right-wing split from MAPU — and the President himself, maintained that confrontation must be avoided and that there was a real possibility of preventing it by institutional and legal means. Allende had convened this meeting to find out the views of the various groups. After hearing them, he said that if the parties could not agree, he would decide himself. The ideas of the left-wing of the UP had no place in this scheme, which was to avoid civil war at all costs. He presented three alternatives. The first was a referendum; this had the support neither of President Allende nor of the parties. The second was confrontation. Allende rejected this; he didn't want a bloodbath, and said that we were bound to lose in a confrontation, given the relations of forces at that time. He did not analyze the situation deeply. He simply wanted to avoid bloodletting and civil war. He stressed this repeatedly. He stuck to the idea that it was indispensable to maintain control of the government until the 1976 elections and even to convene a referendum earlier with mobilization of the masses. Thirdly, he proposed what seemed to him the correct solution, the only positive solution to this situation. He said he had talked to the CDP and that they had reached a direct understanding to solve the crisis through the formation of a military cabinet. The condition posed by the CDP was that the Armed Forces must come into the government, with the participation of civilians. 'Since you cannot agree, I ask you to leave me free to act. I have talked to the Christian Democrats and I have the solution for next week.' (We were three days away from September 11.)" (190)

3. Errors of the Petty-Bourgeois Opposition

The petty-bourgeois opposition to the dominant trend within the UP and the Allende government suffered, as we have said, from a number of errors and weaknesses which prevented it from offering a revolutionary alternative despite very favourable conditions. We will now point out some of these erroneous conceptions.

1. One of the main faults of the radical tendency in the UP and of MIR was that they were incapable of understanding (and many still do not understand today) the plan of the "C"P leaders and their conscious supporters for phony socialism and the underlying reasons for the revisionists' indirect strategy of alliance with the CDP, a strategy deriving from the nature of their plan given the conditions of U.S. imperialist hegemony in Chile. They believed that the "C"P leaders' plan was a genuine plan of advance towards socialism, but a plan implemented under the leadership of those who mistakenly used reformist and opportunist methods. MIR, for example, whose differences with the dominant group in the UP were the most pronounced, stated in its documents that: "They are taking a road different from ours and have never regarded our development sympathetically. But, despite everything, nothing makes them our enemies . . .", thus forgetting that according to the teachings of Lenin, the revisionist leaders are *"better defenders of the bourgeoisie than the bourgeoisie itself"* and that *"if they did not lead the workers, the bourgeoisie could not remain in power"*. Because they did not understand the profoundly reactionary nature of the revisionist leadership (falsifiers of Marxism), they thought revisionism was merely a reformist trend (and still today call it "worker reformist"). They believed it was possible to correct or to bypass the line of the revisionists, without exposing them or depriving them of mass support, without fighting or breaking with the hegemony they exercised over the UP and the government. Although they promote some reforms in order to use the mass movement to their advantage and to demagogically deceive the people, the revisionists are not mere bourgeois reformists, much less "worker reformists". The various strata of the petty and middle bourgeoisie, to the extent that they are reformist, aspire to develop (towed along by the proletariat) at the expense of the big bourgeoisie and imperialism and to take power for themselves. On this level the proletariat can and must use these objective contradictions to liquidate domestic and imperialist big capital, on condition it maintains supremacy and leadership in the process. This strength and leading role must ensure that the petty and middle bourgeoisie do not lead the process, for this would result in compromise and defeat; and that they do not take advantage of it to convert themselves into a big bourgeoisie when victory is won. In reality, in our country, given the weakness of the petty and middle bourgeoisie and their close links with imperialist and internal monopoly capital, the first outcome is the most likely if they lead the process — that is, capitulation and compromise with imperialist and domestic big capital.

Bourgeois reformist leaders of the revisionist or phony Marxist type, on the other hand, attempt to distort the historic role of the proletariat, to distort its ideology and to deceive it for the benefit of their plan for state capitalism. On the one hand, they strive to wipe out the revolutionary mission of the proletariat through false ideological and political concepts; to suppress its leading role; to prevent it from leading the people in the destruction of the bourgeois state and the real conquest of power. On the other hand, they work to promote certain reforms, to use their influence on the proletariat (and even the alliance of the proletariat with the small and middle bourgeoisie) to occupy with their upper bureaucracy the position of exploiters that was held by the big bourgeoisie and the imperialist monopolies. They propose to take over the economy and political power either by replacing some of these old exploiters or by temporarily associating themselves with them. It is this process of replacing domestic and imperialist big capital with a new bureaucratic bourgeoisie coming from their ranks, that they call "building socialism". Because of their reactionary nature, they must carry out this plan without destroying the basic institutions and laws of the bourgeois state. Consequently, the proletariat cannot agree to an alliance with the revisionist leaders, with these phony Marxists, it cannot consider them as "bourgeois reformists", for they want nothing less than to supplant the proletarian leadership and to falsely claim to be the ideological and political representatives of the proletariat so as to betray its interests and take the place of the big exploiters.

Moreover, at the present time, when false Marxists of this type are in power in a number of countries and have created one of the two superpowers, a social-imperialist bureaucratic bourgeoisie, their role as political swindlers has become more dangerous and effective throughout the world. They no longer represent only their local interests and ambitions to become a big bureaucratic state bourgeoisie, but also voracious interests of international domination and exploitation of the peoples of the world, the interests of the Soviet social-imperialist bureaucratic bourgeoisie. This makes them doubly dangerous and distinguishes them still more clearly from the traditional bourgeois reformist circles.

Obviously, in characterizing the phony communists, we are referring to the leading circles of the "C"P. In its rank and file there are many militants — and in Chile, they include many workers — who are duped by these leaders and who must be won over by and to a genuine proletarian leadership. In this sense, the fact that there are many misled workers in the ranks of the phony communist parties, a fact that has led some to label them "worker reformist" parties so as to justify an alliance with them, far from justifying this label and this alliance, only shows the urgency of exposing and fighting such leaders. The fact that they succeed in leading on and duping working class militants testifies precisely to their role of political swindlers and to the difference between them and the genuine, traditional bourgeois reformist trends.

This failure to understand the reactionary essence of revisionism led the radicalized section of the UP and MIR to "fight" the government and the leading group in the UP (both under the hegemony of the "C"P leadership) by criticizing secondary defects of their policy, such as their sectarianism, their tendency to compromise, their role as a brake on the struggle of the masses and so on; or by trying, without breaking with their leadership, to present them with *faits accomplis* so as to divert them from their scandalously opportunist course. These radicalized elements did not see that there was total incompatability between the "C"P leadership's phony plan of "advance towards socialism", or rather, its plan for state capitalism, and the revolutionary mobilization of the people to win political power under the leadership of the proletariat. They did not understand that its phony strategy of "peaceful road to power", its veneration of the legality and institutions of the bourgeois state, its praise for and subordination to the reactionary Armed Forces, and its obsession with concluding an agreement with the CDP, that all this was inherent in and inseparable from its plan to replace one system of exploitation by another, by a system over which it dreamed to rule.

2. Another aspect of the errors that governed the behaviour of the radicalized group in the UP and of MIR was their false concept of unity. Failing to understand the essentially reactionary nature of the phony "communist" leaders, they did not understand the necessity of breaking with them and of creating a new pole of regroupment under revolutionary leadership. They forgot Lenin's teaching: *"The only Marxist line in the world labour movement is to explain to the masses the inevitability and necessity of breaking with opportunism, to educate them for revolution by waging a relentless struggle* *against opportunism . . ." (191)* They let themselves be taken in by a false unity, a unity which, in the last analysis, meant maintaining the revisionist domination over all these political forces by means of the blackmail of calling any attempt at independence "splittist". They did not see that if the "unity" is with an anti-proletarian and anti-popular line, then the more the masses are dragged into this "unity", the more there is a split with the real interests of the proletariat and the people. If the people as a whole follow it, then it is the people as a whole who have been cut off from their interests and linked to the interests of the bourgeoisie (whether the old bourgeoisie or the one that wants to replace it). They did not understand that the only correct unity with respect to the "C"P was unity with its misled rank and file in order to win them over to a correct line through an uncompromising struggle in principle and in practice against these opportunist leaders. This was precisely the tactic followed by Lenin and the Bolsheviks when they temporarily united in the Soviets with the Mensheviks who controlled the leading bodies. They did so in order to resolutely fight the Menshevik leadership and win over the masses to break with this leadership, bringing revolutionary, insurrectional politics to the Soviets.

The false concept of "unity", "unity" around the reactionary line of the "C"P leadership (which always won out in the end), gave rise to the false build-up of numbers that characterized the UP. These great numbers of people were united on the basis of the systematic paralysis of their struggles; on the basis of gigantic parades, which in face of the reactionary opposition were an innocuous display of numbers; on the basis of relegating the workers to the sole task of increasing production; for the purpose of further electoral contests; and finally, on the basis of a verbal repudiation of civil war, a blind confidence in the Armed Forces, and a rejection of any preparation against the coup d'état. What purpose did this "unity" serve? What did this build-up of numbers serve, except to open up the road in the longer term to the plans of the phony "communists"? A pathetic example of its uselessness (from the standpoint of the interests of the people) was the fact that on September 4, 1973, a week before the coup d'état, the UP organized the biggest demonstration in Chilean history, mobilizing about a million people. Just as it serves no purpose to give a sick person millions of units of an antibiotic that is unsuitable for him, it does not serve the interests of the people to build up numbers, to "unite", on the basis of a line and policy contrary to its interests.

Despite the blows they received, the radicalized trend in the UP and MIR did not understand that while it was blackmailing them in the name of "unity", the "C"P leadership actually implemented a brutal policy of splitting and liquidating any trend that deviated from its reactionary designs. It did not hesitate to go over the heads of its "allies" whenever this was convenient; to provoke splits within these parties by means of infiltrators; to falsify the results of the CUT elections; to implacably oppose, and even violently repress, timid attempts to unite the masses around a line more militant and less opportunist than its own. Dealing in this manner with the radicalized wing of the UP, the "C"P leaders dragged it into a shameful "unity" with the reactionary opposition through the approval of the Arms Control Act and the negotiations on the government programme with the CDP.

This false concept of "unity" also led to blind hostility toward the forces (such as the RCP) which were developing a fundamentally correct position and were vigorously calling for the creation of a pole of mass regroupment based on a really revolutionary alternative. A regroupment of this sort, which of course involved breaking with the opportunist "C"P leadership, would have made it possible to offer a clear perspective of action to the rising mass struggle in order to effectively oppose the putschists and really advance the struggle for political power. Objectively, while the radicalized trend was the receptacle for a large number of elements opposed to the opportunist leadership, it stopped these elements halfway and prevented them from making an in-depth critique so as to reach a consistent revolutionary position. By giving critical support to the UP leadership and the government, it kept these elements attached to the revisionists' plan for state capitalism; at most, it offered as an "alternative" certain diversionary actions that did not represent a correct road. Thus this trend played the role of a buffer between revisionism and Marxism-Leninism, for the benefit — consciously or not — of the former.

3. Another basic aspect of the erroneous ideas of this petty-bourgeois trend was rooted in its mistaken and ambiguous conception regarding the nature of the government and, in general, regarding socialism. The partisans of this trend confused nationalization and socialism, often describing as "socialist" a government such as Allende's, which although it nationalized companies was in no way the expression of the dictatorship of the proletariat, and which had not taken power away from the traditional exploiters. They frequently confused the masses by presenting the activity of the government (which despite the good intentions of some, essentially implemented the plan of the "C"P leadership for state capitalism) as the building of socialism. For example, MIR put forward slogans such as "More factories for the people" or "Not just one factory or one estate: all the factories, all the estates for the people, that is socialism!", which implied that the country was advancing toward socialism through mere economic reforms, without the prior destruction of the reactionary state power, without the real seizure of political power. Formulated in this manner, these slogans were false even as agitational slogans, for they led the masses to believe that the government expropriations put the factories and other means of production into the hands of the people and actually integrated them into a socialist sector. Aside from the fact that these formulations ignored the true nature of the revisionist plan, which was opposed to socialism, they expressed an economist and reformist conception of the advance toward socialism, separating it from the decisive political question: the seizure of power. In this manner, believing that one could advance toward socialism by simply nationalizing, the partisans of this petty-bourgeois trend only succeeded — under the conditions of an acute crisis and a ferocious reactionary offensive — in tying an increasingly heavy rock around the government's neck, speeding up its collapse. This is not counting the fact that, under Trotskyist influence, pretenses were made of correcting the inconsistencies of the government in its "socialization" of enterprises by attacking *all* sections of the bourgeoisie and demanding their nationalization. Such demands only recruited more allies for the opposition's coup d'état command.

Paradoxically, this same economist and reformist conception

of "advance toward socialism" led to underestimating and not taking advantage of the fighting spirit and movement of the workers against the shifting of the burden of the crisis onto their backs. Instead of politicizing this movement and transforming it into a struggle for power, those who upheld the conception of "advance toward socialism" even went so far as to condemn it as "economist" and "anti-socialist", in accordance with the judgement of the "C"P leadership. Thus the putschist opposition was allowed on several occasions to demagogically use this fighting spirit to involve some sections of the masses in its subversive plans.

4. Another error common to the radicalized current in the UP and to MIR was to pose the problem of conquering political power in an erroneous manner. Overshadowed or inhibited by the praise of the "C"P leaders for the Armed Forces, they did not understand that the conquest of political power necessarily involved organizing and arming the masses to destroy these Armed Forces. Closing their eyes to this fact, essential for a Marxist, they propagated the illusion that political power could be had by developing, in quantity and quality, a supposed parallel power — built in the shadow of the government — which they called the "people's power". What was this so-called "people's power"? It consisted of organizations uniting a part of the masses of workers, peasants, squatters and students, organizations relatively independent of the CUT and the trade union federations dominated by the "C"P bureaucracy. The concrete organizational forms were: the "Industrial Cordons" (assemblies of delegates from the trade unions in a district of high industrial concentration); the "Communal Commandos" (the Cordons, plus delegates from the shantytowns and the student centres in the district); and a few "Peasant Councils", which were formed democratically by the rank and file. The JAP's in each district were also considered an expression of the "people's power". The main features of these organizations were their links with the rank and file; their functional character, since they brought together the various struggles and demands of a sector of the population; their greater preoccupation with the problems of the masses (wages, supplies, price control, etc.); and the ideological and political influence held in them by trends that did

not consider themselves interpreters of the official UP and government policy.

Using Trotskyist-type speculation to create the illusion that these were organizations "of political power", the petty-bourgeois opponents of the dominant line in the UP tried to brandish the experience of pre-revolutionary Russia, where the Soviets constituted a power parallel to that of Kerensky's bourgeois government, or rather, in Lenin's definition, an "embryo of power". The only problem was that these theoreticians forgot that the Soviets were the product of hard insurrectional struggles by the masses, of the smashing of the tsarist police forces in certain cities, of the rallying of important contingents of the army to the side of the people, and of the absence of the bulk of the reactionary armed forces, which were engaged on distant fronts in the 1914 imperialist war. All this culminated in the overthrow of tsarism and the temporary appearance of two parallel powers: the bourgeois government and the Soviets. Even then, to transform these "embryos of power" that were the Soviets into real power, the Bolsheviks had to defeat the opportunist leadership within them and carry out armed insurrection to actually seize power from the hands of the bourgeoisie. Only the Mensheviks and the Trotskyists (there too) were content to unilaterally proclaim the Soviets a parallel power and to demand that the bourgeois government give them greater prerogatives. Thus they downplayed, and went so far as to fight against, the preparation and initiation of the insurrection, which for Lenin and the Bolsheviks were an urgent task.

In Chile, the prerogatives which these mass organizations exercised (partly with government tolerance), during the October 1972 employers' strike, such as the direct distribution of commodities to the trade unions and shantytowns, the surveillance of merchants and hoarders through the JAP's, the delivery of raw materials to the factories; and other prerogatives resulting directly from mass initiative, such as the confiscation of means of transportation immobilized by the strike, the reopening and management of striking commercial establishments, the distribution of food and raw materials, the formation of vigilante teams in the factories, etc. — all this further helped to generate the illusion that these organizations were a form of "people's power". However, most of these prerogatives were drastically suppressed by the government itself at the demand of the military cabinet formed following the agreement between the government and the opposition that was credited with ending the employers' strike. Following this agreement, most of the UP members who had participated in the Cordons and Commandos during the strike deserted them on the orders of their leaders and concentrated on preparing for the March 1973 parliamentary elections.

The truth is that most of the activities of the Cordons, Commandos and Peasant Councils were basically defensive. These organizations did not play the really important role that they might have taken on: that of transmitting a revolutionary line to the masses in order to mobilize them, unite them and prepare them to stand up — with all the means available — to the military coup d'état that everyone saw coming. Still less did they play the role of centres to guide and unite the people in order to conquer political power. The fact that they did not play any such role was in large part due precisely to the erroneous orientation we have discussed, contained in slogans such as "Create, create the people's power" which implied that political power — which even the UP government did not control — would be won by a mere build-up of numerical strength in these organizations, which would allow them to exercise certain prerogatives such as those we have listed and by virtue of these prerogatives to proclaim themselves as the "people's power". It was precisely the illusion that "this *is* power" that greatly helped to hide and obscure a fact it was vital and urgent the people understand: *that they did not have power,* and that those who did have it were hurriedly preparing to punish them ferociously and to take away everything they had won. Thinking about this today, after all that has happened since the coup d'etat, there is no doubt that mere development of what was called the "people's power", conceived as a substitute for the real necessity of preparing to confront putschism and actually conquer political power, would, rather than preventing the coup d'état, as some still believe today, only have resulted in the death of a hundred to two hundred thousand people or more, instead of thirty or forty thousand.

Another factor that increased the confusion these so-called "people's power" organizations created concerning the necessity to seriously prepare for the struggle for power was the unending ambiguity of their relations with the government. This ambiguity resulted from the confused and erroneous ideas of many who participated in these organizations as to the nature of the UP government. Thus the members of the UP and MIR who participated in them always had an ambiguous and confused position as to whether they represented a "people's power" independent of and parallel to the government; or whether, in accordance with the idea promoted by the official UP groups that tolerated them, they were only instruments of a "people's power" supposedly represented by the government. The UP and MIR members never allowed the question to be fully clarified: were they trying (even through the minor prerogatives won by these organizations) to build a "power" independent of the government and its opportunist leadership, or organizations designed to support the governmental "power"? The struggle between these two conceptions not only paralyzed the development and effectiveness of these organizations to a great extent, but also prevented their adopting a correct interpretation of the role they could play in the struggle against putschism and for the conquest of power.

As we stated at the beginning of this chapter, the erroneous ideas on the nature of the government and the Armed Forces, originating in the baleful influence of revisionist ideology, managed to hide, almost completely, the necessity of mobilizing the masses for the struggle for power. Although the groups in question considered that power had not been completely won following the 1970 electoral victory, and although they made ever more frequent allusions to the inevitability of a confrontation, preparing for this confrontation was never — as it would have been if they had been following a Marxist line — the centre of their politics. In practice, they conceived the "conquest of power" as a system of connecting vessels through which power would be transferred from the hands of the exploiters to the hands of the people through intensification of the expropriations. During the first stage, when the opportunist orientation imposed on the UP by the "C"P leadership was not yet very clear, the mass struggle was conceived as a way to put additional means of production into the hands of the government and to consolidate its mass base. This was why the "people's power" organizations were not at that time (1971) thought of as parallel to and independent of the government. Later, as the clashes became more intense between radicalized UP-MIR and those who exercised opportunist domination over the UP, the struggle of those who wished to develop these organizations independently of the government intensified, although an open break with the opportunist leaders was never considered. The "transfer" of power was then thought of as a double system of connecting vessels: the government would increase its control of "power" by nationalizing, and the organizations of "people's power" would progressively transfer it into their own hands by extending their prerogatives and stepping up rank-and-file participation in the state enterprises and "workers' control" in private enterprises.

To illustrate the first stage, we will quote statements made by MIR to the French journalist Catherine Lamour concerning the assassination of one of its peasant leaders: "It *(the government)* does not understand, or pretends not to understand, that our policy is not limited to demanding more land. What must be done is to arouse the revolutionary initiative of the peasants. They should not receive the land passively, as a right, but should have the feeling of having won it; they should become conscious of the struggle for power that is being waged in this country." Then, showing what it meant by "conquest of power" in this period, MIR added: "This is the only way for the Popular Unity to obtain real mass support in the countryside, as elsewhere." *(192)* In October 1971, as part of this same homage to Moises Huentelaf, Miguel Enriquez, the supreme leader of MIR (who was to be assassinated by the Military Junta), stated at a meeting that: "The policy of making concessions and sacrificing the people on the altar of legality in no way strengthens the Popular Unity." *(193)* In the same speech, although criticizing the "reformist tendencies" of the government, he did not show their inseparable link with a plan leading not toward socialism but toward state capitalism. Instead, he described these tendencies as "incomprehensible" on the part of a government "that incorporates large sections of the masses in the struggle for socialism". "But everything is not clear for the workers," he said. "There have been some actions and measures taken by the government that confuse them, that trouble them, that they don't understand, that nobody explains, and that only a few try to justify." After listing various anti-popular measures taken by the government, he was satisfied to threaten: "Despite this government's positive measures, despite the advances achieved by the Popular Unity, the weaknesses, concessions, and temptations of some elements in it to set themselves up as arbitrators of the class struggle leave the workers no other choice but to take back part of the trust they have given and, by supporting the government's positive measures and fighting its concessions, to begin to define for themselves a road of their own."

Of course, starting from a critique of this kind, it was impossible to "begin to define for themselves a road of their own", and right up to the coup d'état, MIR continued trying to bring about a rectification of the dominant policy in the UP and the government. MIR took a step forward in its critique of the government in November 1972, following the appointment of the military cabinet to "solve" the October strike. It stated: "As a result, a new relationship between the government and the mass movement has been created. Beginning with this cabinet change, the workers will have difficulty aspiring and struggling to make the government an instrument to serve their struggles and a lever to build new forms of people's power . . . Today, when the reformists are attempting to block the road to the creation of the People's Power by forming this UP-generals government, the working class and people must more than ever struggle to strengthen and develop the Coordinating Committees, to convert them into embryos of power, into Workers' Communal Councils, which will culminate in a People's Assembly and a Revolutionary Workers' and Peasants' Government . . . Struggle to defeat the policy of the new UP-generals government, which will lead to the regulation and paralysis of the people's struggle and to concessions to the bosses!" *(194)* Finally, in May 1973, Miguel Enriquez stated: "We maintain that the fundamental task is to build up enough strength, starting from the masses, to prevent civil war or to win it if it is unleashed by the reaction. We will only achieve this build-up of strength by upholding a people's revolutionary programme, which will come out of discussion among the working class and people, and by developing and strengthening mass organs which, because they incorporate all sections of the people, will allow the working class to exercise its role of vanguard in relation to the other sections, within the perspective of developing a people's power replacing the bourgeois order and independent of the government, that is, the Workers' Communal Commandos." *(195)* Only on August 4, 1973, following the dialogue between President Allende and Aylwin, did the Secretary-General of MIR state: "The dialogue that has been initiated with Aylwin and Frei has as its objective the unconditional surrender of the government . . .". He concluded: "As of today, the capitulation has not yet been consummated, but no one can have any illusions: the product of this capitulation will not be a left-wing government, a people's government or a petty-bourgeois left-wing government. The capitulation is not only a setback, it actually means a new government: it means that the government is converting itself into a bourgeois government." *(196)* Unfortunately, this thesis that the government was "converting" itself into a bourgeois government was not formulated by MIR until a month before the coup d'état, despite the fact that MIR was the organization with the most independent positions among those we are discussing.

5. Another basic error of the radicalized trend was not fully understanding the role of the imperialist superpowers in the Chilean problem. The struggle against U.S. imperialism, the main backer of the coup d'état, was relegated to a secondary position. The partisans of this trend accepted in its general lines the partial and limited anti-imperialist programme formulated by the UP, and, what is most serious, they made no contribution to correcting the government's error of confronting the U.S. government's offensive in a conciliatory manner, without vigorously mobilizing the masses. We have already seen the consequences of this capitulationist policy and the perspectives which would have been opened up by a firm anti-imperialist struggle.

Furthermore, failure to understand the goals pursued by Soviet social-imperialism in Chile, as well as the direct or indirect ideological influence of social-imperialism on the radicalized section of the UP and on MIR, were decisive factors in the failure of these groups to understand the reactionary nature of the plan social-imperialism was carrying out in Chile through the "C"P leadership. This influence expressed itself in their refusal to break with the opportunist leadership and in their submission to various forms of falsification of Marxism proper to these revisionists. This "neutralist" attitude (which the Soviets actually encouraged elements they had not succeeded in bringing around to their positions to adopt) had already manifested itself in the reticence of these groups to take, and their opposition to taking, a stand in the great international debate between the Marxist-Leninists and modern revisionists which was initiated by the Party of Labour of Albania and the Communist Party of China in the sixties.

It was particularly through the Cuban leaders that the Soviet bureaucracy exercised ideological and sometimes other kinds of influence on the "rebel" sections of the UP and on MIR. These leaders, especially Fidel Castro, gave their approval to the three basic aspects of the Chilean "C"P leaders' plan for state capitalism: their subordination to the social-imperialist bureaucratic bourgeoisie; their deception as to the possibility of conquering political power and advancing toward "socialism" by the "peaceful road"; and their farce of passing off a form of state capitalism (as in the USSR) as socialism. On the first point, not only do the facts show that the Cuban government went so far as to support the invasion of Czechoslovakia, but there are statements such as this one by Fidel Castro on May 1, 1972: "We have full and absolute confidence in the foreign policy of the USSR", or his earlier statement that he agreed with this policy "right down to details". With respect to the second point (the "peaceful road"), Fidel Castro declared in an interview he granted the "C"P-run newspaper *Puro Chile* on August 4, 1970: "Categorically, yes. At this particular moment in Chile, I believe it is possible to move toward socialism by the ballot, that is, by means of an election victory. Chile is one of those rare countries in Latin America where constitutional political struggle is carried out within the established order, and the only advantage of the right is that it has greater economic means. The struggle is within the constitutional framework, and that is why I repeat: in this particular case, in Chile in 1970, socialism can win through an electoral victory."

Finally, with respect to the third point (that of considering what happened in Chile as "revolutionary"), Castro stated in the course of his visit to Chile during the UP administration that: "We have sometimes been asked in an academic tone whether we believe that what we are seeing here is a revolutionary process. And we have said unequivocally: yes." *(197)* The number two man in the Cuban "C"P hierarchy, Carlos Rafaël Rodriguez, pulled the rug out from under any sympathizers of the Cuban process who upheld the necessity of another road to seize political power, telling them: "For us, there is no revolutionary alternative outside the Popular Unity and its government." *(198)*

Furthermore, it is known that Cuban influence on the radicalized sections of the UP and on MIR was not only ideological. It also took the form of very tangible pressure to get in line with the revisionist leadership, any time they showed inclinations toward independence. Thus the Cuban leaders filled to perfection the role assigned to them as servants of the reactionary line of the Soviet social-imperialist bureaucracy: to neutralize dissidents, and ultimately to bring them around to the line of the Soviet leaders.

One of the serious consequences of the reticence of the radicalized groups to take clear stands and to denounce the phony Marxism of the Soviet leaders and their disciples and the phony socialism that hides a ferocious state capitalism in the Soviet-dominated countries, a consequence that still weighs in the difficulties of forming a broad anti-fascist front, was that this reticence made it easier for Frei and company to deceive large sections of the population and drag them into their pro-U.S. policy. The influence of Frei and his team on large sections of the workers, peasants, employees and middle strata is based on "anti-communism": they make people believe that the fascist dictatorships and the harsh systems of state exploitation in the USSR and the Warsaw Pact countries are examples of what they can expect if socialism is established. Naturally, large sections of the masses refuse to fight and risk their lives to go from one system of exploitation to another that everyone sees is worse. To the extent the repression and fierce exploitation in these countries is known, the baleful "model" of socialism that the pro-Soviet "communist" parties offer their peoples has created a strong "anti-socialist" consciousness, to a point where many "communist" parties faithful to Moscow have had to adopt the tactic of simulating differences with their ideological mentors, and go so far as to criticize the repression in these countries, when they cannot succeed in hiding it. In Chile, however, the problem is more serious, for the Chilean "C"P continues to defend what goes on in these countries and to present them as "models of socialism". Consequently, the lack of a clear ideological and political position toward the two superpowers has not only obscured the indispensable denunciation of what the "C"P leaders intend to do in Chile, but has prevented large sections of the masses (including the misled rank and file of the "C"P) from being won over and mobilized under genuine proletarian leadership.

6. Another of the fundamental errors of the radicalized current in the UP and of MIR was that they did not understand the stage of revolution that Chile was going through and the nature of the united front that had to be built to fight imperialism, the big landlords and the big monopoly and financial bourgeoisie. Although the UP programme only proposed the expropriation of these interests, and that only to open up the road to state capitalism, the UP's achievements in this direction were forever being presented as "building socialism". Trotskyist infiltrators in the UP parties and MIR had a big influence on this strategic definition. It was felt one could verbally compensate for the weaknesses shown in the work of annihilating the big exploiters as a class and seizing power from them merely by defining what was happening as a "socialist revolution". In reality, even if the proposed changes had been the result of a real conquest of political power, even if the expropriated power and wealth had really been in the hands of the people, this would only have been a step toward a People's Democratic Revolution (anti-imperialist, anti-monopolist and anti-latifundist in character) and not the immediate establishment of socialism. And this goal is completely correct, for the People's Democratic Revolution is a necessary first stage in a country that is at a low level of capitalist development and that is dependent on imperialism, such as Chile. A "leftist" definition of the strategic goals, combined with a reformist practical strategy and tactics (such as the UP implemented) is the best formula for total ruin, which is exactly what occurred. While verbally "burning stages" in the purest Trotskyist style, the UP in practice did not even secure the minimum conditions for the accomplishment of the People's Democratic Revolution. On the one hand, attempts were made to expropriate certain imperialist companies, the latifundia, banks and the main monopoly enterprises in order to build state capitalism and not a genuine people's democracy. All this was done in an absurd manner, without seizing political power from the owners of the means of production and without developing a people's movement really capable of seizing it. On the other hand, by defining what it was trying to do as "socialism", the UP opened fire on all those who in one way or another, directly or indirectly, in a big way or a small way, lived off the labour of others, and who therefore hated or feared socialism. In this way, through mere talk and without any purpose (for the proposed changes, even if the dominant intentions had been different from the revisionists', would not have created a socialist society), the UP made hundreds of thousands of enemies, while the real exploiters, who retained political power and their dominant influence in society, opened their arms to receive the support of the middle strata. If the proletariat is strong and maintains a correct orientation and a just policy of alliances, these middle sections can be led in varying degrees to oppose imperialism, the latifundists and the monopoly bourgeoisie; but they will do so in order to better themselves as owners at the expense of the big exploiters, and not through the threat of being expropriated along with them by the immediate establishment of socialism.

Lenin, in his epoch, (although Russia was a capitalist country, albeit with semi-feudal survivals), had already answered the Socialist-Revolutionaries who asserted: " *'Why was it necessary (. . .) first to support the peasant in general against the landlord, and then (i.e. at the same time) to support the proletariat against the peasant in general, instead of at once supporting the proletariat against the landlord; and what Marxism has to do with this, heaven alone knows' "* — by pointing out: *"This is the standpoint of the most primitive, childishly naive anarchism. For many centuries and even for thousands of years, mankind has dreamt of doing away 'at once' with all and every kind of exploitation. These dreams remained mere dreams until millions of the exploited all over the world began to unite for a consistent, staunch and comprehensive struggle to change capitalist society in the direction the evolution of that society is naturally taking. Socialist dreams turned into the socialist struggle of the millions only when Marx's scientific socialism had linked up the urge for change with the struggle of a definite class. Outside the class struggle, socialism is either a hollow phrase or a naive dream. In Russia, however, two different struggles of two different social forces are taking place before our very eyes. The proletariat is fighting against the bourgeoisie wherever capitalist relations of production exist. (. . .) As a stratum of small landlords, of petty bourgeois, the peasantry is fighting against all survivals of serfdom, against the bureaucrats and the landlords. Only those who are completely ignorant of political economy and of the history of revolutions throughout the world can fail to see that these are two distinct and different social wars. To shut one's eyes to the diversity of these wars by demanding 'at once', is like hiding one's head under one's wing and refusing to make any analysis of reality." (199)*

In Chile too, it was (and is) an absurdity to attempt to mobilize more than 30,000 owners of private non-monopoly industries, more than 150,000 non-latifundist agricultural landowners, more than 100,000 non-monopoly tradesmen, and several hundred thousand professionals, handicraftsmen and white-collar workers and other non-proletarian elements who live directly or indirectly from the exploitation of the proletariat, and on whom social ambitions and bourgeois anti-socialist influences weigh heavily, to mobilize these strata to accept the establishment of socialism "at once". Lenin points out that the proletariat will rely for socialist revolution only on the·*"mass of semi-proletarian elements of the population, in order to destroy the resistance of the bourgeoisie by force and to paralyze the instability of the peasants and the petty bourgeoisie."* This will be done, of course, after the proletariat has solidified its position by turning large sections of the middle and petty bourgeoisie in the city and countryside against the landlords and the most reactionary sections of the society.

In formulating revolutionary strategy for Chile, it was (and is) necessary to take into account the class aspirations of large intermediate sections and even of numerous petty-bourgeois and semi-proletarian strata wanting to get out of poverty or to better themselves, not through socialism but for individual prosperity. They will seek this prosperity by aligning themselves either with the big bourgeoisie and imperialism, or with the proletariat, depending on which of the two shows the most strength and carries out the most correct policy of alliance. But under the UP government, practically all the parties in the coalition, (including those which did not share this strategy), as well as MIR, spoke of "socialist revolution". Thus they greatly facilitated the alliance policy of imperialism and the big bourgeoisie. This was doubly serious in a country dominated by imperialism and located in its sphere of direct influence. In fact, the Trotskyist influence managed to make it seem shameful to speak of anything other than the establishment of socialism, and even the phony "communists", with their inveterate opportunism, adopted this phraseology.

The Trotskyists justified their rejection of any possible alliance between the proletariat and the non-monopoly sections of the bourgeoisie (agricultural, industrial and commercial) by pointing to the close economic ties between these sections and imperialism and big monopoly capital. From this they derived their fatalist, one-sided thesis that the proletariat could not mobilize these sections against imperialism, the landlords and the big bourgeoisie. However, although it is certain these ties exist, it is equally certain that they are contradictory in nature, that they also reflect the various methods by which big monopoly capital (domestic and foreign) spoliates and ruins for its own profit the weaker non-monopoly capitalists. The latter, when they see the proletariat in a position of weakness (as it was under the UP government), make up their losses, caused by imperialism and the monopoly bourgeoisie, at the expense of the proletariat, and ally themselves with big capital.

Another simplistic argument of the Trotskyists, no less false than the preceding, was to maintain that the policy of forming broad fronts led by the proletariat to smash its enemies step by step was inherent in the opportunist and reformist strategy of revisionism, in its line of opposing armed struggle and the destruction of the bourgeois state. However, this thesis is totally absurd, for all revolutions, without exception, that have defeated the bourgeoisie, (despite the fact that some have since degenerated), have done so thanks to a policy of united front and of revolution by stages. The united fronts promoted by the phony Marxists, by the revisionists, are profoundly different from those led by Marxist-Leninists. The revisionists want the proletariat to achieve an "alliance" with the bourgeoisie on the basis of abandoning its leading role in the alliance, of making only concessions to the bourgeoisie, of abandoning revolutionary methods of struggle, and of respecting the legality and institutions of the bourgeois state. On the other hand, the united front around a proletarian line is based first of all on the revolutionary strength of the proletariat, on its ability to prove through facts that it can smash the big bourgeoisie and, because of this, can give certain guarantees to the middle bourgeoisie if the latter supports its struggle.

The military coup in Chile, and especially the policy of the Military Junta, which brutally turned against large numbers of capitalists, driving them to ruin after having used them politically against the UP government, has had the virtue of showing not only who are the main enemies against whom the fire has to be concentrated in the first stage, but also the fragility of the links between the middle strata and big capital and their eminently contradictory nature. The big bourgeoisie and imperialism first took these allies away from the UP (which was unable to win them over because of its weakness) in order to overthrow the Allende government, then brutally turned against them and drove them into bankruptcy so as to concentrate more capital in their own hands. The ferocity of the fascist repression in the service of big capital today allows it to act in a bare-faced manner and to sacrifice the entire people to its voracity, including the middle bourgeoisie. This shows that the economic struggle between big monopoly capital and the middle bourgeoisie is deeper and more permanent than the alliance between them, an alliance they put into practice when they need to isolate the proletariat.

Events since the coup d'état have caused ideological embarrassment to the Trotskyist theoreticians, whose dogmatism leads them to refuse the middle strata any place in a front led by the proletariat and to deny the necessity of revolution by stages. Concrete facts show that it is the monopoly bourgeoisie and imperialism themselves which are trying to push these str'.ta toward the proletariat. The ultra-reactionary nature of the policy of the dominant strata in Chile is actually creating the united front that these theoreticians reject "in principle". By demonstrating the economic strength and repressive force of the strata that actually controlled (and continue to control) political power, without *up to now* even having to rely on military intervention by imperialism, the coup d'état has shown still more clearly the absolute necessity of defining these strata as the target of revolution in the first stage and of building the broadest united front against them under genuine proletarian leadership.

4. The Revolutionary Communist Party of Chile

The fundamentally correct Marxist-Leninist position taken by the Revolutionary Communist Party (RCP) toward the UP government cannot be confused with the petty-bourgeois opposition to the UP experiment.

The RCP, in contradistinction to the radicalized trend we have just analyzed, characterized the Popular Unity government in a manner that was in essence correct. Its opposition to the revisionist plan of "peaceful road to socialism" is long-standing; as an open public difference, it dates back to 1963. But this struggle began even before inside the old "C"P, from the moment its leaders adopted the openly opportunist line of the 20th Congress of the CPSU.

As soon as the Allende government was elected, the RCP pointed out (in its organ *El Pueblo,* in the review *Causa M-L* and in innumerable pamphlets) the reactionary nature of the "C"P leadership (which had a decisive influence in the UP) and the opportunism of its politics. It pointed out the error of those who believed that this leadership would advance toward socialism. It indicated the failings and limits of the Popular Unity programme. It showed the necessity of making the main enemies of the Chilean people the target of struggle by building a united front against them under proletarian, and not opportunist, leadership. Almost all these theses are contained, for example, in Issue No. 20 of the review *Causa M-L,* dated November-December 1970, immediately after Allende's accession to the Presidency of the Republic. With respect to the future politics of the UP and the government, these articles pointed out what the line of demarcation between the most advanced sections of the UP and the "C"P leadership would be: the attitude of support for the struggle of the masses. Using all available means, the "C"P leaders would strive to keep the mass struggle in check, in pursuance of their plan for state capitalism. *Causa M-L* stated: "It is not only the Allende government's attitude towards imperialism, but also its attitude towards the masses, that will enable us to decide what it should be called. We will judge according to the opportunities that this government and the parties supporting it offer to the proletariat, the exploited masses and to all the revolutionary sections of our society to broaden, deepen and develop their struggles and to channel them towards the conquest of all the instruments of power. This attitude, this readiness to firmly support these struggles to defeat the enemies of the people, is the only consistent attitude for those who call themselves progressive and revolutionary. On the other hand, if they want to block the struggle of the masses and to promote class conciliation by giving the masses the illusion that they are in power and that their problems can only be solved from above *(this was precisely what the "C"P leaders and their supporters would do),* they will demonstrate that their goal is not to serve the people and to help them open up the road to their liberation, but to strengthen and consolidate the system of exploitation and to survive by adapting to the rules laid down by the enemies of the people."

This article pointed out to the revolutionaries (and in particular to the members of the RCP) that it was necessary to unite with the UP rank and file in order to promote the positive aspects of the government's programme and, at the same time, to advance the struggle of the masses, combat the opportunist lines and put forward more advanced programmatic objectives. One of the ways this rank-and-file unity was established was by giving the call to join the Popular Unity Committees (CUP's), 15,000 of which had been formed by the UP during the election campaign, on condition that the masses belonged to these committees and that there were guarantees of democratic procedure. However, after having been used in the 1971 municipal elections, these organizations were dissolved, mainly at the demand of the "C"P, precisely to avoid pressure from the rank and file against its opportunist line.

In June 1971, eight months into the UP administration, *Causa M-L* published an important interview with the RCP leadership. Already this interview contained an exact and complete characterization of the UP government dominated by the "C"P and its supporters. Refuting those who claimed to be building socialism with this government, it stated: "Socialism is achieved by overthrowing imperialism and the bourgeoisie and replacing the dictatorship of the bourgeoisie with the dictatorship of the proletariat. To build socialism, it is not enough for the means of production to be in the hands of the state. It is also necessary for the state to be in the hands of the proletariat. This is not the case in Chile. The UP government, although it tries to claim it represents the proletariat and to make believe that the proletariat is in the government, must accept the presence of imperialism in any of the workings of our economy that interest it. It must accept the economic and therefore the political survival of the big national exploiters by expropriating them with compensation. It must accept the existence of numerous bourgeois institutions controlled by the oligarchy (such as the Supreme Court); and, what is fundamental, it must accept the maintenance of the armed force created by the bourgeoisie. This last point is particularly important because, armed force being the main component of state power, the class character of the state is determined by the class character of the armed force that defends it."

Further on, clearly characterizing the plan of the "C"P leaders and their conscious supporters for state capitalism, the RCP leadership states: "Down this reformist road they are seeking to develop themselves economically and politically, to set themselves up as a new bureaucratic bourgeois stratum. They think they can achieve this by managing the state and mixed sectors of the economy." And, further on: "This, moreover, is not new. It corresponds exactly to the situation which the regression towards capitalism has created in the 'socialist' countries governed by the revisionists."

The same document sets out a correct position towards the reformist plans of the government, a position inspired by Lenin's idea that: *"The real motive force of history is the revolutionary class struggle; reforms are a by-product of this struggle, inasmuch as they are the result of vain efforts to attenuate this struggle, to blunt it",* and by his statement that: *"The only firm support for reforms, the only serious guarantee that they are not a fiction, that they are useful to the people, is the independent revolutionary struggle of the proletariat, which does not give up its slogans." (200)* The call is given in the interview to uphold and defend reforms that are positive for the masses, to prevent them from being used to check the mass struggles, to refuse to allow them to be conjured away by the bureaucratic bourgeoisie, and to refuse to submit, in tactically supporting these reforms, to the reformist programme of the UP, but on the contrary to hold ever higher the revolutionary programme of the RCP.

Further on, the RCP leadership points out the danger of a coup d'état and the plan by U.S. imperialism to use the local armed forces to impose its interests throughout Latin America. "At present, we are witnessing throughout Latin America a process of increasing participation of the military in politics, which is leading them to exercise ever more direct and intensified control over the state apparatus. In most Latin American countries, the armed forces have for a long time exercised power and governed directly. In other countries, where this has not yet come about, things are heading towards the same situation. Formerly, those who governed and enacted laws relied on the support of the armed forces; in the future, it will be those who have the arms who will govern and enact the laws . . . The recent past shows us that the coup d'état — violent or non-violent — is more and more becoming a chronic disease in Latin America." Then refuting the old revisionist lie that the threat of a coup d'état can be averted through compromise, the RCP leadership states: "To promote class appeasement and sacrifice the interests of the masses is neither a correct nor an effective means of checking attempts at a coup. The only valid way to confront subversive machinations and advance along the revolutionary road is to firmly support the struggle of the masses and bring about conditions such that, through this struggle, they are able to smash and liquidate the putschists. The armed 'momios' must be confronted by the armed people."

Lastly, the RCP leadership stated the following policy towards the bourgeois Armed Forces, at a time when the UP and the government were lavishing praise on them: "There are nationalist and anti-imperialist sections in the Chilean Armed Forces. The only way to enable them to oppose the schemes of U.S. imperialism and ultra-reaction and to win them over to the side of the people is not to weaken the struggle of the masses, but on the contrary, to advance it vigorously forward. Only the most resolute fight by the masses, up to and including armed struggle, can polarize a section of the Armed Forces on the side of the people. This is what international historical experience teaches us. Reformism is incapable of blocking the advance of fascism. Reformist social-democracy has always been the anteroom to fascism. Only the revolutionary struggle of the masses can block the road to fascism." In addition, numerous documents and articles of the RCP (as well as its actual programme), before and during the UP administration, pointed out the ultra-reactionary nature of the high command of the Chilean Armed Forces and police and recounted the innumerable massacres and acts of repression against the people since Chile became an independent country. As the reactionary offensive and plans for a coup progressed and the UP leaders' praise for the Armed Forces intensified, these denunciations became more and more vigorous.

In proportion as the masses experienced opportunism in action, from a government dominated by the influence of the phony communists, the RCP's denunciations of the latter intensified, showing them to be counter-revolutionaries and not merely "mistaken reformists". The Party clearly demonstrated the necessity of breaking with such leaders, of creating a new pole of popular regroupment, based on a really revolutionary programme and strategy. It also pointed out the inconsistency of those who, inspired by the Cuban leaders, considered them to be revolutionary forces, however vacillating and reformist.

Numerous RCP publications combatted the "left" adventurist ideas and practices — inspired by Trotskyism — with which certain elements claimed to oppose the dominant reformism. These publications pointed out the necessity of making the main enemies the target of the struggle: U.S. imperialism, the landed oligarchy and the monopoly and financial bourgeoisie. They demonstrated the necessity — in the first stage of the revolution, the people's democratic stage — of not dispossessing the urban and rural middle and petty bourgeoisie; on the contrary, while defending the interests of the workers they exploit, it was necessary to offer them guarantees and assurances to win them over to the side of the proletariat, or at least to prevent those who could not be won over from being actively mobilized by the putschist opposition. The RCP publications criticized the erroneous Trotskyist ideas, which tended to isolate the proletariat and which, while paying lip service to "socialism", sabotaged it in practice and led the proletariat to defeat.

Many analyses by the RCP pointed out the error of those who believed that a sort of gradual, mechanical transfer of power to the people could be accomplished by simply forming bodies that proclaimed themselves "people's power", rather than mobilizing the masses to smash the reactionary forces and actually conquer power. These analyses showed that the reactionary forces understood more clearly than many "revolutionaries" that "political power grows out of the barrel of a gun": they forced the UP to approve the Arms Control Act, and actively used this act to reaffirm their control of power by means of a coup d'état. During the final months of the Allende administration, a document of the RCP Central Committee gave an urgent and dramatic call to all those who wished to bar the route to the putschists not to stop at forming small armed groups, (which is what was taking place), but to form a united anti-revisionist political leadership, to establish a pole of revolutionary regroupment able to mobilize, organize and arm the broad masses to resist the coup d'état that was being mounted.

Finally, we may say that the policy elaborated by the RCP with respect to the two superpowers was also essentially correct. From the moment the UP government took office, the RCP pointed out that in Chile "one can only govern against U.S. imperialism or with imperialism", and that there was no middle ground on this issue. At the same time, it promoted a consistent anti-imperialist programme aimed at completely eliminating the imperialist presence in Chile through the mobilization of the people.

As for Soviet social-imperialism, the RCP denounced its intentions of penetrating our country and exposed it as the father of the plan for state capitalism disguised as socialism that the "C"P leaders were attempting to implement.

These correct ideas of the RCP on all the fundamental aspects of the UP policy are not the opinions of "generals who criticize after the battle"; they were put forward in good time, before and during the UP experience. What is more, they were the reasons that had prompted a group of militants to break with the old "C"P in 1963; they were expressed in the programme approved at the Founding Congress of the RCP held early in 1966.

The fact that these fundamentally correct ideas were put forward at the right moment is beyond any doubt. Hundreds of documents are there to prove it: pamphlets, newspapers, posters, leaflets, etc. To deny this fact and present oneself now, after the coup d'état, as a pioneer in criticizing the UP or as a "discoverer" of its political and ideological mistakes, to deny that there existed a Marxist-Leninist party with a correct position of principle, is only an additional demonstration of opportunism. What needs to be clarified is the reason why these correct theses did not have a significant influence on the politically more advanced groups within and outside the UP and amongst the broad masses of the people. While the RCP unquestionably played the role of proletarian vanguard on the ideological level, it did not succeed in doing so on the practical level; that is, in grounding its ideas in a powerful mass movement.

To shed some light on the causes of this, I now propose to put forward some personal opinions on the question.

In the first place, there were, in my opinion, various manifestations of sectarianism in the concrete political activity of the RCP and in some of its tactical formulations. The target of attack was not always centred with the required force and emphasis on the main enemies of the Chilean people, U.S. imperialism and the most reactionary forces, while at the same time gauging the necessary and correct attack against the opportunist "C"P leaders according to the level of understanding of the masses and the practical possibility of exposing them through concrete facts. A clear distinction was not always made — although it was in general made in the materials from the RCP leadership — between the consciously opportunist leaders and the rank and file they misled, and between those who helped the opportunists and those who tried to fight them, albeit in an erroneous manner and without understanding their nature. There was sectarianism in practical action with respect to the honest rank and file and leaders of the Popular Unity, the Christian Democratic Party and other political forces; practical action to reach agreements, even partial ones, with those who were not in complete agreement and to forge joint action on the points of accord. Often the necessary ideological struggle was confused with practical action and those who disagreed were shunned.

This lack of more active contacts with the rank and file and leaders of other forces was the result of a sort of complex of a small, marginal party in the face of the two big blocs in which most political activity was concentrated. In general, the RCP worked in a plane that was parallel and in a certain way collateral to the activity of the UP forces or to that of other forces whose members were elements of the masses and with whom joint action was possible. There were, of course, contacts and joint actions, but recognition from these groups, a great direct influence on them and broader joint activity were not sought with the required energy and initiative. Amongst other reasons, this was due to the error of not freeing some RCP cadres, particularly on the national level, to take up the responsibility of openly representing the Party, not only for such contacts but also to try to break the blockade and conspiracy of silence against the RCP.

Because of its lack of political experience, the RCP had difficulty translating the ideas it put forward into political reality. For example, it did not understand in time the necessity of creating broad fronts on the national scale which would unite the forces around definite platforms of struggle and allow greater contact to be made between the Party and the broad masses. Some attempts at the regional level, such as the formation of "Netuain Mapu" to advance the struggles of the native people, gave good results. In the absence of a clear policy on this question, the activity of the basic organizations of the Party was diluted in numerous mass fronts and did not achieve the political presence and weight that come from the unification and coordination of many such actions and that are expressed in united fronts of greater proportions.

Because of this inexperience and the lack of a structure more steeled in the defense of the Party line, errors or shortcomings were committed in the resolution of internal contradictions in the RCP. The Party was unable to win over ideologically and politically a considerable number of members influenced by bourgeois ideas (and to separate them from the real enemy infiltrators), and would break with them for want of the strength to convince them, re-educate them and win them over again to the Party line. This weakness was cleverly taken advantage of by a revisionist agent who had infiltrated the RCP leadership at the Founding Congress; without showing his face, he went about sharpening to the maximum all the internal contradictions that could harm the RCP, and used them to bring in other revisionist agents and mount a secret plot to destroy the Party. Although getting rid of this handful of provocateurs taught profound lessons to all the members and was extremely useful to the Party, the mobilization against them — at the height of the reactionary offensive in the middle of 1972 — required a hard internal struggle, with the resulting setback in the Party's work amongst the masses.

In addition to these errors and internal problems which in my opinion the RCP encountered, and others which will be brought to light as the analysis of its work progresses, it must be said that the Party confronted tremendously powerful objective obstacles to the success of its political work. In the first place, it had to carry on its work — especially at the beginning of the UP administration — amidst the euphoria and illusions (not only on the national level but also internationally) resulting from the election victory and from certain reformist advances made by the UP and its government. Many honest elements working with the RCP let themselves be carried away by those who maintained that Chile would inaugurate a "new road to socialism". Others were won over by less "idealistic" incentives and obtained positions in the overstuffed state bureaucracy, or were seduced by offers of privilege and profit from those who occupied these positions.

Moreover, the fierce hostility towards the Allende government of imperialism, the most powerful internal exploiters and the most reactionary political forces (who had an interest in presenting the government as "Marxist") helped to deceive many people and make them believe that this plan undertaken by the renegades from Marxism was really revolutionary. The fierce offensive of the opposition against the attempt to establish state capitalism (which both opposition and government called "socialism") produced an extreme polarization of forces between the government and the opposition. One was with the government or against it, with the opposition or against it. Under these conditions, although neither of the two really represented the interests of the people, it was extremely difficult to propose a true revolutionary alternative.

In the framework of this polarization, the RCP had to struggle against the reformist deception and against the ultra-reactionary forces leading the opposition under the conditions of a system of relatively full bourgeois democracy, but, as a revolutionary party, it could not adopt the style of work of the bourgeois parties. While almost all the other parties and organizations worked legally and openly, with offices, meetings of members, thousands of employees, completely legal publications and wide-scale commercial-type propaganda, the RCP had to maintain an essentially clandestine organization. And it had to do so not only because its members were followed and fired from their work, but mainly because it had a really revolutionary line and was fully conscious of the temporary nature of bourgeois democracy. Both the opposition and the forces supporting the government took advantage of this clandestinity to create a veritable wall of silence around the activities of the RCP and even about its existence. Since it was difficult to criticize the RCP's positions, it was more convenient to deny its existence. Both sides had an interest in preventing the masses from learning about its ideas and actions. Wanting to show that the government and the UP were trailing behind MIR or even that they were led by it, in order better to attack them, the opposition press often quite consciously credited struggles organized by the RCP to MIR or to others. While the newspaper of the big landlords in Cautin province, for example, screamed loudly and ran headlines almost every day against the peasant struggles led by "Netuain Mapu", pointing out that it was led by the RCP, these news items were reproduced by the other newspapers without any mention of these organizations, or crediting these struggles to others.

The participation of the RCP delegates in the CUT Congress, where for the first time, amidst the attacks and threats of the revisionists, they put forward revolutionary ideas, was totally ignored by the press. The RCP workers and students who distributed leaflets to the delegates at the CUT Congress were brutally repressed by the police, and some of them were jailed. The newspaper *El Siglo* described them as "fascist provocateurs". In the CUT leadership elections, not only was the RCP prohibited (on the sly, after it had already printed its propaganda materials) from running a slate under its own name, an absolutely arbitrary measure contrary to the CUT Statutes, but also, in a scandalous fraud carried out in connivance with the CDP, which switched the marked ballots, virtually all the ballots in favour of the RCP candidates were destroyed. In fact, instead of carrying out a public count of the ballots immediately after the election, the "C"P and SP leaders met with the CDP leaders behind closed doors and for nearly a month carried on a discussion on how the main leadership positions would be shared among them. Then, to "guarantee" this top-level allotment, they gave themselves more than 80 percent of the vote. To the RCP, which during a previous election had won two seats on the CUT Provincial Council in Santiago, where there is the highest concentration of workers in the country, they only gave something like 0.5 percent of the vote. The RCP presented as candidates for the Provincial Councils and the National Council of the CUT over 200 members, all leaders of mass organizations.

However, there were unions whose president, running as candidate for the CUT, appeared as having received no votes, not even his own. The fraud was that brazen, for its cowardly perpetrators were certain of not getting caught. In fact, this election was one of the most shameful swindles carried out by the agents of social-imperialism and by some of their accomplices in the UP and it was done with the connivance of the agents of U.S. imperialism. This shows, by the way, that they have no trouble getting together when it comes to deceiving the workers.

The campaign of ostracism and silence against the RCP (that in many respects is still going on today) was not only waged by the opposition parties and instruments of propaganda and by those on the government side who were most connected with the "C"P leadership. Because of their sympathy or links with the Cuban revolution, this policy was also practised by the small parties in the UP who expressed differences with the "C"P and by MIR. The hostility of the Cuban leaders towards the entire Latin American and world Marxist-Leninist movement is very well-known. Not only did they refuse the Marxist-Leninist organizations the right to participate in the "anti-imperialist" meeting in Cuba that gave birth to the Latin American Solidarity Organization (OLAS), but they also made enormous efforts to organize factions within these organizations and destroy them. Putting forward false "revolutionary alternatives" inside and outside the Marxist-Leninist organizations, they played the role of splitters, a role that the phony "communist" parties could not play in these circles because of their undisguised opportunism. The Cuban leaders' hostility toward the Marxist-Leninists, and particularly toward the RCP, which was one of the first in the world to denounce their opportunism and their role as servants of Soviet revisionism, (at a time when this was not as obvious as it is now), could not but influence certain political forces closely linked to these leaders. Thus, for example, MIR did not stop at passively and enthusiastically accepting the credit for struggles organized and led by the RCP, but in some cases went so far as to claim RCP members assassinated by the police as its own. This was the case with Eladio Camano, a member of Spartacus, the RCP youth organization, whom MIR attempted to accompany to the cemetery with the banners of the FER, claiming he was a member of this organization created by MIR.

Finally, the RCP could not, both because of the interests it represented and for reasons of principle, adopt the big business advertising style that was used by both the opposition and the government parties. These parties, either because they represented powerful economic interests or used the apparatus of government, or because they were supported by one of the two superpowers (or by satellite institutions of the superpowers, such as the CIA, the Vatican, the KGB, social-democracy, etc.), could count on multi-millionaire means to deceive public opinion. They had television programmes, hundreds of newspapers and magazines, control of almost all the printing shops and publishing houses in the country, a network of party offices, and thousands of political, trade union and administrative functionaries at their service; in short, they used a gigantic machinery of deception oiled with millions — not of escudos but of dollars. Against this colossal array of political and public relations instruments, the RCP had to (and preferred to) apply the policy of actually linking itself with the masses, of helping them to struggle for their liberation by relying mainly on their own forces. In this way, to serve the work right amongst the masses, it published national newspapers and periodicals, leaflets, pamphlets and posters, as well as many regional newspapers and other instruments of propaganda, in which the workers themselves expressed their point of view and helped sustain the publications. Although this propaganda could not in the short term compete with that of the other parties from the point of distribution and technical quality, it had the advantage of being born in the heart of the people, who day after day experienced the deception and demagogy of the suffocating propaganda of the various bourgeois trends. This is why, although its mass influence was more limited in scope and effectiveness in the short run, it was and is deeper-rooted, more solid and stable. Sustained by the masses, this propaganda has not disappeared, as has virtually all of the political propaganda of the parties that was adapted to the conditions of legality existing before the coup d'état. On the contrary, protected and disseminated by the people, the propaganda of the RCP has become more regular and has increased in quantity under the present conditions of clandestinity. From the coup d'état to this date (April 1977), to mention only the RCP newspaper *El Pueblo,* more than fifty issues have appeared, published underground in Chile.

Despite the shortcomings in its activity and the enormous objective obstacles that hindered its political work, the RCP has achieved significant development and mass influence. It has waged and continues to wage battles whose scope far exceeds the publicity the Party has received from them. Back in the Frei period, the RCP was already leading some of the big occupations of land by the peasants, which at the end of the Frei administration led to the declaration of a state of emergency in an entire region. By creating the Worker-Student Solidarity Committees, which worked in the big industrial concentrations, coordinating and politicizing the trade union struggles betrayed by the opportunist CUT bureaucracy, it sowed the seeds of the future Industrial Cordons and Communal Commandos. Moreover, before the UP administration, through APAN (Association of Trade Unions at Pan-American North) and the Nunoa Communal Commando, the RCP in fact created the first two Industrial Cordons in Santiago. In Valparaiso, the Worker-Student Solidarity Committee had to be recognized because of its activity as the CUT Provincial Secretariat for Labour Conflicts.

Coordinating the activity of these mass organizations, the RCP initiated, developed and led to total victory one of the most important political battles waged in Santiago province, against both the Frei government and the opportunist CUT leadership: the struggle to free the workers of the "Saba" factory. In one of the most filthy trials known to class "justice", these workers were sent to jail for nearly a year. The factory, occupied by the workers, had been set on fire by bombs thrown by the police to dislodge them. But the government and bourgeois justice intended to set an example against all factory occupations by charging the workers with setting the fire. The struggle began when the injustice committed against these workers which had been jealously covered up by the trade union bureaucracy, was made known. A "Commando" was formed to defend them and, under the signatures of thousands of trade union leaders, a call was given for mass action to free them. On May First, a parade of workers was organized to demand the liberation of the "Saba" workers and to popularize the issue amongst all who attended the meeting to commemorate this anniversary. Weeks of struggle in the streets culminated in a hunger strike by the families of the imprisoned workers on the grounds of Congress. A militant demonstration of thousands of workers and students was held in front of Parliament and police cars were burned. The workers were freed the following day. At a meeting held on the grounds of Congress to celebrate their liberation, a CUT leader who tried in opportunist fashion to take advantage of the outcome of this struggle, which the CUT had all along opposed, was loudly hooted down.

During the Allende administration, the RCP led hundreds and hundreds of struggles in the factories, fields and shantytowns and amongst the students. One of these struggles was the militant first strike at the Bata shoe monopoly. The workers blocked the streets surrounding the factory and in the course of a battle lasting several hours, sent to hospital more than 70 police who were attempting to dislodge them. Later, a militant demonstration was organized around the courthouse where the lawyer of the Bata workers was being held prisoner; he was set free.

The RCP led the struggles of many sections of the masses and won the leadership of a large number of unions, some of which had several thousand members. It led a metalworkers' federation and headed many student organizations, mass organizations in the shantytowns, and peasants' and employees' organizations. It won the leadership of some of the Provincial Councils of the CUT, and led the Student Federation on the Osorno campus of the University of Chile and the Federation of Native Students in Cautin, as well as one of the most militant Industrial Cordons in Santiago.

But because of the subjective and objective factors we have mentioned, its work did not attain the scope necessary to break the wall of silence erected through tacit agreement by both the government and opposition forces and to become a force to be reckoned with in the bourgeois politics, so that its positions, its development and its struggles would bear on this politics.

However, the RCP not only continues to live amongst the masses in the midst of the fascist dictatorship, but has grown substantially. The correctness of its positions, which after the coup d'état began to be widely understood by the masses, as well as its clandestine structure, today allow the RCP to play an important role in the organization of the anti-fascist resistance. Keeping nearly all its members and leaders inside the country, it has developed and strengthened its links with the masses. These successes under the hard conditions of dictatorship prevailing in Chile are also to be explained by the high revolutionary morale of the members of the RCP, who have faced death and torture without flinching and who have not left the country unless the leadership specifically asked them to.

Thus, neither repression nor the conspiracy of silence have worked. Of course, a revolutionary party does not advance in spectacular fashion, as the bourgeois and opportunist trends do when millionaire resources backing their demagogy make them "the rage". But each advance it does make, each step forward, is infinitely more solid amongst the masses. How many bourgeois and petty-bourgeois parties have been "the rage" in Chile, achieving a success as striking as it was ephemeral! But the mass influence won by a revolutionary party, if it remains faithful to principles and continues to serve the people and lead their struggles, is not a temporary development, nor a formal winning of votes through public relations, it is a real advance by the people themselves, who under its leadership are beginning to open up the road, relying on their own forces. In a certain way, such an advance is irreversible. Thus the bourgeoisie's room to manoeuvre through deception and demagogy is shrinking day by day and the people are advancing towards the conquest of power.

Part VI
Prospects for
the Struggle against
the Fascist Military Junta

Chapter XII
Evolution of the Anti-Junta Parties
After the Coup d'état

Although it was difficult to analyze the anti-putschist political trends for the period of the Allende government, it is even more difficult to do so for the period after the coup d'état. For one thing, the defeat has resulted in much fluidity in the political positions of each party, which are continually being rectified through intensive internal discussion and polemics with other forces. For another, the divisions between the various trends within each party have intensified, adding to the effect of the geographical dispersal of their representatives throughout the world, and this has even given rise to different regional party centres, frequently with differing opinions. This fragmentation of forces and of ideas is not just spontaneous; it has been directly induced by revisionism in order to make its viewpoint prevail over the ex-Popular Unity.

Although in a very incomplete way and on the basis of a great proliferation of official and unofficial documents, we have attempted an approximate reconstruction of the evolution of the various political trends in all the important parties opposed to the Military Junta. This analysis has allowed us to come to some general conclusions and to outline some prospects, however provisional and incomplete, for the anti-fascist struggle.

1. Position of the Christian Democratic Party

As is well known, Frei and the CDP leading group publicly supported the Military Junta at the beginning. It was natural for them to do so initially, for, misled by the Armed Forces, they had cooperated in bringing about the military coup, hoping that after ridding them of their enemies, the Army would hand over the government to Frei. The military had promised this to Frei so that he would sabotage the Allende government's plan to capitulate to the CDP, a plan that had prevailed shortly before the coup d'état. As we have already shown, however, the putschist High Command of the Army agreed with the idea expressed in the Rockefeller Report of replacing party rule with military rule, and aspired to become a ruling force itself; it therefore pulled the rug out from under Frei and his disciples. Thus Frei suffered all the disgrace of having been complicit in the junta's genocide, to which were gradually added the effects of the spectacular collapse of its economic policy. All this for nothing, not even permission to operate as a party in Chilean politics. The National Party, on the other hand, has placed some of its men in important public positions, and, (although its activities as a party are suspended), it has been able to continue operating through its control over the Society for Industrial Development, the National Agricultural Society and other such organizations.

After having tacitly agreed to be an accomplice in the bloodiest stages of the repression, Frei is now taking advantage of the disastrous economic washout of the junta, its internal isolation and its international discredit and isolation. He has begun to criticize the dictatorship and to present himself as an alternative who would "restore democracy" and lead the country out of economic crisis. Thus he is trying to save the fascist Military Junta from overthrow at the hands of the people; to salvage the prestige of the U.S. government, which is steadily declining as the injustice committed by the military it put in power becomes known; to save his party, which is suffocating under illegality and is attacked by the junta; to benefit from the crisis of certain sections of the bourgeoisie that exploited mainly the internal market and now face bankruptcy; and to take advantage of and put in his service the broad masses who are hit by the repression and the crisis that has cruelly been dumped on their backs. He longs to be accepted as a pinch hitter by imperialism; once again deceiving the masses, he offers the imperialists fresh guarantees of continued control over the Chilean economy without short-term risk of popular uprising. At bottom, his aim is to preserve fascism as a last resort to crush the people, keeping it in reserve behind a democratic facade, postponing it to a later stage, so as to prevent the people from directly confronting the last recourse imperialism and the most reactionary forces possess to remain in power: military dictatorship. In the conditions of acute crisis and savage superexploitation of the popular masses, and in face of a people with traditions of struggle and exercise of bourgeois democracy, military dictatorship as a system of government in Chile is an extremely dangerous solution for the reactionaries, despite the brutality of the repression.

To carry out their plan, Frei and company need the goodwill of the Armed Forces or of a decisive section of them. A Frei government would share its "democratic" image with them, but they would have to supply it with force to repress those whom this image failed to convince. Frei also needs the support of the U.S. government to convince the army of the need to change governments. Neither imperialism, because of its interest in maintaining its hegemony in Latin America against the USSR, nor the army, which is linked to the most reactionary domestic and imperialist interests, will accept involvement of "C"P in this plan, much less forces they consider left of "C"P. Aylwin pointed this out clearly to Renan Fuentealba in a letter sent on August 18, 1975. The letter takes Fuentealba to task for Leighton's attendance at the meeting at Colonia Tovar in Venezuela, where a rapprochement between the CDP and the UP was attempted through the intermediary of the CDP leaders in exile. Aylwin writes: "According to the information you yourself send us, it clearly follows that an attempt was made to establish possible bases for the 'formation of a regroupment of all the opposition forces', including the Communist Party, all of the Socialist Party, the two MAPUs, and eventually even MIR. But you cannot be unaware that this proposal is in open contradiction with the position adopted by the Party, which has definitely rejected any possibility of a front with the Marxist-Leninist parties." Further on he states: "Once again, at the risk of appearing tiresome, I must remind you that the Party has defined its objectives: the rebuilding of democracy in Chile, and at the same time, I am pointing you the way: by reaching an agreement between the democratic political and social forces and the Armed Forces for the restoration of democracy." He adds as an argument: "No one has the right to forget the universal experience, confirmed in Chile and now in Portugal, of the totalitarian manner in which the Communist Party exercises power every time it wins it."

The last argument given by Aylwin demonstrates the key used by Frei and his pro-U.S. group to maintain their influence over tens of thousands of people who are active in the CDP or who vote for it: namely, the example, whose reality is recognized even by the pro-Soviet "C"Ps in Europe, of the savage repression practiced by the "socialist" regimes of the USSR and the Warsaw Pact countries. If we add to this a fact that although not recognized by these parties is nonetheless certain, namely the exploitation of the people of these countries by their bureaucratic bourgeoisies, we have filled in the whole picture of the arguments which allow the CDP leadership to continue to deceive many workers, peasants, white-collar employees, students and middle strata. This proves, moreover, that so long as the leaders of the UP parties and of MIR, through a spirit of false unity or through open opportunism, refuse to adopt clear positions on the restoration of capitalism in the revisionist countries, on the false nature of what is called "socialism" there and on the reactionary character of the political line of the Soviet leaders, it will be impossible to bring important sections of the population into a broad front against the dictatorship and for the seizure of power by the people: not only the honest rank and file of the CDP, but also hundreds of thousands of workers and petty and middle bourgeois strata who know the facts and with good reason will not accept a destiny of the revisionist sort for Chile. They will put no trust in leadership such as that of the SP External Leadership, which paid public homage to the Fifteenth Congress of the "Communist" Party of Czechoslovakia, a congress presided over by those who agreed to the invasion of their country by Soviet social-imperialism, which the SP protested against at the time.

Another sentence that Aylwin slipped into his letter reveals the role the Christian Democrats are willing to give the UP in their "democratization" plans: "For our part, although we are fully conscious that the consolidation of a stable democratic regime in Chile will require, when the time comes, the broadest base of support politically and socially, we think that this cannot be obtained by means of agreements between the superstructures of antagonistic forces, adopted abroad, outside the reality we are experiencing. This type of agreement only serves the objective of the Marxist-Leninist parties to identify themselves in the eyes of the world with Chilean Democracy, going against historical truth and ridding themselves of blame, without facilitating any viable solution for a return to democracy." That is, while refusing any compromise, the CDP would accept the unconditional political and social support of the "C"P and the other parties for its actions, support offered for the sole purpose of avoiding a return to military government. The "C"P leaders strongly desired to publicly accept these shameful conditions, but they were able to convince neither their allies nor even their own members. Such is the actual prospect for the sake of which the "C"P leaders keep the UP divided, corrupt many leaders of allied parties and openly sabotage the organization of resistance for the overthrow of the dictatorship. Such is the true goal of the "generous solidarity" of the USSR and the dependent "socialist" countries "in support of the Chilean people".

2. Position of the "Communist" Party

The leadership of the "Communist" Party of Chile has made no self-criticism on its ill-fated attempt to establish state capitalism in Chile, the attempt that led the Chilean people into their present hell; on the contrary, the "C"P leaders tried hard at the outset to prevent any critical analysis of the past. Not succeeding in this, they shifted all responsibility for the defeat onto MIR and what they call "ultra-leftism". From time to time they also lay this responsibility at the door of their most "appreciated" ally, the SP, accusing it of being infiltrated by MIR and charging that "extremist positions have often found an audience in the SP". In the document I refer to, instead of "explaining" the failure of social-imperialist strategy in Chile, the "C"P leadership tried to refloat this strategy, the goal of which is joint exploitation of Chile by the two superpowers through a pact with the pro-U.S. section of the CDP. Now that Frei's "anti-junta" inclinations are known (Frei's document criticizing the junta appeared one month after the "C"P document), the "C"P leaders want to offer "ultra-leftism" to Frei and to military repression as a "scapegoat", in exchange for their being allowed to enter into Frei's plans, even if only as the caboose in his train. In fact, the document against "ultra-leftism" and the documents in which they offer to collaborate in Frei's plan to prettify the dictatorship are fully complementary.

In the eyes of the "C"P leadership, the basic cause of the defeat was the policy of the "ultra-leftists", which isolated the UP from the middle strata, blocked the pact with the CDP, and prevented the Armed Forces High Command from rallying to the constitutional government.

Thus they accuse the "ultra-leftists" of having prevented them from capitulating in time, before the coup d'état, and from completely betraying the UP programme. If it had not been for the "ultra-leftists", Nixon, Kissinger and the multinationals would have accepted the UP's surrender; the High Command that had been conspiring since the beginning of the 1960s and had attempted a coup when faced with a mere possibility Allende would be elected — this High Command would have changed into a pillar of government; the landlords, big industrialists and bankers would have willingly agreed to be expropriated; Frei and his group would have agreed to an alliance with the "C"P. The "C"P leadership's analysis was so shameless and cynical that even the SP leadership, having a stronger sense of responsibility and honour, replied to it. In a document dated May 1975, the SP states in part: "The bourgeoisie and its ultimate expression, imperialism, do not make mistakes in defending their particular historical interests. What caused imperialism, international reaction and the big national monopolies and oligarchs to support Frei in 1964? MIR did not exist then; extremism appeared to have no audience in the Socialist Party; the election campaign was low-key in content. . . In short, there was every reason to believe that the changes would be made 'in freedom'. Why, then, did the enemy play all his cards against the will of the people? Clearly because, owing to what we stood for, we were a danger."

These questions can be repeated in relation to 1970. Why was *Patria y Libertad* organized immediately after September 4? Why was terrorism at once unleashed? Why did Andres Zaldivar announce that the economy was in chaos, touching off nation-wide panic? Why did they attempt to prevent Allende from taking office? Why did they assassinate the Army Commander-in-Chief, General Schneider? Extremism had not "come onto the stage". The SP statement continue: "The posture of the classes in the struggle for power is not defined by the 'excesses' of the opposing forces but rather by the essential danger represented by the antagonistic interests each class stands for. The case of Chile is typical of the attitude of the privileged classes when they see themselves endangered. This has happened before, and it is happening now. Their arsenal is infinite, kept up to date by the sophisticated methods made available by modern development, added to 'traditional' elements such as slander, corruption, terrorism and assassination." Further on the SP criticizes the "C"P leadership's thesis according to which the basic cause of the defeat was "the isolation of the working class". "We maintain that there was no 'isolation' of the working class and we reject the idea that such 'isolation' constituted a decisive cause of the defeat." On this subject the SP states: "MIR obtained about 2 percent of the votes in the elections for the leadership of the United Workers' Federation (CUT), as against around 56 percent for the Socialists and Communists. The UP forces as a whole received more than 65 percent of the votes cast by the organized workers. Whom did imperialism and the bourgeoisie fear? The 2 percent or the 3 percent controlled by the extreme left, outside the popular alliance, or the 65 percent led by the workers' parties that held the reins of government in their hands? If we say that the petty-bourgeois trend that controlled 2 percent of the class caused the working class to be isolated, we must as a consequence recognize the impotence of the workers' parties and the UP in leading the people's movement. Hence we suffered from a twofold incapacity: incapacity to prevent the excesses of the 2 percent and incapacity to lead and develop our powerful forces so as to defeat the enemy and solve the problem of power.

"On the electoral level, which only gives a partial picture of social reality, we received 51 percent of the vote in April 1971 and dropped to 44 percent in March 1973. But what was the qualitative worth of these forces? We maintain that the 44 percent had a qualitative worth greater than that of the 51 percent in 1971. The latter reflected support for the victor, the former represented the working masses and their highly conscious desire to take on all the responsibilities required by the seizure of power. The collective attitudes of courage, dynamism and initiative which the Chilean workers displayed during the October employers' strike in defeating the resistance of the bourgeoisie and imperialism are only possible in great moments of social exultation. Only a mass with high revolutionary consciousness could have voted for its government in March 1973, when bread, milk, meat, coffee and other basic commodities were lacking. The majority of the people knew that this shortage was artificially caused by their class enemies against their interests, and they demanded the law be applied in all its rigour. They asked for penalties: an iron fist. Thus they displayed intuition and class consciousness. It was clear to them that only if the enemy were hit could he be driven back. At the same time, these 44 percent represented the vast majority of the labour force, a majority that had production and a large part of the services in its hands."

The statement continues: "Did these forces abandon their government in the final stage, leaving the working class isolated? Those who claim so forget that seven days before the coup d'état, on the third anniversary of the victory, grand demonstrations in support of the government were held in every corner and every city in the country. In Santiago, no less than 800,000 people paraded in front of the Moneda shouting, 'Allende, the people are on your side', 'Show your fist', 'We haven't come for nothing', 'Create, create the people's power'. If these hundreds of thousands of demonstrators all belonged to the working class, then the responsibility of the workers' parties is even greater, insofar as they were unable to lead a quantitatively and qualitatively well-developed class to its destiny. In fact, of course, the demonstrators were not exclusively workers. There were bank, credit union, postal and telecommunications employees, as well as employees of CORFO and all the other public bodies. There were members of liberal professions. These, of course, were a minority. But has there been a single revolution which the majority of the people in these strata have supported? Did not the Bolsheviks have problems with postal employees, civil servants and railwaymen?

"As for the truckers and small tradesmen, we had minority sections with us until the very moment of the coup d'état. Let us not forget how certain truckers and small tradesmen asked for help. The truckers asked that worker pickets accompany them on their trips so that they would not be attacked by Vilarin's gangsters; the tradesmen asked for protection from the *Patria y Libertad* hordes and to be able to open their shops."

The statement concludes: "No, the working class was not isolated. Those who were strangers to a policy of defending the revolution were ourselves, the Popular Unity. And on this there has been very little self-criticism."

The SP then maintains: "It has also been said that another of the decisive causes of the defeat was the lack of a 'Unified Leadership'. We consider that this formulation hides serious political responsibilities behind a euphemism. Let us suppose that there had been a single leadership or even a United Party of the revolution. If this united command had done the same thing we did — that is, attempt to make revolution while subordinating ourselves to the legal mechanisms of the bourgeoisie, put trust in the 'patriotism' and 'neutrality' of the Armed Forces, fail to prepare to defend the revolution, fail to strengthen the People's Power; in short, if it had lacked a strategy and a real disposition to fully take over political power — we would have achieved the same result. On the other hand, if this hypothetical United Leadership had had a strategy for political power, if it had started from the fact that the enemy would not permanently accept the establishment of a new regime and would inevitably resort to violent counter-revolution, we would have been able to prepare ourselves to go from maximum use of our legal powers to the formation of a legitimate force to defend the process. We would have prepared for the qualitative leap which was justified by the daily acts of subversion by the advancing counter-revolutionary front. However, the latter hypothesis was also possible with a leadership made up of many parties. The problem was for the members of the Popular Unity or its main components to agree on such a strategy. Unfortunately, this did not happen. There was no consensus within the Popular Unity to map out a strategy defining the problem of political power.

"We cannot confuse 'United Leadership' with correct leadership. One can have a united leadership that maps out an erroneous course. One can have a multi-party leadership that agrees on a correct line."

The SP statement concludes: "The fundamental question is the problem of political power. We had won government through an election without an absolute majority and the task of winning over the masses and taking over political power in its entirety was before us. (. . .) In specifying responsibility for the conduct of the process led by the Popular Unity, one must delimit the positions of each of its constituent parties on the fundamental problem: the problem of political power and defence of the revolution. One must determine who thought that the confrontation was inevitable and that as a result it was necessary to prepare to defend the revolution; who was for the defence of the revolution by seizing the initiative if necessary; who was for the development of the people's power in order to defend the government. In regard to these crucial problems of the revolution, the Socialist Party can be blamed for not having been able to or not having known how to make them the common perspective of the entire Popular Unity. (. . .) On these problems, two main lines shaped up within the Popular Unity, around each of which appeared one or more variations that did not differ fundamentally. One line believed in the peaceful transition to socialism, in adding on social forces so as to obtain a majority and thus to consolidate the achievements, win the next presidential election (which was to have taken place in 1976) and carry on with the changes by means of the democratic mechanisms.

"The other line considered that the laws of class struggle in the end inevitably manifest themselves in military terms, which meant, insofar as we were consistent with the programme, that the enemy would choose the forms and the right moment to unleash counter-revolution. Consequently, while deepening the process and making it irreversible, it was necessary at the same to create and develop conditions for the defence of the revolution. This required breaking the legal mechanisms — which the reaction was systematically breaking anyway — and making a qualitative leap that could lead us to the total seizure of power." *(200)*

We have reproduced several paragraphs from the SP statement because they reveal the extent to which the responsibility of the "C"P leaders in the events, and the impudence of their attempt to shift the blame onto others, are beginning to be understood. In the SP leaders' analysis, one also notes that they have not reached the point of elucidating the basic causes of the attitude of the phony communist leaders, the reasons for their opportunist line. They still consider them to be "making mistakes in good faith". This, in conjunction with the opportunism of certain leaders of the SP, means that despite everything they still lend themselves to the manoeuvres of the "C"P leading group, which is following the same plans and same line that led to military dictatorship in Chile.

The line of the "C"P leaders is still to make an alliance with the pro-U.S. section of the bourgeoisie represented by Frei (and not with the middle strata, as they profess). Tangible proof of this is given by the documents made public by the "C"P leaders following Frei's criticism of the Military Junta. These documents, which timidly criticize Frei for his support for the coup d'état and the junta and for his initial silence in face of the repression give as their main impression the idea that Frei might have acted differently. In essence, the "C"P leaders blame him for not including them in his plan for "democratization". They repeatedly call on him in the most servile manner not to leave them out of his plans. They try to pluck Frei's "Catholic" string, writing: "If only the truth will set us free, let us also practice it in regard to ourselves with humility, a humility that in Christians can go so far as self-humiliation. We believe that all Chileans who are now against the junta (including those who joyfully hailed the coup d'état and hoped it would be the anteroom of their return to power) must unite around the common denominator of putting an end to fascist dictatorship." The "C"P leaders agree to reduce the struggle against the imperialist and reactionary bourgeois interests represented by Frei to "ideological clarification among those who, starting from different positions, are confronting a common adversary, in order to avoid confusion."

Then, with lyrical phrases, the "C"P leaders give Frei a guarantee that behind his throne he can keep the Armed Forces that carried out the coup d'état, with a few little touch-ups. They assert: "Rejection of the Junta pierces the hearts of the believers.

It penetrates like a consciousness awakening in the depths of the Armed Forces, where the drama is building today, and who are crying out to leave a road of blood onto which they were pushed at bayonet-point by a crazed minority, manipulated from abroad, that took advantage of the secret rainfall — now made public — of treasonous dollars." One should ask them: "Isn't Frei part of this minority?"

The "C"P leaders implore Frei to "unify" them around his sinister plans to rescue the dictatorship by giving it his hypocritical image of a democrat. They state: "Frei modestly proposes that he be the centre. But from time to time, he does not act like a centre for unification, but as a sower of discord within the opposition at a time when what is in fact most needed is unity and a crystal-clear attitude toward despotism." Then, blotting out the wishy-washy criticisms they had of Frei, they applaud him for his attitude, the devious motives of which are plain to all. They state:"All this shows how the junta is inexorably isolated. This rectification of (Frei's) stand has been late, but we hail the fact that it has finally come about. Likewise, it is symptomatic and positive that Frei is now concurring in a world-wide verdict, when he maintains that the international policy of the junta 'deeply wrongs the interests of Chile'." The "C"P leaders then try to draw arguments from Frei's own words to convince him that they are indispensable to his plan. They state: "Frei has written something reasonable in expressing the view that 'not through hunger for power and still less through sectarianism will Chile find its way and achieve accord. Nor can any isolated party successfully face up to this difficult undertaking. To overcome its current problems, this country needs all its men.' "

Further on, in a sort of code language, the "C"P leaders suggest to Frei that they are ready to agree to his continuing to repress the so-called "ultra-leftists." "These freedoms that were unrestricted and unchecked in Allende's day, when the entire situation was being disturbed and falsified by the enemy conspiracy financed and led by the CIA orchestra leader, died with the coup d'état, which did not save Chile and its democracy. What will resuscitate it is respect for the person, freedom in all its aspects and domains, lucid democracy that will learn from its own experience and draw lessons from its naivete. Therein, " they conclude, "lies a possible ground for fruitful convergence." Coming from those who have shifted all responsibility for the coup d'état onto the "ultra-leftists", it is easy to imagine against whom they are offering to exercise (along with Frei and his team) this "lucid democracy" in which "unrestricted" and "unchecked" freedoms "died with the coup d'état".

Then, applauding some other denunciations by Frei of the most obviously criticizable aspects of the junta, the "C"P leaders stress that: "We are in agreement with these propositions. So why not unite all those who want the same thing in order to achieve it?"

Further on, they complain of Frei's "anti-communism", the reason why he excludes them from his plans. They remind him of how they supported his government, in particular when it was threatened by Viaux's coup d'état, and repeat the tributes that Frei paid them on that occasion. What is more, they try to convince him that this "anti-communism" is being overcome in the Armed Forces, and that, if he wishes, he can arrange for the military to admit the "C"P into their plans. (What is tragic for them is that not even Frei himself figures in these plans.) "Within the Armed Forces," they write, "in the private consciences of those who wore the uniform, there is a heterogeneous collection of ideas and feelings. The majority now think that the coup d'etat was the most tragic error in the history of the Army and of Chile. Many are beginning to understand that the anti-communist and anti-Popular Unity campaign was an essential part of this great error." It would be interesting to learn how they have managed to penetrate "the private consciences of those who wear the uniform", especially after the coup d'état and the repression, since they were flatly mistaken before the coup, with the result that everyone knows. Could it be that the Church has revealed to them the secrets of the confessional? Next, they again assure Frei that if he delivers them from Pinochet and a few "big guilty ones", he can use the reactionary Armed Forces, as "the vast majority of the Armed Forces — who are truly patriotic and humane — not only have nothing to fear, but will have an honourable place in the reconstruction of the country, its institutions, its freedom and its progress, within the Armed Forces. Worthy of their mission, the latter will also contribute as a guarantee that today's hecatomb will never again be repeated." This cynical "naivete" breaks all records!

Further on, the "C"P leaders persist in their entreaties and praise directed to Frei. "This is why we appreciate all the positive changes in those who did not adopt this position from the beginning. We applaud those who are drawing nearer to correct positions, positions that the Popular Unity adopted from the onset of the coup d'état. There is no partial solution. There is only the global alternative which excludes no one and which is carried out with the people." Thus their differences with Frei are only differences in "positions", not in class interests. A sincere statement for once!

Finally, this document, written by a member of the "C"P secretariat, Volodia Teitelboim, reminds Frei that the "C"P has always stood for unity with him and with what he represents. "Let us not forget," it states, "that we have been seeking this joining of forces, this saving convergence, for a long time, since before the coup d'état; that the Communist Party a thousand and one times proposed the necessary dialogue, but was ignored by people with too much influence." (201)

In March 1976 (the text by Volodia Teitelboim is from January of that year), following Frei's refusal to accept them as even the caboose of his plan, the "C"P leaders published another document, in which they try desperately to convince him. They implore him "above any other consideration or ideological divergence that may have separated us in the past". However, Frei justified his real anti-communism by the rejection that the phony socialist regimes in the USSR and the neighbouring subject countries inspire; he declared himself to be against "communism", "because we have seen that the society the communists support has invariably led to a totalitarian type of state in the countries where it has won out". Given the extent of their subordination to the chieftains of the Soviet social-imperialist bureaucratic bourgeoisie, the leaders of the Chilean "C"P do not have sufficient autonomy to present themselves as independent of the "models of socialism" that their European brothers are beginning to repudiate. Thus, by persisting to defend the Eastern bloc countries and to present them as an "example" for Chile, the "C"P leaders allow Frei to maintain his influence over large sections of the population which rightly reject these regimes. In the document we are analyzing, after a defence of the USSR's economic performance and of its "democracy", the "C"P leaders state: "We are fully within our rights in demanding this genuinely human, democratic system, superior to any humanity has known before, as a banner of the Chilean people's struggle." While Frei drags large sections of the people along behind his policy in the service of imperialism, the "C"P leaders give him pretexts by proposing that Chileans try out their model of "socialism" and describing as "anti-communist" anyone who rejects the treason against communism perpetrated in the USSR; together, the two keep the Chilean people divided and block real anti-fascist unity and real progress toward socialism.

In the UP, only the MAPU-OC led by Gazmuri, which was created by the "C"P in order to voice its positions from another platform, completely goes along with the "C"P leaders in their adventure of asking Frei to carry them along at the tail end of his plans. A long document written by MAPU-OC on behalf of the "C"P deplores the fact that Frei-ism, although advocating "democratic ideas", suffers from an "anti-workerism and anti-communism that leads it to present itself as an alternative to fascism and to 'communism', thereby distorting the real nature of the choices facing the nation". The document merely repeats the arguments of the "C"P, with literary efforts being used to make them appear as an independent line.

3. Trends within the Socialist Party

Within the Socialist Party, although ideological confusion and factional struggle (the official trend, the National Coordination of the Regions, etc.) still exist, positions on the reactionary plans of the "C"P leadership seem to be gradually improving, at least in what is written. In a document we have not been able to date, in Chapter III on the "Political Line of the SP", the leaders of this party still speak of the socialist character of the Chilean revolution. "The coup d'état carried out by the fascist forces," they state, "has not changed the nature of the Chilean economic system. On the contrary, the fascist military dictatorship representing the interests of the big bourgeoisie and imperialism has given stronger proof of its nature. These are the objective elements that determine the socialist character of the Chilean Revolution." For them, the struggle against the dictatorship is a mere tactical phase in the struggle for socialism. But earlier in the same document, in pointing out the objectives of the broad anti-fascist front they advocate, they promote "open struggle for a new, people's democratic system of institutions which will make the resurgence of fascism impossible and wipe out its germs from the entire body of society, while at the same time serving as an adequate framework to get back on the socialist course of the Chilean Revolution". They continue: "The new forms of political power, to the extent that they forcibly prevent the rebirth of fascism and replace the institutions supporting it, signify the establishment of a revolutionary democracy. This new system of institutions must guarantee the effective control of state leadership on behalf of the majority of the people. It will be necessary to destroy the institutions fascism has developed, and in particular, to transform the Armed Forces and police into instruments of the people."

It is clear that this formulation presupposes actual destruction of the state apparatus controlled by the fascists and the "establishment of a revolutionary democracy" with "state leadership on behalf of the majority of the people". All this, combined with the indispensable economic measures against the interests protected by the Military Junta (the imperialist monopolies, the internal monopoly bourgeoisie and the big landlords), is precisely the people's democratic stage of the revolution, a fact the document refuses to explicitly recognize.

Further on in this document, showing that they do not understand the nature of the "Communist" leadership, the SP leaders advocate Socialist-"Communist" unity as the axis of the anti-fascist movement. They believe it will be possible to achieve a "united policy" through a "serious and far-reaching debate conducted with a view to delving deeply into our respective positions". As for MIR, they believe it must participate in the anti-fascist front and consider that "the content of the open letter from MIR to the Communist Party augurs well" — despite the fact that the "C"P leaders indignantly rejected this letter.

As for the CDP, they describe its participation in the front as "welcome". They add, however, that "one must not expect a consistent posture of anti-fascist struggle so long as the dominant sections (in the CDP) express the interests of big capital and imperialism". They maintain that the front must be advanced "with or without the Christian Democrats". Needless to say, this position is intended to counter the obstinate decision of the "C"P leaders to paralyze any anti-fascist alternative that excludes the CDP led by Frei.

Lastly, the SP leaders add a concept that demonstrates the fruitlessness of the "serious and far-reaching debate" with a view to achieving a "united policy" with the "C"P leaders. They state: "In present conditions, the revolutionary process can only be carried on by means of armed struggle", adding that: "Any formula designed to raise hopes of a so-called peaceful and democratic way out of the present situation simply means weakening the fighting resolve of the people and the will to prepare their political vanguards." The obsessive desire of the "C"P leaders to ally themselves with Frei and company at any price is designed precisely to sabotage any movement aiming at the overthrow of the military dictatorship through popular struggle.

In March 1974, the SP Central Committee published a lengthy document which analyzes the causes of the defeat within the framework presented by the "C"P leadership, tending to hide the deliberate paralysis of the people's struggle. It states: "The basic factor in the defeat of the UP experiment was the resistance of the enemies of the people to the process and the enormous strength they succeeded in building up." In an analysis more descriptive than self-critical, the document then mentions the success the opposition had in blocking the agreement with the CDP, in ideological struggle against the UP, in penetrating the Armed Forces, etc. Speaking in the negative and failing to mention the very real predominance of a policy that reduced the UP and its government to impotence, the SP leadership gives what in its opinion were the reasons why the anti-government offensive was not successfully countered: "The political defeat of the people's movement" was "caused by the degree to which the working class was isolated and the lack of a real leading force able to successfully make use of the revolutionary potential latent in the strength of the masses and in the tools of institutional power within the government's reach." The report then gives an academic and abstract analysis of the errors that were made, without showing the link between the official opposition to the "revolutionary potential latent in the strength of the masses" and the isolation of the working class, and of course without discerning either the basic causes of this or who was responsible for it.

Further on, showing how little they are aware of the essence of the opportunist policy into which they let the "C"P leadership drag them, the SP leaders state that SP-"C"P unity "was completely insufficient to face the very decisive circumstances in which a qualitative change in the relations of political forces was at stake, the problem of political power itself". However, the role played by the SP leadership in "unifying" the UP under the hegemony of the "C"P leadership was an important factor that impeded the development of the process and led to the catastrophe.

Still further on, the SP correctly defines the nature of the Chilean revolution for the first time in one of its official documents. It states: "There is a strict relationship between the nature of the revolution (anti-imperialist, democratic, popular, with a socialist perspective), the main enemy (imperialism, monopoly bourgeoisie and big agrarian bourgeoisie) and the proletariat's policy on alliances (broad anti-fascist front)." The SP then argues that: "The Chilean revolution still has a basically democratic, anti-imperialist and anti-monopoly character, of a very advanced and popular type. This is a function of the dependent character of Chile and the high monopoly concentration that makes imperialism and the monopoly and agrarian bourgeoisie the central core, axis of support and centre of gravity of capitalist domination in the country." Then, showing that the coup d'état has at least had the virtue of clarifying the identity of the nucleus that held power in Chile and the urgent necessity of isolating it, the SP states: "The concentration of capitalist economic and political power in this dominant nucleus, and the weight of the vestiges of pre-capitalist forms of production (small-scale commodity production) condition a class structure and a system of contradictions such that not only the urban and rural petty bourgeoisie but also the subjugated sections of the middle and small bourgeoisie can be united around the proletariat." Further: "It is not correct to advocate socialist revolution at this stage", and "the nature of our revolution, although not initially socialist, contains the seeds of its transformation into a socialist revolution, in a single process." This formulation is absolutely correct. The SP document goes on to give an essentially correct description of the process of establishing the "New Democratic State" and its socialist future.

On the question of alliances, the document categorically states that the alliance with the CDP can only be established on "the basis of the hegemony of the democratic and progressive partner". It adds that: "The development and strengthening of the process of unification entail the defeat of the CDP's right wing. Frei is simply not qualified to lead the CDP in the anti-fascist alliance." This formulation is far away from the efforts of the "C"P leaders to have Frei accept them, and even further away from their intentions to back him unconditionally.

The SP document goes on to criticize the "errors" in the ideas of the "C"P, particularly its thesis of "the possibility of a peaceful, or unarmed, road". According to the document, this "was blown up, leading to illusions and fatal errors in judging the class character of the bourgeois-democratic institutions." *(202)*

The document concludes by pointing to armed struggle (combined with legal and illegal mass struggles) as the road to overthrow the junta.

On February 7, 1976, an interview was published with the head of the National Coordination of Regional Committees of the SP, a trend which says it has the decisive influence inside the country. While it upholds a more radical position than the SP leadership, it nonetheless maintains organic relations with this leadership, and at the same time is relatively autonomous. In the interview, the head of the SP (NCRC) appears to agree with the SP document just analyzed as to the nature of the revolution. He states: "It is the energy of the masses organized in this new type of front that will make it possible for us, once the obstacle of the Military Junta is swept aside, to move immediately to establish the people's power and to march without interruption toward the construction of socialism in our country."

Intuitively aware of the role played by the "C"P line as a brake on the struggle against the dictatorship, as well as of the paralysis that was forced on the SP leaders by the secret "unity" meetings with the "communist" leaders, the SP(NCRC) leader points out that: "To tell the truth, the statements of the Popular Unity abroad help the revolutionary process inside the country very little." He adds that: "Common actions by these same forces do not yet take place inside the country. And this is very serious. It is one of the reasons why the dictatorship is still in power."

With even more forcefulness than the document by the SP leadership, this interview argues against the alliance with Frei and his group, and warns against the elements in the UP that let themselves be taken in by this phony solution.

In issue No. 13 of *Orientacion,* official organ of the SP External Secretariat, dated June 1976, the SP leadership stepped up its polemic against the "C"P leaders. The issue contains the document cited at length above, refuting an article by the "C"P leadership entitled "Ultra-Leftism, Imperialism's Trojan Horse". With the utmost impudence, this article had attempted to blame MIR and other forces described as "ultra-leftist" for the overthrow of the Allende government. Half of the SP document is intended as a refutation of the "C"P article. Thus the "unity" between the SP and the "C"P, subordinated to the reactionary inclinations of the "Communist" leading group, is beginning to wear thin following the rejection by most of the UP parties, including the rank and file of the SP and many of its leaders, of the "C"P's persistent opportunist line. It is no accident that this same issue contains a two-page letter from the "C"P leadership on the occasion of the 43rd anniversary of the SP, a letter in which the word "unity" is mentioned 18 times. This is in the typical revisionist style of hiding their splittist activities and reactionary plots beneath words of "unity". Issue No. 1 of *Arauco,* the SP newsletter in France, dated August 1976, gives lengthy quotes from the "C"P document designed to seduce Frei, and counters it with various documents by the SP leaders rejecting this reactionary alternative.

To sum up this partial and incomplete look at the evolution of political positions in the SP leading circles, we may say that there has been positive progress on many points: progress in characterizing more correctly the nature of the revolution; in deepening the critical analysis of the causes of the coup d'état; in appreciating the importance of armed struggle for the seizure of political power; and, especially, progress in understanding the opportunist policy which the "C"P leadership dragged them into under the Allende government. This critical advance is becoming more and more dangerous for the revisionist leaders because it is reaching the point where the link between their opportunist line and their farce of "socialism" will become clear for many people.

4. The Ideological Discussion within MAPU

It is very difficult to analyze the stand of MAPU as such, for there has been a great proliferation of official and unofficial documents correcting one another, so lively is the ideological discussion. The first document we know of was a very sectarian and "leftist" one signed by the Political Commission of MAPU and published in March 1974. It puts forward the necessity of unifying the forces opposed to the junta "in the framework of an anti-dictatorial and anti-capitalist programme". It maintains that following a mass political struggle, a second phase "of an insurrectionary type" would be reached, in which "the working class and people put everything on the line". Putting the cart before the horse, the document goes on to state that "in the course of this insurrectionary process . . . the people's army takes shape". *(203)*

However, in September 1974, the Political Commission published another document, one which is broader in its thinking. Called Document No. 3, it was reprinted in the MAPU journal *Unidad Proletaria* in September 1975. It puts forward the necessity of struggling for a People's Revolutionary Government of a provisional nature. The objective of this government would be to "re-establish and extend the political freedoms, allowing the people to control the state apparatus" and to "re-establish and extend the victories won against the monopolies, imperialism and the big landlords". But if they were carried out under proletarian leadership, these changes would in no way be the product of so "provisional" an action as the authors of this document would suggest; they would in fact constitute a People's Democratic Revolution. The tactic suggested by the authors for the overthrow of the junta also reflects a naive underestimation of the enemies' power. According to them, the struggles "in the beginning take the form of partial confrontations in the ideological, economic and political spheres, intensifying and spreading until they culminate in a general political strike combined with an armed mass uprising of an insurrectionary nature".

The document then presents the idea of "the unity of the working class" — just that — through a Workers' United Front made up of the UP parties and MIR. Thus it fails to take into account the petty-bourgeois and frankly reactionary lines of some of the leading groups in these parties. As to the CDP, while recognizing the necessity of making it a part of the anti-fascist front, the authors of the document maintain that this would "presuppose a change in the internal balance of power in favour of the progressive sections and neutralization of its most reactionary sections, the ones that maintain ties with the dictatorship".

The document corrects, although only partially, the "leftist" tendencies of the first document, stating that "to propose the establishment of the dictatorship of the proletariat as the objective in this period, without understanding the necessity for a prior tactical step, without identifying the fascist dictatorship as the main enemy and without recognizing the possibility of building a broad alliance against it, only results in handing potential allies over to the enemy, confuses the people, and in short, holds back the development of the revolutionary process". However, it is not enough to identify "the fascist dictatorship" as "the main enemy"; those who are behind the dictatorship must also be identified as such. One then discovers that enemies such as imperialism, the monopoly bourgeoisie and the landed oligarchy must be confronted, enemies whose overthrow will not be the result of a mere "tactical step" nor of a short-term "insurrectionary uprising".

Document No. 3 contains no critical or self-critical formulation concerning either the UP government or the struggle against the junta. However, it recognizes that there does not yet exist an "alternative political leadership to unite and guide the classes and social forces hurt by the junta, a fact which allows the dictatorship to exercise total control over the situation".

The issue of *Unidad Proletaria* containing Document No. 3 also prints extracts from Document No. 4, dated April 1975, in which No. 3 is criticized for its "over-estimation of the attitude and willingness of the Communist Party to adopt this tactic (resolute struggle against the dictatorship). At that time," the later document states, "we believed that given the objective conditions, the CP would step up to this work and launch actions of resistance. In fact it did not do so, because it has a different conception . . . The political line of the CP in Chile has always been to conserve its strength, not to set its forces in motion, especially not in the working class, to wait for circumstances in which, in its judgment, the contradictions within the bourgeoisie are becoming extremely sharp."

In issue No. 4 of *Unidad Proletaria* (January-March 1976) there appeared a long article on the forms of "people's power" that existed under the Allende government. This article is full of the illusions about these organizations that we criticized in the previous chapter. However, it takes a clear position against the "C"P line of alliance with Frei and his group, criticizing the "C"P leaders' document against MIR but still trying to "show them" that they are reformist and are revising Marxism.

Finally, we have a document written by seven members of the MAPU Central Committee. This document is undoubtedly the most advanced in its formulations and its criticism in respect to the UP experience, the movement to overthrow the junta, and the "C"P leadership. It is entitled, "A Line of Victory for the Proletarian and Revolutionary Resistance", and proposes to be "a basic draft for the discussion taking place inside the Party". It states: "We are openly putting forward a set of theses distinct from the reformist, revisionist or simply opportunist theses which a minority rightist faction inside the Party has advocated."

The document points out that in the UP "the predominant reformist-revisionist leadership . . . found expression at all times and in all fields" and that such ideas "express precisely the strategic and ideological interests of the bourgeoisie and not the proletariat". It then denounces the role played by the USSR in relation to the Allende government, stating that it "did not commit itself in Latin America to the process which, by breaking through certain reformist or bourgeois-democratic limits, endangered the international status quo. The document goes on to state that the USSR "put constant pressure on the UP government to reach an agreement with the Christian Democrats". And it concludes that "the objectively reactionary role of the U.S. and USSR in Latin America must be a basic premise of any revolutionary strategy on our continent".

Although it does not give a correct formulation on the nature of the reactionary plan for state capitalism, inspired by the opportunist line of the "C"P leadership, which dominated the experience of the UP government, the document goes further than any other in demanding self-criticism from those who participated in the government. It rejects the criticism of the process (in the official MAPU documents) as insufficient. It points out that in rallying to the UP, MAPU strayed from its original line, which was to form a revolutionary front and not to join the UP, due to the reformist nature of the UP's concept of the state. The document states that henceforth, "to attempt to build and strengthen an alliance with reformist forces at the price of maintaining and even deepening the ideological and political disarmament of the masses and their vanguard sections is not only naive: it is an error and an act of serious political irresponsibility". However, the document encourages the idea that such an alliance is possible on condition that "the reformist and revisionist nature of the positions which held sway during the three years of people's government and which caused its defeat is pointed out and denounced when necessary (and it is necessary now)". The document also demands a self-criticism from MAPU as a "protagonist" of this opportunist policy.

In the conclusions of the chapter of criticism and self-criticism, the document states, showing, however, the weakness of its analysis, that "a reformist-revisionist dominant leadership among the masses represents a danger and an extremely great obstacle to the advance of the masses to higher phases of revolutionary struggle, and its overthrow and political and ideological defeat is a necessary condition for the decisive victory of the proletariat". This leads one to believe that the authors of the document are willing to coexist with this leadership, even though the final conclusion of this chapter is that "without the hegemony of the proletariat, there can be no consistent and victorious anti-imperialist, democratic or socialist struggle".

The document goes on to analyze the characteristics of the present Chilean government, the interests it represents and its feature of being a model of imperialism's response to its problems in the dependent countries. It rejects the "anti-fascist front" as the "reformists" conceive it. By including groups such as Frei's which appear to be in "contradiction" with the junta, the "reformists" (according to the document) "oppose the development of the forces of the working class and people through the Revolutionary Resistance Committees and the Factory Councils", and they continue to propagate "a reformist concept of the army" and speak of "armed struggle" as a "mere possibility". "They must do all this in order to give guarantees to the bourgeoisie and achieve an alliance with it."

In their international analysis also, the authors of the document go further than any other section of the UP in their criticism of the system prevailing in the USSR, although their denunciation of it is still incomplete. They point to "the evolution of the USSR in a direction ever further removed from socialism and the international revolutionary camp". They state: "Inside the country, the abandonment of proletarian ideas is increasingly more definite and obvious, and is expressed in a process of growing capitalist restoration. The dictatorship of the proletariat was progressively abandoned, particularly after the Twentieth Congress of the CPSU in 1956. The state took on an increasingly more repressive role against the working class and people. And the party, army and state apparatus are increasingly controlled by a bureaucratic bourgeoisie." In short, for the authors of the document, the USSR has only been "moving away from" socialism for the last 20 years, and there has been "growing capitalist restoration", which according to them is apparently not yet complete. They do not point out the social-imperialist superpower nature of the USSR and its plans and attempts at world domination in collusion and contention with U.S. imperialism. It follows that they are unable to give a clear formulation concerning the model of state capitalism and subordination to Soviet social-imperialism that was the soul of the reactionary line promoted by the "C"P leadership during the UP administration and still promoted by it today. It follows that they consider the USSR as an "obstacle and an enemy (albeit a secondary one) of the development of the revolutionary struggle of our peoples", not because of its efforts at world domination and promotion of regimes like itself, but "basically by virtue of its compromises with U.S. imperialism", which are expressed "in its policy of 'peaceful coexistence' and 'detente' and in its tacit recognition of the fact that Latin America is part of the U.S. 'sphere of influence' ". This failure to understand the reactionary model that the Soviets and "pro-Soviets" want to establish in Chile leads them to believe that the opportunist policy of the "C"P leadership was only the application of the line of "peaceful coexistence" dictated by the USSR. They do not see that it reflected the need to preserve the bourgeois state in order to establish state capitalism. The truth is that in Chile, as we have shown, the line of compromise for the redivision of the world into spheres of influence between the USSR and the U.S. took the form of the demand to advance toward state capitalism in alliance with the pro-U.S. populist sector and its leaders: Frei and his group. Wherever suitable conditions exist, as in Czechoslovakia and Angola, the social-imperialists do not hesitate to abandon their "peaceful road" and their "peaceful coexistence".

Moreover, the reason the USSR is an enemy of the Latin American peoples is not just that it is promoting a line of conciliation with U.S. imperialism there, but follows directly from its designs to dominate, beginning by exploiting the peoples of the continent jointly with the U.S.

Further on, the document characterizes in a relatively correct manner the tasks of the "present strategic stage" and its targets: "the big monopoly bourgeoisie (central core of the bourgeoisie and of dependent national capitalism), U.S. imperialism and the big landlords", and states that: "The strategic tasks are still the expropriation of big monopoly capital, the expulsion of U.S. imperialism, the expropriation of the big landlords, and the destruction of the bourgeois state." However, it maintains that with these tasks will be achieved "the establishment of socialism and the beginning of socialist construction". And, while advocating the direct establishment of a proletarian state and socialism, the authors of the document want to win over not only the proletariat and poor peasantry but "the impoverished sections of the petty bourgeoisie and certain sections of the middle and small bourgeoisie". Thus the objectives proposed are very narrow for the strata they want to win over, and these strata are defined in a very restricted way in relation to the amply demonstrated strength of the main enemies to be overthrown.

The problem of separating the stages of the revolution (people's democratic and socialist) being too complex for them, due to the Trotskyist prejudices that subsist in the most honest strata of the Chilean left, the authors of the document end up with a confused, eclectic formula. They write: "We speak of the national people's democratic and socialist character of the revolution in a Leninist sense." And they go on to state: "Even during the period of struggle against the dictatorship, the monopolies, imperialism and the big landlords, the content of the struggle will not only be national and people's democratic, but also strictly proletarian and socialist." They "justify" this by stating that it is socialist "in the sense and to the extent that it is at the same time a struggle for political power, and in the sense and to the extent that the essence of socialism itself is nothing other than the realization of the dictatorship of the proletariat, not only in the political and ideological, but also in the economic and social fields." They add: "In this sense, we say that the present strategic stage of the revolution in our country is at the same time national people's democratic and socialist." In support of this strange conclusion, they quote a passage from Lenin which in fact says just the opposite of what they conclude (and this is not counting the numerous statements by Lenin in which he clearly and explicitly distinguishes between the two revolutions). They write: "Lenin himself stated clearly and emphatically in 1921: *'We solved the problems of the bourgeois-democratic revolution in passing, as a "by-product" of our main and genuinely* proletarian-*revolutionary, socialist activities . . . We said — and proved it by deeds — that bourgeois-democratic reforms are a by-product of the proletarian, i.e., of the socialist revolution. Incidentally, the Kautskys, Hilferdings, Martovs,*

Chernovs, . . . were incapable of understanding this *relation between the bourgeois-democratic and the proletarian-socialist revolutions. The first develops into the second. The second, in passing, solves the problems of the first. The second consolidates the work of the first. Struggle, and struggle alone, decides how far the second succeeds in outgrowing the first.' " (204)* The only thing Lenin is pointing out here, as against Kautsky and others who sought to mark time in the bourgeois democratic revolution and hold back its transformation into a socialist revolution (a transformation which is accelerated under the conditions of relatively advanced capitalist development obtaining in a country such as Russia), is that the fundamental objective of the Marxists is proletarian revolution and that it is not necessary, once the first revolutionary objective is achieved, to wait for the complete fulfilment of all the bourgeois-democratic demands before going on to the stage of struggle for socialism. However, Lenin speaks clearly, in this passage as always, of *two* revolutions. These revolutions (and this is valid today for the people's democratic revolution, which is not a mere bourgeois-democratic revolution, but nor is it a socialist revolution) have distinct programmes, are directed against or have as their main target different class enemies, and are carried out with distinct class alliances. Moreover, the forms of political power they give rise to are not the same. The people's democratic revolution gives rise to a particular form of dictatorship of the proletariat, which the proletariat exercises, while maintaining its leadership, together with the whole of the people against the main enemies; while under socialism, according to Lenin himself, the proletariat exercises "unshared" dictatorship over the entire bourgeoisie. Just as it is vitally important, once the first stage of revolution is accomplished, to struggle against the rightist tendencies to freeze the process, to separate the two stages with a "Chinese wall", it is extremely important before this first stage to fight the "ultra-left" tendencies, which attempt to confuse the two stages, isolating the proletariat and assigning it tasks which are impossible to fulfil "at once".

The correct formulation of the objectives corresponding to the first stage of revolution (particularly in countries such as Chile which are at a low level of capitalist development) and to the policy of alliances which the proletariat must promote is an indispensable condition for the success of this stage and for rapid advancement to the socialist stage. "Revolutionary" phraseology, the verbal burning of stages, not only does not hasten the coming of socialism but prevents the completion of the first stage of revolution. Consequently, to argue in favour of confusing the two stages by saying that "the essence of socialism is nothing other than the realization of the dictatorship and hegemony of the proletariat" promotes neither the advance of the proletariat toward its future unshared dictatorship nor the hegemony which it must establish over broad sections of the people in order to overthrow the main obstacles in its march towards socialism.

Paradoxically, while attempting to mix up the two revolutions, the document points to "the absurdity and childishness of attempting to expropriate all the bourgeois classes or sections completely and immediately, particularly the entire middle and petty bourgeoisie". However, to stay away from this "absurd and childish" position means to put forward a programme in which one specifies clearly that only the interests of imperialism, the latifundia, the banks and the monopoly industrial firms that are key to the economy will be expropriated; the others, within the framework of certain limitations and requirements that the revolution will impose and of certain guarantees it will grant, will be respected. The programme must also specify which strata, of those which will not be the target of the revolution, will participate in the government and the new institutions which will replace the old reactionary state, and so on. Otherwise, even if one manages to avoid the "absurd and childish" measures, one will implement the even more "absurd and childish" strategy of making all these sections (which are not the main enemy) believe that they are also the immediate target of revolution and that they will be wiped out when political power is seized in the same way as the main enemy, even though one actually has no intention of doing this. The reason why this blunder must not be committed is not only that these strata, because of the great strength of the main enemies and their international allies, have to be drawn to the side of the proletariat or at least neutralized, but also that the proletariat, which as the leading force takes over the management of the key sectors of the economy, is not in a position, in the short term, to administer the hundreds of thousands of industrial, commercial, agricultural, craft and service enterprises controlled by small and medium private owners.

The example of the UP government, which did not even succeed in administering the big state enterprises with average efficiency (due to the active but foreseeable sabotage, of course), should have led to some conclusions being drawn on this question. Of course, control of political power produces conditions radically different from those of the UP government, but does not eliminate the enormous complexity of the transition to a completely socialized economy. Moreover, the need to reckon — after the smashing of the big exploiters — on a period of controlled and efficient operation of small and medium private industry (as well as of commerce, services, etc.) does not only extend to the people's democratic stage. Even the establishment of socialism from the point of view of political power does not necessarily imply the immediate, simultaneous expropriation of all private business. The pace of the complete socialization of the economy, as well as the procedures to achieve it, must be determined by the proletariat in power. This makes it all the more indispensable to win over or neutralize these bourgeois strata through an alliance made with them by the proletariat in the People's Democratic Revolution.

The MAPU document we are analyzing takes a sectarian line on the tactical tasks of the proletariat, setting up the People's Democratic programme as the (purely tactical) minimum programme for the overthrow of the dictatorship. It states: "The present dictatorship must be overthrown through popular insurrection and replaced by a people's democratic dictatorship". This programme would be implemented by a Provisional Revolutionary Government.

In regard to methods of struggle for the overthrow of the dictatorship, the authors of the document mix up the concepts of insurrection and protracted people's war. While recognizing that "it would be completely idiotic and criminal for a leading group to drag the people into a decisive general confrontation when the combat units are still weak and inexperienced, or in any case, weaker than the enemy forces", they also maintain that "in the course of the revolutionary war not just one but several general insurrections may occur". But if one recognizes the principle of building up the forces through a process of protracted war until strategic superiority over the enemy is attained, it is absurd to foresee, in the same breath, "several general insurrections". Such insurrections would only be transgressions of the overall strategy, and their defeat (which is presupposed when one speaks of "several"), would be a destructive blow against the people's forces and would therefore mean a decisive setback in the development of protracted people's war. In fact, because of the importance of the cities in Chile, one can only conceive of a single insurrection, the culmination of a protracted war.

After having defined the People's Democratic Revolution as a mere tactic and not a strategic objective, the document nonetheless presents a sort of sub-tactic, an "Immediate Platform against the Junta", which emphasizes democratic freedoms, defence of the basic natural resources against imperialism, and defence of the standard of living of the masses. The truth is that a platform of this type, which includes certain aspects of the People's Democratic programme and stresses those having to do with democratic rights and freedoms and the standard of living of the masses, is the true tactic of the anti-fascist movement, a movement broader still than the front fighting for People's Democratic Revolution. The struggle against the dictatorship and against the most aberrant aspects of its policy constitute the present tactical step, which will open the way for the strategic objective of establishing a People's Democracy. Their devaluation of the strategic character of the People's Democratic Revolution leads the authors of the document to think up this sort of sub-tactic, which underestimates the objectives to be attained after and through the overthrow of the junta; their People's Democratic programme is only a "tactic" of a provisional government.

Finally, the document states that "the reformist and revisionist groups are the main enemy of the revolutionary forces and positions within the working class. But on the national scale and in face of the main enemy of the proletariat and the people as a whole, they are today an objective ally. Consequently, we should in no way hesitate to consciously and responsibly seek alliances or joint action with them, on the basis of the Immediate Platform or, in general, on the basis of democratic objectives, but without subordinating ourselves to them, without losing our ideological and political independence, without ceasing to wage the clearest ideological struggle against the positions or actions promoted by these groups which hold back or harm the struggle of the masses against the dictatorship". Thus presented, this position is dangerous unless one clarifies various factors that condition the tactics of dealing with the revisionist leaders. It is true that they are not at the moment so dangerous as the Frei group, which represents the dominant imperialist power in Latin America and in our country in particular; but their character as a false proletarian leadership, their plan to replace the big exploiters through the establishment of state capitalism, and the objective tendency to ally with the group representing U.S. imperialism oblige us to be very cautious in taking advantage of their contradictions with U.S. imperialism and the Chilean big bourgeoisie. What forces us to take them into consideration in the present struggle against the dictatorship is not their soundness as "allies" but the popular masses whom they have succeeded in deceiving and keep under their influence, masses who must be won over to proletarian leadership. In any case, one cannot agree to participate with them in a so-called "anti-fascist front" on which they would impose their reactionary leadership and their reactionary strategy and tactics. This would only be justified if there were a real prospect of rapidly unmasking them and taking away their mass influence, as Lenin did by participating in the Menshevik-led soviets. However, the "C"P leaders are daily using their influence to paralyze the organization of a resistance front to overthrow the junta, with a view to making the coveted pact with U.S. imperialism through Frei and his group. Therefore, the fundamental task is to create this broad front *under proletarian leadership* by putting an end to the revisionist sabotage. Only the development of a front of this type will give the proletariat sufficient strength and dominance to profitably make use of the contradictions between revisionism and its main enemies, and especially the mass base deceived by it. It is therefore not enough to allow oneself to be dragged into a phony anti-fascist front in which the revisionists would retain hegemony, on condition one is authorized to criticize them and to "wage ideological struggle" against their reactionary line. A very important step forward in this respect was the joint statement signed by the representatives in Sweden of the SP (National Coordination of Regional Committees), MIR and MAPU in September 1976. The statement points out that "the reconstruction of the ex-Popular Unity abroad does not reflect the unifying process experienced in Chile and is in fact an obstacle to building the broad unity against the dictatorship with a revolutionary line and leadership".

5. MIR's Line after the Coup d'Etat

MIR has not learned any lessons from the strength of the main enemies of the Chilean people, nor from the junta's policy against broad sections of the middle and petty bourgeoisie; it still gives the slogan of socialism as the immediate stage. In June 1974, Enriquez, former leader of MIR, stated during a press conference held in Cuba: "The Chilean working class has drawn an indelible lesson from the September 11th defeat. This is why, when it manages to overthrow the 'gorilla' dictatorship, it will be content only with complete victory over the big bourgeoisie and imperialism. It will destroy the bourgeois state to its very foundations and establish a workers' and peasants' state in place of the old state."

However, in the journal *Correo de la Resistencia* (No. 5, January 1975), MIR published an article in which it stated that, without abandoning the "people's programme" (socialist in nature), it had drawn up a "platform of struggle" centering on four points: democratic freedoms, defence of the standard of living of the masses, overthrow of the dictatorship and establishment of a new government, through the formation of a Popular Resistance Movement. It added that "the demands contained in the Programme are not an immediate objective of the struggle. It suits no one at present to establish the seizure of political power and the construction of socialism as a direct and immediate objective for the working class and the masses."

In April 1975, *Correo de la Resistencia* published a document by the Political Commission of MIR which it said had been written in December 1973. This document also states that "in a period such as the present, for an entire initial stage, our socialist programme will basically take on the character of a propaganda objective, due to the enormous difficulties of advancing it in practice".

Finally, in June 1975, MIR stated: "The thing most likely to happen is that in the course of the struggle to overthrow the dictatorship, a provisional government will appear, made up of all the classes which are fighting in a consistent manner to overthrow the 'gorilla' dictatorship. In this government, the proletariat must have decisive strength and win the leadership". This document puts forward a series of objectives broader than those contained in the "platform of struggle", including several basic aspects of a People's Democratic Revolution, although it refuses to recognize them as such.

Concerning the road for the overthrow of the dictatorship, the document corrects many "focist" trends which held sway in MIR in the past. It advocates the "military mass line, by which we mean that our military action will be oriented mainly towards incorporating broad sections of the mass movement in the forms of armed struggle, not restricting it exclusively to vanguard groups which act militarily 'in the name of the masses' and with their 'sympathy'."

The leaders of MIR made many fruitless efforts after the coup d'état to convince the leaders of the UP parties (notably the "C"P leaders, who were the most opposed to their plan) of the necessity of forming a Political Front of the People's Resistance, comprising the UP parties, the progressive circles in the CDP, and MIR. In essence, that is, they aspired to be admitted into a Popular Unity with prospects of expansion to include the anti-Frei elements of the CDP. They wanted to accomplish after the establishment of the dictatorship what was not possible before it. But they had committed the "crime" (in the eyes of the "C"P leaders) of criticizing the UP experience as reformist and of upholding the necessity of building up the forces for the overthrow of the dictatorship; and — as if that were not enough — they opposed the alliance with Frei and his acolytes ardently desired by the "communist" leaders. The "C"P leaders might temporarily pardon such sins in the ex-UP allies, but not in MIR, which they chose as scapegoat for the catastrophe into which they had led the Chilean people. For its part, the MIR leadership has persisted in its blindness, considering the pro-Soviet "C"P leaders as honest, mistaken reformists, and for more than four years has been making pathetic and naive efforts to convince them of their errors and to unite with them.

Orlando Millas, in an interview published in *L'Humanité-Dimanche* in early September 1974, attempted to silence the MIR leaders by exploiting their desire to unite with the UP and be admitted to it. He stated: "I must say that the difficult, dangerous and sometimes heroic work of the anti-fascist resistance is seriously hindered by the obstinacy of the ultra-leftists in maintaining a posture of division and provocation. For example, the fascists exploit the propaganda of MIR attacking the Popular Unity in imprudent and odious terms. The itch to form 'Resistance Committees' outside the parties by trying to mislead a few isolated activists seems designed more to undermine the anti-fascist forces than to trouble the fascists . . ."

The MIR leader Edgardo Enriquez answered Millas in *Politique Hebdo* (No. 142), stating: "The members of the left-wing parties are already carrying out joint action. They are overcoming in practice at the rank-and-file level the slowness of certain left-wing parties in understanding the urgent necessity of building the Political Front of the Resistance. The left-wing activists have nothing in common with those who are still delaying the formation of this front, hoping to incorporate in it a political party of the big bourgeoisie that is openly collaborating with the junta!" Still believing he can "convince" Millas and other reactionaries of his ilk, Enriquez states: "We are certain that the working class and people will eventually convince Orlando Millas and those who think as he does of the profound reality of the struggle: what the fascists exploit, what serves the 'gorillas', is the unbelievable delay in the formation of this Political Front of the Resistance with all the political forces ready to struggle for the overthrow of the Military Junta . . ." However, the MIR leaders and others who persist in believing that the "C"P leadership is "ready to struggle for the overthrow of the Military Junta" have greatly contributed to the "unbelievable delay" in organizing a resistance front to overthrow the dictatorship. It seems that the tragic experience of the UP government has gone for naught: the desire for "unity" with the renegades from Marxism and the failure to understand what they represent allow them to continue to hold sway.

In December 1974, the leaders of MIR stepped up their criticism of the orientation of the UP during the Allende administration. Andrès Pascal, Secretary-General of MIR after the assassination of Enriquez, stated in a press conference: "According to MIR, the downfall of the UP was due precisely to the fact that its government was not 'revolutionary'. What predominated within the UP government were reformist policies, the belief that it was possible to achieve socialism through a process of reforms in the framework of the bourgeois state, the tendency to conciliate with the enemies, the illusion they could reach agreements with sections of the bourgeoisie (the Christian Democrats) and the absurd faith in the 'constitutionality' and 'professionalism' of the reactionary Armed Forces officers' corps. In return, the UP lost the basis of its own power: the working masses. In their desire to compromise with the bourgeoisie, the reformist leaders held back the forward march of the mass movement, opposed the development of the people's political and military power, cultivated legalist illusions among the masses, and disoriented and disarmed them, thus creating conditions for the victory of the bourgeois coup d'état." Further on in this interview which he granted to various agencies and newspapers, Pascal stated: "In 1972 and 1973, we even held joint meetings at MIR's suggestion with the UP leaders and President Allende, for the purpose of reaching an agreement for joint struggle against the bourgeois reaction. But each time, these attempts were boycotted by the reformist leaders in the UP, who preferred to combat the mobilization of the people and seek illusory agreements with the CDP. The vacillations of the centrist sections of the Socialist Party and other UP parties also contributed to the failure."

He added: "But the most dramatic of these attempts was the one made by the leadership of MIR on the very day of September 11, 1973, when, in the middle of the coup d'état, we met with the leadership of the SP and CP to decide on joint resistance action.

But the CP leader present at this meeting opposed the development of the resistance, rejected any coordination with MIR, and declared that we had to wait and see whether the military would close down Parliament or not." Demonstrating that even this "dramatic" attempt did not allow MIR to understand the reactionary essence of what it calls "reformism", Pascal states that after the coup d'état, "to achieve this unity, the leadership of MIR met, both inside and outside the country, with the leaders of the UP parties and the democratic petty bourgeoisie of the CDP, with the exception of the leaders of the Chilean CP, who refused to meet with MIR. Again our efforts were boycotted by the resurgence of reformist positions within the leading groups of the traditional left-wing parties, which seemed to have learned nothing from the bloody defeat to which they led the Chilean people, and who are once again sacrificing the unity of the workers and of the left to their vain attempt to subordinate themselves to sections of the bourgeoisie, in particular to the Frei wing of the Christian Democrats." There is also no doubt that the leadership of MIR is continuing to "sacrifice" the genuine unity of the Chilean people to overthrow fascism, for the sake of false unity with those who have betrayed the people's interests.

In 1975 the MIR leadership carried on with its "self-denying" efforts to convince the "C"P leadership of the "inappropriateness" of subordinating everything to the alliance with Frei, although, like all the advanced sections of the UP, it put more stress on the necessity of not waiting for this "unity" to come from the top and of promoting it among the rank and file through the formation of Resistance Committees.

At the end of 1975 the "C"P leadership launched attacks against MIR and published its document on the "Trojan Horse". In this document, MIR is in fact only a pretext: the real purpose is to attack the opposition to the "C"P's reactionary line, which was on the rise in almost all the UP parties. The proof of this is that not only MIR, but also the SP, MAPU and other forces that reject the line of the phony communists, replied to the document. In its periodical *El Rebelde* (No. 114, June 1976), MIR observes that "the reformist leaders . . . preferred to obstruct the unity of the left and seek unity in submission with Frei and his section of the bourgeoisie. They preferred to maintain the division of the left, the working class and people, and the popular resistance movement, attempting to line up part of the people's resistance forces behind the objectives of a section of the bourgeoisie in order to seek unity with Frei and his clique." In spite of all this, MIR still says: "We call on the CP leadership to form the political front of the entire left, including MIR and the progressive sections of the CDP." Moreover, in No. 118 (June 1976) of *El Rebelde,* MIR denounces the fact that "these groups (the ones it calls reformist) are even trying to divide certain left-wing parties in order to impose non-proletarian domination of the people's movement, subordinating the proletariat and the people to Frei-ist demagogy". From this MIR concludes that "the most important lesson . . . (is) the fact that the unity of the left, like the strengthening and development of the resistance, will be a slow and gradual process". It still hopes that these fully conscious reactionaries will convince themselves that they are nothing more than "reformist", and, pressured by a unity built among the rank and file, will one day agree to mend their ways. How long will the rank and file of MIR and other forces whose leaders share this stubborn naivete continue to accept it as such, without denouncing it as complicity with the sabotage of the anti-fascist struggle by the revisionists? Certain recent symptoms, such as the joint statement cited above by representatives of MAPU, the SP(NCRC) and MIR in Sweden (September 1976), indicate that the time is not far off when this will begin to occur, to the benefit of the formation of a genuine front against the dictatorship, a front which is prepared to fight at the head of the masses and in which proletarian leadership will little by little win out.

6. The Anti-Fascist Position of the Revolutionary Communist Party

The RCP is in a qualitatively different position from the other parties which oppose the dictatorship. Even though self-criticism of the tactical aspects of its policy is necessary and inevitable, events have entirely confirmed the correctness of its main political principles and its strategic line. The coup d'état has thus contributed to ideologically strengthening the RCP and uniting it even more solidly around its line and its leadership. The basically clandestine nature of its organizational structure (maintained since its inception) has enabled it to avoid the virtual annihilation which the UP and MIR have suffered; not only are the bulk of its forces still in action, but — what is more important — in action inside Chile. Because of this, the RCP has gained tremendous weight in the present struggle against the dictatorship. To mention only one aspect, in the field of propaganda, with more than 50 issues of its newspaper published secretly since the coup d'état in Chile, with hundreds of leaflets, slogans on the walls, publications of the resistance committees, etc., there is no doubt that the RCP holds first place inside Chile in the propaganda against the Military Junta.

For the RCP the strategic goal at the present stage is still the People's Democratic Revolution, which (through the hegemony of the proletariat) opens the road to socialism. And in fact, the coup d'état in the service of U.S. imperialism, the monopoly and financial bourgeoisie, and the landed oligarchy, which has crushed not only the workers but also the middle strata, confirms this thesis entirely.

Events confirm the steadfast position of the RCP that the conquest of political power by the people is possible only if the main enemies are isolated, if they are opposed by the whole people under the leadership of the proletariat. Likewise, they confirm the principle which the RCP has always upheld, that this victory over the main exploiters is possible only by destroying their state apparatus (especially its Armed Forces) through armed people's struggle. This armed people's struggle, in the opinion of the RCP, taking into account the power of the enemy to fight and the geographic situation of Chile, must be conceived of as a protracted war.

For the people, the ideal would be a speedy annihilation of their adversaries; but their military, economic and political power and the necessity to develop these aspects step by step among the people rules out any adventurist action which could lead to annihilation of the forces. Consequently it is necessary to gain an overwhelming tactical superiority in each battle against the adversary and in this way build up the forces, avoiding premature destruction, so as to gain strategic superiority.

The RCP also believes that a consistent struggle against the main exploiter and, through this struggle, the build-up of forces to wipe them out, are impossible without exposing and strongly fighting against the false Marxists (whether of the "left" or of the right, although in Chile the latter present the most urgent danger). The masses must free themselves from their fatal influence and break away from them. The advantages in the RCP's favour which we have stated, as well as its independence with respect to the paralyzing influence exerted by the leadership of the "C"P over the UP, enabled it to contribute to organizing in Chile (and abroad) the first basic organizations of an anti-fascist united front: the People's Front.

The policy of encouraging the development of a broad and unified anti-dictatorial front, with a minimum programme, complies with the existing concrete conditions in the struggle for the People's Democratic Revolution. This policy is developing under the conditions imposed by the coup d'état: terrorist dictatorship, the rescinding of almost all bourgeois democratic rights, and the application of a policy of superexploitation of the people in the service of the big landlords and the monopoly bourgeoisie, both internal and imperialist. It is being applied under conditions of a big downturn in the people's struggles, caused by revisionist treachery and by the repressive savagery of the putschist Armed Forces. This latter aspect constitutes the major contradiction facing the people, to enforce their rights, to paralyze the thoroughly reactionary policy of the junta, and to find a way out of the crisis into which it is leading the country. Consequently, the primary tactical objective is to smash through struggle the repressive instrument of the junta's policy — a policy which is pro-imperialist and which favours the landlords and the monopoly bourgeoisie — in order to begin to impose another policy which favours the people. Consequently, the anti-fascist front constitutes the present tactic in the strategy of the People's Democratic Revolution. This tactic consists of uniting the broadest sections of the population in the struggle to overthrow the Military Junta, to smash the instrument of repression which supports the big exploiters of the Chilean people: the reactionary Armed Forces. In line with this tactic, the People's Front has worked out its minimum programme, with which the RCP agrees. This is not the programme of the People's Democratic Revolution worked out by the RCP, but certain demands represent significant progress towards realizing it (especially the creation of political conditions much more favourable to the development of the struggle to achieve it. Foremost in the People's Front programme is the overthrow of the dictatorship, the return of democratic rights and freedoms, and the elimination of the dictatorship's instruments of repression. It advocates also, through the overthrow of those who impose an ultra-reactionary policy by force of arms, the beginning of a policy favourable to the people (including the middle strata) and opposed to U.S. imperialty, the big landlords, and the monopoly and financial bourgeoisie.

The People's Front also advocates the formation of a Democratic Government of Anti-Fascist Unity after the overthrow of the dictatorship. The primary task of this government will be to carry out the minimum programme of the anti-fascist front, that is essentially, the restoration of democratic freedoms for the people, the complete demolition of the repressive apparatus of the dictatorship (whatever still exists after the struggle to overthrow it), and the repression of the classes it serves. It will also begin a policy favourable to the people and opposed to the big exploiters.

Once the dictatorship is overthrown, another tactical phase begins, in which the RCP in keeping with the leading role which the proletariat will have obtained in the struggle to overthrow the dictatorship and in the new government which will rise from it, will present, completely or in part (depending on the situation), its programme for the People's Democratic Revolution in the broad organizations.

Both in the anti-imperialist, anti-monopolist and anti-latifundist policy which the Democratic Government of Anti-Fascist Unity will initiate and in the prospect of not merely eliminating the repressive instruments of the dictatorship, but also completely destroying the bourgeois state in all its aspects and establishing a form of dictatorship of the proletariat in alliance with other forces, the hegemony of the proletariat in the struggle is decisive. The founding of a genuine People's Democracy and its prospect for an uninterrupted march toward socialism depends on this struggle and on this hegemony. This will be a sharp struggle, not only against the main enemies and against the attempts of various bourgeois sectors to take over the leadership of the movement, but especially against the falsifiers of Marxism, who will try to take advantage of the progress of the people to set up their state capitalism and open up Chile to Soviet social-imperialism. We say "especially" because they act deceitfully and underhandedly, presenting themselves as revolutionaries.

The People's Front is engaged in creating unified organizational forms in keeping with its anti-fascist policy, thus responding with deeds to the paralysis created within the UP by the influence of the phony "communists". However, the People's Front is not — nor does it claim to be — a closed or exclusive front, either on the organizational or the political level. The clandestine unified resistance committees, deeply rooted in the mass organizations, have as their mission only to unite the most advanced sections of the masses in the most reliable and effective form, to give them a common leadership in the anti-fascist struggle. They do not try to replace the masses, who must be the main protagonists in the anti-fascist struggle, nor the parties which send activists to the committees or operate outside of them. There is no discussion in the committees of the political differences among the parties which favour the overthrow of the junta; instead they contribute to uniting their mass political leadership on the points of agreement. Furthermore, the resistance committees are not intended to be the sole bases of the People's Front; there are also the mass organizations (unions, sports centres, cultural centres, residents' associations, etc.) which are in agreement with its minimum programme. Moreover, the anti-fascist front policy of the People's Front goes much beyond its organizational forms. It is open to joint action on one, several or all the points of its programme, and even on concrete demands (temporary or permanent) which bring forces into the struggle to overthrow the junta. Furthermore, it is open to joint action of amalgamation (depending on the situation) with other anti-fascist fronts put forward by other organizations which are working towards the same goal.

However, the policy of the People's Front is clearly aimed at the overthrow of the junta. To achieve this, it considers it essential to promote the most varied forms of mass struggle, especially the form which is the most advanced, important and decisive to attain its goal: armed struggle. It aims to smash and overthrow the repressive armed force which imposes the dictatorship on Chile. So long as that has not happened, it will not consider that its goals have been achieved. Consequently, as long as the armed instrument of the dictatorship continues to exist, the People's Front is not ready to accept that the anti-fascist struggle be defused in exchange for certain democratic guarantees handed out by the military or by some civilians who are less bloodthirsty in appearance than Pinochet and his followers. Fascism must be smashed by the people, not prettified to make it more acceptable while allowing it to keep the means necessary to massacre the people all over again whenever it finds it necessary. This is why the People's Front rejects the falsely "democratic" solution of Frei and rejects the false anti-fascism of the leadership of the "C"P, which would be satisfied if the fascists agree to restore certain legal and democratic rights, which would be satisfied with the punishment of a small number of individuals who are responsible for the repression, while the High Command of the Armed Forces, the officers and the sections of the troops who agreed to massacre, torture and imprison the people simply sneak off into the background, ready to act again. Neither does it agree to dilute itself inside the so-called anti-fascist front represented by the ex-UP, in which the "C"P leaders still have enough influence to sabotage the struggle to overthrow the junta in the hope of convincing their allies to unite with Frei or anyone else that the military would agree to use as a screen in order to preserve their capacity for repression. The People's Front is in favour of developing a broad anti-fascist front, excluding no one, but clearly guided by the slogan of mobilizing the masses to overthrow the dictatorship. Although it is necessary to take as much advantage as possible of the contradictions between these inconsistent anti-fascist sections and the Military Junta, one must not give in to their capitulationist line. These contradictions must be used to overthrow the dictatorship.

If it should happen that the anti-fascist struggle, the economic crisis and other factors mean that the military force of the bourgeois dictatorship moves into the background and a government is installed which concedes certain democratic guarantees without the overthrow of the dictatorship, the RCP believes that at all costs this "democratic" force must be prevented from demobilizing the people to make them accept the survival of the armed instruments of the military dictatorship. In this situation, the struggle against the phony "communists", who will occupy themselves totally, at least insofar as their leadership is concerned, with restraining the mass movement in exchange for these "democratic" crumbs, will take on particular importance.

Unlike other fronts proposed by various political organizations, the People's Front has not remained on the level of a mere theoretical formulation. The clandestine organizations are multiplying, despite the savagery of the repression, as are their activities among the masses. Over and above their propaganda work, the resistance committees have already led numerous demonstrations and mass struggles, and have also participated in actions organized by other forces and in spontaneous actions. Many rank and file members of the UP parties (including the "C"P), of MIR and the CDP work with those of the RCP in these clandestine resistance committees. At times these committees are organized without the presence of party members, through the sole influence of the propaganda and the circulation of instructions on the way to organize them. The development of these committees, their struggles, and their anti-fascist propaganda are a living testimony to the popular masses' growing interest in organizing themselves to fight effectively to eliminate the dictatorial government.

Chapter XIII
Two Lines in the Struggle Against
the Military Junta

At the present time, as in the past, one of the main obstacles to uniting the people against fascism and against the interests which it protects is interference in Chile of the policy dictated by the Soviet leaders and carried out slavishly by the leaders of the "C"P. As if nothing had happened, they stubbornly continue to search for a formula of conciliation between the two superpowers, so as to establish the joint exploitation of Chile demanded by Soviet social-imperialism. They continue to operate within the framework of dividing the world into spheres of influence between the two superpowers. This framework forbids the Soviets and their followers to openly defy U.S. imperialism in Latin America, and requires that, to promote their model of state capitalism, they make a "historic compromise" with the political representatives of U.S. imperialism in Chile. This is why they reacted so enthusiastically when U.S. super-spy Eduardo Frei presented himself as an alternative to the junta. The fact that the SP, MAPU, the CL, not to mention MIR, the RCP, etc., are all opposed to this empty alternative which essentially changes nothing; the fact that Frei himself and his group, obeying definite instructions from U.S. imperialism, reject this compromise with Soviet social-imperialism and its agents; none of this disturbs the leaders of the "C"P. They have instructions about this, and they are monolithic, at least on the leadership level, in their obedience to the Soviet bureaucratic bourgeoisie. They do not care that they have created deep division within the ex-UP and the parties which are part of it. They do not care if they sabotage the resistance movement aimed at overthrowing the junta. Once again, they intend to use the phony support of the USSR and other revisionist countries for the Chilean people, and the substantial sums of money which they give to activists who are of use to their policy, to try (once again) to involve the leadership of the SP and, through it, the rest of the UP, in their plans to support the man with whom imperialism wants to replace the junta.

In the context of the evolution of the parties which oppose the junta, which we have analyzed, two opposing lines have appeared on how to confront the military dictatorship. On one side, there is the line of all the honest forces inside and outside the UP, who are in favour of forming a broad anti-dictatorial front, united around a common platform (in which the essence, for everyone, is the destruction of the repressive machine which oppresses the Chilean people). These forces want to mobilize the broad masses (including the Christian Democrats) to *overthrow* the Military Junta through the most varied forms of struggle, including mass armed struggle. This line presupposes a clandestine united-front organization of the advanced sections of the masses in resistance committees (or other forms), and the use of all open organizational forms which are possible under the dictatorship. It presupposes that the main thrust of action will be *inside* the country, and that international support is an indispensable, but secondary, complement.

On the other side is the line advocated by the leadership of the "C"P (and through them by the Soviets), which consists of making every concession which may be required so that a group acceptable to the military and to imperialism can get into government and act out the farce of calling for the restoration of bourgeois democratic guarantees — with the Armed Forces standing right behind them, of course. The supporters of this "solution", faced with an ever more isolated military government, have come out publicly to oppose the formation of clandestine united-front resistance committees which can orient the mass struggle toward the overthrow of the junta. They continue to foster hopes about the Armed Forces, presenting them as repenting what they did, and persistently saying that they were led astray from their "purely professional" role by a small group of traitors. Moreover, they put the centre of activity "against" the junta on the international level, and spread the illusion that the U.S. government would help get rid of the military dictatorship, if it were offered certain guarantees.

Essentially, they have aspirations that U.S. imperialism and its agents sooner or later will again bestow on them a small "place in the sun" in Chile.

1. The Capitulationist Line of the "C"P

The underlying reasons for this political position of the "C"P leadership are found not only in their obedience to social-imperialism's strategy for Latin America, but also in the features of the plan for state capitalism which they want to implement in our country. Essentially, although they want the junta overthrown, in the hope of gradually recommencing their legal activity in Chile, their foremost activity is to prevent the overthrow of the junta by the armed people. Sabotage of the people's struggle is more important for the "C"P leadership than having a pro-U.S. bourgeois government interested in re-establishing certain democratic guarantees. This latter is simply the logical way to stop the former, in the same way that sabotaging the struggle to overthrow the junta is one of the conditions for a relatively stable change. The reasons for this policy are obvious. They are basically the same reasons, which, during the Allende government, led the "C"P leaders to sabotage every popular struggle aimed at crushing the putschists and their instrument: the reactionary armed forces. The overthrow of the Military Junta and destruction of the armed instrument of the arch-reactionary interests by the people, especially nowadays, with the experience the people have with reformism and fascism, would make it almost impossible for the leaders of the "C"P to establish the state capitalism which is their strategic goal. It would make more difficult the system of joint intereference in Chile by the two superpowers which the Chilean phony communists are commissioned to develop by means of the CDP-"C"P pact.

At the present time, the rejection by Pinochet and his group of the Frei solution has caused the "C"P leaders to lower their sights. In respect to the solution proposed by Frei, they at least demanded not to be left out, and to be included among the forces which were to replace the junta. Today they are not even asking for that. They hope for it, but they are ready to unite with the CDP (no matter what section leads it) on the sole basis of putting an end to the rule of the junta. In a "C"P leadership document (September 1976), they put forward three proposals, essentially to the CDP, making it clear that the first of the three has absolute priority and is not conditional on agreement on the other two. They state: "Since we are against the dictatorship, let us act together with the sole aim of putting an end to it; and once this aim is realized, let the country decide its future and elect its rulers by democratic procedure, with no prior arrangements between us." And they add: "If there were agreement only for this one aim, it should be concretized." The anti-junta position of the group which leads the CDP and contributed actively to the coup d'état is well known. Its only aspiration is to preserve the image of bourgeois dictatorship and the prestige of imperialism, to serve as "democratic" window-dressing for the Armed Forces. It has never considered joining a movement to overthrow the junta and deprive the ultra-reactionary sections of their armed instrument. This instrument is necessary to enable them to re-establish the military dictatorship at a moment's notice. In its document, the "C"P takes certain literary precautions so as not to frighten its allies in the UP; however, it makes it clear that the "C"P is also for replacing the junta and not for its overthrow. It states that "the dictatorship remains standing and commits as many misdeeds as it can, more because of the fragmentation of the democratic forces (listen carefully) than because of the force of arms." In the same document the "C"P leaders had already stated that: "Inside the Army, the Navy, the Air Force and the Carabineros, the discontent is plain to see, as is the desire to put an end to the repression as soon as possible, to close the concentration camps, and to free the political prisoners" because "this repressive attitude has nothing to do with the real function of armed institutions." *(205)*

What a remarkable Marxist thesis! What does it consist of, then, this priority commitment offered by the "C"P leaders to Frei (and through him indirectly to the military) with the object of putting an end to this repressive policy which has "no part in the function of armed institutions" and which the latter would like to see terminated "as soon as possible"? Naturally, since there are no conditions attached to their offer, it does not involve an agreement opposed to the interests which gave rise to the coup d'état. It does not involve an agreement to struggle to overthrow the fascist regime. It does not involve an agreement with a political group which would be willing to govern with the "C"P, and anyway the "C"P leaders are very far from demanding such a thing. So what concretely are the "C"P leaders offering, as their contribution to this alliance, to Frei and the military who, while they will not be overthrown, must agree to pass on their mandate? Without a doubt, what they are implicitly offering (implicitly in this document at least) is to use all their energies and those of any allies whom they can manage to involve in this disgraceful scheme, *to restrain every mass struggle which could warrant military repression, in exchange for a return to legal political activity for the "C"P.* That is to say, the "C"P no longer even attempts, as in the past, to ally with the CDP by using its mass influence (including that which comes from certain struggles), in order to govern with it. What it is offering now is its ability to demobilize the masses, with the sole condition that it is allowed to do this legally. Then, having gained the opportunity to show its servility and its good behaviour, it hopes for the other opportunities put forward in the document — that is, to come to an understanding about the political system to establish in Chile, and even, if possible, to govern with the CDP, which is led by the group most subservient to imperialism. These last two objectives, however, are only aspirations put forward as what could be done after the first objective is realized.

The "C"P leaders are making this new step towards even greater capitulation right at the time when the Military Junta finds itself extremely isolated on the national and international levels, and when the country is in the midst of a catastrophic economic crisis. That is, when its social base of support is decreasing at an accelerated rate and is approaching zero; in conditions when the sections from whom the junta can hope for obedience because its power and influence are greatly reduced and when it can impose its will only through terror and repression; in short, when excellent conditions exist to transform the generalized discontent into resolute opposition, and this opposition into struggle to overthrow the fascist junta. In such conditions (worsened for the junta by the victory of a Democrat in the USA), the "C"P leaders reckon that the fascist military has a pressing need to find a way out which will enable them to escape destruction and to regain through deceit and demagogy a larger social base of support. And through the intermediary of a so-called "opponent" like Frei, they are eager to offer them such a way out. One again, they are tempting the military with the "Frei solution". They guarantee that in exchange for this they will do everything to restrain the hatred of the popular masses for fascism and its evil practices. Their only condition is that someone (Frei or someone else) take power with whom they would be less ashamed to make deals than with the junta itself. But it is the junta, which imperialism and the ultra-reactionary sections installed, with whom they are negotiating, since Frei and the other CDP leaders have never considered or wanted the overthrow of the military or the elimination of their armed presence.

Being familiar with the revisionists' past activity, it is easy to imagine what they will do once they get such a "democratic" government to replace the military. Every day they will present the people with the spectre of the return to fascism as a pretext to restrain all struggles. They will make use of the country's widespread economic crisis as an argument to call on the workers to make sacrifices for the reconstruction of the country and to put all their demands off until later. They will accept the bloody repression of every struggle owing to "ultra-leftism", the real culprit (according to them) responsible for the institution of fascism. In short, they will do everything to show the military that they do not demand that Frei (or whomever they would choose as a replacement) govern jointly with them, and that in spite of this, they cooperate to restrain every outburst of the masses.

In fact, the policy of sabotaging the resitance and paralyzing the parties that made up the UP — a policy that the revisionist leaders apply by taking advantage of the influence they retain and by speculating with a misunderstood slogan of "unity" is designed to allow the junta to "painlessly give birth" to a new government, one which will save it and offer it guarantees. Holding back the struggle for the overthrow of the junta, opposing the formation of resistance committees, concealing the advances made by the people's protests, and highlighting only the tortures and repression, so as to terrorize the masses, the revisionist leaders are trying to demonstrate that there is no popular will to overthrow the junta and that, as a result, a negotiated "solution" must be accepted.

In order to make use of as many forces as possible in their capitulationist policy, they corrupt leaders, offer asylum in revisionist-controlled countries, finance costly trips for activists, offer work in capitalists countries where they have influence through other pro-Soviet parties, and in general use every propagandistic and economic means that social-imperialism and its accomplices afford them. The more that they are isolated and rejected by the rank and file of the UP parties and by their own rank and file, the more that they try to stage farcical "united" meetings of the ex-UP and to sign joint top-level statements with leaders who do not understand (or have no interest in understanding) that by going along with the "C"P chieftains they are sabotaging any real united front movement to smash the dictatorship. Thus, while the resistance has advanced in spite of such leaders thanks to the activity of the rank and file, we have had the Budapest Statement, the Berlin Statement, the Mexico Statement, and so on. The most recent was the Belgrade Statement of September 1976. These statements cannot help reflecting the ideas of the rank and file and the masses opposed to the capitulationism of the "C"P leaders. By failing to expose the latter, they serve as a smokescreen for their sabotage of the struggles and allow them to speculate on behalf of the UP, looking for a deal with reactionary, two-bit politicians such as Frei. Moreover, because they are statements of "unity" with those who refuse to mobilize the people to overthrow the junta, they do not provide a clear orientation for the people's anti-fascist struggle but rather are necessarily ambiguous and full of opportunist contraband. The most recent statement, for example, while pointing out that "there is no way out of the Chilean crisis on the basis of support for imperialism", criticizes the "Frei solution" as an "anti-unity formula proposing 'restricted democracy' " and goes on to maintain that "the attempt to exclude any left-wing party means keeping alive the roots that sustain the junta", as though the replacement of the junta by Frei would not keep alive these roots. Further on, the statement gives the view (a step back relative to the analysis made by the leaders of the SP and other parties) that the UP government was overthrown "because the allied forces did not have a common strategy". This ignores what was said earlier in the same statement; namely, that total "unity" around the line of the phony communists would only have hastened the defeat of the government or its total surrender to the Frei wing of the CDP.

The statement makes some concessions to those who are fighting to overthrow the junta, by admitting that "to crush all fascism, all necessary forms of struggle (must be used), none can be ruled out *a priori"*, and by accepting the rank-and-file resistance committees, which already exist despite their rejection by the revisionists. At the same time, it leaves the way open for negotiations with the CDP led by Frei. So as not to prolong "Chile's martyrdom", the authors of the statement propose "to the Christian Democrats and all conscious anti-fascists, joint action in the struggle against the dictatorship in a wide variety of fields". With the intention of further obscuring the question of whether they are proposing joint action with the Christian Democratic rank and file or with the Frei-dominated CDP, they add: "Although there are different ways of thinking within the CDP and although a group of leaders supported the coup d'état, the decisive factor is that the vast majority are opposed to the junta." They "forget" here that Frei and his group are not merely some "group of leaders" who "supported" the junta, but *the* group which leads the CDP and which aspires only to replace the junta, not to overthrow it. The statement ends suspiciously, advocating "immediate unity in action" for the sole purpose of putting an end to the junta; and like the "C"P leadership, it qualifies unity on essential matters — that is, the struggle against the classes that imposed the dictatorship — with "we can" and "we must". In sum, with a few touch-ups and minor concessions designed to prevent the complete break-up of the UP forces, the most recent statement seems to be nothing other than an effort to drag this coalition and MIR (with which discussions are under way) along behind the line of the "C"P leadership.

2. The Fascist Junta Can and Must be Overthrown by the People

The Chilean people, particularly the working class, have long traditions of organization and struggle. It is no accident that the Armed Forces has had to resort to many brutal massacres to check their struggles and to systematic repression of the revolutionary trends. Through their struggles, the Chilean people have won important gains and democratic rights, which now have been completely wiped out by the fascist dictatorship and super-exploitation. The main protagonists of these struggles, the masses of the people, are in Chile and will never resign themselves to oppression by the dictatorship, nor to the cruel setback that the junta has brought about in their living conditions, to the prevailing hunger and poverty. They have had to retreat in face of the brutality of the repression because owing to the defeatist and paralyzing influence of powerful opportunist trends, they lack the means necessary to confront it. The mass struggle during the UP administration reached a high level in numbers and in fighting spirit, but because of this opportunist influence, it did not combine with revolutionary ideology and leadership so as to become capable of smashing the reactionary forces.

To evaluate the potential of the Chilean people's struggle and the future it would offer, if it were oriented by revolutionary ideology, as the main weapon for the overthrow of the Military Junta, we must recall some of its features under the Allende government and even before, under the Christian Democratic government.

The impetuous advance of the popular struggles was influenced as much by the populist demagogy of the Christian Democratic government as by the demagogy of the UP and its government, which was more intensive for its socialist disguise. In the UP period, there was on the one hand the influence of the improvement in the living conditions of the masses during the first year of the Allende administration; and, in contrast, the acute economic crisis that, beginning in 1972, began to fall onto the backs of the people, with even greater effect on their fighting spirit than the earlier improvement. To these material factors, one positive and one negative, was added the important stimulus to the morale of the exploited strata provided by the Allende government's expropriations, which dealt serious blows to the main exploiters. While making many people believe that the government was actually ready to establish socialism, these blows to the exploiters encouraged the fighting spirit of broad sections of the population. Even in the countryside, or rather, especially in the countryside, where for many centuries the despotic and arbitrary spirit of the big landlords had held sway, the peasants were aroused to defy them. Not only did they win substantial material gains from them, including the land itself, but they defied their semi-feudal privileges and prerogatives, refusing to greet them, often shutting them up in their estate offices, invading their private houses or gardens, insulting them, imposing prohibitions on them, and in general making them pay for years of humiliation. Another factor in the growth of the fighting spirit of the people was that the Allende government refused to use the more brutal forms of anti-popular repression practiced by previous governments. This was one of the things that the reactionary opposition and U.S. imperialism never forgave the government, and it was decisive in prompting them to overthrow it as soon as they could.

As we pointed out, the growth in the fighting spirit of the masses was especially strong in the countryside. The contradictions there were sharper and of longer standing, and the opportunist trade union bureaucracy of the "C"P had less influence. For purposes of comparison, let us note that in 1969, when the Frei government began its demagogic agrarian reform policy, 118 occupations of land took place. In 1970, the last year of the Frei administration, the number of occupations climbed to 365. But in only the first eight months of the Allende government, there were 990 occupations, an average of more than four a day. This upsurge of peasant struggles continued throughout the Allende administration.

However, the mass struggles under the UP government were not limited to the countryside. "Occupations" also became popular in the cities as a method of action. Hundreds and hundreds of factories and other businesses were occupied by the workers, either to request their expropriation or to force the employers to accept the workers' demands. The occupations frequently received logistical support (coordinated by the "Industrial Cordons" and "Communal Commandos") from workers in neighbouring enterprises. The same thing happened in the countryside: each occupation could rely on the solidarity and practical support of the workers from neighbouring estates, both when it was carried out and in its subsequent defense. Factory occupations, which had numbered only 23 in 1969, increased to 133 in 1970 and to 513 in the first eight months of the Allende government. During the employers' strikes of 1972 and 1973, the workers occupied almost all the factories. In the countryside (and to a lesser extent in the factories of the city), in conjunction with the occupations, defense teams with elementary weapons were organized and, in the rural zones, succeeded in repulsing the attempts by the latifundists' armed groups to recover their lands. Tools were used as improvised weapons, along with hunting rifles and, in the native people's districts, even primitive spears. In the region where the native peasantry is the main group, when the armed police began to retake the occupied lands, *Netuain Mapu* (led by the RCP) used the tactic of handing over the land when surrounded by a superior force only to take it back again when the police left. In some places there were as many as four or five successive expulsions and re-occupations. These struggles ended in victory for the peasants, because the government obviously did not have sufficient armed forces to permanently guard the land of each latifundist.

Alongside the occupations of factories and landed estates, there were occupations of vacant lots in the cities by homeless people wanting to build temporary dwellings. Although they previously took place on a smaller scale, there is a long history of such actions in Chile, as in other Latin American countries. The population in these countries was rapidly and steadily concentrated in the cities, particularly the capital cities. This concentration was the result not of the rapid development of industry, as was the case in the big capitalist countries, but basically of acute crisis in a pre-capitalist system of agriculture, which forced the population of the countryside to emigrate. Thus, shantytown "belts" were formed on the outskirts of the cities, called *Villas Miseria* in Argentina, *Favelas* in Brazil, *Callampas* in Chile. They consisted of closely-crowded "houses" built by their inhabitants out of boxes and old bits of wood. After the war, the intensification of imperialist·exploitation and the deepening of the crisis forced urban workers, and even white-collar employees no longer able to feed themselves and at the same time pay the lowest of rents, to join these emergency settlements or to occupy new lots. They live there with the lumpen proletariat and the peasants who arrive in search of work. One of the first major struggles of the homeless people took place in January 1969: a group of 300 families (almost 2,000) people occupied vacant lots and with their own hands built the encampment that was named after the day they occupied it: "January 26th". These occupations continued throughout the Frei administration. One of the bloody massacres perpetrated by the Frei government was against people who had occupied lands in the region of Puerto Montt.

Under the Allende government, dozens and dozens of *callampas* were set up and joined with the neighbouring Industrial Cordons to become important centres of struggle, the Communal Commandos. The Commandos even resisted the coup d'état, which was the reason the military bombed and annihilated many shantytowns. A movement for the "takeover" of recently constructed houses also came up during the UP administration. But most of these occupations were incited by the CDP to make problems for the government, as the dwellings in question had usually been built for workers, white-collar employees or the middle strata. The President of the Housing Council, an opposition-controlled organization, stated on December 1, 1970, that 5,700 mass dwellings (1,700 of which belonged to the private sector) had been occupied during the months immediately preceding the election of Allende and up to November 24 of that year.

Occupation as a method of struggle also extended into the student milieu, where it was also used by the opposition, resulting in sharp clashes during successive "takeovers" and expulsions. It was almost inconceivable under the UP government to put forward demands without "taking over" the establishment in question and barricading the roads and lanes giving access to it. A left-wing Catholic movement called the *Iglesia Joven* (Young Church) even went so far as to occupy

Santiago Cathederal.

The Office of the Director-General of the Carabineros, in a report submitted to Senate as a petition on July 1, 1971, stated that in the five and one half months from January 1 to June 15 of that year, 658 agricultural estates, 339 factories, 514 educational institutions and 218 city lots (already settled) and public buildings had been occupied.

This extraordinary militancy of the masses, which developed as a result of the UP victory and whose character and orientation was of course very different from that of the employers' and "professional" movements organized by the opposition, had a decisive influence (not always recognized in the post-mortem analyses) on the fate of the UP. Even more than the government's reforms, it was the fear of this mass mobilization that hastened the union of the opposition forces to overthrow the government. The potential danger it represented was one of the main reasons why the CIA and the State Department stepped up their plans for a coup d'état in Chile. The phony communists' increasing loss of control over this movement and their inability to keep it in check determined the ever more openly opportunist and conciliatory policy they and their supporters inside the UP followed.

In fact, the popular militancy that developed (mostly in spite of its leaders) during the reformist UP experiment created an actual possibility for the people to seize political power, smashing the armed and unarmed forces that stood in their way. This would have been possible if a genuine proletarian leadership, welding Marxism-Leninism to the fighting energy of the masses, had been at the head of these struggles. This orientation would have led the mass movement to break with the dominant opportunist trend in the UP, to march right over its constant opposition to the mass struggle, to clearly identify the main enemies and the false friends, and to understand what weapons to use in crushing them. The reason the UP government can be said to have represented a fairly good opportunity for the people to seize power and hold onto it was not so much that reformism had fragile control of the executive branch as that the people took advantage of this situation to advance their struggles. The possibility of the people seizing power, which frightened not only imperialism and the arch-reactionary forces but also those who aspired to establish state capitalism, failed because of the strong mass influence of revisionist opportunism, because of the errors of the petty-bourgeois trends that opposed the revisionists inside and outside the UP, and because of the inability of the genuine Marxist-Leninists to overcome these obstacles and put themselves at the head of the mass struggle.

One of the permanent objectives of the policy of the phony communist leaders, one which they succeeded in having even President Allende and other political forces adopt, was to tenaciously oppose the people's initiatives and struggles. Their policy of conciliation went to such an extreme that even the reactionary opposition had some success in demagogically "leading" some struggles. The only reason the "C"P leaders did not brutally repress the mass struggles, as do their ideological mentors in Poland, the USSR, Czechoslovakia, etc., is that they were under fire from an extremely aggressive opposition and were afraid the latter would capitalize on these struggles to a greater extent. But, as we have seen, they did use the traditional forms of repression, and, if they had consolidated their position, they would have used them with a savagery equal to, if not greater than, that of the old exploiters.

However, because they could not use open repression in the way they would have wished, they redoubled their propaganda efforts to oppose the mass struggles and any manifestation of initiative or fighting spirit by the masses. Even President Allende tried to convince the latifundists of the National Agricultural Society that by carrying out a legal process of agrarian reform, the government was saving them from what would happen if the fighting spirit of the peasants were unleashed. In an interview in mid-December of 1970, Allende told the latifundists that "he wanted the farmers to become fully aware that his government was like a *riverbed,* meant to serve not only as a dike but as a channel for just social revolts which, if it were not there, would break out in violence, as has occurred in other countries." "And", he concluded, "although no one believes that we are a factor for the defence of the social order and indeed we are not, nor will we ever be, we want it to be understood that our presence allows things to be run in accordance with our tradition, our history, and our temperament." *(206)* As we have seen, the reactionary elements had very different ideas on the ability of the government to hold back the people's struggle, as well as on this tradition, history and temperament, for they themselves did not hesitate to destroy them in order to protect their interests and arrest the people's struggles.

The "C"P leaders were of course in the van of all the initiatives and actions to restrain the struggles, both in the city and in the countryside. On February 14, 1971, *El Siglo* published the following statements by Luis Corvalan: "No, we do not justify these takeovers (referring to the occupation of landed estates). We can explain the problem, we understand that the reason why peasants in some regions and the *Mapuches* in the South are participating in these actions is that there is a drama going on there, a social situation that cannot be ignored. But the CP is not in favour of the occupation of lands under conditions of a people's government." Corvalan adds: "None of the UP parties is promoting these takeovers, and, so far as I know, not even MIR is officially promoting them. It is possible that some elements in MIR who have escaped the control of its leadership, and perhaps some elements from other left-wing organizations, are participating in these actions. Whoever is promoting them, they seem to us a mistake. It seems to us that this situation should be ended as soon as possible."

A little later, on February 25, *El Siglo* published extracts from Corvalan's speech to the Senate on the occupation of lands. He took the trouble to explain to the members of parliament representing the affected latifundists that: "In Cautin, the UP government has intervened to stop the process of takeovers that broke out there a few weeks ago. Everyone knows that a few left-wing and extreme left-wing elements participated in this. But I would like to add that according to my information, even MIR has officially come to the conclusion that this road must not be followed. It follows that it must have been, or might have been, elements escaping MIR's control." To calm the landlords represented there, Corvilan added: "We have therfore committed ourselves to continue working in this direction (i.e. sabotaging peasant struggles). In particular, we communists are in favour of speaking frankly to the peasants, of explaining our position to them and of pointing out to them that, from the viewpoint of successful agrarian reform, it is a mistake to follow this path." At the same session of the Senate, a Socialist senator, Maria Elena Carrera, read a statement from a peasant federation in Colchagua province supporting the occupation of lands. The statement denounced various arbitrary acts by the landlords against the peasants, as well as "the many landlords who are sabotaging production. They are not preparing to sow this year, and this will lead to increased unemployment and greater spending of dollars to import food. We also denounce the holding of nocturnal meetings in the province. Strange airplanes bring parcels to the estates, many of which have landing strips. Thus it is to defend production and the government that we have taken over the estates." The statement ended by demanding that agrarian reform be accelerated "in order to solve our problems and guarantee production for next year", and also that "the Internal State Security Act be applied against subversive employers who boycott production". What was Corvalan's reaction to this magnificent lesson in vigilance and class spirit that the peasants were giving him? Just what one had to expect: he used the statement to continue to calm the landlords' representatives and give them servile explanations. He said: "The facts which the Honourable Senator Madame Carrera has made known to us confirm what I have already stated: these occupations are not so numerous. Consequently, the veritable sabotage of certain landowning groups cannot be justified." Corvalan added: "As for the statement that the UP is not preventing these occupations, I must point out that it has done so to such an extent that in Colchagua province, for example, as the Honourable Madame Carrera has reported, conditions existed such that 300 estates in the area might have been occupied in three or four days, instead of only 20 or 28. This is what the workers wanted. The UP parties, especially the SP, which is the most influential in this region, prevented things from going further. Such are the real facts." And the person who talks this way is supposed to be a "Marxist" and a "Communist"!

Like the sorcerer's apprentice, the official UP government circles, inspired by the "Marxism" of Corvalan and his ilk, did not know what to do with the forces they had helped unleash.

They feared the mobilization of the masses; on the other hand, they believed that their strict submission to the bourgeois laws and institutions and the "constitutionalist" and "professional" spirit of the Armed Forces were the key factors that would allow them to expropriate imperialism, the big bourgeoisie and the landlords. While the opposition press clamoured hysterically about "guerillas" and "armed bands" in the countryside, the government tried to play down the importance of the peasant struggles and at the same time to put a brake on them. On January 22, 1971, the National Agricultural Society expressed its astonishment that 250 estates had been occupied since the beginning of the Allende administration. The Minister of the Interior, José Toha (whom the hangmen of the Military Junta later "suicided"), declared: "Under no circumstances, in no region of the country, will the government tolerate the existence of armed bands attempting to organize outside public order and safety." He asked the opposition members of parliament who claimed such groups existed to provide concrete information on them to the government, for "we will not be slow to act". Daniel Vergara, undersecretary in the Interior Ministry and an eminent member of the "C"P, became the favourite target for the attacks and ridicule of the opposition because of his ostrich-like policy in regard to the peasant struggles, the importance and even existence of which he systematically denied. This attitude was maintained not only during the government's first year in office, when the legal and institutional measures of the Executive appeared to be succeeding and when the subversive plans of the opposition were not so evident, but right up to the very moment of the coup d'état. In the months preceding the coup d'état, as we have already mentioned, the appeasement turned into more active preaching and took the form of open calls for capitulation to the putschists. To the "Marxist" ideologues of the UP, the people no longer counted for anything; they were a hindrance to their attempts to "save" the government by conciliating with the main enemies. They counted for nothing even when the putschist offensive in the Armed Forces became evident and the opposition allowed itself the luxury of taking to the streets to organize mass demonstrations.

The militancy of the Chilean popular masses and particularly of the working class, which opened up a real opportunity to conquer political power for the people during the Allende administration, has now become the main instrument for the overthrow of fascism. Since the coup d'état, despite the terror, the paralysis caused by opportunism, the assassination or imprisonment of many mass leaders, the mass movement has begun in a thousand ways to find its way forward. It has not allowed the junta to adopt demagogic positions; it has not allowed it to create organizations linked to fascism among the workers; it has not allowed it to improve its image by giving in to repression; it has not allowed it after more than three years to lift the night curfew. The savagery of the dictatorship has not prevented strikes, sabotage, public protests, clandestine propaganda, the punishment of informers, mass refusal to pay for public services, and other expressions of anti-fascist struggle.

3. A United Leadership of the Struggles Must be Wrought

To develop the struggles of the people and to advance them to a higher level of organized mass resistance to fascism, all the consistently anti-fascist forces must be brought into play, their activity must be coordinated and their points of view unified in order to create a broad anti-fascist front. The SP, MAPU, CL, RY, MIR and RCP, as well as many sections of the "C"P and CDP rank and file, have shown their desire to fight and to coordinate their efforts to advance the struggle to overthrow the junta. Most of these political forces have drafted basically similar minimum programmes, aimed at uniting all groups opposed to the dictatorship in the broadest possible manner. These programmes demand the institution of rights and freedoms for the people; advocate the overthrow of the dictatorship and the destruction of its apparatus of repression; demand the improvement of the living conditions of the people; and call for severe measures against the latifundists, the capitalist monopolies, and U.S. imperialism — the inspirers of the coup d'état, supporters of fascism and sole beneficiaries of its policies. In regard to strategy and tactics, most of these political forces agree that these main enemies, and particularly the dictatorship which represents them, must be made target of the struggle. Likewise, most of them have come out in favour of overthrowing the dictatorship through a variety of forms of mass struggle, both legal and illegal, including the most decisive form: people's armed struggle. Almost all these political forces, even though they have not all made a thorough-going analysis, recognize that the coup d'état was made possible by the predominance during the Allende administration of an opportunist trend which refused to resolutely mobilize the masses and arm them; which promoted faith in the possibility of a pact with forces over which Frei had decisive influence; which widely propagated the myth about the "professional" and "constitutionalist" nature of the Army; which demanded unreserved respect for the laws and institutions of the bourgeois state. The evolution of most of the anti-fascist parties is leading them to deepen their critical analysis and to understand ever more clearly the mistakes they made and the treacherous and reactionary nature of the revisionists, whose line held sway in the UP. There exist, therefore, ample conditions to create a united anti-fascist leadership, which will be the vanguard of the aspirations of the masses to fight and smash fascism, and which will develop their will to fight and their struggles and transform them into organized and generalized struggle against the junta.

However, four years have passed since the establishment of the dictatorship, and despite the desire of the rank and file of the anti-fascist parties to coordinate their actions for the struggle, their leaders — still under the influence of revisionism, blinded by the myth of a false unity with those who refuse to fight — are still trying to revive the UP through press releases and to ensure the survival of fascism behind the facade of Frei or others of his ilk, who would replace it with pseudo-democracy. Instead of taking the leadership of the struggles, as the rank and file and the broad masses demand, the leaders of these parties concoct formula after formula, attempting to "pull the chestnuts out of the fire" instead of advancing the mass struggle for the overthrow of fascism. They remain under the influence of (or let themselves be corrupted by) those who have capitulated, hoisted the white flag and surrendered to fascism without a fight, those who would prefer any solution whatever to the militant mobilization of the masses to liberate themselves from the fascist yoke. They have drawn no lessons from the reactionary (and not simply "reformist" and "mistaken") motives which induced the phony communist leaders to oppose the resistance of the masses to fascism during the Allende administration and to promote the capitulation of the government. They squander the generous international aid, given by genuine anti-fascist groups to organize resistance and struggle in Chile, on trips and secret meetings designed to promote the "historic compromise" with the agents of imperialism — the solution desired by the Soviets and their supporters in order to prevent a popular uprising against the dictatorship. In this way, they are more and more showing themselves to be accomplices of those who aspired to impose their own system of exploitation disguised as socialism on the Chilean people, rather than victims of revisionist deceit.

It is certain that the broadest possible unity of political forces and especially of the masses is necessary to overthrow fascism, and that the masses influenced by the CDP and "C"P must be counted in. But these masses and these political forces can only be useful if they are united to fight for the overthrow of the junta. How does it serve the people to create a broad "united" front around a plan such as the "C"P leadership promotes, offering militaristic fascism the opportunity to hide behind a pseudo-democracy so that it can return to massacre and repress the people whenever it thinks fit? Why do forces that have come out for the overthrow of the junta block any possibility of giving a big boost to the struggle, of creating a political command ready to fight? Why do they resign themselves to preserving "unity" with the capitulationists, to waiting for another secret meeting that will constitute another betrayal of the people?

The task at hand is to forge this political agreement among the forces which are genuinely for the overthrow of the dictatorship and to take the leadership of the people's struggles as soon as possible. This is the unity we need, not unity to capitulate. This resolute struggle will undoubtedly draw the sincere elements from the rank and file of the CDP and the "C"P itself into the anti-fascist struggle and isolate the leaders, who are playing the game of the superpowers. It will speed up the disintegration of the reactionary armed forces. The political agreement for the overthrow of the dictatorship requires that activity be centred inside the country; that the various organizations support one another to defend against repression; that solidarity be channelled in support of the resistance in Chile; that propaganda be focussed mainly on the progress and development of the struggle, and not almost exclusively on repression and tortures, as is done by those who seek to justify capitulation to and collaboration with the junta by terrorizing the people. It requires that joint discussions be held on the most effective tactics of struggle; on mutual stimulation of revolutionary morale, in order to put an end to informing and to fear; on ways in which militants who were forced to go into exile abroad can return when opportunities arise. There has been enough preaching to convince those who refuse to struggle against fascism that they are "mistaken" and that they should deign to agree to unite to overthrow fascism. How long are we going to let them sabotage our fighting unity? It is questions such as those we have listed that the anti-fascist forces should discuss, and not methods for getting accepted by Frei or another of his ilk who would give guarantees to the junta.

There is no doubt that a fighting anti-fascist unity will create the basis of agreement to lead the people toward the annihilation of their main enemies and the establishment of socialism in Chile. Through this discussion and this action, genuinely proletarian ideas on the future of the country must be put in command. In this discussion and through our practice of joint struggle against fascism and against the interests it represents, the nature of the people's democratic regime which must be established in advancing toward genuine socialism will be clarified. Thus will be laid the foundations of a regime which must achieve thoroughgoing democracy for the people and firm dictatorship of the proletariat, in alliance with other popular forces, over the main enemies and exploiters of the Chilean people. Dictatorship also over those who disguise themselves as revolutionaries and falsely invoke Marxism in order to clear the way for state capitalism and penetration by the social-imperialist superpower. We must guarantee that, through the political forces which represent them honestly and faithfully, it is the Chilean people themselves who exercise dictatorship over their class enemies while ensuring the fullest democracy for themselves. We must prevent the rise of a new bureaucratic bourgeoisie on the backs of the people, a bourgeoisie which in the name of a phony popular or proletarian dictatorship would exercise its own dictatorship over the people and the proletariat for the sake of its own interests as the new ruling group. We must define and advance toward the eventual establishment of a genuinely socialist system, completely different from the caricature of socialism that exists in the USSR and the countries dominated by it. It must be a system in which not only are the means of production in the hands of the state, but the state is in the hands of the proletariat. This definition and this struggle for a genuinely democratic and popular regime, followed by a socialist one, will undoubtedly arouse the resolute support of the broad masses of the people of our country. This will take away any basis of support from those who, like Frei, do anti-communist work by presenting dictatorial and exploiting regimes as communist, and will also allow us to win over the masses who were misled by the phony communist leaders.

In this struggle against fascism, for people's democracy and socialism, we must consolidate the genuine vanguard of the proletariat, the genuine communist party, which is indispensable for the success of the struggles. It must not only be an ideological vanguard, but, by tearing the broad masses of the people away from the opportunist influence, from phony Marxism, and by taking the leadership of their struggles, it must become the actual vanguard of the proletariat and people. It must be a party of a new type, firm in its ideology, clever and flexible in its tactics, and endowed with deep revolutionary conviction, a conviction which will serve it not only in resisting the blows of the enemy and the hard conditions of the struggle, but also in providing the people with an *advance* model of genuine socialism. It is not enough for it to cultivate in its own ranks the revolutionary virtues of courage, the spirit of sacrifice, initiative, discipline, flexibility of tactics and firmness of principles, etc. The heart of its revolutionary conviction must be the concept of "Serving the People Wholeheartedly". It is not enough for it to know *how* to seize power, it must understand *for whom* it is seizing power. Inadequate understanding of the fact that the party seizes power in order to serve the people, as their vanguard and the expression of their interests, was an important factor in the development of the phony socialist regimes which have caused so much damage to the concept of socialism in the minds of the broad masses throughout the world. Even before the seizure of power, the principle of "serving the party" and its sectarian objectives, instead of "serving the people" above all else, represented essentially by the proletariat, has cut off many well-intentioned parties from the masses and from their revolutionary orientation.

To transform society in a thoroughgoing and revolutionary manner, purely economic changes are not enough; those who are participating in this process, and especially those leading it, must transform themselves, liberate themselves from the influence of bourgeois ideology and morality. This dialectical truth is decisive for the success and the future of the revolution. At present, the questions of firmness on principles and of revolutionary morality have acquired even more importance. The regression to state capitalism (and in the case of the USSR, to social-imperialism) of certain countries in which the proletariat had seized power is directly related to the abandonment of revolutionary principles and morals. The economic changes arising from the expropriation of the bourgeoisie do not of themselves lead mechanically to the transformation of the consciousness and morals of the members of society. The party of the proletariat has the duty to carry on class struggle on the ideological, cultural and moral fronts. Marxist ideology and its use in solving the daily problems of the broad masses must be reaffirmed and propagated. Egoism, individualism (personal as well as national "individualism" or chauvinism), the mercenary profit-seeking mentality, bureaucracy, servility, careerism and many other vices inherited from the bourgeoisie must be combatted. We must create the new man, capable of placing the collective interests above his own egotistical interests which are opposed to the former. The fulfillment of the individual must be achieved in conformity with the collective interests. If the opposite is the case, if the struggle in the superstructure is not waged firmly, both in the society and in the leading party itself, a reactionary counter-current will appear and there will be a return to a system of exploitation and oppression of the people. Principles will be compromised for the sake of petty interests and Marxism distorted to restore exploitation.

A deep split took place in what formerly constituted the socialist camp and in the old International Communist Movement. This has given rise to different conditions in the revolutionary struggle of the peoples of the world today. We are not only dealing with the consolidation and open promotion on the world scale of a line which distorts Marxism and does great damage to the revolutionary struggle, but also with the existence of phony "socialism". The existence of this phony "socialism" does not only concern those countries and peoples which have suffered this regression. It has a considerable negative influence on the countries which are still struggling for national independence and socialism. These negative "models" of phony socialist systems can only contribute to the revolutionary struggle insofar as they are unmasked and fought by distinguishing them from genuine socialism. On the other hand, if the masses believe that the exploitation and oppression which exists in these countries *is* socialism, these "models" can only demoralize them and divert them from the struggle for genuine socialism.

By the same token, it is natural for the proletariat and people in the capitalist world to demand *today* that the Marxist-Leninist Communist parties which are leading their struggles to end the system of exploitation give a clear definition of genuine and phony socialism. It is natural for the masses to demand, before putting confidence in them, before the seizure of power, that those who aspire to lead their struggles show evidence of a new morality. They cannot be parties built on the model of bourgeois parties, on the basis of money, demagogy, careerism, an army of bureaucrats, and adaptation to bourgeois legalism. They cannot be parties whose members, rather than selflessly serving the people, are seeking personal or individual fulfillment as "heroes" detached from the masses or merely as political mercenaries and profiteers. The apolitical mentality among the masses is due largely to their contempt for the bourgeois politics and for the "left" or right-wing parties that practice it. It is legitimate for them to seek a party which right now, before the seizure of power, is made up of activists who are ready to become (not in isolation but in the heat of revolutionary struggle) faithful servants of the people's interests.

Our intention in this book was none other than to analyze and expose the role played by the falsifiers of Marxism and by falsified socialism in the tragedy that the Chilean people are experiencing. They are not for the time being the main enemy of our people; but to fight the main enemy and advance toward genuine socialism, it is essential to unmask them, to break with their reactionary orientation and to help the people get rid of their influence. It is not Marxism which was defeated in Chile; it is not genuine socialism which was smashed by fascism. It was falsifications of Marxism and socialism. We must uphold the ideology of the proletariat, scientific socialism, and the genuine socialist and communist ideals. That is why the analysis and criticism of the events in Chile must be carried out in a thoroughgoing manner. From this analysis will come the correct ideas which will lead to the national and social liberation of the Chilean people. This book is meant as a modest contribution to this discussion and to the struggle that the Chilean people are waging against fascism and for their socialist future.

In conclusion, it will suffice to quote Lenin on this question:

"... there is a socialism that is dying and a socialism that must be reborn; this death and this rebirth, however, comprise a ruthless struggle against the trend of opportunism — mot merely an ideological struggle, but the removal of that hideous excrescence from the body of the working-class parties, the expulsion from those organizations of certain representatives of this tactic, which is alien to the proletariat, a definite break with them. They will die neither physically nor politically, but the workers will break with them, will throw them into the cesspool of the servitors of the bourgeoisie. The example of their corruption will educate a new generation, or, more correctly, new proletarian armies capable of an uprising." (207)

Notes

(Translator's note: Where possible, quotations from English-language sources have been restored from the originals. Where this has not been possible, and a quotation has had to be retranslated from the Spanish, the reference is marked with an asterisk (*) below.)

1. The numbering of this congress as 10th and not 14th, which would have been the correct number, was due to a resolution by the "C"P leadership changing the date of the founding of the party.

2. Marx and Engels, "Circular Letter", *Selected Correspondence,* (Moscow: Foreign Languages Publishing House), p. 391.

3. Lenin, "They do not see the wood for the trees", *Collected Works,* Vol. 28, (Moscow: Progress Publishers, 1964), p. 252.

4. Lenin, "The Proletarian Revolution and the Renegade Kautsky", *Collected Works,* Vol. 28 (Moscow: Progress Publishers, 1965), p. 108.

5. Lenin, *The State and Revolution,* (Peking: Foreign Languages Press, 1970), p. 28.

6. *El Siglo,* October 9, 1970, p. 7.

7. ibid., November 27, 1970

8. ibid., January 11, 1971.

9. ibid., October 5, 1971, p. 2.

10. ibid., March 8, 1973.

11. ibid., May 13, 1973.

12. ibid., June 26, 1971, p. 3.

13. ibid., November 7, 1970.

14. ibid., November 21, 1970.

15. ibid., May 22, 1971, p. 4.

16. ibid., March 29, 1971, p. 4.

17. ibid., October 6, 1971, p. 7.

18. ibid., March 20, 1971, p. 5.

19. ibid., March 22, 1971, p. 6.

20. "Focism" is the form of armed struggle promoted by the Cubans in Latin America. In focism, the masses are replaced by small petty-bourgeois groups which open up "guerrilla zones" to "stimulate the people to make revolution".

21. *El Siglo,* May 31, 1971, pp. 4-5.

22. ibid., August 20, 1971, p. 3.

23. ibid., August 11, 1973.

24. ibid., September 7, 1973.

25. ibid., October 11, 1970, p. 2.

26. ibid., October 13, 1970, p. 7.

27. ibid., October 17, 1970, p. 4.

28. ibid., November 22, 1970, p. 7.

29. ibid., December 22, 1970.

30. ibid., December 2, 1970.

31. ibid., December 1, 1970.

32. ibid., December 27, 1970.

33. ibid., January 31, 1971, p. 4.

34. ibid.

35. ibid., November 17, 1971.

36. ibid.

37. ibid., April 25, 1971, p. 6.

38. "Pourriture de la société soviétique", *Pekin Information,* No. 7, February 16, 1976.

39. " 'La propriété commune' selon Moscou", *Documents du Mouvement communiste international,* (Paris: September-October 1975).

40. "Soviet Revisionists' Sinister Programme of Neo-

Colonialism", *Peking Review,* Vol. 17, No. 16, April 19, 1974.

41. *Covert Action in Chile 1963-1973:* Staff Report of the Select Committee to Study Governmental Operations with respect to Intelligence Activities, United States Senate, (Washington, D.C.: U.S. Government Printing Office, December 18, 1975).

42. J.E. Garcés, *Allende y la experiencia chilena,* (Barcelona: Editorial Ariel), p. 175.

43. *El Mercurio,* December 14, 1972.

44. *Covert Action.*

45. ibid.

46. ibid.

47. ibid.

48. Garcés, op. cit., P. 304.

49. ibid., pp. 213-216.

50. ibid., p. 245.

51. "Tancazo": name popularly given to the attempted uprising by an armoured regiment of the Chilean Armed Forces under the Allende government.

52. Garcés, op. cit., p. 304.

53. *El Siglo,* June 22, 1972.

54. *Actas de Sesiones del Senado de Chile,* May 1972.

55. Lenin, "What Next?", *Collected Works,* Vol. 21, (Moscow: Progress Publishers, 1964), p. 110.

56. JAP's (Juntas de Abastecimientos y Precios: Boards of Supply and Prices): organizations for the control of pricing and supplies, created in various districts by the Popular Unity.

57. "Industrial Cordons" (Cordones Industriales): assemblies of delegates elected by the workers of each of the factories in a given industrial district. These Cordons, plus delegates from the settlers' encampments and the student centres in the district, made up the Communal Commandos (Comandos Comunales).

58. In J.J. Sebreli, *Tercer Mundo mito burgués,* (Argentina: Editorial Siglo Veinte).

59. *Covert Action.*

60. ibid.

61. ibid.

62. ibid.

63. ibid.

64. ibid.

65. ibid.

66. ibid.

67. ibid.

68. ibid.

69. ibid.

70. ibid.

71. ibid.

72. ibid.

73. ibid.

74. ibid.

75. Les complots de la CIA, (France: Stock, 1976), p. 34.*

76. ibid., p. 34.*

77. ibid., p. 35.*

78. ibid., p. 45.*

79. ibid.*

80. *Covert Action.*

81. Garcés, op. cit., p. 260.

82. A. Joxe, *Le Chili sous Allende,* (Gallimard), p. 57.

83. Garcés, op. cit., pp. 254 and 256.

84. *Covert Action.*

85. O Millas, Minister of Finance, *Report on government economic policy and the state of the public finances,* presented to the Senate Joint Commission on the Budget, November 15, 1972.

86. *Hearings before the Subcommittee on Multinational Corporations,* U.S. Senate, (Washington, D.C. U.S.

Government Printing Office, 1973), pp. 656 and 657.

87. Garcés, op. cit., p. 258.

88. *Covert Action.*

89. ibid.

90. Garcés, op. cit.

91. Statement by Kissinger to U.S. television, May 6, 1975, *(Le Monde,* May 8, 1975).*

92. *Covert Action.*

93. For all these data on economic aid granted by the 40 Committee, see *Covert Action.*

94. Ministry of the Economy, Studies by the Undersecretariat of the Economy, 1971.

95. *El Mercurio,* January 14, 1973.

96. ibid.

97. ibid., April 3, 1973.

98. ODEPLAN, *Résumen del Plan de la Economica National 1971-1976,* p. 38.

99. *El Mercurio,* February 13, 1972.

100. ibid., December 19, 1972.

101. L. Gotuzzo, Minister of Finance, *Report on the state of the public finances,* October 1973, p. 14.

102. *El Mercurio,* July 1, 1971.

103. ibid., December 7, 1971.

104. ibid., October 10, 1972.

105. ibid., July 1, 1971.

106. ibid., November 11, 1971.

107. ibid., February 13, 1972.

108. ibid., September 12, 1972.

109. ibid., January 5, 1973.

110. Gotuzzo, op. cit.

111. *El Mercurio,* January 5, 1972.

112. ibid., January 9, 1973.

113. ibid., May 11, 1972.

114. ibid., June 20, 1972.

115. ibid., February 19, 1973.

116. ibid., November 20, 1972.

117. ibid., January 27, 1973.

118. ibid., February 3, 1972.

119. ibid., June 12, 1972.

120. ibid., December 26, 1972.

121. A. Baltra, *Gestión Economica del Gobierno de la Unidad Popular,* (Chile: Editorial Orbe), p. 61.

122. ibid., p. 60.

123. *El Mercurio,* August 25, 1972.

124. ibid., September 15, 1972.

125. ibid., November 13, 1972.

126. ibid., May 14, 1973.

127. ibid., July 16, 1973.

128. "momios" ("old mummies"): popular term for right-wing personages.

129. *El Mercurio,* July 18, 1972.

130. ibid., October 25, 1972.

131. Lenin, "Theses on the Fundamental Tasks of the Second Congress of the Communist International", *Collected Works,* Vol. 31 (Moscow: Progress Publishers, 1966), p. 186.

132. *Covert Action.*

133. J. Petras, "Estados Unidos y el nuevo equilibro en América Latina", *Revista de Estudios Internationales,* (Santiago, Chile, January -March 1969).

134. ibid.

135. R.A. Hansen, *Military Culture and Organizational Decline: Un estudio del Ejercito de Chile,* University of California at Los Angeles, 1967.*

136. Lenin, *The State and Revolution,* (Peking: Foreign

Languages Press, 1970), p. 25.

137. *El Siglo,* October 26, 1970, p. 4.

138. ibid., October 27, 1970.

139. ibid., September 19, 1970.

140. ibid., March 30, 1973.

141. Hansen, op. cit.*

142. *Hearings,* op. cit., p. 701.*

143. *Les complots de la CIA,*op. cit., p. 28.*

144. ibid., p. 45.*

145. ibid., p. 46.*

146. ibid., p. 52.*

147. ibid., p. 64.*

148. ibid., p. 65.*

149. ibid., p. 67.*

150. ibid., p. 69.*

151. ibid., p. 73.*

152. ibid., p. 74.*

153. *Covert Action.*

154. ibid.

155. ibid.

156. ibid.

157. ibid.

158. ibid.

159. ibid.

160. ibid.

161. *Les complots de la CIA,* op. cit., p. 54.*

162. *El Mercurio,* August 19, 1973.

163. Garcés, op. cit., p. 294.

164. ibid., p. 66.

165. ibid., p. 171.

166. ibid., p. 77.

167. *Les complots de la CIA,* op. cit., p. 60.*

168. *El Siglo,* October 6, 1971, p. 7.

169. ibid., September 6, 1971, p. 4.

170 ibid., December 4, 1971.

171. ibid., December 5, 1971, p. 14.

172. ibid., October 1, 3 and 4, 1971.

173. ibid., January 26, 1973, p. 7.

174. ibid., July 9, 1973.

175. Garcés, op. cit., p. 381.

176. ibid., p. 395.

177. *El Mercurio,* August 2, 1973.

178. Lenin, "From a Publicist's Diary", *Collected Works,* Vol. 25, (Moscow: Progress Publishers, 1964), p. 296.

179. L. Corvalan, *27 horas,* (Santiago de Chile: Quimantu, 1972), p. 13.

180. Joxe, op. cit., p. 188.

181. M. Toer, *La vïa chilena: un balance necesario,* (Argentina: Tiempo Contemporaneo), p. 181.

182. ibid., p. 191.

183. Joxe, op. cit., p. 193.

184. Toer, op. cit., p. 195. "Locatelis": political expression indicating unconscious people.

185. ibid., p. 197.

186. ibid., p. 214.

187. *Chile Hoy,* August 17, 1973, p. 3.

188. Toer, op. cit., p. 232.

189. *El Mercurio,* August 14, 1973.

190. Toer, op. cit., p. 236.

191. Lenin, "Imperialism and the Split in Socialism", *Collected Works,* Vol. 23 (Moscow: Progress Publishers, 1964), p. 120.

192. C. Lamour, *Le pari chilien,* (Stock, 1972), p. 142.

193. ibid.

194. Toer, op. cit., p. 181.

195. Joxe, op. cit., p. 212.

196. ibid., p. 226.

197. ibid., p. 101.

198. Toer, op. cit., p. 198.

199. Lenin, "Petty-Bourgeois and Proletarian Socialism", *Collected Works,* Vol. 9, (Moscow: Progress Publishers, 1965), p. 443.

200. "Una clarificación necesaria", *Orientación,* official organ of the External Secretariat of the Socialist Party.

201. "El documento de Frei", duplicated article by Volodia Teitelboim, January 1976.

202. Duplicated document by the Socialist Party.

203. Duplicated document by the Political Commission of MAPU, March 1974.

204. Lenin, "Fourth Anniversary of the October Revolution", *Collected Works,* Vol. 33, (Moscow, Progress Publishers, 1966), p. 54.

205. "Frei: de espaldas al pueblo", *Boletín Informativo,* No. 89 (March-April 1976), Havana.

206. *El Siglo,* December 18, 1970.

207. Lenin, "The Voice of an Honest French Socialist", *Collected Works,* Vol. 21 (Moscow: Progress Publishers, 1964), p. 356.

List of Abbreviations

AMPICH — Asociacion de Medianes y Pequenos Industriales de Chile (Association of Small and Medium Manufacturers of Chile).

API — Accion Popular Independiente (Independent Popular Action).

CDP — Christian Democratic Party (PDC, Partido Democrata Cristiano).

CERA — Centro de Reforma Agraria (Agrarian Reform Centre). Production units combining various reformed estates, whose workers form a production cooperative with a common investment fund.

CL — Christian Left (IC, Izquierda Cristiana). Party formed by a left-wing split from the CDP in 1971.

CODE — Confederación de la Democracia (Democratic Confederation). United front in opposition to the Allende government formed in 1973 by the CDP, NP, RLP and RD.

CORFO — Corporation de Fomento de la Produccion (Production Development Corporation). Public body to promote industrial development; administered nationalized enterprises during the Allende administration.

CORA — Corporacion de la Reforma Agraria (Agrarian Reform Corporation). State organ responsible for agrarian reform.

CODELCO — Corporación de Cobre (Copper Corporation). State organ responsible for administering the nationalized copper companies and for marketing copper.

CORVI —Corporación de la Vivienda (Housing Corporation). Public body for financing and promoting the construction of workers' housing.

"C"P — "Communist" Party of Chile (P"C", Partido "Comunista" de Chile). Revisionist, pro-Soviet party which openly abandoned Marxism following the 20th Congress of the Communist Party of the Soviet Union.

CUP — Comités de Unidad Popular (Popular Unity Committees). District electoral committees formed for the 1970 presidential election and dissolved following the 1971 municipal elections.

CUT — Central Unica de Trabajadores (United Workers' Federation). Trade union federation formed in 1953, with a membership of over one million during the Allende administration.

DIRINCO — Direccion de Industria y Comercia (Industry and

Commerce Administration).

FRAP — Frente de Acción Popular (Popular Action Front). Electoral coalition of the "C"P and SP; later expanded through the incorporation of other parties to form the Popuiar Unity (UP).

FRENAP — Frente Nacional de la Area Privada (National Front of the Private Sector). Federation of various employers' associations.

INDAP — Instituto Nacional de Desarrollo Agropecuario (National Institute for Agricultural Development). State organ for agricultural development.

JAP — Juntas de Abastecimiento y Precios (Boards of Supply and Prices). Local bodies created by the UP government to combat speculation and facilitate distribution.

MAPU — Movimiento de Accion Popular Unitaria (United Popular Action Movement). Party formed by a left-wing split from the CDP in 1969.

MIR — Movimiento de Izquierda Revolucionaria (Revolutionary Left Movement). Movement of Castroite inspiration founded in 1967.

NP — National Party (PN, Partido Nacional). Party of the monopoly bourgeoisie and landed oligarchy.

PL (or FNPL) — Frente Nacional Patria y Libertad (Homeland and Liberty National Front). Fascist movement founded in 1970 following the victory of Allende.

RCP — Revolutionary Communist Party (PCR, Partido Comunista Revolucionario). Genuine Communist party founded by the Spartacus group, which came out of a split in the old "C"P at the time the latter publicly adopted the anti-Marxist theses of Khrushchov. The RCP was founded in 1966.

RDP — Radical Democratic Party (DR, Democracia Radical). An extreme right-wing group which split from the Radical Party in 1969.

RLP — Radical Left Party (PIR, Partido de la Izquierda Radical). Right-wing faction of the RP which, on CIA instructions, pretended to support the Allende government in order to sabotage it.

SOFOFA — Sociedad de Fomento Fabril (Society for Industrial Development). Federation of employers in manufacturing industry.

SP — Socialist Party (PS, Partido Socialista de Chile). The UP party with the greatest electoral strength; includes a wide variety of political tendencies.

UP — Popular Unity (UP, Unidad Popular). Coalition of the SP, CP, MAPU, RLP, RP, API and CL, which was the political foundation of the Allende government.

USOPO — Union Socialista Popular (Popular Socialist Union). Socialist faction which remained outside the Popular Unity in 1970.

Index